LightWave 3D 5

Character Animation

LightWave 3D 5

Character Animation

Doug Kelly

VENTANA

LightWave 3D 5 Character Animation f/x
Copyright © 1997 by Doug Kelly

Library of Congress Cataloging-in-Publication Data

Kelly, Doug
   LightWave 3D 5 Character Animation f/x / Doug Kelly.—1st ed.
      p.   cm.
   Includes index.
   ISBN 1-56604-532-0
   1. Computer animation. 2. Computer graphics. 3. LightWave 3D. I. Title.
   TR897.7.K45 1996
   006.6—dc20   96-35108
                                   CIP

First Edition 9 8 7 6 5 4 3 2 1

Printed in the United States of America

Ventana Communications Group, Inc.
P.O. Box 13964
Research Triangle Park, NC 27709-3964
919.544.9404
FAX 919.544.9472
http://www.vmedia.com

About the Author

Doug Kelly has written articles and tutorials on 3D animation software for a variety of publications, including *Video Toaster User* and *3D Artist* magazines. He wrote the manuals for Envisage 3D and SoftF/X while managing those products' development, and also contributed to the manuals for Animation Master. He is currently a principal at Kelly Computer Consultants.

Acknowledgments

A project this size is never a one-man show. Thanks to everybody who contributed, intentionally or otherwise, including: JJ Hohn and the rest of the Ventana crew, for making it happen. Mike Comet, for technical direction above and beyond the call of duty. Pat Kelly, for faith and composition. Brian Kelly, for art and overachieving. Rick May, founder of the Computer Graphics Character Animation Mailing List (CG-CHAR), and all contributors to the list, for a wealth of advice, support, and encouragement. Bill Allen, for my first byline. Dave Duberman, for valuable advice on writing tutorials. Dr. R. Stuart Ferguson, for an invaluable education in the labyrinth of CGI software and a shining example that some people can't be bought. Finally, to Frank Thomas, Ollie Johnston, Shamus Culhane, Tony White, Harold Whitaker, John Halas, Preston Blair, Chuck Jones, Eli Levitan, Kit Laybourne, John Lasseter, and all the other animators who recorded their techniques and experience for future generations.

> *"If I have seen farther it is because I stood on the shoulders of Giants."*
> —Sir Isaac Newton

Dedication

To Carrie: best friend, cheering section, constructive critic, touchstone, and wife; and Roxanne, who reminds me to take breaks by dropping her toys on my feet.

Contents

Introduction

Animation is a special form of that most human of arts—story-telling. It is perhaps the furthest extrapolation of the hand gestures used by the fireside storyteller to draw pictures in the minds of the audience. Just as the storyteller uses a physical language to emphasize and embellish their tale, animation can use a variety of techniques to accomplish the same goals.

An animator creates the illusion of motion with a series of images. Whether those images are created by the pen of a cartoonist, the knife of a sculptor, the posing of a living body, or the pixel manipulation of the computer artist, the principles of animation are the same. Every branch of animation can learn from every other. Computer generated imagery, or CGI, is the youngest shoot on the family tree, and therefore has the greatest amount to learn from the older forms.

The last 30 years have seen great advances in CGI—from abstract light patterns on vector graphic displays to the photorealism of *Jurassic Park* and character development of *Toy Story*. Older forms of animation were restrained by the limits of the physical materials they relied on, whether paper, cel, clay, or even the film itself. Now it is possible for CGI to overcome the limits of that materiality, to literally animate anything we can imagine, to make our dreams and fantasies live on the screen.

CGI animation development has thrived in the area of motion picture special effects—animating spacecraft and astronomic phenomena, and energy weapons and the explosions they produce. These effects have pushed CGI to very high levels of cinematic realism, but they cannot tell an engaging story by themselves. People aren't interested in watching special effects unless they advance the story line. Effects are window dressing, not premise.

If CGI animation is to tell an engaging story, it must be a story about anthropomorphic characters: digital models of humans, creatures, artifacts, or even inanimate objects caricatured into the semblance of life. This is the highest and most difficult form of CGI: character animation.

Character animation has always been the apex of any form of animation. Even in the most abstract of line drawings or the most minimalist of stop-motion cinematography, the creative workload of character animation is overwhelming. Each image must first be composed with the obsessively detailed care of any other animation. On top of this, the animator must give the characters that breath of life, the posing, timing, and expressiveness that will convince the audience that the characters are moving of their own volition.

This is a talent so rare that recent surveys have shown character animation to be one of the most popular careers. *The Wall Street Journal* and *The New York Times* have published profiles of top animators. Salaries for lead animators have more than doubled in the last few years, and every major animation house is actively recruiting.

For the CGI character animator, the prospects have never been better. The viewing public has responded so well to the use of CGI character animation that advertising agencies, video game developers, and motion picture studios are pushing the demand for character animators to unprecedented heights.

Training for CGI character animation has been almost exclusively on the job or by way of traditional animation approaches. Until very recently, the hardware and software necessary for CGI character animation have been prohibitively expensive, animation schools have been slow to offer programs in CGI, and there have been few books or videos on the topic.

LightWave 3D & Character Animation

NewTek's development of LightWave 3D has made character animation tools affordable for even the beginning animator. The hardware necessary to run LightWave 3D can currently be purchased for a fraction of the price of a good used car. You can afford to buy LightWave 3D for a hobby, and the program's power will continue to support you in a growing animation business all the way up to television and feature films.

LightWave 3D has been used to produce character animation for television programs, including *Hercules: The Legendary Journeys* and *seaQuest DSV*, and advertisements, including Will Vinton Studio's Blue M&Ms series. The commercial success of LightWave 3D for character animation has helped build a demand for character animators who can use this software.

Who Needs This Book?

This book is intended to bridge the gap between the CGI artist and the traditional animator. It is designed to introduce the vocabulary and techniques used by both approaches. If you are already an animator, you will learn the LightWave 3D software tools designed to support character animation. If you are a CGI artist, you will learn the essential techniques of character animation as they apply to LightWave 3D.

If you are a beginner in both fields, I suggest that you complete the exercises in *NewTek's LightWave 3D User Guide* before you start to work through this book. NewTek has done an excellent job of assembling introductory tutorials for the major functions of LightWave 3D. The *Reference* and *User Guides* also contain the technical information you need regarding system requirements, software installation, and troubleshooting. Once you have worked through the NewTek materials, you will be better prepared for the exercises in this book.

Throughout this book, each concept is reinforced with exercises designed to build your expertise without overwhelming you. Completing all the exercises will enable you to produce complete character animation, from storyboard to video or film. This book also shows you how to assemble a demo reel and look for employment as an animator or technical director.

What's Inside?

Chapter 1 is your guide to using this book to your best advantage. The path you should follow through the exercises depends on what you already know and what you want to learn. Whether you are a beginner, an expert CGI artist, or a traditional animator, you should read this chapter first.

Part I, Chapters 2 through 11, describes the work and tools of the character animator. Essential principles like squash-and-stretch, anticipation, follow-through, and timing are explored in theory and as they apply to working with LightWave 3D. Each software function that applies to character animation is summarized with simple examples, then incorporated into exercises of gradually increasing complexity. You will learn LightWave 3D character animation techniques in small, easy steps, and almost before you know it you'll be creating professional-level character animation.

Exercises explore realistic character animation, as well as caricatured or "cartoony" styles. Whether you want to animate a photorealistic animal for an educational video or a minimalist blob for a five-second station ID, the techniques are explained here. Each exercise closes with tips on practicing, sometimes recommending that you repeat the exercise (with interesting changes) and sometimes referring you to other activities that will help hone your skills.

Along the way, you'll find advice from professional animators about the business of animation. You'll learn what to expect from studio, freelance, or independent work, how to get your career started, and when not to take a job or project. You'll also find maps through the minefield.

Part II, Chapters 12 through 18, explores the responsibilities of the technical director (TD). The TD is the CGI counterpart of most of the skilled trades that support traditional cel or clay animation. Even if you want to concentrate on animation, you would be well advised to learn about the TD's job by working through the exercises here.

A TD must be able to use LightWave 3D's Modeler and Layout to create models for the animator. You'll learn guidelines for working with the director, animator, and layout artist to design characters. The exercises in this part teach LightWave 3D techniques for constructing objects that can be animated as easily as possible, whether mimicking natural motion or the exaggerated behavior of a Saturday morning cartoon character. More exercises show you how to color, texture, and clothe the characters, again designing for their easiest possible animation.

"Stock" LightWave 3D scenes are the starting point for the animator, and the TD is usually called on to stage them. Exercises show you how setting up default poses, camera angles, and other details can save the animator a lot of time.

The TD in many shops is largely responsible for the look of the finished animation through the design of sets, props, and lighting. Tweaking the final rendering can make a major difference in both look and production time, and is the responsibility of the TD as well. Exercises teaching techniques for building sets, lighting them, and rendering final output complete Part II.

Part III is a grab bag of everything required for an animation production that is not contributed by either the animator or TD. Exercises show you how to create a production from the original story idea through script, layout, storyboards, and bar sheets, to the animator's exposure sheets and the TD's character and layout sketches. This part wraps up with exercises that teach you how to do titles and credits, compositing, and transferring your work to the final output format.

As you might expect, at the back of this book you'll find a glossary, index, and a number of useful appendices.

About the Companion CD-ROM

Inside the back cover you will find the Companion CD-ROM. It contains all the electronic files you need to complete the exercises. You will also find examples of completed work from the exercises for you to compare to your own efforts. In addition to scripts, storyboards, sounds, exposure sheets, models, backgrounds, images, and scenes, there are finished animations, artwork, software, and other samples from a number of vendors and artists.

About Ventana Online

Software changes rapidly, so Ventana Online offers free Online Updates to exercises and files from this book as software development continues. When NewTek or third-party developers announce a new feature or plug-in for LightWave 3D, you can count on Ventana Online to show you how to use them. Ventana Online also provides links to various LightWave 3D resources on the Internet, including discussion groups, newsgroups, databases, and more. Plus—enjoy access to free services on Ventana Online. You'll find the Online Updates at:

```
http://www.vmedia.com
```

Hardware & Software Requirements

To complete the exercises in this book, you'll need whatever hardware is necessary to run LightWave 3D version 5.0 on your platform of choice. Some of the exercises, especially in Chapters 19 and 20, will use additional software written for the Windows NT Intel platform, and equivalent tools for the DEC Alpha, MIPS, PowerMac, or Amiga may not be available. In each case, sample output from the exercise is provided on the Companion CD-ROM so you can complete any dependent exercises.

So What Are You Waiting For?

By now, I'm certain you're eager to get started. When you've completed all the exercises, or just have a few nice examples you want to show off, I'd like to hear from you. You can reach me via e-mail at kcc@apk.net or c/o Ventana Communications Group.

Best of luck, and welcome to the wonderful world of character animation!

Doug Kelly

How to Use This Book

This book is intended to bridge the gap between the computer graphics artist and the traditional animator, introducing you to the vocabulary and techniques used by both approaches.

The path you follow through this book's exercises depends on what you already know about character animation and LightWave 3D, and what you want to learn. This chapter is your guide to using this book to your best advantage.

For the specific guide you should follow in using this book, refer to the section below that most closely describes you: CGI Artist, Traditional Animator, or Beginner.

CGI Artist

If you are already an experienced CGI artist, you only need to learn the essential techniques of character animation as they apply to LightWave 3D. Some of the functions explained in exercises dealing with Layout and Modeler may seem familiar to you. Even if you feel you already know how to use a particular function, remember that each of these exercises is designed to interpret each technique as it relates to traditional animation approaches.

When you have completed all the exercises, you will not only be able to use LightWave 3D to create character animation, but you will also be able to use the traditional animation vocabulary of a studio production team. This can be crucial to landing a job! If your demo reel is great, but you don't understand the director's or lead animator's jargon, you will not be taken seriously.

You probably should start with Part I. This part introduces the character animator's work and the traditional techniques of character animation as they translate to LightWave 3D. Part I gives you a better understanding of why objects and sets need to be built a certain way to support character animation. Once you understand these concepts, it will be easier for you to work through the Layout and Modeler exercises in Part II.

If you are feeling ambitious, you can start with Part III, Chapter 19, then follow up with the appropriate chapters from Part I and Part II in actual production order, as you create a demo reel or short motion picture. For details, refer to the chapter-by-chapter content descriptions immediately following the Beginner section.

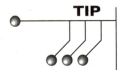

TIP

The basic production cycle is usually: story, script, storyboards, overall layout and design, bar sheets, model design and construction, sound and vocal track recording, story reel, exposure sheets, animation, lighting, rendering, compositing, editing, dubbing, titles and credits, final edit, output to media. And most of these processes go on in parallel, each affecting the others in a way that is impossible to track linearly. The production scheduling charts for a feature film are really something to see.

Traditional Animator

If you are a traditional animator working in cel or stop-motion media, you have a great advantage. You are already familiar with the toughest parts of character animation and only need to learn how to translate your existing skills in characterization, composition, and timing to the CGI medium. Compared to developing those skills in the first place, learning computer graphics is a snap!

You may want to begin with Part I, but you can probably jump to Chapter 3 for an overview of the LightWave 3D functions you will use most. From there, the remainder of Part I shows you how to translate your character animation skills into LightWave 3D procedures.

Once you are comfortable with the basics of LightWave 3D character animation, I suggest you move on to Chapter 19. If you choose to create your own story and script, rather than using the provided examples, it will be more work for you to learn modeling, set design, and lighting design.

In either case, plan to spend extra time working through the chapters in Part II in the order they are required in production. These exercises, intended for the technical director, give you a better understanding of the nuts and bolts of LightWave 3D. They take you through a computer analogy of the cels, paint, armatures, clay, lights, and cameras that you have worked with in the past. You don't need to master their theoretical details, but it is to your benefit as an artist to understand something about how your tools are constructed.

When you finish Part II and have all your demo reel scenes animated, move on to Chapter 20 to wrap it up and transfer your finished animation to video or film.

When you have completed all the exercises, you will not only be able to use LightWave 3D to create character animation, you will also be able to use computer graphics jargon as part of a studio production team. This can be very helpful in working with technical directors, as most of them come from a more computer-oriented background. The ability to speak their language makes it easier for you to express your needs and shows them that you have some understanding of their job as well.

Beginner

If you are a newcomer to both character animation and LightWave 3D, you have a great deal to learn. Don't worry, this book will guide you through it!

I recommend that you start off in Chapter 19 for an introduction to the production processes used in animated films. It won't be until later that you get into animating characters, but the grounding you acquire in storytelling and the production process will serve you well later on. Learning a particular software function makes a lot more sense when you can mentally tie it in to the larger process of creating a motion picture. For your first project, it would be a good idea to stick to the script, storyboards, and other examples provided. After you've been through the whole production process (and made the usual mistakes) with somebody else's story, you'll do a better job when you produce your own.

After Chapter 19 you should work through Chapters 2 and 3 so you understand the tools of character animation with LightWave 3D.

At this point, you may have developed a preference for the more technical side of the work. If that is the case, proceed to Part II and work through those exercises before returning to Chapter 4 and the rest of Part I.

If you find you prefer animating characters rather than building them, stick with Part I. Continue to use the example materials provided on the Companion CD-ROM to animate the example story. After you complete the animation, work through Part II to learn the nuts-and-bolts procedures used to build the models and sets you've been animating.

After you complete Parts I and II, wrap things up by working through the exercises in Chapter 20 to complete your demo reel.

If you still want a career in character animation after all this, go back to Chapter 19. Start the whole process again, but this time use all original materials—story, models, sounds, the works. Pay special attention to the demo reel guidelines in the introduction to Part III. If you still prefer the modeling, texturing, and rendering part of the work, you may want to consider looking for a job as a technical director rather than an animator. Whichever career you choose, make sure your demo reel targets the job you are looking for, and give it your best shot. Good luck!

Chapter Summaries

Part One

Chapter 2

This chapter describes the job of the character animator, either in an animation production house or for individual clients as a freelance artist. If you have never worked as an animator before, this is a good place to find out what the job is like.

This chapter includes a discussion of working environments, coworkers (director, technical director, lead animator), typical and alternative workflows from different shops, and guidelines and advice for independent and freelance animators. Overviews and definitions of basic animator tools and "raw materials" include bar sheets, exposure sheets, models, storyboards, and film footage to be matched. The chapter also examines requirements of the animator's output: complete animated shots ready for lighting and rendering.

Chapter 3

This is a guided tour of the LightWave 3D tools that can be used to create character animation, with examples and exercises illustrating each concept and cross-references to more detailed exercises elsewhere in this book.

This chapter translates traditional animation approaches such as replacement, displacement, and hybrid puppet animation to LightWave 3D techniques. Brief demonstrations of LightWave 3D functions include Replace Object, ObjList, ObjSequence, Metamorphosis, MTSE, Parenting, and Bones.

Chapter 4

This chapter begins the detailed examination of character animation techniques using LightWave 3D. Here you learn how to mimic the natural path—the arc or slalom—that living creatures follow in all their movements. You also begin to learn principles of facial animation, beginning with motion of the eyes and eyelids and the attitude of the head as a whole.

Chapter 5

Chapter 5 explores the essentials of timing, with examples of extreme variations, tools to manipulate timing in LightWave 3D, advice about studying and developing your own sense of timing, and information about other resources available to assist you.

This chapter explains traditional animation terms such as key poses, interpolation, inbetweening, pose-to-pose vs. straight-ahead animating, ease-in/ease-out, snap, moving holds, "on twos," exposure sheets, and frame rates.

Chapter 6

Through the creation of walk cycles, this chapter teaches the fundamentals of hierarchical animation. Exercises include layers of the animation hierarchy, hip action, extremes, passing position, heel strike position, dynamic balance, and fixed foot placement.

This chapter also includes a quick overview of LightWave 3D's Inverse Kinematics (IK) functions; more detail is available in Part II in the technical director section on modeling.

Advanced tips include creating reusable motion cycles, easing the animation burden with plug-ins like Lock & Key, and adding personality to a walk.

Chapter 7

Chapter 7 expands the concepts you learned through walk cycles by exploring other gaits, their application to four-legged as well as bipedal characters, and recommending resources for motion studies, bimechanics, and kinesiology. This chapter points out differences between classes of creatures, proposes appropriate solutions for character animation, and discusses motion capture, rotoscoping, and other techniques designed to aid in or replace manual keyframing. The chapter wraps up with techniques for changing gaits, which leads to the subject of Chapter 8.

Chapter 8

The logical step beyond Chapter 7's study of natural motions is the extrapolation of natural to caricature motion. The exercises and examples in this chapter explore the concepts of takes, double and extreme takes, sneaks, staggers, and zips. This chapter also discusses caricature of anticipation, weight, overlapping action, and squash-and-stretch, plus techniques for extension of basic movement principles to the animation of fantastic creatures.

Chapter 9

Chapter 9 covers the theory and practice of camera direction to compose the shot. Exercises illustrate staging the action, selection of camera angles and lens parameters, and animation of camera motion to frame the character effectively. A discussion of the camera as an actor explores the importance of camera movement in telling a story. A number of cinematography terms and their CGI counterparts are defined, including shot, pan, tilt, dolly, traveling shot, tracking shot, zoom, focal length, focal plane, wide-angle, telephoto, medium shot, and close shot.

The director uses the camera to control what the audience sees, to set the mood, and to advance the story. This chapter examines the options for lens selection, field of view, depth of field, and shot composition.

Camera movement limitations for direct computer playback are important for multimedia and game applications of character animation; this chapter lists the trade-offs between currently available options.

This chapter also covers composing considerations for character animation including defining the line of action, testing key poses in silhouette, avoiding twins in posing, and staging the main actions through introductory or preliminary movements.

Chapter 10

This chapter teaches the acting technique as it applies to character animation; it covers posing, gesture, emphasis, and anticipation. This chapter emphasizes analyzing real-world actions to find the essence of each gesture.

Chapter 11

The last chapter of Part I goes into detail about animating the face and head, including lip sync, timing emotional transitions, and realistic versus caricatured facial actions.

This chapter is about the finishing touch, the last tweak to the animation that makes all the difference. The pantomime and composition may get your main point across, but it's the subtlety of the facial animation that really sells the shot to your audience.

Part Two

Chapter 12

Chapter 12 shows how to use LightWave 3D's Modeler and Layout to create models usable by the animator. It also presents guidelines for working with the director, animator, and layout artist to design characters.

Numerous exercises and examples explain specific techniques used to build Metamorph libraries, object hierarchies, Boned articulation, and other animatable models. This chapter also presents an overview of natural and caricature proportions for human, animal, and fantastic creature modeling.

This chapter recommends and explains useful utilities including Glenn Lewis' SIMILAR model library duplicator. Special issues, such as modeling of hands, are examined in detail through several exercises.

Chapter 13

Chapter 13 elaborates on the techniques introduced in Chapter 12, expanding them to include Boning of heads for the most versatile facial expressions. It also reviews criteria for realistic and caricature expressions, and examines trade-offs between the different approaches to facial animation through a series of exercises.

This chapter explains the observable musculature and skeletal structure of the human face. Exercises relate this information to the object geometry and bones placement that can be used in LightWave 3D to emulate the natural structure, including dimples, wrinkles, flab, and fat.

Chapter 14

This is the equivalent of the wardrobe and makeup departments of a motion picture studio. Once the basic character is designed and modeled, it comes here for the coloring, texturing, and embellishments that add the realism—or that extra touch of fantasy—that is the finishing touch. This chapter explains boning, model library creation, and other techniques for animating fabrics, and also the matching of various map types to animate character faces. It includes exercises to produce model and map libraries for lip sync and emotional transitions. This chapter also discusses special applications for maps and shaders including photorealistic work to match live-action footage.

Chapter 15

This chapter explains the various techniques that the TD can use to make life easier for the animator. It provides exercises for: setting up stock scenes for characters, Parenting Lights to provide useful Layout views, communicating crucial data to the animator, and organizing and documenting files. A lot of these tips apply to sets as well, which are covered in Chapter 16.

Chapter 16

This chapter is about building sets and backgrounds. This is where the artistic judgment of the TD really shines; the techniques taught here are intended as a take-off point for the creative TD. Exercises cover texturing, modeling, and the animation of repetitive or machine elements.

This chapter discusses background procedures including fixed background images, images locked to the camera field-of-view, and matching live-action footage photographed with moving cameras.

The chapter concludes with tips on building generic sets that can be reused with only superficial modifications.

Chapter 17

Lighting design, as explained in this chapter, ranges from the basics of three-point lighting to using subtle effects to establish mood or emphasize character action. Several exercises teach you to use lighting to match live-action footage, shadows, and sun angle, and also show you how to duplicate (or fake) them.

Chapter 18

Chapter 18 details the tips and tricks necessary to minimize rendering time in a production environment. It discusses technical issues of hardware requirements, memory management, output formats, resolution, aspect ratios, and the special requirements of game developers, feature films, and television.

Part Three

Chapter 19

Chapter 19 leads you through the steps necessary to produce the model sheets for the TD and the exposure sheets for the animator, beginning with the very first idea for a story. You'll produce premise, story, script, storyboard, layouts, sound, bar sheets, and exposure sheets in a logical, easy-to-follow sequence that will teach you a great deal about the production of animation and, incidentally, help you produce a really good demo reel.

Chapter 20

The final chapter wraps up all the work you've done in the preceding 19 chapters and ties it with a pretty bow. Here you'll find compositing techniques, title design, and the nuts and bolts of making VHS duplicates of your finished demo reel.

Compositing exercises explain the concepts of key, chroma key, luma key, mattes, transitions, effects, fade in, fade out, wipes, and dissolves. This chapter also discusses how you can save time and labor by compositing layers for complex scenes.

Title design explores techniques and criteria for titles and credits, typographic design, text-safe areas for video transfer, and building animated technical end-credits.

The explanations of final output formats familiarize you with film recorders, service bureaus, hard drive recording devices and single-frame VTRs, direct computer playback, and computer-to-video scan converters.

Appendix A: About the Companion CD-ROM

The Companion CD-ROM contains all the electronic files you need to complete the exercises in the book. You will also find solutions and examples of completed work from the exercises for you to compare to your own efforts. In addition to scripts, storyboards, sounds, exposure sheets, models, backgrounds, images, and scenes, there are also finished animations, artwork, software, and other samples from a number of vendors and artists.

Appendix B: About the Online Updates

The *LightWave 3D Character Animation f/x Online Updates* on Ventana Online provides updated and supplementary files for this book. It also provides links to various LightWave 3D resources on the Internet including discussion groups, newsgroups, databases, and more. Plus, enjoy access to free services on Ventana Online. You'll find the Online Updates page at http://www.vmedia.com.

Appendix C: Resources

When you are ready to send out a demo reel, you'll find a list of potential employers, their expectations, and application procedures in Appendix C. Along with that, you'll find contact information about various professional organizations and unions for animators and TDs. Finally, there is a list of trade publications, magazines, and scholarly journals that you may find useful to your research and daily work.

Appendix D: Sample Script

This appendix contains a short script appropriate for a three- to five-minute character animation demo reel. It also can be used to complete the exercises in Chapter 19.

Appendix E: Sample Storyboards

These storyboards are expanded from the example script in Appendix D. The story sketches are representative of the kind of storyboards an employer or client would want to see, or that a studio production team might work from. They can also be used to complete some of the exercises in Chapter 19 if you don't want to draw your own.

Appendix F: Exposure Sheets

This appendix contains filled-in exposure sheets to be used in several exercises that explain lip sync. There is also a blank exposure sheet that you can photocopy and use to record your own track analyses.

Appendix G: Creating Custom Exposure Sheets

If you want to create your own exposure sheets, this appendix explains the procedures used to build the example sheet in Appendix F and tells you how to modify it to suit yourself.

Appendix H: Track Analysis Using Magpie

Miguel Grinberg's Magpie shareware program is a wonderful tool to aid in track analysis for lip sync. This appendix is a thorough tutorial in Magpie's use, and ties in with several of the lip sync exercises elsewhere in the book.

Glossary

The glossary provides brief definitions of the technical terms used in this book. Terms are culled from the fields of drama, cinematography, photography, art and design, computer science, optics, anthropology, biology, advertising, media production, animation, and others. Terms are generally defined the first time they appear in the text, but if you run across an unfamiliar word or phrase it will most likely be defined in the glossary.

Bibliography

The bibliography is not intended to be an exhaustive guide to the field of animation. Entire volumes have been published on that subject, and one or two of them are included in this more selective list. This bibliography is annotated with my personal opinions, and is intended to recommend only the most useful books for the beginning character animator. If you want to research deeper into one of the subjects summarized in this book, this bibliography is a good place to start.

Index

If you are having difficulty in finding a definition or exercise to illustrate a particular function, check the index. It has been extensively cross-referenced, so even if you don't know the exact term you are looking for, the See and See Also references should help you find what you need.

Moving On

If you are a CGI artist you can proceed to Chapter 2 to begin learning the foundations of character animation. If you are a traditional animator you can skip to Chapter 3 and start digging into LightWave 3D techniques. If you are a beginner, I recommend you go directly to Chapter 19 for an introduction to animation production.

Whichever route you follow through this book, if you complete all the exercises, you will learn how to create character animation with LightWave 3D.

The Animator

An animator is someone who makes inanimate objects appear to move. This is simple; almost anyone can set up a stop-motion camera or low-end animation software and make an object move between one frame and the next.

A character animator is one who can use inanimate materials to create the illusion of life. This is a lot tougher than just animating. The audience must believe the character is moving of its own volition. The timing of each motion can maintain or destroy that illusion. It takes a great deal of practice and skill to animate a believable character, but even a child can spot a character that has been animated badly.

A Brief History of the Art

The topic of this book is character animation as created using LightWave 3D, but the sources for the techniques you'll learn go back far beyond the invention of LightWave 3D, computer graphics, or even written language. Character animation is an outgrowth of storytelling, a very ancient art form. Like most forms of storytelling, when a new form is created, the old ones survive.

The earliest form of character animation for storytelling was probably done by cave dwellers who made shadow pictures on the wall by firelight. The retelling of the day's events, perhaps a successful hunt, might have been the evening's entertainment. The shadow-maker had to mimic the characteristic movements of the animals and persons portrayed, but also had the ability to transform one shadow character into another—the first special effects. Modern animators still test their creations in silhouette (see Chapter 9) to judge the strength of the performance.

Puppetry was a natural outgrowth of shadow play. In some traditional branches of puppetry, it is still the shadows that are watched; the audience never sees the actual puppets. Puppeteers still need the ability to mimic natural motion, just as character animators do, but the puppets serve as tools to extend the hands' dramatic range.

Animating for Posterity

Probably the first instance of animators recording their work for later exhibition was the flipping tablet or *thaumatrope*. If you draw or engrave two different pictures on opposite sides of a flat object, then loop a string through holes in the objects' edges, you can twist and untwist the string to rapidly flip the object. A visual phenomenon called *flicker fusion* makes the two images appear to be a single image at higher speeds. At lower speeds, the motion between the images is visible and you can make a two-pose animation. Nobody knows the earliest example of this technique, but it was popular in the early 1800s, and children still play with similar toys.

It wasn't until the 1830s that devices were developed to show a longer series of images. The phenakistoscope, zoetrope, and praxinoscope are all simple mechanical devices designed to display drawn animations of eight or ten frames. This enables the animator to create simple looping actions or motion cycles (see Chapter 6) such as walking or running figures. Kit Laybourne's *The Animation Book* (see the Bibliography) includes detailed instructions for making your own zoetrope animations.

Flipbooks gave animators the ability to create drawn animations of up to several hundred frames, limited only by the amount of paper the binding or viewer could hold. Flipbooks are still popular; Disney recently published short flipbooks from its animated feature films. If you wrap the spine of a flipbook of a thousand pages or more around a cylinder, so the first card follows the last, then add a crank to turn the cylinder and flip the cards, you have a Mutoscope. This invention gave the animator even more range for expression. The last time I checked, there were several working Mutoscopes in the Main Street Arcade in Disneyland. They're worth looking for.

The invention of cinematography enabled the animator to create stories limited only by the amount of film that could run through the projector. At first a novelty for vaudeville acts, the animated film soon became a medium in its own right. Short films of both drawn and puppet animation became a standard item on cinema marquees, and animation studios proliferated to meet the demand.

The Disney studio pioneered the feature length animated film, with its emphasis on storytelling and character development rather than the slapstick comedy of the shorts. This was a mixed blessing for animators, for although a single feature production might employ many animators, the sheer volume and expense of the work kept feature films beyond the reach of most independent animators. The Disney studio also formalized most of the principles of character animation that this book attempts to teach, and established a training program that has produced some of the best 2D animators in the business.

Animation Goes Digital

Most recently, the development of computers powerful enough to process graphic images gave the character animator another tool. Computer generated imagery (CGI) at first was horrendously expensive and required more programming skill than animation talent. Few CGI pioneers were animators, so early CGI animation rarely showed knowledge of basic animation techniques. As computer prices dropped, more animators acquired CGI animation tools, and the general quality of CGI animation improved. CGI software developers eventually enhanced their products to handle the complexities of character animation.

The length of a CGI animation, as with film, is limited only by the capacity of the storage medium. As of this writing, a CGI animator can acquire a complete video production system—computer, software, and video recorder—for less than the price of a good used car. With talent and perseverance, an animator can create a complete CGI animation with a fraction of the resources of older methods.

The CGI animator can then sit back and enjoy the audience's reaction from a quiet corner, as they watch animated shadow pictures cast by a tungsten filament fire onto the wall of a multiplex cinema cave. The more things change, the more they stay the same.

An Animator's Work

If you have never worked as an animator, this chapter is a good place to find out what the job is like, either in an animation production house or for individual clients as a freelance artist.

Meet the Team

Most production studios have an organizational structure with similar job titles, although the actual responsibilities of the people vary from studio to studio. Generally, the larger the organization, or the bigger the project, the more people will specialize. For smaller shops and shorter projects, each person may handle several different jobs. Whatever the size or scope of the production, there are a few basic job descriptions you can depend on.

The Animator

When you strip away the technology, finance, and politics of making an animated film, the animator's job is the heart of it. Whether working solo or as part of a production team, the animator's task is to breathe the illusion of life into a model by creating a sequence of poses that communicate character. You can program a computer to make a model lip sync any line of dialog, but if the accompanying action is not convincing, the characterization fails. The rest of the production team relies on you to get the animation right.

The materials you, as an animator, use to create a LightWave 3D animation can include storyboards, exposure sheets, model sheets, film footage to be matched, and LightWave 3D objects and scenes. Who provides these varies from studio to studio. For this book's exercises, the necessary materials are included in the appendices and the Companion CD-ROM. The results you are expected to produce are finished animation files, ready to be lighted and rendered.

The Technical Director

The technical director (TD) can make or break your animation work. In most shops, the TD builds, textures, and lights the models you animate, and may develop custom software tools as well. The TD provides you with the model sheets and other notes on the construction of the characters. This information can make your work much easier, so cultivate your TD and treat him or her well. TDs tend to have more computer skills and a more analytical and engineering approach than animators, which has led to industry stereotypes about cultural conflicts between the two "tribes."

When you take a problem to a TD, be diplomatic (as with all team members), and make an attempt to understand the TD's side of the problem. One of the goals of this book is to teach you the professional vocabulary of the TD, since people are generally more receptive to suggestions if you speak their language. As an animator, you do not need to know absolutely everything about LightWave 3D or the particular computer hardware you use, just as you don't need to know how to make a pencil in order to use it effectively. However, knowledge can be a good thing; just as in other arts, artists who does not understand how their tools function and are made is at a disadvantage.

The Supervising Animator

If the project is a large one, you may be working under a supervising animator. Job titles and authorities vary, but typical examples are directing animator, lead animator, or animation supervisor. Usually, these are senior animators who act as deputies for the director. You will probably receive your shot materials from the supervising animator rather than the director. If you are new to the profession, the supervising animator may become your mentor, helping you out on problem shots and giving you the benefit of experience. Take advantage of the opportunity to learn from that person!

The Track Analysis Specialist

Track analysis has traditionally been performed by specialists, with the director or supervising animator transcribing the completed analysis to exposure sheets, which are then passed on to the animator. Software developers have recently produced several different tools that automate most of the track analysis process (see Chapter 19 and Appendix H), so this specialty may not survive much longer.

The Layout Artist

Layout artist is a job title that you will only find in larger organizations. In smaller ones, the job is generally split between the director, TD, and animator. The layout artist translates each 2D story sketch to one or more composed 3D shots (see Chapter 9), setting the scene with camera, characters, sets, and basic lighting. This is the CGI equivalent of cinematic or theatrical blocking.

Layout can be a difficult job, especially if the storyboard artist "cheated" shots in ways that can't be modeled in 3D. Once the layouts are done, it's possible to substitute rendered frames for the story sketches in the story reel (see Chapter 19). In some studios, "layout" can also refer to character layout—the job of setting up default scenes for the animator (see Chapter 15).

The Storyboard Artist

The storyboard artist translates the written script to a series of sketches (see Chapter 19), and revises, adds, or deletes sketches during story sessions. Since storyboard artists work in 2D, they can "cheat" or draw character actions that are difficult to animate. If you see a story sketch that is going to be a problem, point it out at the first opportunity. It's a lot easier to get a story sketch revised than the finished model and exposure sheets!

The Art Director

The art director (and the entire art department, in larger organizations) is responsible for developing the overall look of the product—the visual style. Like the storyboard artist, the art director can create 2D drawings that are nearly impossible to replicate in 3D. Character design is especially difficult to adapt; you need to work closely with the TD in negotiating with the art director to make sure the proposed characters can be built and animated.

The Writer

The writer develops the script. Unless there are rewrites, the writer has the least influence on the difficulty of your work as an animator. In many cases, once the script has been translated to storyboards, all further development is done visually and the script is obsolete. The writer may still participate in story sessions, but any revisions from that point are collaborative efforts.

The Director

The director is the person responsible for the overall product—for keeping the "big picture" clearly in sight. In smaller shops or on shorter projects, the director hands you the storyboards and exposure sheets, and goes over the intent of the shot to make sure you understand the characterization they are looking for. The director also passes final judgment on your animation.

In effect, the director is a minor deity, answerable only to the executive producer or the client. Some directors—especially the insecure type—remind you of their exalted status at every opportunity.

Others remind you of their rank only if you do something inadvisable, like continuing to disagree with them after they've made a decision. Voice your opinion once, diplomatically, then go along with whatever the director decides. That's what the director gets paid for.

Working With a Team

Production workflows seem to be one of the most closely guarded secrets in the animation business. As I was researching this book, I found questions about production practices to be the one sure way to get a source to clam up. Whenever you have a job interview, be sure to ask questions about workflow and creative opportunities; it shows you are interested in doing the work, and the answers you get tell you a lot about the organization.

Every shop is different, and even the same shop can vary from project to project. An advertising project may come from a micromanaging client or agency with very specific ideas about everything, or they may ask the production team to come up with the whole concept. A feature or short may start out very nebulous, with the creative team soliciting story ideas from everyone down to the janitor, or the director may have one of those crystalline, burning visions that dictates every detail. You need to stay flexible and adapt your working style to your employer or client.

Depending on shop policy (and your seniority), your supervisor may simply hand you exposure and model sheets and tell you to animate them. This kind of creative restriction is intolerable to some animators, but others don't seem to mind. In more flexible shops, you may be allowed to contribute ideas in story meetings, storyboard sessions, and other creative collaborations. These are good opportunities to practice your diplomacy and teamwork skills.

You should also keep in mind the ground rules for these meetings, which vary a great deal between shops, teams, and even directors. One common approach is to separate the creative, brainstorming part of a meeting from the analytical, critical part. If a meeting is being run with this approach, the fastest way to make yourself persona non grata is to break the rules, either criticizing during the brainstorming session or throwing in new ideas after the analysis has begun. In any case, don't hare off on topics that aren't on the agenda, don't chime in if you don't have anything constructive to contribute, and never play devil's advocate just for the sake of starting an argument. Try not to think out loud, either; give yourself a moment to phrase an observation or suggestion as concisely as possible, and think about the effect your suggestions may have on the other people in the meeting. You want to build a reputation as a person of few words and good ideas, so that when you do speak up, your team members listen.

Working on Your Own

Of course, being an employee of an animation studio or game developer has several advantages: you don't have to manage the business, you can concentrate on your animation, and you (usually) get a steady paycheck and benefits. The pay, however, can be a fraction of what you could make on your own.

Independent animators are generally either freelance, subcontractors, or consultants. To succeed as an independent animator, you need the basic know-how of any successful small business owner: accounting and finance, customer relations, legal risk management, and estimating, for starters. As a person, you need to be self-starting, diplomatic, persistent, entrepreneurial, thorough, and organized. That's all in addition to your skills and talent as an animator. Do you see why most animators are not in business for themselves?

Freelance animating is usually work-for-hire, which means you are essentially a temporary employee on a project basis. Freelancing can bring in good money, but you have to market your services and pay more attention to business matters than a regular employee does.

Being a subcontractor is like running your own production house, with a little less responsibility and a lot less creative control. Your client, the main contractor on the project, hands you a piece of work and tells you when the finished product is due. Where, when, and how you do the work is usually up to you. With this freedom comes added risk: if you don't deliver as contracted, the client (and sometimes even their client) can sue you for damages. Think about insurance, and don't promise what you can't deliver.

Being a consultant can be lucrative and relatively low risk, but you need a solid reputation and a lot of friends and colleagues in the business who know the quality of your work and will recommend you. Don't plan to start off as a successful animation consultant; you can only get there after a lot of solid professional work and sustained networking.

Unless you enjoy working hard for little money, or having your work stolen outright, get yourself a competent animation attorney and an agent. An agent only makes money if you do, and a good agent can get you far more than you could negotiate for yourself. Agents also network for you, keeping track of where the work is and who's doing what—an invaluable resource when you are hired project by project.

Animation is a specialized business, and even an experienced media attorney can stumble over the quirks of an animation contract. And for your sanity's sake, don't ask the "family lawyer" to draft or review any legal document pertaining to this business. Family law, or even standard business practice, is a far cry from what you'll be doing. I've seen a contractor's attorney actually revise a production subcontract in my favor, just because he didn't know the business well enough to look out for his client's interests. If you are doing original work, and the contract is not work-for-hire, you also need to look out for your copyright interests. Character designs can be worth more than film rights.

Even if you are just starting out as an animator, resist the temptation to do work "on spec" or for free. If the potential client is a non-profit organization, insist on some sort of compensation, whether it's free tickets or other services, access to equipment, or a tax-deductible receipt for pro bono services rendered (calculated at your full rates). If the client is a for-profit, insist on either a cut of the gross, a barter for services or product, or payment on delivery. Any other arrangement will most likely add your name to the long list of animators who have been ripped off by unscrupulous or inexperienced clients.

Dealing With Clients

Ah, clients. Where would animators be without clients? Broke and unemployed, but probably less stressed.

The client/animator relationship is a simple one. They have money, which you need. You can create animation, which they want. Try not to lose sight of this basic fact, especially when a difficult client's head games cloud the issue.

The best way to deal with client problems is to prevent them from occurring. Make sure your contract spells out all the details. Have a written schedule of the deliverables you need from the client, and base your delivery dates on your receipt of those deliverables. That is, your deadlines should be something like "20 business days following receipt of approved storyboards," rather than "no later than February 12." If you suspect (or know from prior experience) that a client will drag their feet on approvals, add on held work fees that are high enough to compensate you for your waiting time. If a client wants to make changes after approvals, your contract should spell out exactly what fees must be paid for you to do the work over.

Nothing is impossible, just expensive. If the client is willing to pay for it, you should be willing to do it. If a particular piece of work is going to be unpleasant, quote them a high price and long delivery schedule. If they're willing to pay your asking price, at least you'll be compensated well for the unpleasant work.

If an approval deadline is approaching and you have not heard from the client, call them. Stay in touch. More client delays are due to oversight than intentional stonewalling or indecision. Make sure the client knows the deadline is coming up and that you are ready to go. When your own deadlines are looming, don't talk to the client as much. Filter your incoming calls with an answering machine and reply to the client's answering machine after hours, when you won't have to speak to them directly. Every time you interact with the client, they may see it as an opportunity to make changes. Even if you convince them not to make changes, those negotiations come out of your production time. Stick to the approvals spelled out in your contract and don't let the client micromanage you.

When you are presenting materials for approval, make sure there is one obvious glitch to fix. Clients need to feel useful. Don't bring other problems to their attention; just fix them. Pointing out a problem to a client can lead to a whole chain of revisions. Anticipate changes you think the client will request, but if you finish them ahead of time, hold the changes in reserve. In fact, you should always hold work in reserve. If you finish work ahead of schedule, don't try to deliver it because the client may ask for more changes, right up to the original deadline. Deliver work exactly when it is due.

Dealing with a client when a problem occurs is the acid test of your diplomacy skills. Even the best clients can be difficult, just because they don't understand your business or your problems. If the client is reasonable, your best approach is to explain the problem—and your proposed solution—in plain English and with just enough detail to get your point across. If the client is unreasonable, your only defense is your contract.

Remember, they have money, which you need. You create animation, which they want. If they are difficult, pad the bid on the next job enough to pay for the aggravation. If a client becomes more trouble than they are willing to pay for, just politely turn down the job.

Maintaining Your Space—and Yourself

If you are a typical animator, you spend more time at work than away from it. With that in mind, make sure you are going to be comfortable. Windows? What windows? Get used to the idea of not seeing the sun very much. Sunlight glaring off your monitor's screen and the cost of commercial office space mean you will usually be working in a windowless cubicle or sharing a room with other animators or TDs.

You'll probably spend more time decorating your cubicle than you spend furnishing your home. Animators are famous for cluttering their workspace with toys. It may be a good idea to arm yourself—there have been hair-raising reports of Nerf™ wars in some shops. Try to keep a sense of humor; when deadlines are tight and nerves are thrumming, the catharsis of a good Nerf™ battle can save your production team's sanity.

Animation can be a bit of an endurance sport, physically and mentally, and you have to make sure you're up to it.

Make sure you take care of yourself physically. CGI animators, like other computer workers, are prone to Repetitive Stress Injury (RSI), including carpal tunnel syndrome, Dequervaine's, and related maladies. Set up your workstation to provide proper support, and if you have already injured yourself, follow the directions of your therapist. A lot of animators use wrist braces and ergonomic supports. Get yourself a good chair with proper back support. After searching unsuccessfully for decent workstation furniture, I finally designed and built my own. It's a standing-height work surface for my keyboard and tablet, with my monitor at eye level, and a matching draftsman's stool. I alternate standing and sitting on about a 20-minute cycle to keep from stiffening up over the course of a 16-hour workday.

Take especially good care of your eyes. Staring at a monitor for hours can exhaust the focusing muscles of your eyes, getting them in a rut that can affect your ability to change focus rapidly. Try to have a brightly colored object within view at least twenty feet away, and periodically (every 15 minutes or so) look up and focus your eyes on it. Looking out a window is best, but if your work area is too enclosed, set up a mirror on the far wall to double your line of sight. If you ever have any doubts about the effect your job is having on your vision, talk to your optometrist or ophthalmologist.

Even if you love your job, you need to keep a balanced perspective. Set aside some time, on a regular basis, to keep up your personal life.

Moving On

I hope this chapter has given you a better idea of what the day-to-day work of an animator is like, and that it hasn't scared you away from being an animator. Like most art forms, the thrill of seeing your animations played for an appreciative audience is worth any sacrifices. In the next chapter, you begin learning and practicing some of the animation skills you'll use every day as an animator.

Basic LightWave 3D Tools for Character Animation

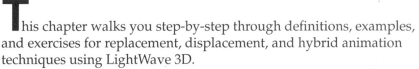

This chapter walks you step-by-step through definitions, examples, and exercises for replacement, displacement, and hybrid animation techniques using LightWave 3D.

If you are an experienced LightWave 3D user, you may be able to get by with skimming these tutorials. Even if you are expert with the functions discussed, however, you should read through the exercises for the discussions and critiques, and learn how to apply these basic techniques to character animation.

If you are a beginning or intermediate LightWave 3D user, you definitely should work through each of the following exercises, in order if possible. Later exercises assume some basic familiarity with these functions, and are easier to follow if you complete these exercises first.

If you are a traditional animator making the transition to computers, I hope you will find these exercises relatively painless and expressed in terms more familiar to you than most computer jargon.

This book is not intended to replace any part of the official NewTek documentation you received with your copy of LightWave 3D. I assume that you have at least worked through the exercises at the end of the LightWave 3D User Guide, and therefore have a basic familiarity with the functions and screens of Layout and Modeler. If you have not completed the exercises in the User Manual, I suggest you do so before attempting any of this book's exercises.

Learn From Others' Mistakes—It's Much Cheaper!

As I noted earlier, there are many similarities between CGI character animation and the more traditional forms used in the past. I've always believed in the wisdom of learning from other people's experience and mistakes, as it is much cheaper and less painful. That said, let's take a look at what we can learn from the masters of character animation.

3D CGI animation has more in common with clay or puppet animation than with 2D drawn animation for a number of reasons. In three-dimensional animation, you must set before the camera models of everything the audience will see, whether you use CGI, clay, or puppets. You have, in compensation for this extra effort, a great deal of freedom in moving your camera to compose your shots. The correctness of perspective and depth, so difficult to attain with drawn animation, is also integral to 3D, whether physical or CGI. And, 2D animation generally relies on the laborious redrawing of anything that must appear to move. This is a huge burden; enormous resources have been poured into developing production shortcuts to reuse as much hand-drawn artwork as possible. In 3D formats, you have the comparative luxury of reusing almost everything in nearly every frame; changes between frames are incremental or piecemeal, rather than substantial or total.

This is only to say that puppet or clay traditions have more bearing on nuts-and-bolts techniques for CGI character animation. For theory and example, we will still rely heavily on the much larger body of work supporting 2D character animation.

So what does puppet animation have to offer?

First, let's get the terminology straight. There really isn't an official name encompassing puppet, clay, and related forms of animation. The phrase "stop motion" is used by a lot of people, but this term was originally used for a larger body of special effects that were performed in the camera, including optical dissolves, split screens, and others that have nothing to do with animation. The alternatives of "dimensional animation" and "puppet animation" have their drawbacks. More recently, market forces have bred neologisms such as Claymation™ and Go-Motion™ in an effort to differentiate one studio's or animator's techniques from the others. For the sake of consistency, I use the term *puppet animation* to refer to puppet, clay, and all other forms of physical 3D animation. If the term offends you, feel free to scratch it out and insert your own favorite term—but only after you've purchased this book!

There are two major divisions in puppet animation techniques: replacement and displacement. Each has advantages and disadvantages, depending on the needs of a particular animation sequence. They are often combined in hybrid replacement/displacement animation, which can use the strengths of one technique to shore up the weaknesses of the other.

Replacement Animation Techniques

Replacement puppet animation uses a complete model for each pose, swapping out the model for each change, sometimes for each frame. The models are generally cast or similarly mass-produced in batches of one pose, then deformed, sculpted, or otherwise modified to create the individual poses. As you can imagine, this method requires a large number of models for even simple actions. The advantage is that the actual staging and shooting of the animation proceeds very quickly, as the entire sequence of models has been determined in advance and can be rapidly swapped out during photography.

For a noncharacter example of this technique, you can look at the peach glop in *James and the Giant Peach* (1996).

One of the few examples of this technique being used for a complete character in a feature film is the Tyrannosaurus Rex in "The Beast of Hollow Mountain" (1956). The replacement models of T. Rex were used for walking and running sequences; the cyclical actions were a good match for the strengths and limitations of replacement puppet animation.

LightWave 3D has a number of tools you can use for replacement animation. Each has strengths and weaknesses. You can benefit from learning and practicing each of them, as you never know which one will be perfect for that rush job the boss dumps on you. The exercises in this chapter cover the LightWave 3D functions that are most useful for replacement animation:

- Replace Object
- ObjectSequence
- ObjList
- Metamorph
- Multiple Target Single Envelope (MTSE)

Replace Object Function

At the most basic level, you can mimic single-frame replacement animation by using the Replace Object function to swap out objects, while manually stepping through each frame of the animation. This produces a numbered image sequence for later assembly or compositing. It's possible, but I have to ask, "Why?" Nevertheless, for completeness' sake and to provide a contrast to more useful techniques, I have included a step-by-step exercise to illustrate the concept.

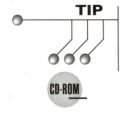

TIP

All the files you need to complete the exercises in this book are located on the Companion CD-ROM. Each chapter has its own directory. The example scene files are set up with the default directory path D:\NEWTEK\OBJECTS\, so if you simply copy the entire chapter directory to that path, the scene files should load into Layout with no trouble. If you can't set up a default path to match this, LightWave 3D prompts you for alternative object and image paths when you first load each scene.

I recommend that you do not try to load the files into Layout directly from the CD-ROM because you will not be able to save any changes.

Exercise 3-1: Animating the Desk Lamp Using Replace Object

1. Load the EXER0301.LWS scene file, from the Chapter 3 directory of the Companion CD-ROM, into Layout. Your screen should look like Figure 3-1.

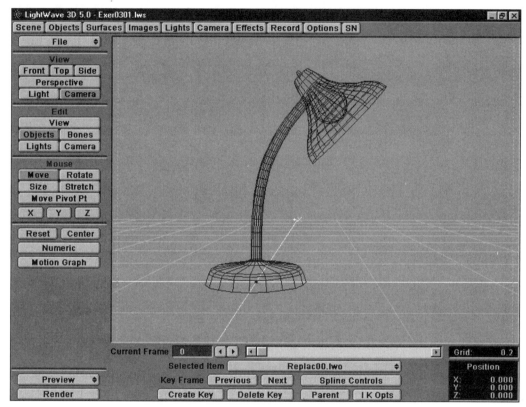

Figure 3-1: EXER0301.LWS scene file loaded and ready for replacement animation exercise.

2. Click the Record button at the top center of the Layout window. The Record Panel appears, as shown in Figure 3-2.

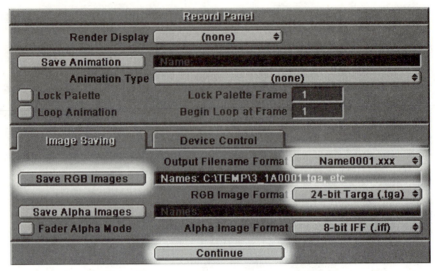

Figure 3-2: Record Panel.

3. Click the Save RGB Images button. An operating system dialog titled "Save RGB Images Prefix" appears. Select the drive and directory path where you want the image files to be saved, and type the filename prefix you want to use. For this example, I used C:\TEMP\3_1A to remind me these files are from Exercise 3-1, version A. Press Enter to accept your entry and close the dialog.

4. Back in the Record Panel, pull down the RGB Image Format drop-down list and select 24-bit TGA, or whatever other image file format you prefer to work with. From the Output Filename Format drop-down list, select Name0001.xxx. This names rendered image files with the four-letter prefix you specified in Step 3, adds the four digits corresponding to the frame number, and finishes up with the three-letter file format suffix. Click the Continue button at the bottom center to save your changes and close the panel.

5. Click the Camera button at the top center of the Layout window, just left of the Record button. The Camera Panel appears (see Figure 3-3).

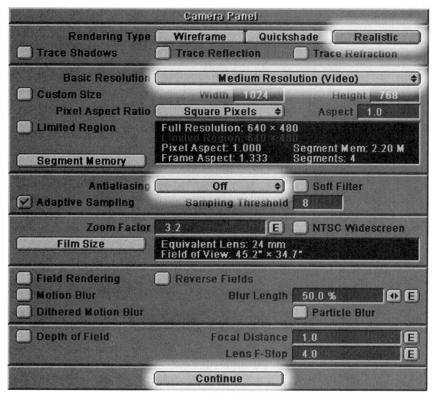

Figure 3-3: Camera Panel.

6. Select the rendering type, resolution, and other settings for the images you will be rendering. (If you'd like more information on LightWave 3D's rendering options, refer to Chapter 18 of this book or to Layout Tutorial 8 in the LightWave 3D User Guide.) Click the Continue button at the bottom center to save your changes and close the panel.

7. Click on the frame advance button or press the right arrow key to advance to frame 1 of the animation. Click on the Render button at the bottom left of the Layout window. The Render Scene Panel appears (see Figure 3-4).

Figure 3-4: Render Scene Panel, all set to render frame 1.

8. Change the First Frame setting to 1, Last Frame to 1, and press Enter to accept your changes and render the image. This renders just frame 1 and saves it using the path and filename you specified.

9. When the rendering of frame 1 is complete, click the Abort button or press Enter, if necessary, to close the Render Scene Panel. In Layout, click the frame advance button or press the right arrow key to advance to frame 2 of the animation. If you stayed at frame 1, LightWave would overwrite every old file with each new one, since they would have the same name. When you make changes and then render from frame 2, LightWave correctly renumbers the new image file so it doesn't overwrite the old one.

10. Click the Objects button in the Edit area of Layout, then press p to bring up the Objects Panel (see Figure 3-5).

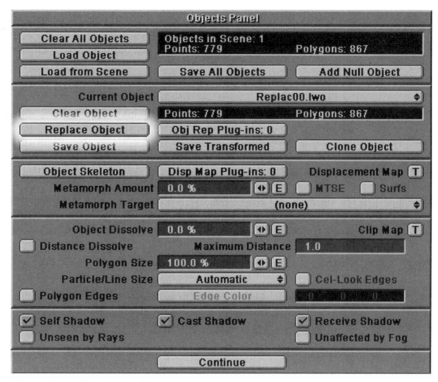

Figure 3-5: Objects Panel.

11. In the Current Object section, click the Replace Object button. An operating system dialog titled "Replacement Object File" appears (see Figure 3-6).

Note: The appearance of these dialogs depends on the operating system you are using. All the screen shots in this book were taken from computers running Windows NT 4.0, but the other operating systems should be similar enough that you will have no trouble following these directions. Other LightWave 3D screens are identical for all operating systems.

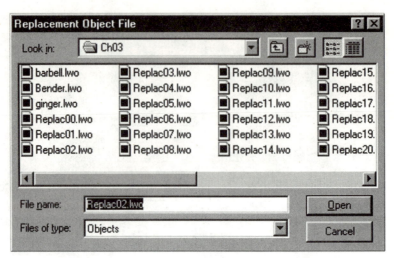

Figure 3-6: Replacement Object File dialog.

12. Select the REPLAC02.LWO object file and press Enter. Click the Continue button or press p to close the Objects Panel. The replacement object is loaded into Layout in the same position and with the same settings as the original object.

Note: These objects were created by the process detailed in Exercise 12-4 later in this book. They are basically modified duplicates of the DESKLMP.LWO tutorial object that comes with LightWave 3D. If you'd like to try creating your own objects for this exercise, skip ahead to that exercise and return to this one when your own object library is complete.

13. Press Enter or click the Create Key button at the bottom center of the Layout window to save the keyframe. The Create Motion Key Panel appears. Press Enter to confirm the keyframe save and close the panel.

14. Click the Render button at the bottom left of the Layout window. The Render Scene Panel appears again (see Figure 3-7).

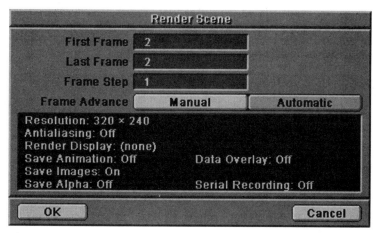

Figure 3-7: Render Scene Panel, all set to render frame 2.

15. Change the First Frame setting to 2, Last Frame to 2, and press Enter to render the image.

16. When the rendering of the image is complete, click Continue or press Enter to close the Render Scene Panel, if necessary. In Layout, click the frame advance button or press the right arrow key to advance to the next frame of the animation.

17. Repeat steps 10 through 16 for frames 3 through 30, selecting the REPLACXX.LWO object with the matching number for each frame.

When you have completed this exercise, you should have 30 images in a numbered sequence. Unfortunately, using this technique prevents LightWave 3D from saving the images as an AVI file, since each image is a separate render operation. You can load them as a background image sequence in an otherwise empty LightWave 3D animation and render it out as an AVI; or use one of the available freeware or shareware video tools to assemble the separate images into an AVI or FLC file for playback.

You should end up with an AVI file similar to the example file you find in the Chapter 3 directory of the Companion CD-ROM, EXER0301.AVI.

18. Play back either the sample animation (see Figure 3-8) or your own while you read and think about the following critique.

Figure 3-8: Frames 1, 15, and 30 from EXER0301.AVI animation of Exercise 3-1 results.

Even though the motion of the bending lamp seems smooth enough, it depends on having one complete pose for each frame. If you tried to stretch the animation out to 90 or 120 frames but still used only 30 objects, you would see jerks or *strobing* each time the pose changed. Since the objects are not really connected from frame to frame (the way Bones or Metamorph objects are), there are no in-between poses for LightWave 3D to render. Even Motion Blur won't help, since the object is not actually moving. This is one reason other techniques are generally more useful than single-frame replacement animation.

One potential advantage to this technique depends on how large and diverse your library of objects is, and oddly enough is related to 2D rather than 3D animation traditions. The 2D technique known as *straight-ahead action* consists of drawing each pose as you come to it, working out timing, and posing on the fly. This results in a zany, impromptu look that is difficult to produce in a preplanned sequence. Animating using the Replace Object function enables you to exert the same freedom as straight-ahead action, limited only by the range of objects you have available to throw into the mix. If you work with a particular character over any length of time, creating objects for expressions and actions as you go, you may eventually collect enough objects to make Replace Object animation feasible.

As you work with a character, you may collect enough objects to make Replace Object animation feasible.

Another major disadvantage of this approach is that the animation is not readily edited or repeated. Just as straight-ahead action leaves no key drawings to connect revised actions with, Replace Object animation loses the preceding frame information every time you save the current keyframe.

ObjSequence Plug-in

The ObjSequence plug-in works a lot like the Replace Object exercise you just completed. This is like lining up all the objects you are going to use on a shelf, in order, with duplicates where necessary. You just work down the row, swapping out the next object in line without having to think about it. The only difference is that the "shelf" you use is a directory on your computer, and the plug-in does the replacement for you.

This works exactly like setting up an Image Sequence. You make copies of the object file for each frame where you want it to first appear, and name the copy to match the frame number. For example, if you want the object REPLAC05.LWO to appear in frames 25, 37, and 42, you duplicate the REPLAC05.LWO file three times, and name the copies REPLA025.LWO, REPLA037.LWO, and REPLA042.LWO.

This approach is easy to use because LightWave 3D doesn't require you to specify an object for each frame in a sequence; it "holds" the last used object until the next higher number in the sequence is reached. For example, if the file order is:

1, 2, 5, 10, 11

the displayed file sequence will actually be:

1, 2, 2, 2, 5, 5, 5, 5, 5, 10, 11.

Obviously, this can save you a great deal of work in laying out an object sequence. You only have to specify the changes, not the holds!

Exercise 3-2: Animating the Desk Lamp With the ObjSequence Plug-in

The approach we're going to use is simple, requiring only a bit of typing. Since there are only 31 objects to choose from, we'll simply write a *batch file*, a text file containing a list of DOS commands, to make the required number of copies of the object files, numbered in the order we want them to appear. The completely manual approach would be to use your system's Copy and Rename functions for each and every file, which would get tedious.

1. Set up a new directory for the sequence objects.

2. Copy the REPLAC00.LWO through REPLAC30.LWO objects to the new directory.

3. This exercise is fairly simple, so we won't bother with an exposure sheet. All we will do is make the lamp bend forward, then bend more slowly back up to its original position. This means the

first 30 frames will call for the objects in their original numerical order, and the last 60 frames will call for them backwards, at two-frame intervals. You might want to write this out to help you visualize it.

4. Using Windows Notepad or another text editor, create a new batch file named for this exercise (EX0302.BAT). Type

```
REM BATCH FILE FOR EXERCISE 3-2
```

for the first line and save it in the new directory along with the objects.

5. The first frame of the animation calls for the REPLAC00.LWO object file. Add a second line to the batch file, reading:

```
COPY REPLAC00.LWO OBJSQ000.LWO
```

This command duplicates the original object with a new name. This means the original object will appear in frame 0 of the animation. Note that the ObjSequence plug-in requires the file name to end in a three-digit number sequence.

6. Select the second line (including carriage return), copy it, and paste it as many times as the first object is called for, which in this case is only twice. For some animations you may end up duplicating a single object several dozen times. You should end up with this:

```
REM BATCH FILE FOR EXERCISE 3-2
COPY REPLAC00.LWO OBJSQ000.LWO
COPY REPLAC00.LWO OBJSQ000.LWO
```

7. Select the number part of the new filename in the third line. Type the number of the next start frame for this phoneme object. Since we are animating one "ping-pong" cycle with a total of 90 frames, and objects in the last half of the animation are all held for two frames, this object should appear in frames 0, 89, and 90.

```
REM BATCH FILE FOR EXERCISE 3-2
COPY REPLAC00.LWO OBJSQ000.LWO
COPY REPLAC00.LWO OBJSQ089.LWO
```

Note that we don't have to make a copy for frame 90, as the plug-in holds the last object until a higher number comes along.

8. Repeat these steps for the rest of the objects. When you're finished you should have a list to make 61 copies, thus:

```
REM BATCH FILE FOR EXERCISE 3-2
COPY REPLAC00.LWO OBJSQ000.LWO
COPY REPLAC00.LWO OBJSQ089.LWO
COPY REPLAC01.LWO OBJSQ001.LWO
COPY REPLAC01.LWO OBJSQ087.LWO
COPY REPLAC02.LWO OBJSQ002.LWO
COPY REPLAC02.LWO OBJSQ085.LWO
COPY REPLAC03.LWO OBJSQ003.LWO
COPY REPLAC03.LWO OBJSQ083.LWO
COPY REPLAC04.LWO OBJSQ004.LWO
COPY REPLAC04.LWO OBJSQ081.LWO
COPY REPLAC05.LWO OBJSQ005.LWO
COPY REPLAC05.LWO OBJSQ079.LWO
COPY REPLAC06.LWO OBJSQ006.LWO
COPY REPLAC06.LWO OBJSQ077.LWO
COPY REPLAC07.LWO OBJSQ007.LWO
COPY REPLAC07.LWO OBJSQ075.LWO
COPY REPLAC08.LWO OBJSQ008.LWO
COPY REPLAC08.LWO OBJSQ073.LWO
COPY REPLAC09.LWO OBJSQ009.LWO
COPY REPLAC09.LWO OBJSQ071.LWO
COPY REPLAC10.LWO OBJSQ010.LWO
COPY REPLAC10.LWO OBJSQ069.LWO
COPY REPLAC11.LWO OBJSQ011.LWO
COPY REPLAC11.LWO OBJSQ067.LWO
COPY REPLAC12.LWO OBJSQ012.LWO
COPY REPLAC12.LWO OBJSQ065.LWO
COPY REPLAC13.LWO OBJSQ013.LWO
COPY REPLAC13.LWO OBJSQ063.LWO
COPY REPLAC14.LWO OBJSQ014.LWO
COPY REPLAC14.LWO OBJSQ061.LWO
COPY REPLAC15.LWO OBJSQ015.LWO
COPY REPLAC15.LWO OBJSQ059.LWO
COPY REPLAC16.LWO OBJSQ016.LWO
COPY REPLAC16.LWO OBJSQ057.LWO
COPY REPLAC17.LWO OBJSQ017.LWO
COPY REPLAC17.LWO OBJSQ055.LWO
COPY REPLAC18.LWO OBJSQ018.LWO
COPY REPLAC18.LWO OBJSQ053.LWO
COPY REPLAC19.LWO OBJSQ019.LWO
COPY REPLAC19.LWO OBJSQ051.LWO
COPY REPLAC20.LWO OBJSQ020.LWO
COPY REPLAC20.LWO OBJSQ049.LWO
```

```
COPY REPLAC21.LWO OBJSQ021.LWO
COPY REPLAC21.LWO OBJSQ047.LWO
COPY REPLAC22.LWO OBJSQ022.LWO
COPY REPLAC22.LWO OBJSQ045.LWO
COPY REPLAC23.LWO OBJSQ023.LWO
COPY REPLAC23.LWO OBJSQ043.LWO
COPY REPLAC24.LWO OBJSQ024.LWO
COPY REPLAC24.LWO OBJSQ041.LWO
COPY REPLAC25.LWO OBJSQ025.LWO
COPY REPLAC25.LWO OBJSQ039.LWO
COPY REPLAC26.LWO OBJSQ026.LWO
COPY REPLAC26.LWO OBJSQ037.LWO
COPY REPLAC27.LWO OBJSQ027.LWO
COPY REPLAC27.LWO OBJSQ035.LWO
COPY REPLAC28.LWO OBJSQ028.LWO
COPY REPLAC28.LWO OBJSQ033.LWO
COPY REPLAC29.LWO OBJSQ029.LWO
COPY REPLAC29.LWO OBJSQ031.LWO
COPY REPLAC30.LWO OBJSQ030.LWO
```

9. Save the batch file and make a backup copy. It's fairly easy to rebuild the directory structure if you accidentally delete some object files, but if you lose this batch file you'll have to go back and type it all over.

   Also, once you have a particular object sequence worked out (and some of them can be very complex), you can apply it to any compatible set of objects. Just use your text editor's Find and Replace functions to change the source filenames in the batch file. This can save you the time and bother of having to retype the whole thing from scratch.

10. Make sure you've got plenty of disk space available. Multiply the number of lines in your batch file by the size of the largest file you are duplicating to get the total required. When you are ready, execute the batch file.

11. Now you get to do some preemptive quality control. Browse the object sequence directory. Did the files end up where you expected them to? Are all the file numbers you expected actually there? Open a few files in Modeler as a spot check and compare them with the batch file. This quality control is not so crucial for this exercise, but it's a good habit to develop. It's better to catch any mistakes now than after rendering an entire animation.

12. Reload the EXER0301.LWS scene file in Layout. This is to save you the trouble of setting up the camera angle in a new scene. Click the Objects button at the top left of the Layout window to open the Objects Panel.

13. Click the Replace Object button. The Replacement Objects File dialog appears. Select the first object file in the sequence, OBJSQ000.LWO, and press Enter to close the Replacement Objects File dialog and return to the Objects Panel. The Current Object button now shows the file name OBJSQ000.LWO (see Figure 3-9).

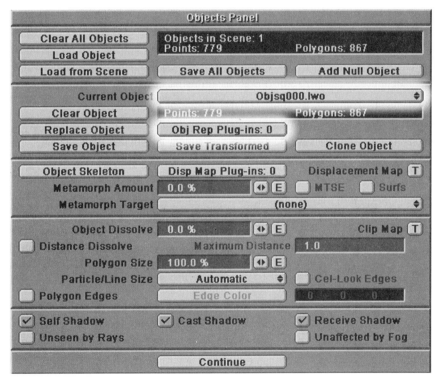

Figure 3-9: OBJSQ000.LWO, the first object of the sequence, is loaded in the Objects Panel.

14. Click the Obj Rep Plug-ins button just beneath the Current Object button. The Object Replacement Plug-ins Panel appears, with the Plug-in 1 drop-down option reading (none) (see Figure 3-10).

Figure 3-10: Object Replacement Plug-ins Panel, with no plug-ins loaded.

15. Drag down the Plug-in 1 drop-down button and select ObjectSequence. Click Continue to close the Object Replacement Plug-ins Panel and return to the Objects Panel. The Obj Rep Plug-ins button now shows one plug-in loaded.

16. Press p or click the Continue button at the bottom of the Objects Panel to close it and return to Layout.

17. Create a keyframe at frame 0, then create another one at frame 90 for all items. Save the scene. In Layout, frame 30 should look like Figure 3-11.

18. Make a preview for all 90 frames. Play it back at a variety of speeds and observe it closely. Is the action smooth enough? Did any objects get out of order, causing strobing?

    Note that the motion of frames 1 through 30 is apparently smoother, even though frames 31 through 90 are using the exact same objects in reverse order. This is because the first 30 frames are animated "on ones," that is, every frame has an increment of motion. The last 60 frames are animated "on twos," since each object replacement is held for two frames. This is just long enough to be perceptible as strobing to most people, if the movement is large enough.

19. Manually delete alternating object files between OBJSQ031 and OBJSQ089 (33, 37, 41, etc.), then return to Layout and redraw the preview animation.

    Now you can see how jerky the last part of the preview becomes when it's animated on fours.

    Most cel or 2D animation, especially Saturday morning cartoons aimed at children, is animated on twos, and sometimes even as high as fours, in order to save money. 2D seems to be able to get away with longer intervals without strobing. Puppet animation, with the higher realism of sets and modeled characters, generally can't even get away with animating on twos because the audience is expecting smoother, more realistic motion.

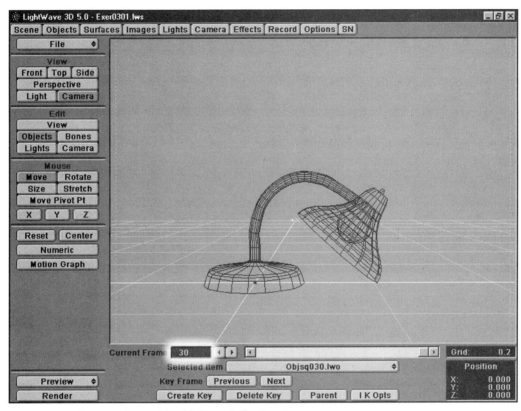

Figure 3-11: Scene at frame 30 with lamp fully flexed.

You need an object for every frame, or your audience will begin to see strobing.

You need to keep this in mind when planning an animation sequence. If you are thinking about using one of these replacement techniques, remember that you will have to have an object for each and every frame, or your audience will begin to see strobing.

20. If you like, render the animation in AVI format.

You should end up with an AVI file similar to the example file in the Chapter 3 directory of the Companion CD-ROM, EXER0302.AVI (see Figure 3-12).

21. Play back the sample animation or your own while you read and think about the following critique.

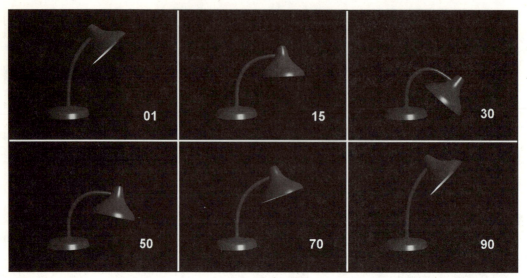

Figure 3-12: Frames 1, 15, 30, 50, 70, 90 from EXER0302.AVI animation of Exercise 3-1 results.

The ObjectSequence technique apparently shares the strobing problem of the Replace Object technique you learned in Exercise 3-1. The advantages of ObjectSequence seem to be simplicity, repeatability (just run the batch file again, and repeat the loading of the first object and the ObjectSequence plug-in), and editability (just edit the batch file to copy as many objects to as many frame addresses as you need).

One major disadvantage of the ObjSequence approach should be obvious. If you've got a long shot, with a lot of action, the number of copied files can get very large, very quickly, and demand a lot of hard disk space. The rule of "one object, one frame" is an expensive one to observe when individual object files grow large. If this becomes a problem, you may have to render the animation in segments, limited by how many objects your system can store at one time. Also, as with all replacement techniques, you are limited to the objects you have on hand. If you need a new pose, you will have to model one or have your TD model one for you.

While not exactly a drawback, it is especially important with this approach to keep your files organized. If you mess up a directory name, you could end up with one object being systematically replaced with the target objects for another!

Incidentally, this technique is an excellent one for generating an animation or a series of stills of all the objects in a library—a handy reference when you have dozens or even hundreds of objects to choose from!

ObjList Plug-in

The ObjList object replacement plug-in works a lot like ObjectSequence, except you don't have to change or duplicate the object files. You still get to write up which object you want to appear in a particular frame in advance, and the plug-in does the replacement for you. Where the ObjSequence plug-in loads the objects in numerical order, you can tell the ObjList plug-in to load any file in any order you like.

Exercise 3-3: Animating the Desk Lamp With the ObjList Plug-in

This approach is also a simple one, again requiring only a bit of typing, with the same 31 objects to choose from. We'll simply write a properly formatted text file that calls for the object files in the order we want them to appear. If you are used to working with exposure sheets, this will be a piece of cake.

1. The Object Replacement List text file has to have a particular format. Use Windows Notepad or your favorite text editor to create a new text file with the first line:

   ```
   #LW Object Replacement List
   ```

   This header must be used for every Object Replacement List.

2. Each object replacement requires two lines in the text file. The first one sets the frame where the replacement is made. The second provides the full path and filename of the replacement object. We want the animation to start at frame 0, with the lamp at its normal position, so add these two lines to the text file:

   ```
   0
   d:\newtek\objects\ch03\replac00.lwo
   ```

3. To add a little variety, this time let's make the desk lamp stop part way through its bend, come back up slightly, then continue down to nearly touch the ground. To do this, objects 0 through 20 need to be in their usual order, then repeated in reverse order back to object 10, then forward again all the way to object 30, like this:

   ```
   #LW Object Replacement List
   0
   d:\newtek\objects\ch03\replac00.lwo
   1
   d:\newtek\objects\ch03\replac01.lwo
   2
   d:\newtek\objects\ch03\replac02.lwo
   ```

```
3
d:\newtek\objects\ch03\replac03.lwo
4
d:\newtek\objects\ch03\replac04.lwo
5
d:\newtek\objects\ch03\replac05.lwo
6
d:\newtek\objects\ch03\replac06.lwo
7
d:\newtek\objects\ch03\replac07.lwo
8
d:\newtek\objects\ch03\replac08.lwo
9
d:\newtek\objects\ch03\replac09.lwo
10
d:\newtek\objects\ch03\replac10.lwo
11
d:\newtek\objects\ch03\replac11.lwo
12
d:\newtek\objects\ch03\replac12.lwo
13
d:\newtek\objects\ch03\replac13.lwo
14
d:\newtek\objects\ch03\replac14.lwo
15
d:\newtek\objects\ch03\replac15.lwo
16
d:\newtek\objects\ch03\replac16.lwo
17
d:\newtek\objects\ch03\replac17.lwo
18
d:\newtek\objects\ch03\replac18.lwo
19
d:\newtek\objects\ch03\replac19.lwo
20
d:\newtek\objects\ch03\replac20.lwo
21
d:\newtek\objects\ch03\replac19.lwo
22
d:\newtek\objects\ch03\replac18.lwo
23
d:\newtek\objects\ch03\replac17.lwo
24
d:\newtek\objects\ch03\replac16.lwo
```

```
25
d:\newtek\objects\ch03\replac15.lwo
26
d:\newtek\objects\ch03\replac14.lwo
27
d:\newtek\objects\ch03\replac13.lwo
28
d:\newtek\objects\ch03\replac12.lwo
29
d:\newtek\objects\ch03\replac11.lwo
30
d:\newtek\objects\ch03\replac10.lwo
31
d:\newtek\objects\ch03\replac11.lwo
32
d:\newtek\objects\ch03\replac12.lwo
33
d:\newtek\objects\ch03\replac13.lwo
34
d:\newtek\objects\ch03\replac14.lwo
35
d:\newtek\objects\ch03\replac15.lwo
36
d:\newtek\objects\ch03\replac16.lwo
37
d:\newtek\objects\ch03\replac17.lwo
38
d:\newtek\objects\ch03\replac18.lwo
39
d:\newtek\objects\ch03\replac19.lwo
40
d:\newtek\objects\ch03\replac20.lwo
41
d:\newtek\objects\ch03\replac21.lwo
42
d:\newtek\objects\ch03\replac22.lwo
43
d:\newtek\objects\ch03\replac23.lwo
44
d:\newtek\objects\ch03\replac24.lwo
45
d:\newtek\objects\ch03\replac25.lwo
46
d:\newtek\objects\ch03\replac26.lwo
```

```
47
d:\newtek\objects\ch03\replac27.lwo
48
d:\newtek\objects\ch03\replac28.lwo
49
d:\newtek\objects\ch03\replac29.lwo
50
d:\newtek\objects\ch03\replac30.lwo
```

4. Save the list file. You should also save a backup copy if you intend to do any editing of the original list.

5. In Layout, load the EXER0301.LWS scene file again.

6. Click the Objects button in the Edit section at the middle left. Since there is only one object, REPLAC00.LWO, in the scene, it is listed as the Selected Item.

7. Press p to call up the Objects Panel (see Figure 3-13).

Figure 3-13: REPLAC00.LWO is loaded in the Objects Panel.

8. Click the Obj Rep Plug-ins button just beneath the Current Object button. The Object Replacement Plug-ins Panel appears, with the Plug-in 1 drop-down option reading (none) (see Figure 3-14).

Figure 3-14: Object Replacement Plug-ins Panel with no plug-ins loaded.

9. Drag down the Plug-in 1 drop-down button and select ObjList. Click the Options button to call up the Object Replacement List dialog. Select the List file you saved in step 4 and press Enter to close the dialog and return to the Object Replacement Plug-ins Panel.

10. Click Continue to close the Object Replacement Plug-ins Panel and return to the Objects Panel. The Obj Rep Plug-ins button now shows one plug-in loaded.

11. Press p or click the Continue button at the bottom of the Objects Panel to close it and return to Layout.

12. Create a keyframe at frame 0 for all items. Save the scene.

13. Make a preview of frames 1 through 50.

Note: The lamp makes an abrupt stop at frames 20 and 30 when it reverses direction. This is because we did not put in any ease-out, a technique we'll cover in more detail in another chapter. For now, all you need to concentrate on is the basic replacement technique. We'll fine-tune it later.

14. If you like, render the animation in AVI format. You can also try rewriting copies of the list file to create other variations on the basic bending motion of the desk lamp.

15. Play back the sample EXER0303.AVI animation from the Chapter 3 directory of the Companion CD-ROM (see Figure 3-15), or your own results, while you read and think about the following critique.

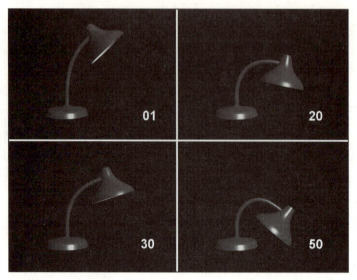

Figure 3-15: Frames 1, 20, 30, and 50 from EXER0303.AVI animation of Exercise 3-3 results.

The ObjectList technique shares the strobing problems of the Replace Object and ObjectSequence techniques you learned in Exercises 3-1 and 3-2. One object per frame for any changes is still necessary to prevent visible jerks.

However, you don't have to create a duplicate object for every frame. You can choose a series of objects by their original filenames, repeatedly, and in any order you like. This saves hard drive storage space and makes file management a lot easier. Also, making changes to the sequence or timing of objects only requires the editing of the List file; you don't need to clear off the previous setup's objects and re-execute a batch file. This means you can work faster, especially when experimenting.

Metamorph Function

The common problems of straight object replacement are (1) the requirement of an extensive and varied library of objects and (2) visible strobing in the animation if an object is replaced on twos or higher. Metamorphosing solves the second problem and goes a long way toward reducing the first one.

The Metamorph function calculates an in-between position for each point for every frame.

Just as for other replacement techniques, you specify a beginning object and the object that is to replace it. But instead of popping directly from one object file to the next, the Metamorph function calculates an in-between position for each point for every frame. This makes the changes very smooth, even when the object and target are hundreds or thousands of frames apart. It also means that objects to be used with Metamorph must share the exact same number of points. This makes creating complex Metamorph objects more of a challenge (see Chapter 12 for details).

Unfortunately, Metamorph doesn't know that objects sometimes move in arcs. When you provide the two objects to Metamorph, all it can do is calculate a straight-line change, or interpolation, in the position of each point relative to that point's counterpart in the target object. This can cause problems, as the following exercise demonstrates.

Exercise 3-4: Animating the Desk Lamp Using Metamorph

1. Load the EXER0301.LWS scene file into Layout again (see Figure 3-16).

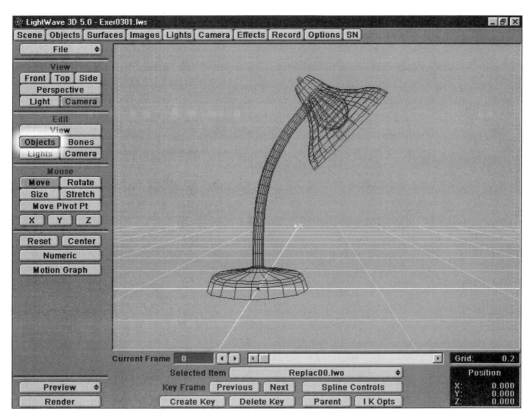

Figure 3-16: EXER0301.LWS scene file loaded and ready for replacement animation exercise.

2. Click on the Objects button in the Edit area at the middle left. Since there is only one object in the scene (REPLAC00.LWO), it is shown as the Selected Item in the drop-down button at the bottom of the window.

3. Press p to open the Objects Panel (see Figure 3-17).

4. Click the Load Object button at the upper left. Select object file REPLAC05.LWO, and press Enter to close the file dialog and return to the Objects Panel. Set the Object Dissolve value at 100 % and press Enter to accept the change. This keeps the object invisible during renderings. We don't want to see it, we just want to use it to change the original object.

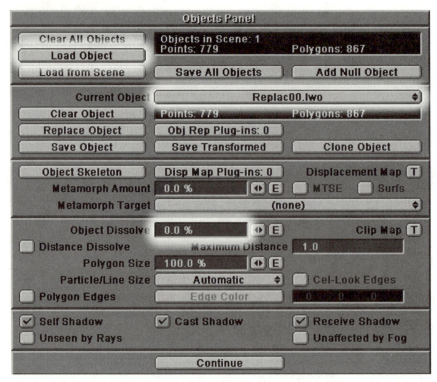

Figure 3-17: REPLAC00.LWO is loaded in the Objects Panel.

5. Repeat step 4 for object files REPLAC10.LWO, REPLAC15.LWO, REPLAC20.LWO, REPLAC25.LWO, and REPLAC30.LWO. These are the different Metamorph target objects you'll be using.

6. Select REPLAC00.LWO from the Current Object drop-down list. This is the object the metamorphosis will start with.

7. In the Metamorph Target drop-down list, in the middle of the Objects Panel, select REPLAC30.LWO as the target object. This is the object the metamorphosis will go toward.

8. Click on E to open the Morph Envelope Panel (see Figure 3-18).

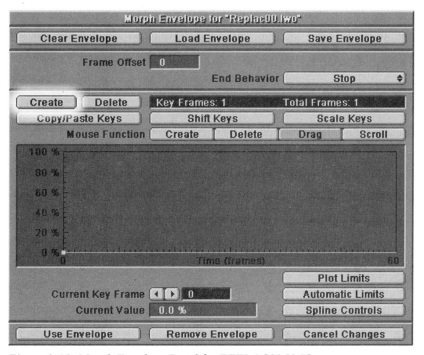

Figure 3-18: Morph Envelope Panel for REPLAC00.LWO.

The Morph Envelope controls how quickly and to what extent the metamorphosis will take place.

The Morph Envelope controls how quickly and to what extent the metamorphosis will take place. This is a very important and powerful animation tool, and we really can't do it justice in this chapter; the tweaks you can perform with the Envelope controls are detailed later in the book. For now, we'll just make the transformation happen smoothly over 60 frames.

9. Click the Create button just above the Copy/Paste Keys button. The Create Key at Frame Panel appears. Type **60** and press Enter to accept the input; close the panel and return to the Morph Envelope Panel (see Figure 3-19).

Figure 3-19: Create Key at Frame Panel for Morph Envelope.

Notice the new yellow dot at frame 60. This represents the keyframe you just created, and shows that it is currently selected.

10. While the keyframe at frame 60 is still selected, type **100** in the Current Value field at the bottom center and press Enter. This puts the keyframe dot right up at the top right corner of the Envelope graph (see Figure 3-20).

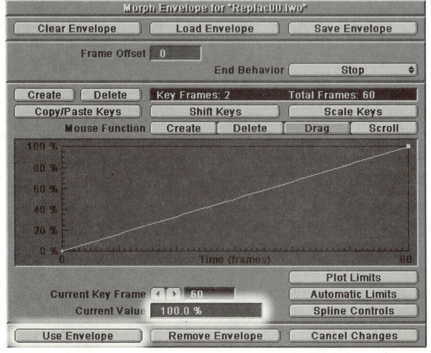

Figure 3-20: Envelope graph for REPLAC00.LWO, after editing.

This straight-line graph means that the metamorphosis will go smoothly from 100 percent REPLAC00.LWO to 100 percent REPLAC30.LWO, over the course of 60 frames.

11. Click the Use Envelope button at the bottom left to close the Morph Envelope Panel and return to the Objects Panel. Press p again to close the Objects Panel and return to the Layout window.

    You'll have a screen full of overlapping objects. Even though you set all but one object to 100% Dissolve, their wireframes or bounding boxes are still visible in Layout. To make it easier to see what you are doing, you will probably want to make the target objects disappear.

12. Click on the Scene button at the upper left of the Layout window. The Scene Panel appears (see Figure 3-21).

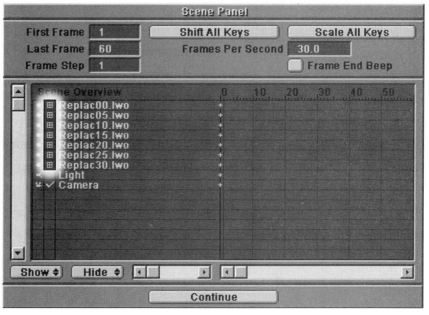

Figure 3-21: Scene Panel showing all objects loaded.

13. If you click on the small icon in the second column of the Scene Overview area the icon changes. This icon represents the object's visual status. If no icon is displayed in this column, the object is Hidden, or invisible. Click on the icon for each object (except REPLAC00.LWO) until they are all Hidden.

If you want to hide most of the objects in the scene, it may be faster to choose Hide All Objects from the Hide pull-down list at the bottom left, then individually unHide the objects you do want to see.

14. Make a wireframe preview of frames 1 through 60. Play the preview.

    What in the world is going on here? The shade, in fact the entire upper part of the lamp, seems to be shrinking in the middle of the animation!

    Remember what I mentioned earlier about Metamorph only handling straight-line changes? If you traced the outline of the lamp from frame 0 over an image from frame 30, and drew a line connecting the frame 0 and frame 30 positions of the outside front edge of the lamp's shade, you would find that an image from frame 15 would also have its lamp shade edge touching that line, exactly halfway between frame 1 and frame 30. Metamorph is taking each point on the shortest path between two points: a straight line.

    As you can see, this distorts the object and produces unrealistic actions. The lamp looks like it is melting from one position to the next.

    To avoid this problem, you need to use Metamorph targets that are fairly close to the original object in shape. The difference between REPLAC00.LWO and REPLAC30.LWO is pretty extreme, but the difference between REPLAC00.LWO and REPLAC05.LWO is not nearly so extreme.

15. Click End Preview to close the Preview Panel and return to Layout. Open the Objects Panel again and select REPLAC05.LWO for the Metamorph target object. Close the Objects Panel and make another preview.

    This one turned out much better. There is not much arc between the original object and the -05 target object, so Metamorph's straight-line interpolation is almost undetectable.

16. Repeat step 15 again, using objects REPLAC10.LWO, -15, -20, and -25, to see how much distortion you can get away with.

The Metamorph technique eliminates the strobing problems of the Replace Object, ObjectSequence, and ObjectList techniques you learned in the first three exercises. Instead of popping directly from one object file to the next, the Metamorph function calculates an in-between position for each point for every frame. This makes the changes very smooth, even when the object and target are hundreds or thousands of frames apart.

Unfortunately, Metamorph can't read your mind. You know that a bending lamp should move in an arc, but Metamorph doesn't know that. When you provide the two objects to Metamorph, all it can do is calculate a straight-line change, or interpolation, in the position of each point relative to its counterpart in the other object.

One way to compensate for this problem is to use enough targets, closely spaced, that the straight-line interpolation is not noticeable to your audience. This is most important with actions like a character's curling fingers or bending arms, where the points describe relatively large arcs between their start and end points. Metamorphosing for facial animation generally doesn't have this problem, as the arcs are much shorter and straight-line interpolation works just fine.

As a matter of fact, facial animation is one of the stronger uses for Metamorph and its big brother, MTSE. You can use either the Metamorph percentage setting or Envelope to precisely control the transition between objects. This gives you the power, for example, to animate a face precisely 65 percent of the distance from an "anger" object to a "rage" object to get the exact emotional nuance you want for your animated transitions.

Metamorph requires four or five targets for a smooth desk lamp bend; the other techniques needed 30.

Even if you have to use more targets to disguise straight-line interpolations, you will still use fewer targets for Metamorphosing than you would have for an equivalent ObjList, ObjSequence, or Replace Object animation. Metamorph requires four or five targets for a smooth desk lamp bend; the other techniques needed 30.

One obvious limitation is that Metamorph is designed to transform from one object to another. What do you do if you have a whole string of targets within a single animation, as in lip sync? That's what the next function, MTSE, is all about.

Multiple Target Single Envelope (MTSE)

We'll wrap up the replacement animation part of this chapter with what I believe is the most versatile and powerful replacement tool of all—MTSE. I use this tool by preference, as I believe it provides the user with the best combination of control, ease of use, power, and flexibility. There are a few character animation tricks you can't perform with this tool, but not many.

MTSE enables you to chain together a number of Metamorph target objects, then control the metamorphosis between the default object and any of the targets by using a single effect Envelope. This is incredibly powerful, as you can manipulate the spline controls of the Envelope graph to interactively put the exact percentages of each Metamorph target exactly when you want them.

For example, if you have an object library of heads for the basic phonemes and emotions (anywhere from 15 to several dozen objects), you can load them all in an MTSE chain and then use the Envelope to make the head lip sync and run through any emotional transition in range. Needless to say, MTSE figures prominently in later chapters. For now, you can concentrate on the basics.

Exercise 3-5: Animating the Desk Lamp With MTSE

1. Load the EXER0301.LWS scene file into Layout one more time (see Figure 3-22). If you made changes to it by mistake, reload the original file from the Companion CD-ROM.

2. Click the Objects button in the Edit area at the left. Since there is only one object in the scene (REPLAC00.LWO), it is shown as the Selected Item in the drop-down button at the bottom.

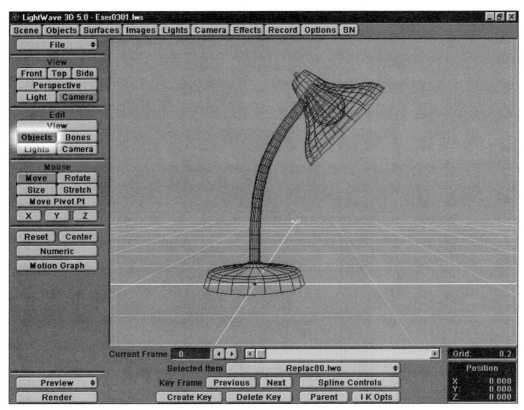

Figure 3-22: EXER0301.LWS scene file loaded and ready for replacement animation exercise.

3. Press p to open the Objects Panel (see Figure 3-23).

4. Click the Load Object button at the upper left. Select object file REPLAC05.LWO, and press Enter to close the file dialog and return to the Objects Panel. Set the Object Dissolve value, just below the center of the panel, at 100% and press Enter to accept the change. Just as in the previous exercise, this keeps the object invisible.

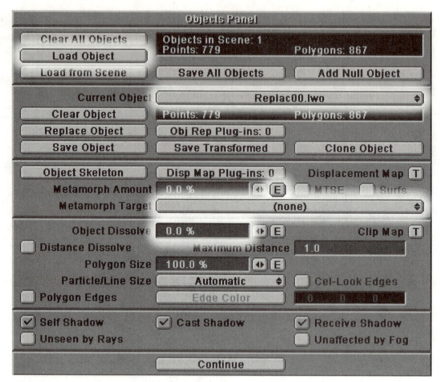

Figure 3-23: REPLAC00.LWO is loaded in the Objects Panel.

5. Repeat step 4 for object files REPLAC10.LWO, REPLAC15.LWO, REPLAC20.LWO, REPLAC25.LWO, and REPLAC30.LWO. These are the MTSE target objects you'll be using.

6. Select REPLAC00.LWO from the Current Object drop-down list. This is the beginning object for the MTSE chain.

7. In the Metamorph Target drop-down list, select REPLAC05.LWO as the target object. This is the object the first metamorphosis in the chain will go toward.

8. Select REPLAC05.LWO from the Current Object drop-down list. This is the second object in the MTSE chain.

9. In the Metamorph Target drop-down list, select REPLAC10.LWO as the target object. This is the object the second metamorphosis in the chain will go toward. Do you see the pattern you are following?

10. Repeat steps 8 and 9 for MTSE object pairs 10 and 15, 15 and 20, 20 and 25, and 25 and 30.

11. Select REPLAC00.LWO from the Current Object drop-down list. Click the E button next to the Metamorph Amount data field to open the Morph Envelope Panel shown in Figure 3-24.

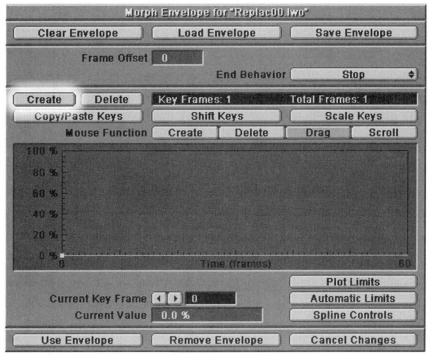

Figure 3-24: Morph Envelope Panel for REPLAC00.LWO.

12. Click on the Create button just above the Copy/Paste Keys button. The Create Key at Frame Panel appears (see Figure 3-25). Type **60**, and press Enter to accept the input, close the panel, and return to the Morph Envelope Panel.

Figure 3-25: Create Key at Frame Panel for Morph Envelope.

13. While the keyframe at frame 60 is still selected, type **600** in the Current Value field at the bottom center and press Enter. The Metamorph values for MTSE target objects are increased by 100 for each object in the chain. If there were only two targets, the top of the scale would be 200%. With six targets, the top end is 600% (see Figure 3-26). 0-100% controls morphing to the -05 object, 101-200% controls morphing to the -10 object, and so on.

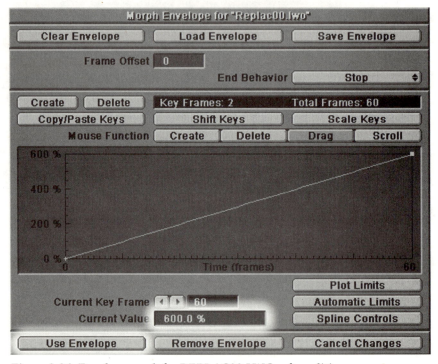

Figure 3-26: Envelope graph for REPLAC00.LWO, after editing.

This straight-line graph means that the metamorphosis will go smoothly from REPLAC00.LWO to REPLAC30.LWO over the course of 60 frames.

14. Click the Use Envelope button at the bottom left to close the Envelope Panel and return to the Objects Panel.

15. Click the MTSE button next to the E-for-Envelope button. This activates the MTSE chain you just set up. Press p again to close the Objects Panel and return to the Layout window.

16. You'll have a screen full of overlapping objects again. Just like last time, click the Scene button at the upper left of the Layout window. The Scene Panel appears (see Figure 3-27).

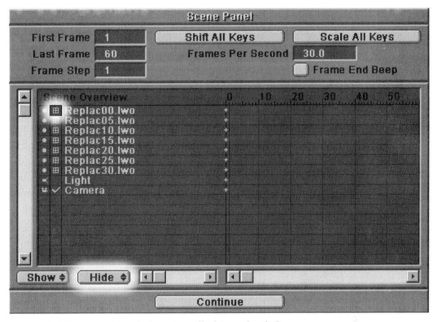

Figure 3-27: Scene Panel showing all objects loaded.

17. Choose Hide All Objects from the Hide pull-down list at the bottom of the panel, then click the icon next to REPLAC00.LWO to reset it to Full Wireframe. This conceals all the target objects while leaving the beginning object visible.

18. Make a wireframe preview of frames 1 through 60. Play the preview.

    Pretty smooth, huh? That's only using 7 objects, and the motion over 60 frames is just as smooth as using 30 objects in ObjList or ObjSequence over 30 frames. Now, let's have a little fun before we wrap this up and move on to displacement animation.

19. End the preview. Press p to open the Objects Panel again. Click the E button next to Metamorph Amount to open the Morph Envelope Panel again, shown in Figure 3-28.

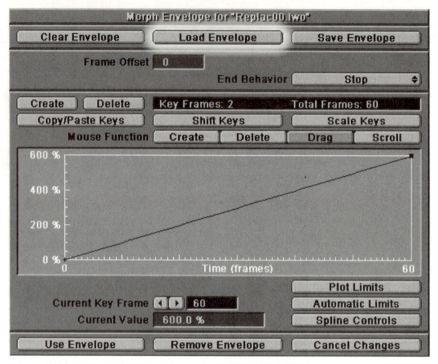

Figure 3-28: Morph Envelope Panel for REPLAC00.LWO.

20. Click the Load Envelope button at the top center. From the Chapter 3 directory of the Companion CD-ROM, select the file STAGGER.LWE. This is a quick little envelope I made just for fun. Press Enter to close the file dialog and return to the Morph Envelope Panel (see Figure 3-29).

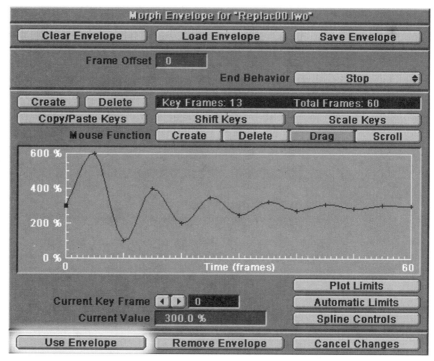

Figure 3-29: Morph Envelope Panel with STAGGER.LWE envelope loaded.

21. Click on the Use Envelope button to close the panel and return to the Objects Panel. Press p to close the Objects Panel and return to Layout.

22. Make a new preview. Play the preview.

MTSE can be tweaked by direct numerical entry, but is still malleable enough for "freehand" animation.

Boing! Isn't that fun? Fiddle with the envelope, create your own—this is a good way to learn something while amusing yourself. This particular envelope was based on something I remembered about a pendulum's period being constant, but the amplitude decreasing over time due to friction. This desk lamp is a flexible pendulum with a lot of friction and a short period.

As you can see, MTSE is powerful and at the same time relatively easy to use. The control it provides is pretty fine and can be accurately tweaked by direct numerical entry, but is still malleable enough for "freehand" animation work. A very nice combination.

The down side is that MTSE is a bit of a RAM hog if your objects are at all complex. All your target objects are loaded at all times, so extensive target libraries can really tax your system. Also, while MTSE and Metamorph animation require fewer objects than ObjList, ObjSequence, and Replace Object, you still need a good-sized object library to have a decent dramatic range for character animation. Add the fact that compatible objects pretty much have to be modified from the same base object, thereby limiting the Modeler tools you can use, and it's pretty much a bed of roses: you have to take the thorns with the blooms.

Displacement Animation

Displacement animation is probably more familiar than replacement animation to most people, because popular characters such as Gumby and King Kong were displacement puppets.

Efficient displacement animation requires a model that is jointed or flexible enough to be posed, but rigid enough to hold the pose while it is being photographed. Clay, rubber, urethane foam, and similar materials are often used for the external appearance of the displacement puppet, but these materials don't hold a pose very well under hot studio lights. That's why almost all displacement puppets have a metal skeleton, called an *armature*, that provides more rigid support. The design and construction of the armature is critical to the puppet's successful use, and there are many rules, guidelines, and trade secrets to building a good armature.

Displacement animation using LightWave 3D is similar in many respects. The exterior appearance of many LightWave objects, especially the organic shapes favored in character animation, is not readily animated. The polygonal structure needed to form the surface details doesn't lend itself well to the deformations—bending, stretching, and swelling—necessary to character animation. Accordingly, LightWave 3D includes a number of functions designed to replicate the effects of an armature.

The simplest form of armature is to string together separate objects in Layout, placing each object in a hierarchy by using the Parent function. This is a lot like assembling a marionette or a bare armature, because all the joints are exposed and very mechanical in action. If joints are required to be realistic, the objects must be modeled with mating surfaces just like an armature's. Ball-and-socket, lap hinge, and other joint constructions are typical.

If a more organic armature is required, the Bones functions are used. Bones is a method of distorting the shape of a single object in a controlled fashion in a defined area. A series of Bones are added to an object to form a skeleton. Some Bones may actually be placed outside the object's surface, but in most cases they are placed approximately where you would put a physical armature—through the center of the body and limbs.

Each Bone in an object's skeleton influences the points in its immediate area, and can also be used to influence the rest of the object, kind of like a configurable magnet. The Bones function in LightWave 3D 5.0 has also been enhanced to mimic the muscular expansion and compression common to most endoskeletal joints; that is, when your arm bends, your bicep swells and your tricep stretches out flat, and vice versa. Bones can also be used to control purely muscular distortion, such as tongues, tentacles, worms, and other invertebrate structures. This is a difficult job with even the best physical armatures, and nearly impossible with other types of CGI hierarchy tools.

As you might have guessed, Bones is a powerful character animation tool, but it does take some extra effort to master its full range. Let's take a look at the more basic Parent functions first.

Displacement Animation Using a Parented Object Hierarchy

The most basic form of displacement animation is a collection of rigid objects, joined together like the pieces of a traditional armature or puppet so they can rotate at the joints. LightWave 3D has a Parent function that can duplicate this effect, enabling you to assemble very complex puppet-like characters.

Exercise 3-6: Animating a Ball & Socket Joint

1. Click the File button at the top left of the Layout window and choose the Clear Scene option. Click the File button again and use the Load Scene option to load the EXER0306.LWS scene file from the Chapter 3 directory on the Companion CD-ROM.

    This scene is set up with no objects loaded, but the camera is set up to give you a good view of the exercise you're about to work through. Just trying to save you a little time!

2. Click the Object button at the top left. The Objects Panel appears. Click Load Object and choose the BARBELL.LWO object from the Chapter 3 directory. Click Load Object again, and again choose

BARBELL.LWO. The barbell object is loaded twice, with the numbers (1) and (2) in parentheses after their names in the drop-down list. Press p to close the Objects Panel and return to the Layout window, and click the Objects button in the Edit area at left center.

3. Make sure BARBELL.LWO (2) is shown in the Selected Item drop-down near the bottom. Click the Parent button at the bottom center. The Parent Object Panel appears (see Figure 3-30).

4. Choose BARBELL.LWO (1) from the pull-down menu, then press Enter or click the Continue button to return to the Layout window. This sets barbell 1 as the Parent of barbell 2. That means that barbell 2 will automatically follow all of 1's movements and rotations, just as if they were physically attached to each other.

    You should always Parent an object before you move or rotate it. If you Parent it afterwards, the changes will be recalculated from the Parent's origin, and the results will probably not be what you intended.

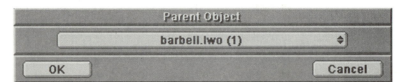

Figure 3-30: Parent Object Panel with BARBELL.LWO (1) selected.

It's not terribly helpful to have both objects completely overlapping each other. Let's move 2 down a bit.

5. Make sure BARBELL.LWO (2) is still the Selected Item. Click the Move button in the Mouse area at the left. Press n to call up the numeric Object Position Panel (see Figure 3-31).

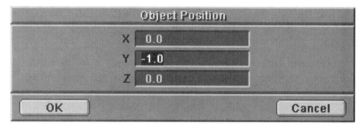

Figure 3-31: Object Position Panel.

6. Leave the X and Z values alone, but change the Y value to -1.0. This makes the second barbell's upper sphere exactly line up with the first barbell's lower sphere, making a nice ball joint. Press Enter or click Continue to save the settings and close the Object Position Panel.

7. Since the second barbell will be following the first one as a Parent, the second barbell doesn't need to move on its own any more. With the Move option still active in the Mouse area, click on each of the X, Y, and Z buttons in the Mouse area until they are grayed out. This locks off the second barbell's movement, so you won't accidentally shift it and mess up the objects' alignment.

8. At this point, you have your basic Parent hierarchy set up (see Figure 3-32). Click Create Key, and when the Create Motion Key Panel appears, choose the All Items option and click OK. You may also want to save the scene under a new name, just in case.

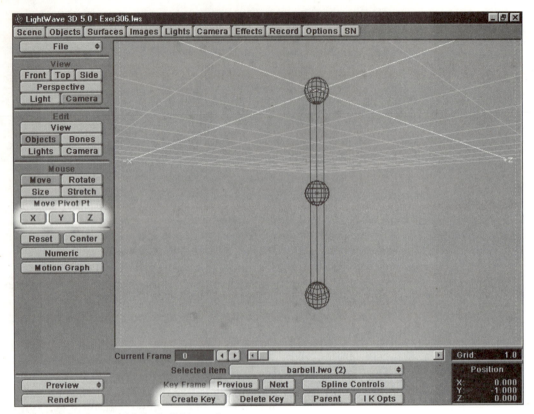

Figure 3-32: Scene with barbell hierarchy set up.

9. Drag the frame slider at the bottom of the view window all the way to the right to move to frame 30. You'll be posing the hierarchy and making another set of keyframes here.

10. With the second barbell still selected, click on the Rotate button in the Mouse area. Press n to call up the numeric Panel. Change the Pitch to 90 and the Heading to -80. Leave Bank set to zero; the barbell is symmetrical along the Bank axis and you probably wouldn't be able to detect the movement. Click OK or press Enter to save your changes and return to Layout (see Figure 3-33).

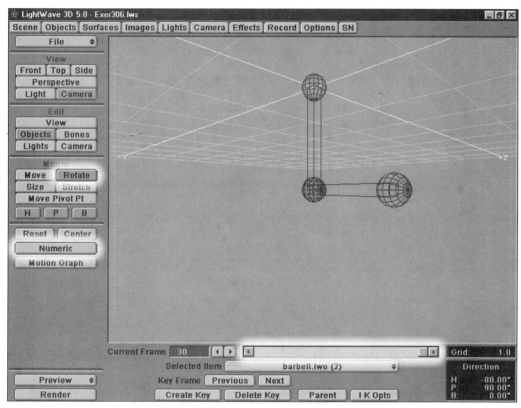

Figure 3-33: Scene with BARBELL.LWO (2) rotated.

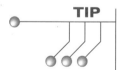

TIP

You could also make these changes by toggling off the B button, and using the mouse in the Heading and Pitch axes to pose the barbell interactively. Try it both ways, just for practice.

11. Choose BARBELL.LWO (1) from the Selected Item drop-down list at the bottom. Use the Move and Rotate options to position the barbell 0.5 meters along the Z axis, and with a Pitch of -30, as shown in Figure 3-34.

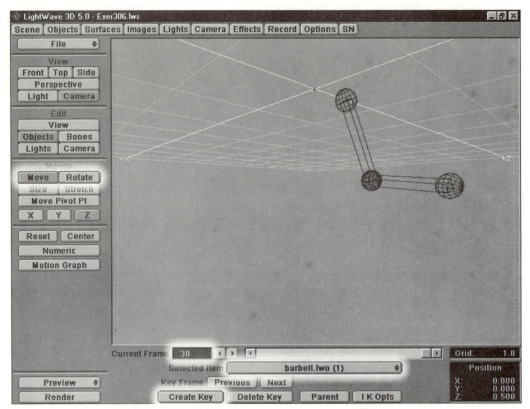

Figure 3-34: Scene with BARBELL.LWO (1) positioned and rotated.

12. Create keyframes for all items again, this time for frame 30. Make a preview.

    The barbells should rotate smoothly and move together, with the second one following the first one's lead. Experiment with posing the two barbells, making new keyframes to create new movements.

13. Once you are satisfied with your results, save the scene. You'll be using it again in the next exercise. Render an AVI of the scene, if you like.

There are several advantages to Parent hierarchical animation. You have very accurate control of the positioning and posing, the motion can be tweaked right down to every frame or bracketed with a single keyframe at each end of an animation, and there is no need to create extensive libraries of Metamorph objects.

Parent animation is limited by a rather mechanical joint appearance that needs to be disguised if used to animate organic objects. Also, the scene setup and posing take more time than replacement animation, assuming you already have the object libraries created.

Exercise 3-7: Animating a Ball & Socket Arm

I hope you saved your results from the previous exercise; you'll be using them here!

1. Click the File button at the top left of the Layout window and choose the Clear Scene option. Click the File button again and use the Load Scene option to reload the original EXER0306.LWS scene file from the Chapter 3 directory on the Companion CD-ROM. This scene is the one you just used, but without any of the changes you made.

2. Click the Object button at the top left. The Objects Panel appears. Click the Load from Scene button (just under the Load Object button), and choose the scene file you saved at the end of the previous exercise. You'll be asked whether you want the lights from the other scene loaded as well; answer No.

3. The two barbell objects load again. Press p to close the Objects Panel and return to Layout (see Figure 3-35).

4. Make a preview and play it.

Being able to save and reload entire Parent object hierarchies makes it much easier to reuse walk cycles and other complex actions.

The Parent hierarchy and the position and rotation keyframes are all loaded from the previous scene file. Being able to save and reload entire Parent object hierarchies makes it much easier to reuse walk cycles and other complex actions. Once loaded, you can edit them just as when you first created them. Just as with replacement objects, the longer you work with a set of objects, the more objects and actions you will have available for reuse. Keep this in mind while you are working, and save as a separate scene any actions that you think you might be able to use again.

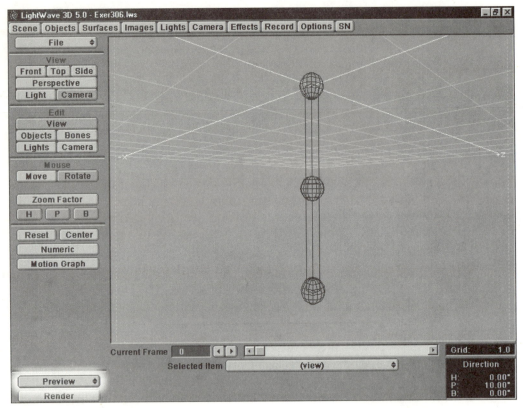

Figure 3-35: New scene with BARBELL.LWO (1) and (2) reloaded from old scene.

5. Move back to frame 0. Open the Objects Panel again, and click the Load Object button. Select a third copy of the barbell object and close the panel.

6. Make sure BARBELL.LWO (3) is shown in the Selected Item drop-down near the bottom. Click the Parent button at the bottom center. The Parent Object Panel appears.

7. Choose BARBELL.LWO (2) from the pull-down menu, then press Enter or click the OK button to return to the Layout window. This sets barbell 2 as the Parent of barbell 3.

8. Just as we did last time, let's move the Child barbell down a bit. Make sure BARBELL.LWO (3) is still the Selected Item. Click the Move button in the Mouse area at the left center of the window. Press n to call up the numeric Object Position Panel (see Figure 3-36).

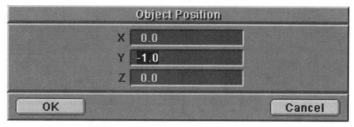

Figure 3-36: Object Position Panel.

9. Leave the X and Z values alone, but change the Y value to -1.0. This makes the third barbell's upper sphere exactly line up with the second barbell's lower sphere, making a nice ball joint. This assumes you did not change frame 0 of your previous scene before saving it; if you did, manually align the top sphere of barbell 3 with the bottom sphere of barbell 2. Press Enter or click Continue to save the settings and close the Object Position Panel.

10. The third barbell, now that it has a Parent to lead the way, doesn't need to move on its own any more. With the Move option still active in the Mouse area, click each of the X, Y, and Z buttons in the Mouse area until they are grayed out. This locks off the third barbell's movement, so it won't accidentally be moved out of alignment.

11. Create a new keyframe for all items at frame 0 and save the scene under a new name, just in case.

12. Move to frame 30 and pose the new addition to the hierarchy in any way you choose. When you are finished, set another keyframe for all items at frame 30 and make a preview.

You can see how useful it can be to have a library of scenes with prebuilt or half-built actions. If you plan ahead, and use the Replace functions to swap incompatible objects, there is a lot of potential to build motion libraries. You also retain precise control of position and attitude for each object, which means every saved action is as adaptable as any you build from scratch.

You still have to deal with the mechanical joint appearance, and using the Reload from Scene function brings in the whole enchilada, whether you wanted it or not. If you think you might want to load just part of an action, save a duplicate of the original and delete all the extraneous stuff. It'll save you time later on when you might really need it.

Displacement Animation Using Bones

A traditional puppet can have visible rotating joints like those you emulated in the preceding exercise; it can also have a flexible outer covering over a jointed armature, or inner skeleton, allowing the puppet's skin to deform without visible seams. LightWave 3D's Bones functions can duplicate this effect, enabling you to assemble complex characters that simulate the appearance of bone, flesh, and skin.

Exercise 3-8: Animating an Elbow Bend With Bones

1. Click the File button at the top left of the Layout window and choose the Clear Scene option. Click the File button again and use the Load Scene option to load the EXER0308.LWS scene file from the Chapter 3 directory on the Companion CD-ROM.

   This scene is set up with no objects loaded, but as before, the camera is set up to give you a good view of the exercise you're about to work through.

2. Click the Object button at the top left. The Objects Panel appears. Click Load Object and choose the BENDER.LWO object from the Chapter 3 directory. Press p to close the Objects Panel and return to the Layout window, and click the Objects button in the Edit area at left center.

   Note that the Bender object is a duplicate of the barbell, but with a lot more polygons near its center. This is where you will build the elbow joint. The more polygons around a joint, the smoother the bend will appear. If you don't have enough polygons in the area, you may end up with sharp corners where you don't want them.

3. Make sure you are looking at the Side view. Click the Bones button in the Edit area, and press p to open the Skeleton Panel (see Figure 3-37).

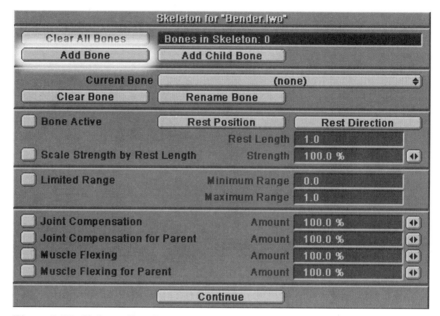

Figure 3-37: Skeleton Panel.

4. Click the Add Bone button, then press p to close the Skeleton Panel. The bone is added at the pivot point of the object, as shown in Figure 3-38.

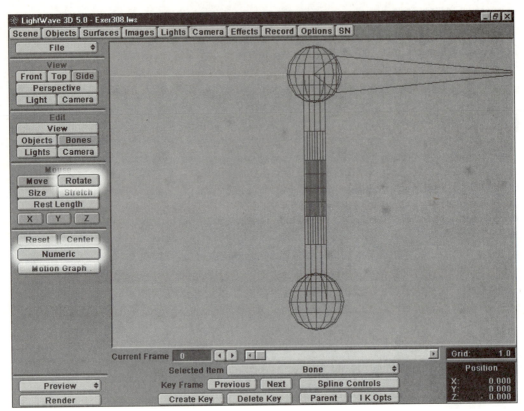

Figure 3-38: Bone added to BENDER.LWO object.

5. You want the bone to be inside the object and end in the middle of the elbow region. Click the Rotate button in the Mouse area and press n to call up the numeric Bone Direction Panel. Set the Pitch to 90, and leave Heading and Bank at zero. Press Enter to accept the change and close the panel. Layout should look like Figure 3-39.

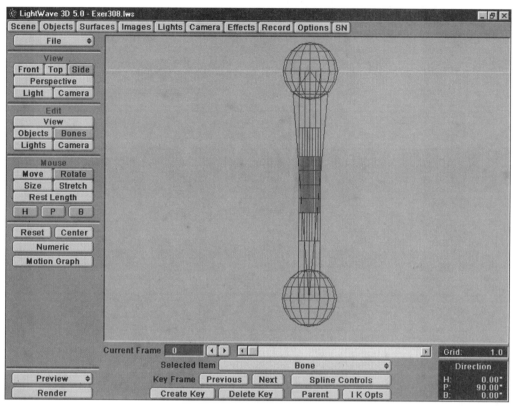

Figure 3-39: Bone aligned with BENDER.LWO object.

6. The bone is now aligned with the object's long axis, but it is obviously too long. Click on the Rest Length button in the Mouse area. Use the mouse to change the length of the bone, or press n for the numeric Bone Rest Length Panel, and set the rest length to 0.5; this produces something like Figure 3-40.

   If you use the Bone as is, it distorts the entire object. Sometimes this is the effect you want, but not if you want a simple elbow bend. Now you'll set the Limited Range to control just how much distortion this bone can produce.

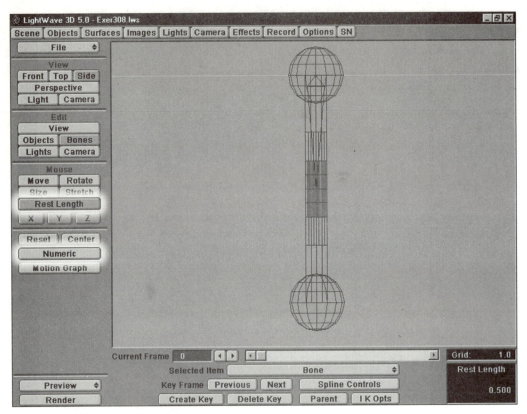

Figure 3-40: Bone Rest Length is set.

7. Press p again to open the Skeleton Panel. Click the Limited Range button at the middle left, then change the Minimum Range to 0.01 and the Maximum Range to 0.3. I found these values by trial and error; you can do the same, if you want to experiment. Press p again to close the panel.

8. With the bone still selected, create a keyframe for the Selected Item. After you create the keyframe, press r to activate the bone. If you had activated the bone before making a keyframe it would have performed all those size and rotation changes on the object!

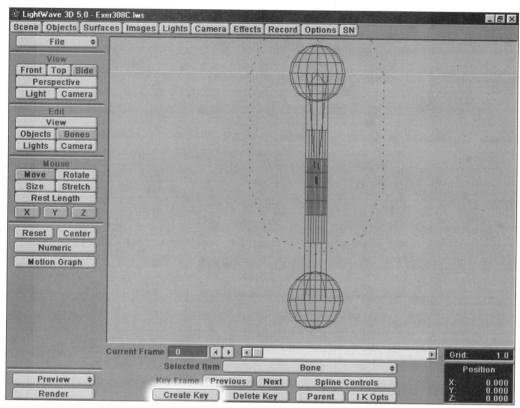

Figure 3-41: Bone Limited Range is set.

The bone is now surrounded by a dotted capsule shape (see Figure 3-41). This defines the area of the bone's furthest effect, as controlled by the Maximum setting. Any points within the Minimum distance are completely controlled by the bone, sort of locked down and immune to the influence of other bones. Any points outside the Maximum capsule are unaffected, and any inside it are affected in proportion to their distance from the Minimum. If you set identical Minimum and Maximum values, there is no falloff in the effect and every point inside the capsule is locked down.

Save the scene, just in case.

Well, that's one bone done. You've been taking regular breaks, I hope. The next step is to add a Child bone to the one you just finished.

9. Press p to open the Skeleton Panel again. Make sure the current bone is selected. Click the Add Child Bone near the top center of the panel. Click it again to add another Child Bone.

10. Use the Current Bone pull-down list to select each of the three bones in turn, and the Rename Bone button to change their names. Rename the first bone Parent, the second bone Child, and the third bone HandBone.

11. While you've got the Skeleton Panel open, set the Child bone rest length to 0.5, turn on the Limit Range, set the Minimum to 0.01 and Maximum to 0.3, and turn off the Bone Active button. Set the HandBone rest length to 0.148, turn on the Limit Range, set the Minimum to 0.15 and Maximum to 0.15, and again turn off the Bone Active button.

12. Press p to close the Skeleton Panel and return to Layout. Select the Child bone and create a Keyframe for the Selected Item. After you create the keyframe, press r to activate the bone. Select the HandBone and create a Keyframe for the Selected Item, and again press r to activate the bone. Save the scene again. You should have something that looks like Figure 3-42.

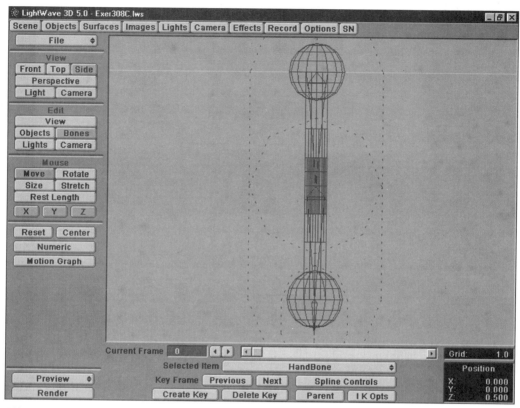

Figure 3-42: All bones sized, positioned, rotated, and limited.

The HandBone was added to stabilize the sphere capping the end of the object, without interfering with the elbow joint. That's why its Minimum and Maximum values are the same, and why the capsule representing the bone effect boundary is as close as possible to the perimeter of the sphere.

13. Go to frame 30, select the Child bone, and change its Heading to 90 degrees. Switch to the Perspective view as shown in Figure 3-43.

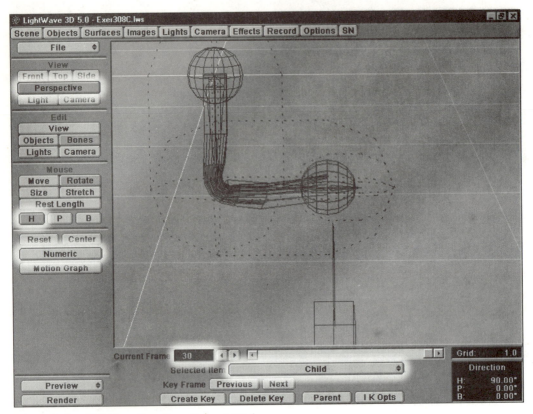

Figure 3-43: Child bone bending elbow at 90 degrees.

Create a key for the Child bone at frame 30 and save the scene again. Make a preview, or if you like, render an AVI file.

You probably noticed that the elbow crimped slightly, like a garden hose that has been bent too sharply. LightWave 3D version 5.0 has a couple of enhancements, Joint Compensation and Muscle Flexing, that are intended to fix this problem and provide better-looking bends for character animation. Chapter 12 has more details on these features.

Bones can be placed individually or in hierarchies, to deform a single joint or provide a flexible armature for an entire creature. Bones are a very powerful tool, and especially useful for the major skeletal joints. Also, the complete object, bones, and motions can be loaded from a saved scene, just as you did with a Parent hierarchy in Exercise 3-7.

Exercise 3-9: Animating Distortion With Bones

This exercise shows you another use for Bones: distorting muscular masses that in reality wouldn't have a skeleton.

1. Click the File button at the top left of the Layout window and choose the Clear Scene option. Click the File button again and use the Load Scene option to load the EXER0309.LWS scene file from the Chapter 3 directory on the Companion CD-ROM.

    This scene is set up with no objects loaded, but as before, the camera is set up to give you a good view of the exercise you're about to work through. This saves you a little bother, because most of this exercise is done in an extreme close-up.

2. Click the Objects button at the top left. The Objects Panel appears. Click Load Object and choose the SWELLUP.LWO object from the Chapter 3 directory on the Companion CD-ROM. Press p to close the Objects Panel and return to the Layout window, and click the Objects button in the Edit area at left center.

Note: The SwellUp object is another duplicate of the barbell, but with a lot more polygons in a cluster at its top.

3. Click the Bones button in the Edit area and press p to open the Skeleton Panel. Click the Add Bone button. Click the Limited Range button at the middle left, and change the Minimum value to 0.01 and the Maximum value to 0.08. Press p to close the Skeleton Panel. The bone is added at the pivot point of the object (see Figure 3-44).

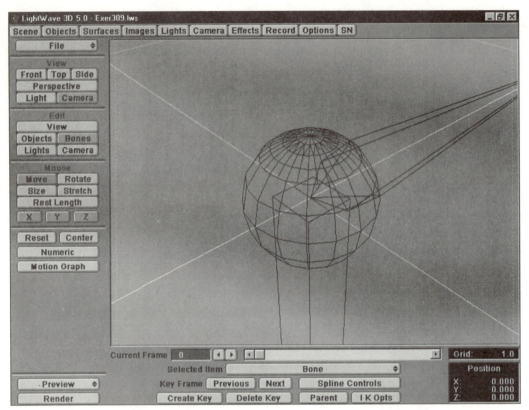

Figure 3-44: Bone added to SWELLUP.LWO object.

4. You want the bone to be inside the object and end in the middle of the cluster of polygons forming the top surface. Click the Rotate button in the Edit area and press n to call up the numeric Bone Direction Panel. Set the Pitch to 270, and leave Heading and Bank at zero. Press Enter to accept the change and close the panel.

5. Click the Rest Length button in the Edit area. Use the mouse to change the length of the bone, or press n for the numeric Bone Rest Length Panel and set the rest length to 0.128.

6. With the bone still selected, create a keyframe for the Selected Item. After you create the keyframe, press r to activate the bone. You should have results similar to Figure 3-45. Save the scene, just in case.

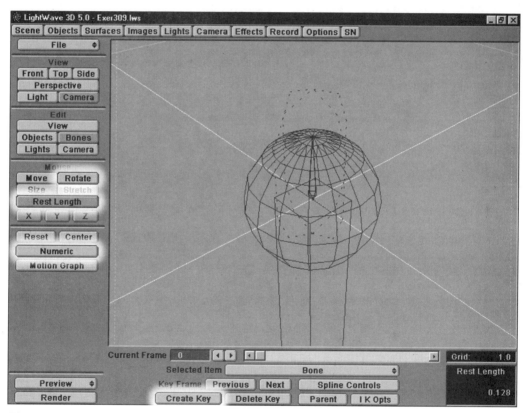

Figure 3-45: Bone sized, positioned, rotated, and limited.

7. Go to frame 30, select the bone, and change its Z-axis size to 1.25 and its X-axis position to 0.038. Make a keyframe for the Selected Item at frame 30, as shown in Figure 3-46. Make a preview, if you like.

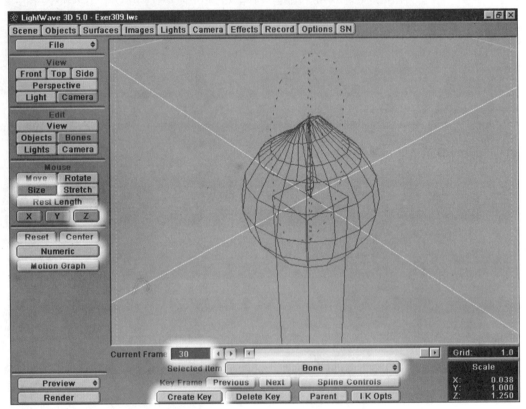

Figure 3-46: Bone pushing up the surface of the sphere.

You can see how a single bone can be used to distort an object's surface, with a great deal of control. Bones can even pull in, as well as push out.

8. Go back to frame 0 and make another keyframe at frame 15. Reduce the size of the bone at frame 0 to 0.5 on the Z-axis, and create another keyframe at frame 0, as shown in Figure 3-47. Make a preview again.

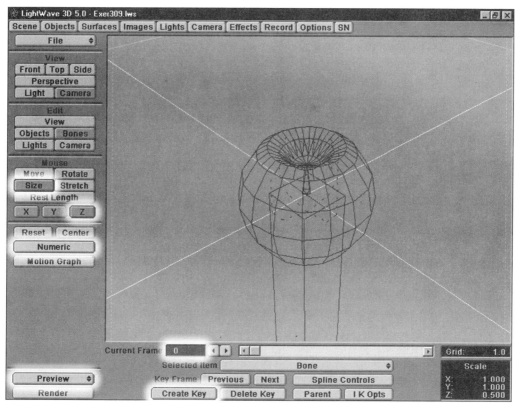

Figure 3-47: Bone pulling down the surface of the sphere.

As you may have surmised, this kind of Bone animation is extremely useful for animating facial expressions. You can place bones to manipulate eyebrows, pucker lips, even set the Minimums to nail down a dimple while the rest of the face bulges. It's very flexible, and we'll be using Bones a lot in the following chapters.

Hybrid Replacement/Displacement Animation

Hybrid puppet animation is, as you might expect, a combination of displacement and replacement techniques. Most puppet animation being done in professional studios is a mixture of techniques; as in any business with deadlines and budgets, it's whatever gets the job done.

Generally, the gross skeletal animation is best handled with a displacement armature. In LightWave 3D terms, that means either Parent (if joints can show) or Bones (if it has to look seamless). There are a few special circumstances—long repetitive sequences, perhaps—where replacement techniques can be used for the whole-body motions, but generally this is done with displacement.

Replacement pieces really shine when there is fussy, detailed yet repetitive animation to be done. Lip sync is a prime candidate; if a character needs to speak, it's a lot easier to swap head or face parts from a library of phonemes than it is to pose the 20 or more Bones necessary to shape a decent-looking mouth.

Sometimes hands are also animated with replacement model parts, as they are smaller than the rest of the armature and the fine wire of their skeleton tends to break more often.

The usual technique, then, is to build displacement armatures with pegs or keys at the extremities, the neck, wrists, and so on, to which the replacement bits are readily attached and removed.

A wonderful example of this technique is *The Nightmare Before Christmas*. The protagonist, Jack Skellington, had approximately 180 replacement heads, covering every permutation of lip sync and emotional expression. His displacement armature, by comparison, had about 18 joints (not including the hands, which used flexible wire rather than machined joints).

> Replacement pieces really shine when there is fussy, detailed yet repetitive animation to be done.

Exercise 3-10: Animating a Hybrid Character

The goal of this exercise is to set up a hybrid animation figure, with a Bones-displacement body and a replacement head. We'll animate objects that are simple extrusions of a Gingerbread Man outline.

1. Click the File button at the top left of the Layout window and choose the Clear Scene option. Click the File button again and use the Load Scene option to load the EXER0310.LWS scene file from the Chapter 3 directory of the Companion CD-ROM.

     This scene is set up with a single object loaded (a headless body, how macabre!) and as before, the camera is set up to give you a good view of the exercise you're about to work through.

2. Click the Object button at the top left. The Objects Panel appears. Click Load Object, and choose the GHEAD000.LWO object from the Chapter 3 directory. This is the head of our Gingerbread Man.

3. Press p to close the Objects Panel and return to the Layout window, and click the Objects button in the Edit area at left center.

4. Make sure GHEAD000.LWO is shown in the Selected Item drop-down list near the bottom. Click the Parent button at the bottom center. The Parent Object Panel appears.

5. Choose GBODY000.LWO from the pull-down menu, then press Enter or click the OK button to return to the Layout window. This sets the body as the Parent of the head (see Figure 3-48). That means the head will automatically follow all of the body's movements and rotations, just as if they were physically attached to each other.

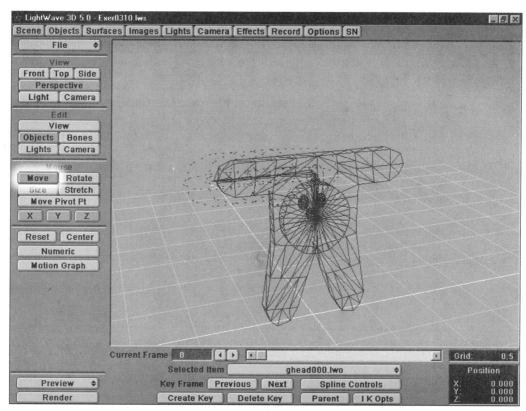

Figure 3-48: Layout with GHEAD000.LWO loaded and selected.

The head is loaded with it's pivot on the pivot of the body. That's just a bit low, I think; let's move it up a little.

6. Make sure GHEAD000.LWO is still the Selected Item. Click the Move button in the Mouse area at the left center. Press n to call up the numeric Object Position Panel (see Figure 3-49).

Figure 3-49: Object Position Panel.

7. Change the X value to -0.0125, Y to 0.805, and Z to 0.115. This puts the head on top of the body's shoulders. Press Enter or click Continue to save the settings and close the Object Position Panel.

8. Unless you're animating the *Legend of Sleepy Hollow,* you won't want the head floating off on it's own. With the Move option still active in the Mouse area, click on each of the X, Y, and Z buttons in the Mouse area until they are grayed out. This locks off the head's movement so that you won't accidentally shift it and mess up its alignment to the body.

9. Click Create Key, and when the Create Motion Key Panel appears, choose the All Items option and click OK. You should have a scene like Figure 3-50. You may also want to save the scene under a new name, just in case.

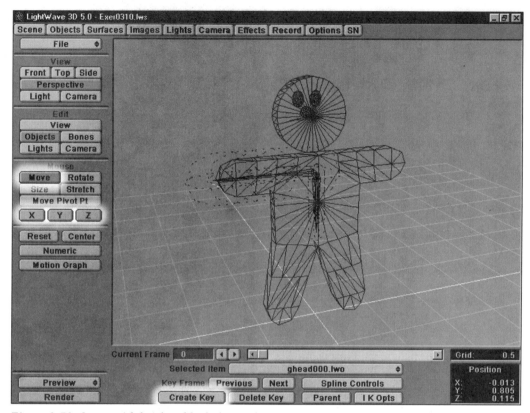

Figure 3-50: Scene with head and body hierarchy set up.

Let's make sure the head is on straight.

10. Select the head and click the Rotate button in the Mouse area. Press n to call up the numeric Panel. Change the Heading to 180. This should line up the head with the body.

11. Leave Bank and Pitch set to zero. Click OK or press Enter to save your changes and return to Layout (see Figure 3-51).

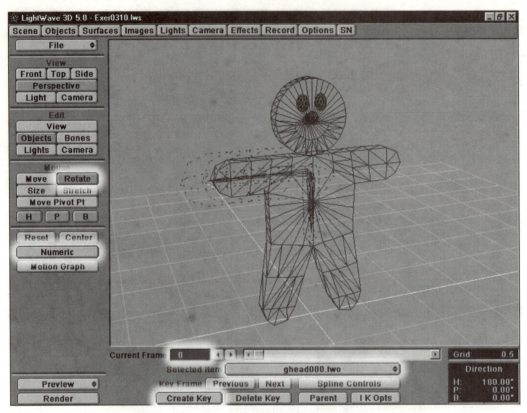

Figure 3-51: Gingerbread Man's head aligned with his body.

12. Create a key for the head at frame 0, then a duplicate at frame 10, then another duplicate at frame 60. This keeps the head aligned with the body, but later we'll stick in a different rotation keyframe somewhere between frames 10 and 60.

    Now let's make the body move in a straight line for the first 30 frames, then pivot from frame 30 to 60. The point of all this is to show that a Child object can follow the Parent through both movement and rotation.

13. Create both a Move and a Rotate key for the body at frame 0.

14. Go to frame 30. Click the Move button in the Mouse area. Press n to call up the numeric Panel. Change the Z value to 1.60. Leave X and Y as they are. Click OK or press Enter to save your changes and return to Layout.

15. Create a Move key and a Rotate key for the body at frame 30, and a duplicate Move key at frame 60. This makes the body move in a straight line along the Z axis from frame 0 to frame 30, then stop there until frame 60.

16. Go to frame 60. Make sure the body is selected and click the Rotate button in the Mouse area. Press n to call up the numeric Panel. Change the Heading to 145. Leave Bank and Pitch set to zero. Click OK or press Enter to save your changes and return to Layout. Create a Rotate key for the body at frame 60.

    Make a preview. Does the body move the way you intended? If not, go back and tweak the keyframes until you are satisfied with the effect.

    Now let's animate the head's rotation, to anticipate or "lead" the body's rotation.

17. Select the head and click on the Rotate button in the Mouse area. Go to frame 40. Press n to call up the numeric Panel. Change the Heading to 160, and leave Bank and Pitch set to zero. Click OK or press Enter to save your changes and return to Layout (see Figure 3-52).

18. Create a Rotate key for the head object only, at frame 40.

    The next step is to animate the Gingerbread Man's arm, which I have set up with Bones at the shoulder, elbow, and wrist.

19. Select the body object. Go to frame 60. Click the Bones button in the Edit area at the left.

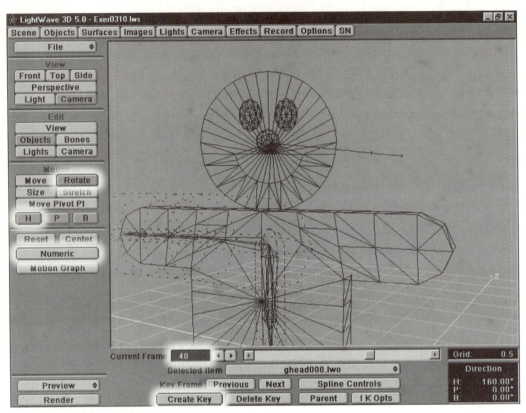

Figure 3-52: Scene with GHEAD000.LWO rotated.

20. Select RBicepBone from the Bones drop-down list at the bottom of the page. Click the Rotate button in the Mouse area and press n to call up the numeric Bone Direction Panel.

21. Set the Bone Direction to 28, -32, 0. Press Enter or click OK to accept the changes, and create a key for this item at frame 60.

22. Repeat the preceding two steps for RForearmBone, setting Bone Direction to 25, -19, 0, and for RHandBone, 0, 39, 0.

    When you're finished you should have a pose like Figure 3-53. Make a preview to check out the motion.

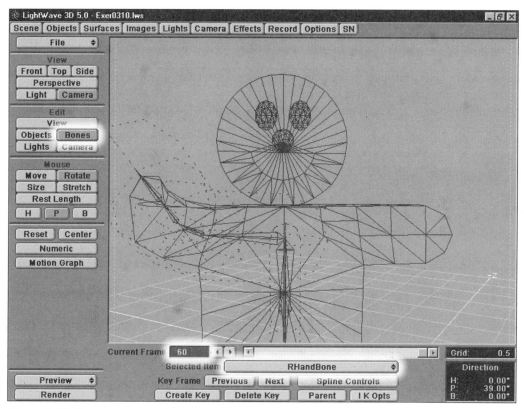

Figure 3-53: Posed arm, complete at frame 60.

OK, the Gingerbread Man can move, rotate, and wave, after a fashion. Now let's give him a little more expressive face, using the Replacement function of MTSE.

23. Click the Objects button in the Edit area at the left center. Select the head object. Press p to open the Objects Panel (see Figure 3-54).

24. Click the Load Object button at the upper left. Select object file GHEAD001.LWO, then press Enter to close the file dialog and return to the Objects Panel. Set the Object Dissolve value at 100% and press Enter to accept the change. Just as in the earlier exercises, this keeps the object invisible.

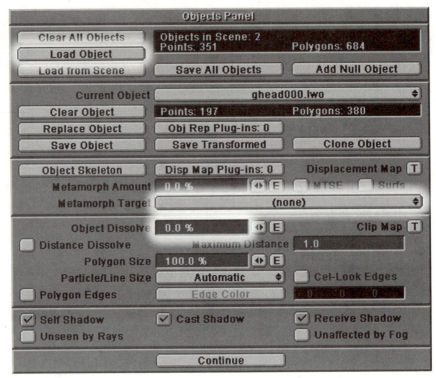

Figure 3-54: GHEAD000.LWO is loaded in the Objects Panel.

25. Repeat the preceding step for object files GHEAD002.LWO, GHEAD003.LWO, GHEAD004.LWO, GHEAD005.LWO, GHEAD006.LWO, and GHEAD007.LWO. These are the MTSE target objects you'll be using.

26. Select GHEAD000.LWO from the Current Object drop-down list. This is the beginning object for the MTSE chain.

27. In the Metamorph Target drop-down list select GHEAD001.LWO as the target object. This is the object the first metamorphosis in the chain will go toward.

28. Select GHEAD001.LWO from the Current Object drop-down list. This is the second object in the MTSE chain.

29. In the Metamorph Target drop-down list, select GHEAD002.LWO as the target object. This is the object the second metamorphosis in the chain will go toward. Do you see the pattern you are following?

30. Repeat the preceding two steps for MTSE object pairs 2 and 3, 3 and 4, 4 and 5, 5 and 6, and 6 and 7.

31. Select GHEAD000.LWO from the Current Object drop-down list. Click the E button next to the Metamorph Amount data field to open the Morph Envelope Panel (see Figure 3-55).

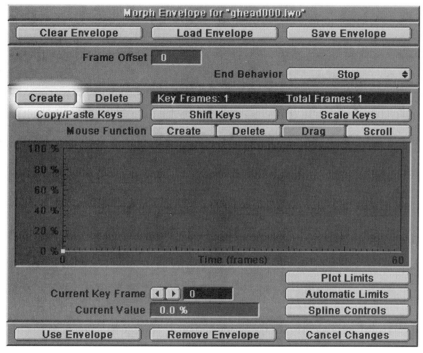

Figure 3-55: Morph Envelope Panel for GHEAD000.LWO.

32. Click the Create button just above the Copy/Paste Keys button. The Create Key at Frame Panel appears. Type **60**, and press Enter to accept the input, close the panel, and return to the Morph Envelope Panel (see Figure 3-56).

Figure 3-56: Create Key at Frame Panel for Morph Envelope.

33. While the keyframe at frame 60 is still selected, type **700** in the Current Value field at the bottom center and press Enter.

As you learned previously, the Metamorph values for MTSE target objects are increased by 100 for each object in the chain. If there were only two targets, the top of the scale would be 200%. With seven targets, the top end is 700%. Values from 0-100% control morphing to the -01 object, 101-200% control morphing to the -02 object, and so on (see Figure 3-57).

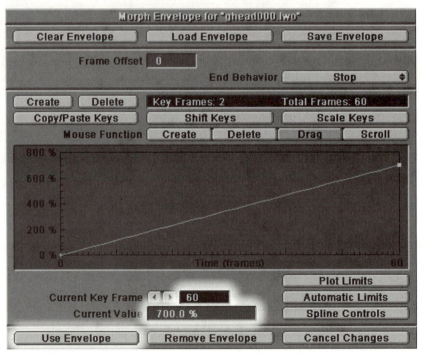

Figure 3-57: Envelope graph for GHEAD000.LWO, after editing.

This straight-line graph means that the metamorphosis will go smoothly from GHEAD000.LWO to GHEAD007.LWO over the course of 60 frames.

34. Click the Use Envelope button at the bottom left to close the Envelope Panel and return to the Objects Panel.

35. Click the MTSE button next to the E-for-Envelope button. This activates the MTSE chain you just set up. Press p again to close the Objects Panel and return to the Layout window.

36. Make a wireframe preview of frames 1 through 60. Play the preview.

    This gives you a run-through of all the expressions available to the Gingerbread Man. Not much, I'll admit; this set of objects was only intended as an example, not the dramatic range necessary for a fully animatable and expressive character.

37. End the preview. Press p to open the Objects Panel again. Click the E button next to Metamorph Amount to open the Morph Envelope Panel again.

38. Go ahead and play with the Envelope. If you are feeling especially ambitious you can try your hand at lip sync; Gingerbread Man has most of the basic mouth shapes in his eight-pose repertoire. In any case, make an effort to control the head's MTSE changes in a logical pattern over the 60 frames.

    When you are satisfied with the Envelope, render an AVI.

Hybrid replacement/displacement animation has its advantages. As with straight replacement, it gives faster layout of fine detail in sequences. As with Bones and Parent hierarchies, you can reuse poses and action sequences. Consistent use over time will build a growing range of retrievable poses. Since only part of the character must be modeled for replacement animation, there can be far fewer total objects to make and track, plus more flexibility in whole-figure poseability using Bones and Parenting.

Of course, hybrid replacement/displacement animation has its disadvantages. Changes in replacement head and hand poses must be saved as separate objects and cannot be tweaked in Layout. It also requires tracking and storage of a larger number of objects than would a pure Bones or Parent method. Additionally, if the replacement objects are to follow the distortions of a Bones-controlled body, you must use a third-party plug-in such as Lock & Key (which we'll explore in detail later) to enable Parenting to Bones.

Moving On

If you've completed all the exercises so far, congratulations! You should now be familiar with the basic tools for LightWave 3D character animation. With this collection of tools, you can animate characters with a surprisingly active and dramatic range. The only limits are your talent, patience, and ingenuity.

You may have noticed that none of the animation exercises so far has produced any really good-looking, or even realistic, action. They are, in fact, rather mechanical. These have been deliberately simple exercises, designed to show you the basics of LightWave 3D tools before we dive into animation techniques. Even the most powerful CGI tools can't make great character animation for you; with that in mind, let's move on to the next chapter and start learning how to put these tools to use.

A Nod Is as Good as a Wink

Eye & Head Motion

This chapter shows you how to apply some of the techniques you learned in Chapter 3 to mimicking natural motions. A logical place to start is the character's eyes and head, the most expressive and closely watched parts of a character. Along the way, this chapter shows you how to partly automate natural eye motion.

Throw 'Em a Curve

The first tool you can get rid of, at least for character animation, is your straight edge. It won't be of any use to you because nothing in the natural world moves in a straight line!

Now you are probably thinking of movements that describe a straight line. Sorry, but you're mistaken; straight-line movement is an illusion. Any simple projectile—whether bullet, spacecraft, or Olympic high jumper—moves in an arc, defined by its velocity, mass, the force of gravity, and the resistance of the air. Over a short distance, the trajectory may appear flat, but it is actually a curve. Generally, the slower the movement, the more pronounced the curve. Billiard balls on a near-perfect table will still exhibit a little bit of table roll, and anything moving in three dimensions is even more prone to follow a curved path.

For any unguided movement, given the starting parameters, you can calculate the curve the object will follow and the impact point, using a class of mathematics called *ballistics*. You can also animate this kind of movement by using a program that simulates physical laws. One such program is a plug-in for LightWave 3D, called Impact!, that simulates ballistics and models *collision detection*, the interaction of physical objects based on their elasticity, movement, and mass.

If any part of an animation calls for accurate physical effects like these, use whatever tools are available to automate as much of the process as possible. It's like photography versus painting in oils: if you want it to be accurate, use technology; if you want it to be artistic, use human judgment. Animating dozens of billiard balls realistically bouncing downstairs is simply a matter of plugging in more numbers, using the right software. If you try to animate all that by hand, you won't impress anybody (animating it in a caricatured style is another matter entirely!).

Adding feedback to the equation, however, changes most movements from a simple parabolic arc to a more complex *slalom*. A slalom is the path followed by any system, natural or machine, that can correct its movement towards a goal. Guided missiles and torpedoes, a hawk swooping down on a field mouse, your feet as you walk toward a doorway, and your hand as you reach for the doorknob are each following a slalom path. Almost every action you take describes a slalom.

The basic components of a slalom are a starting point, a goal, and the limits that trigger feedback correction. Let's take walking toward a door as a simple two-dimensional example.

You start out across a large space, perhaps a plaza or parking lot. You identify the building you wish to enter and begin walking toward it. For the first step or two, you are following a nearly straight line. As you get closer, you notice the door you wish to enter by and turn toward it, bending your path slightly to the right. This adds a little bit of curve to your path, beginning the slalom. As you get even closer, you glance down to make sure you aren't going to stumble over an obstacle. When you look up again, you find that you have stepped a little too far to the right, so you correct your path to the left to line up with the door again. This process of making tiny corrections to your path continues until you actually pass through the doorway, at which point you are right on target—or you bruise a shoulder on the door frame if you aren't paying attention!

The corrections when you are farthest away are mostly approximations, but your estimates are more accurate the closer you are to the target, and each following correction is that much smaller. In this case, you are basing most of your correction limits on visual cues. Your first goal is the building; as long as your planned path appears to intersect the building, that's good enough. Once you spot the door, the limits become much tighter, and you correct your planned path to intersect the door. As you get even closer, you plan to walk through the middle of the doorway, so you correct your path accordingly. The result might look like Figure 4-1.

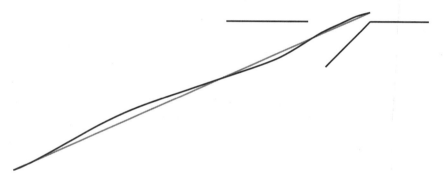

Figure 4-1: Walking toward a goal produces a simple two-dimensional slalom.

Slaloms are not just for movement through three-dimensional space, either. Any natural system that rotates around one or more axes also describes a slalom. For example, the hawk I cited earlier describes a separate slalom with its head as it dives. It keeps its eyes on the mouse by making small, rapid corrections to the angle of its head and eyeballs. If you plotted these rotations on a graph, they would describe a slalom, with larger corrections at the beginning and very small corrections closer to the goal.

What appear to be static poses can make use of slaloms, too. If you hold a heavy object at arm's length and try to keep it level with your shoulder, every joint in your arm and shoulder describes small slaloms. Every time a small twinge or weakness in one muscle causes a joint to vary from the target, another muscle compensates. This is feedback, and feedback expressed mathematically describes a slalom.

So what, you say? So you must animate your characters to follow slaloms, or their actions will seem mechanical and dead, and you will lose that illusion of life you've been working so hard to maintain. Traditional animators have known and practiced this for years; although they have used other terms such as arcs or natural paths to describe these types of motion, they all mean essentially the same thing.

Fortunately, LightWave 3D uses splines to define motion paths, so it is relatively easy to make objects follow slaloms. Let's try animating an object with a slalom motion.

Exercise 4-1: A Slalom Head Turn

1. Load the EXER0401.LWS scene file into Layout (see Figure 4-2). You can find this file in the Chapter 4 directory of the Companion CD-ROM.

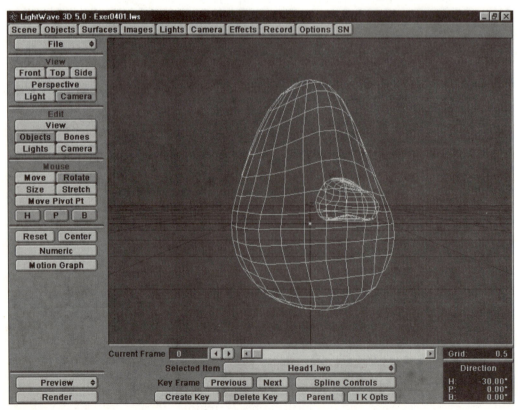

Figure 4-2: EXER0401.LWS scene file loaded.

2. Click the Objects button in the Edit section of the Layout window.

   Note: There is only one object in this scene, HEAD1.LWO.

3. Click the Rotate button in the Mouse section at the left side.

4. Click the Create Key button at the bottom center. The Create Motion Key Panel appears. Make sure the values are set to create a keyframe at frame 0 for the selected item, then press Enter or click OK to create the keyframe and close the panel.
   This creates a keyframe for the head object to remain just as Layout loaded it. It's always a good idea to set up baseline keyframes like this in frame 0. If you make a mistake in another frame, you can always recover the baseline settings from frame 0.

5. Drag the frame slider under the view window to go to frame 15.

6. Press n to call up the Object Direction numeric Panel (see Figure 4-3).

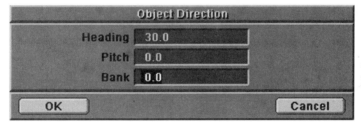

Figure 4-3: Object Direction Panel.

Now you'll turn the head object to the left.

7. Set the Heading entry in the panel to 30 degrees. Press Enter or click the OK button to close the numeric Panel.
   This turns the head object in the opposite direction, at the same angle relative to the camera (see Figure 4-4).

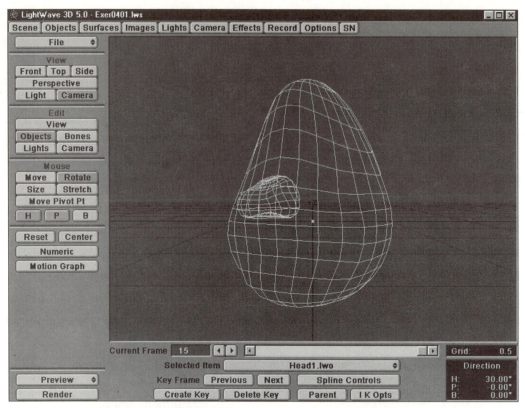

Figure 4-4: Head object rotated to the left.

8. Click the Create Key button at the bottom center. Make sure the values in the Create Motion Key Panel are set to create a keyframe at frame 15 for the selected item, then press Enter or click OK to create the keyframe and close the panel.

9. Choose Make Preview from the Preview drop-down list at the lower left. In the Make Preview Panel set First Frame to 0, Last Frame to 15, Frame Step to 1, and Preview Type to Wireframe. Then click OK to render the preview. When the rendering is complete, play the preview (see Figure 4-5).

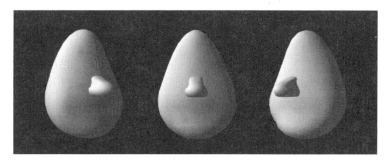

Figure 4-5: Frames 0, 7, and 15 of the head turn animation.

The head moves kind of like a tank turret, doesn't it? This is very mechanical, not lifelike at all. Let's find out why.

10. Click the End Preview button to stop the preview and return to the Layout window.

11. Press m to call up the Motion Graph for Current Item Panel. The Current Channel drop-down list is in the center of the panel, under the graph window. Pull down the list and select Heading Angle (see Figure 4-6).

    Notice that the graph is a straight line, not a slalom or curve.

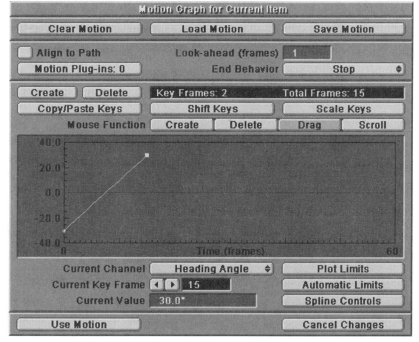

Figure 4-6: Heading Angle motion graph.

12. Click the Create button at the middle left. The Create Key at Frame Panel appears. Type **7**, then press Enter to close the panel and return to the Motion Graph Panel.

    A new yellow dot appears at frame 7 on the graph, representing the new keyframe. The current frame indicator changes to 7 (see Figure 4-7).

13. Change the Current Value for Heading to zero degrees to keep the motion graph straight. Zero is exactly halfway between the -30 degrees of the head's original rotation and the +30 degrees you set it to in frame 15.

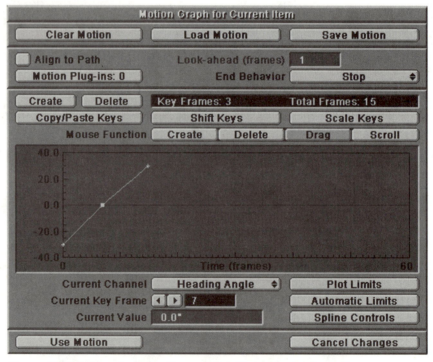

Figure 4-7: Heading Angle motion graph with new key at frame 7.

14. Pull down the Current Channel list again and select Pitch Angle. Now you'll add some rotation in the pitch axis to turn the straight line of the heading motion into a slalom.

15. While you are still at key frame 7, change the Current Value for Pitch to -5.0 degrees (see Figure 4-8).

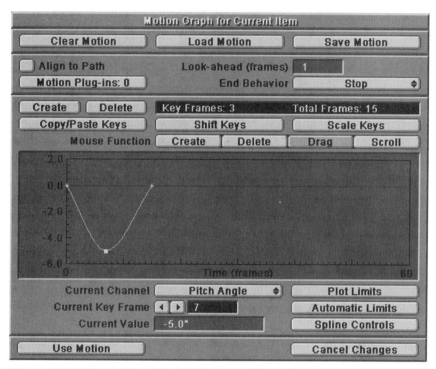

Figure 4-8: Pitch angle keyed to -5.0 degrees at frame 7.

Notice that LightWave 3D automatically interpolates this motion graph as a smooth curve between the old endpoints and the new midpoint you just created. It is possible to shape a curve using only endpoints and the spline controls, but it is usually easier to add midpoints.

16. Press p to close the panel and return to Layout.
    Let's see how changing the pitch changed the animation.

17. Choose Make Preview from the Preview drop-down at the lower left. As before, set First Frame to 0, Last Frame to 15, Frame Step to 1, and Preview Type to Wireframe. Then click OK to render the preview. When the rendering is complete, play the preview (see Figure 4-9).

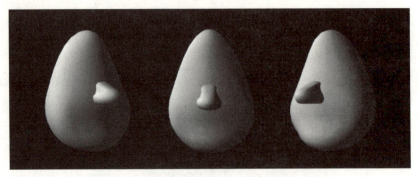

Figure 4-9: Frames 0, 7, and 15, with pitch added to heading.

This looks a little more natural, doesn't it? Just adding a few degrees in another axis is enough to give a more natural appearance.

18. Save the scene with a new filename. You'll be using it in the next exercise.

Experiment with the Pitch keyframe setting. How subtle can you be, and still make the head rotation seem more natural? How extreme can you be, to make the head rotation seem caricatured and over-acted?

In head movements, the slalom rule generally expresses itself as a few curves leading from the starting position to the goal, with the swell of the largest curve pointing down. The only general exception to this rule is when the character is looking toward something well above the horizon line, in which case the largest curve swells upwards. The smaller curves are near the starting position and the goal, and represent the *anticipation* before and the *follow-through* after the main action.

As in the exercise you just completed, the character's head generally pitches down slightly as the head rotates side-to-side, then comes up to the goal pitch angle at the end of the rotation. For simplicity's sake, the origin pitch and the goal pitch in this exercise were the same. If you like, repeat the exercise with different origin and goal pitch angles, and see what effects you can create.

The Eyes Have It

Although it is possible to animate a character with no facial features at all, it's much easier to get your audience to identify with a character if it has eyes, eyelids, and the range of expression that these things make possible. Reflexive eye movement is also fairly easy to mimic and can be a great asset to directing your audience's attention and selling a shot.

The following exercises show you how to add eyeballs and eyelids to a head model, and how to use the Parent, Inverse Kinematics, and Target functions to animate them.

Exercise 4-2: Adding Eyes to a Head

1. Reload the scene file you saved from Exercise 4-1.

2. Click the Object button at the top left of the Layout window. The Objects Panel appears, with HEAD01.LWO selected. Click Replace Object, and choose the HEAD02.LWO object from the Chapter 4 directory of the Companion CD-ROM.

   This replaces the head object you animated in the last exercise with the slightly different head object designed for this exercise.

3. Click Load Object, and choose the EYE.LWO object from the Chapter 4 directory. Repeat this to load a second copy of the eye object. LightWave 3D automatically names the duplicate objects EYE.LWO(1) and EYE.LWO(2). The left eye is (1), and the right eye is (2).

4. Press p to close the Objects Panel and return to the Layout window.

5. Select EYE.LWO(1) from the Selected Item drop-down list near the bottom. Click the Parent button at the bottom center. The Parent Object Panel appears.

6. Choose HEAD02.LWO from the pull-down menu, then press Enter or click the OK button to return to the Layout window (see Figure 4-10). This sets HEAD02 as the Parent of EYE.LWO(1). That means the eye will automatically follow the head's movements and rotations as if they were physically attached to each other.

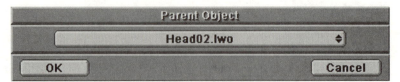

Figure 4-10: Parent Object Panel with HEAD02.LWO selected.

The head looks decidedly odd with the eye stuck in the center like that. Let's move the eye to a more appropriate location.

7. Make sure EYE.LWO(1) is still the Selected Item. Click the Move button in the Mouse area at the left center. Press n to call up the numeric Object Position Panel (see Figure 4-11).

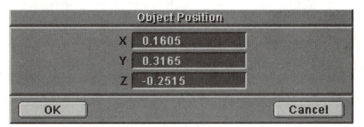

Figure 4-11: Object Position Panel.

8. Change the X value to 0.1605, the Y value to 0.3165, and the Z value to -0.2515. You can also try eyeballing (pun intended) the position yourself and moving the eye object with the mouse. You want to make the eyeball line up with the appropriate spot in the face, as shown in Figure 4-12. Press Enter or click OK to save the settings and close the Object Position Panel.

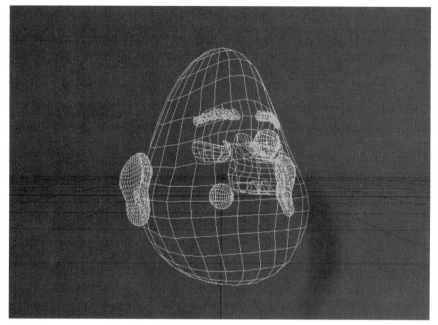

Figure 4-12: Left eyeball, in position.

9. Since the eye will be following the head as a Parent, the eye doesn't need to move on its own. With the Move option still active in the Mouse area, click each of the X, Y, and Z buttons in the Mouse area until they are grayed out. This locks off the eye's movement so you won't accidentally shift it and mess up its alignment to the head.

10. Repeat steps 5 through 9 for the EYE.LWO(2) object, but position it parallel to EYE.LWO(1), at X=-0.185, Y=0.3175, Z=-0.2525.
    So far, so good. Now to save the changes you just made.

11. Click the Create Key button. When the Create Motion Key Panel appears, choose the All Items option and click OK. You may also want to save the scene now, under a new name, just in case (see Figure 4-13).

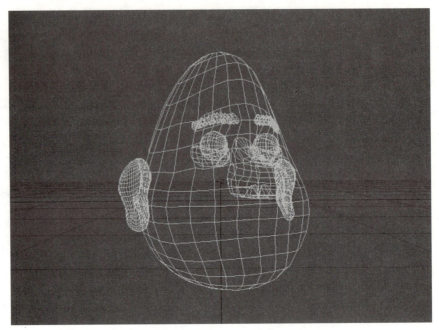

Figure 4-13: Scene with head and eye hierarchy set up.

Giving your character eyes opens up a whole new range of acting capabilities. Aside from emotional expressions and other intentional communication (which we'll cover in Chapter 11), the eyes can convey an extraordinary amount of unintentional or unconscious information. Any parent, teacher, or police officer can tell you how a miscreant's eyes move when they are lying. A loud noise, bright light, or rapid motion also produces an involuntary or unconscious reaction, which is usually readable in eye movement.

If you animate your character to mimic these natural motions, you'll be taking a big step toward convincing your audience. You'll also be able to use those motions to tell the audience what is going on, in a subtle and natural way, and so advance your story. This technique is especially important with animals or creatures that have little facial expression: eye movement and body posture are about all you have to work with.

You've already animated the head to follow a slalom. Now let's do the same with the eyes.

12. Select EYE.LWO(1) again. Press m to call up the Motion Graph for Current Item Panel. The Current Channel drop-down list is in the center of the panel. Pull down the list and select Heading Angle.

13. Click on the Create button at the middle left. The Create Key at Frame Panel appears. Type **0**, then press Enter to close the panel and return to the Motion Graph Panel.

    A new yellow dot appears at frame 0 on the graph, representing the new keyframe. The current frame indicator changes to 0.

14. Change the Current Value for Heading to -30 degrees to match the heading of the head object.

15. Repeat steps 13 and 14, setting the heading to 0 degrees at frame 7 and 30 degrees at frame 15.

16. Go back to frame 7. Pull down the Current Channel list again and select Pitch Angle.

17. Change the Current Value for Pitch to -5.0 degrees. Press p to close the panel and return to Layout.

18. Select EYE.LWO(2) and repeat steps 12 through 17.

19. Make and view a preview. You should end up with an animation like Figure 4-14.

Figure 4-14: Key frames 0, 7, and 15, with eyeballs rotated.

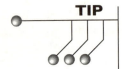

You probably noticed that simultaneous rotation of the head and eyeballs is neither convincing nor realistic.

The eyes can move much more rapidly than the entire head; their purpose is to track rapid movement, to scout ahead of the slower movements of the head and body. When a creature with eyes is nervous or keyed-up, the eyes tend to flicker all over the landscape. If you tried to do that with the entire head, you'd appear to be giving your character whiplash.

A more realistic approach is to animate the eyes' rotation in advance of the head's. If the character is to look up and to the right, the eyes should follow a slalom up and to the right just before the head begins to follow its own slalom. In other words, the eyes should always lead the head. Let's give it a try.

20. Select HEAD02.LWO. Press m to call up the Motion Graph for Current Item Panel. Pull down the Current Channel list and select Heading Angle.

21. Click the Create button at the middle left. The Create Key at Frame Panel appears. Type **5**, then press Enter to close the panel and return to the Motion Graph Panel. Repeat to add another key at frame 12, and again at frame 20.

22. Go to frame 5. Change the Current Value for Heading to -30 degrees, the same as frame 0. Click the Spline Controls button at the lower right to call up the Current Key Frame Spline Controls Panel. Click the Linear check box at the center of the panel, then click OK to close the panel.

This keeps the graph between frames 0 and 5 flat so the head will not move at all. If you left the Linear box unchecked, LightWave 3D's default interpolation would make a curve between the keyframes, which would make the head rotate slightly between frames 0 and 5.

This is a good trick to remember. Any time you need an object to hold perfectly still, set the keyframes at the beginning and end of the hold to identical values, and turn on the Linear option. You can do what you like to the rest of the motion graph, but the line between those keyframes remains straight.

23. Delete the keys at frames 7 and 15. Go to frame 12. Change the Current Value for Heading to 0 degrees. Go to frame 20. Change the Current Value for Heading to 30 degrees. The graph should now be a straight line between keyframes 5 and 20 (see Figure 4-15).

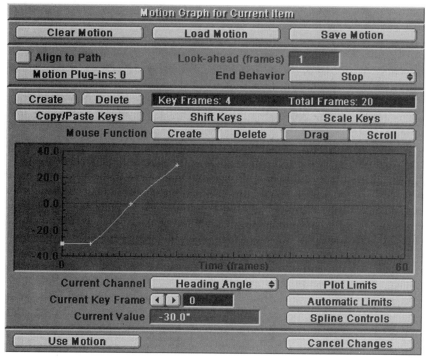

Figure 4-15: Modified Heading graph for head object.

24. Go back to frame 0. Pull down the Current Channel list again and select Pitch Angle.

25. Change the Current Value for Pitch to 0 degrees. Repeat for frames 5 and 20.

26. Go to frame 12 and set Pitch to -5.0 degrees. You should get a graph like the one shown in Figure 4-16.

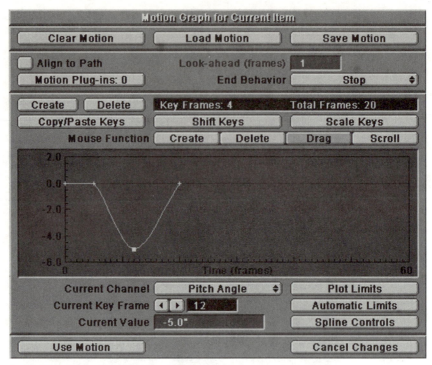

Figure 4-16: Modified pitch graph for head object.

27. Press p to close the panel and return to Layout.

    Test the changes with a quick preview. The head should hold still for five frames, then perform the same slalom rotation you animated before. If not, see if you can figure out what's wrong (and fix it) by looking at the motion graphs.

    The five-frame pause gives you enough time to animate the eyes turning before the head. The next step, reasonably enough, is to animate the eyes leading the head motion.

28. Select EYE.LWO(1) again.

29. Press m to call up the Motion Graph for Current Item Panel. Pull down the Current Channel list and select Heading Angle.

30. Go to frame 0. Change the Current Value for Heading to 0 degrees to match the Heading of the head object.

31. Delete the keyframes at 7 and 15.

32. Add a key at frame 5. Change the Current Value for Heading to 40 degrees, which is a fairly extreme heading angle for normal eye movement.

33. Add a key at frame 20. Change the Current Value for Heading to 0 degrees to bring the eye back into alignment with the head. You should end up with a heading graph like the one shown in Figure 4-17.

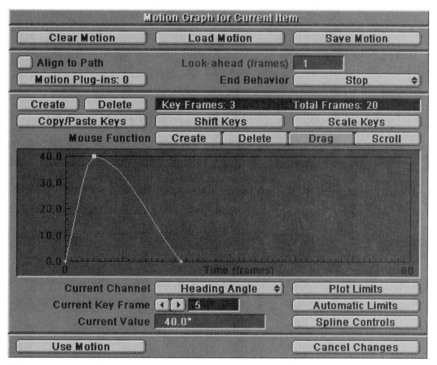

Figure 4-17: Modified heading graph for eye object.

34. Go back to frame 5. Pull down the Current Channel list again and select Pitch Angle.

35. Change the Current Value for Pitch to -5.0 degrees. You should end up with a pitch graph like the one shown in Figure 4-18.

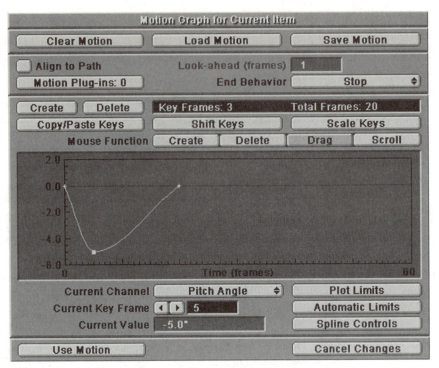

Figure 4-18: Modified pitch graph for eye object.

36. Press p to close the panel and return to Layout.

37. Select EYE.LWO(2) and repeat steps 29 through 36.

38. Make and view a preview. You should end up with an animation like Figure 4-19.

Figure 4-19: Keyframes 0, 5, 12, and 20 for eyes leading head motion along slalom.

This is a more natural motion for the eyes, but something is still missing. The eyelids should always frame the iris (the colored part of the eyeball surrounding the pupil) unless you are trying to show fright, rage, rolling of the eyes, or another extreme effect. Let's get rid of the bug-eyed look by adding some eyelids.

Exercise 4-3: Keep a Lid on It

1. Click Load Object and choose the EYELIDL.LWO object from the Chapter 4 directory of the Companion CD-ROM. Repeat this step to load the EYELIDR.LWO object.

2. Press p to close the Objects Panel and return to the Layout window. Go to frame 0 and click the Objects button in the Edit area.

3. Select EYELIDL.LWO from the Selected Item drop-down list near the bottom. Click the Parent button at the bottom center. The Parent Object Panel appears.

4. Choose HEAD02.LWO from the pull-down menu, then press Enter or click the Continue button to return to the Layout window. This sets HEAD02 as the Parent of EYELIDL.
   Now let's move the eyelid to match the appropriate eyeball.

5. Make sure EYELIDL.LWO is still the Selected Item. Click the Move button in the Mouse area at the left center. Press n to call up the numeric Object Position Panel (see Figure 4-20).

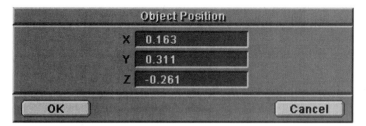

Figure 4-20: Object Position Panel.

6. Change the X value to 0.163, the Y value to 0.311, and the Z value to -0.261. You can also move the eyelid object by using the mouse. You want to line up the eyelid with the eyeball, as shown in Figure 4-21. Press Enter or click OK to save the settings and close the Object Position Panel.

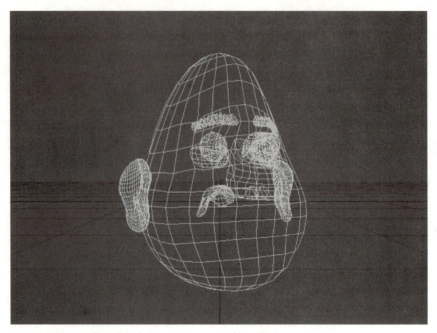

Figure 4-21: Left eyelid, in position over left eyeball.

7. Since the eyelid will be following the head as a Parent, it doesn't need to move on its own. With the Move option still active in the Mouse area, click each of the X, Y, and Z buttons in the Mouse area until they are grayed out. This locks off the eyelid's movement.

8. Repeat steps 3 through 7 for the EYELIDR.LWO object, but position it parallel to EYELIDL.LWO, at X=-0.187, Y=0.311, Z=-0.26. Now save the changes you just made.

9. Click the Create Key button. When the Create Motion Key Panel appears, choose the All Items option and click OK. You may also want to save the scene now, preferably under a new filename (see Figure 4-22).

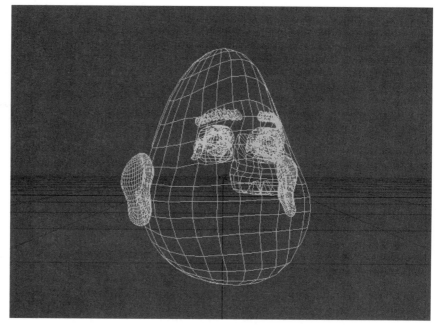

Figure 4-22: Scene with eyelids added to hierarchy.

In most cases, you can get away with animating eyelids in just the Pitch axis. This makes it very easy to pose the eyelids; just lock off the Heading and Bank axes and use the mouse. It's usually best to set the key positions for eyelids with the mouse rather than the numeric Panel, since you will generally be trying to match the edge of the eyelid to the edge of the iris.

The edge of the eyelid should just cover the upper curve of the iris. You should not be able to see the white, or *sclera*, completely surrounding the iris unless you are animating a very surprised look. The eyelid should not cover more of the iris unless the character is squinting in pain, anger, or bright light. The pupil itself always remains visible between the upper and lower eyelids unless a blink or squint closes the eye almost completely.

10. Make sure the EYELIDL.LWO object is selected and that Rotate is active in the Mouse area at the left.

11. Click the H (Heading) and B (Bank) buttons until they are grayed out. This limits mouse actions to rotating the eyelid in the Pitch axis.

12. Use the mouse to align the bottom edge of the eyelid with the top of the iris, as shown in Figure 4-23. When you are satisfied with the result, create a keyframe for the eyelid at the current frame.

Figure 4-23: Positions of the upper eyelid over the iris: No, Yes, No.

13. Go to the next keyframe for the eyeball.

14. Repeat steps 12 and 13 until all the keyframes for the eyeball have a matching keyframe for the eyelid.

15. Repeat steps 11 through 14 for the EYELIDR.LWO object.

16. Make and view a preview. You should end up with an animation like Figure 4-24.

    That's a lot better, isn't it?

Figure 4-24: Keyframes 0, 5, 15, and 20 of eyelids matching eyeball rotation.

17. Save the scene under a new filename. You will use it in the next exercise.

Keep in mind that when the head or eye turns, the eyelid often covers more of the upper part of the iris in a partial blink. The faster the turn, the more of the iris is covered, until a snap turn produces a full blink.

By now you are probably tired of repeatedly posing one eyeball, then matching the rotation for the other eye. Imagine trying to do this for a long shot, in which your character intently watches the erratic and convoluted flight of a mosquito!

The sensitivity of your audience to *sightlines*, the apparent direction of the eyeball, makes your job harder. We learn almost from birth to deduce exactly what someone is looking at by observing tiny variations in the angle of their eyes. Your least mistake in aligning the eyes can shatter your character's credibility.

Of course there is a better way to do this. LightWave 3D has a function called Inverse Kinematics that can make an object in a hierarchy point consistently and precisely at another object.

Inverse Kinematics and Targets

Inverse Kinematics (IK) is, in simplest terms, a tool for posing a hierarchy in reverse. Normal kinematics are what you do with a Parented or Boned hierarchy; for example an arm and hand: rotate the shoulder, then rotate the elbow, then rotate the wrist, then rotate the fingers, until you get the fingertips to point at or touch what you want them to. This is tedious, as you have found out.

Inverse Kinematics, as the name implies, inverts this process. You drag the fingertip to point or touch what you want it to, and the IK software figures out the appropriate angles for all the joints. Magic! you say, but of course there's a catch. For the arm, or any hierarchy with two or more joints, there are several possible poses that will put the fingertip in the same position.

Think about it and try this experiment: touch your finger to the end of your nose and see how much your arm can move while keeping your finger in place.

What usually happens when trying to use IK is that the hierarchy flops all over the place, and you spend a lot of time confining it to a reasonable set of poses. It is useful in certain situations, however, and we'll be spending more time with IK in other chapters.

In the following exercise, we'll work with a very simple hierarchy having only one joint, so there will only be one IK solution for any pose.

Exercise 4-4: Keep Your Eye on the Null

This exercise shows you how to use Inverse Kinematics to keep both eye objects pointed at a single null object.

There are some problems with setting an object to track a target directly. The usual approach is to add a null object to the end of the hierarchy and set the null to track the target. This also gives you better control over how the rest of the hierarchy reacts to the target's movement.

1. Go to frame 0 of the scene you saved from the last exercise.

2. If it is not already selected, click the Objects button in the Edit section at the left side. Press p to open the Objects Panel.

3. Click the Add Null Object button at the upper right. Click the Save Object button. Change the name of the null to EyeNullLeft and press Enter to close the panel and return to the Objects Panel.

    Nulls are not saved as separate objects; they are saved with the Scene file. The Save Object function is used here to change the name of the null.

4. Press p to close the Objects Panel and return to Layout. With EyeNullLeft still selected, click the Parent button at the bottom of the screen. The Parent Object Panel appears. Choose EYE.LWO(1) from the drop-down list, and press Enter to close the panel.

    This Parents the null to the left eyeball object.

5. Make sure the null is still the Selected Item. Click the Move button in the Mouse area at the left center. Use the mouse to position the null (represented by a three-axis crosshair) directly in front of the pupil of the left eyeball, as shown in Figure 4-25.

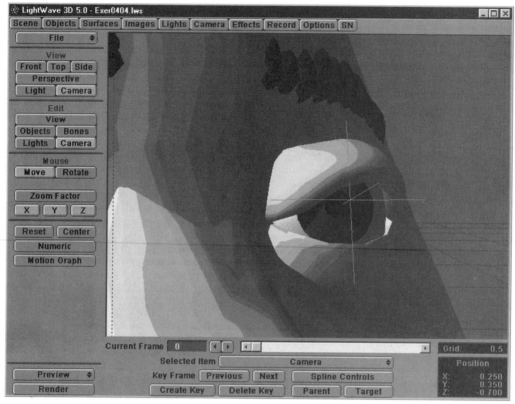

Figure 4-25: EyeNullLeft null positioned in front of left eyeball.

6. Click the Create Key button at the bottom of the screen. When the Create Motion Key Panel appears, choose the Selected Item option; make sure the frame is set to 0 and click OK to create the keyframe and close the panel.

7. Repeat steps 2 through 6 to add Parent, and position a null named EyeNullRight to EYE.LWO(2), the right eyeball.

8. Repeat steps 2 and 3 for a null named EyeTarget. Repeat steps 5 and 6 for EyeTarget, but position the null in front of the nose as in Figure 4-26.

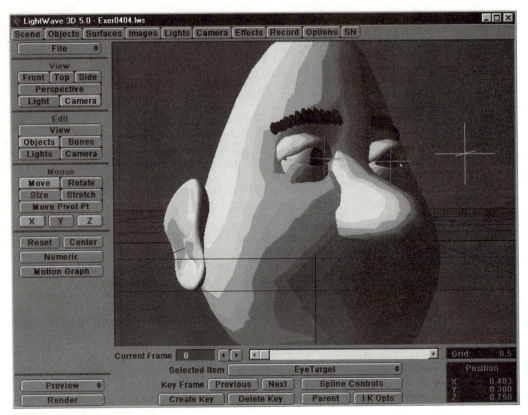

Figure 4-26: EyeTarget null positioned in front of nose.

The next step is to limit the IK effects on the head hierarchy. You want the eyes, not the entire head, to track the target.

9. Select HEAD02.LWO from the Selected Item drop-down list. Click the IK Options button at the lower right of the Layout window. The Inverse Kinematics Options Panel appears (see Figure 4-27).

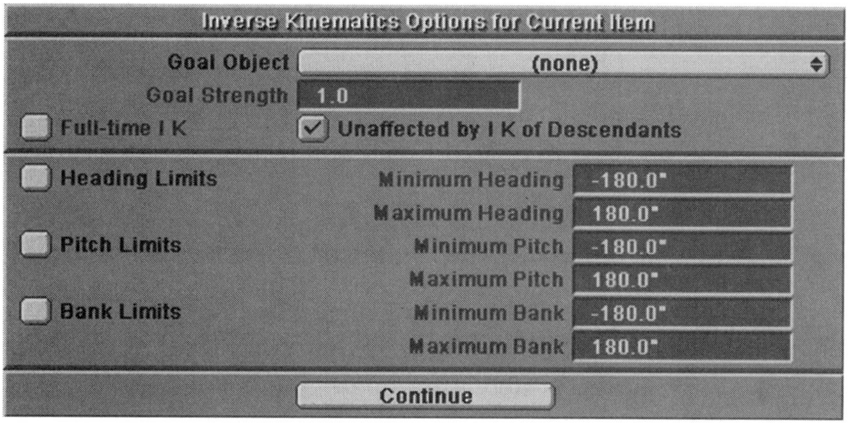

Figure 4-27: Inverse Kinematics Options Panel.

10. Click the Unaffected by IK of Descendants check box, then click Continue to save the change and close the panel.

    This tells the head to ignore any IK effects from the Parented nulls, eyelids, or eyeballs. It only moves according to its own key frame settings.

11. Select EYE.LWO(1) from the Selected Item drop-down list. Click the IK Options button at the lower right. The Inverse Kinematics Options Panel appears again.

12. Click the Full-time IK check box at the upper left.

    This tells the IK routine to run constantly, updating the position of the affected objects whenever you make a change. In general, it's a good idea to use full-time IK whenever possible. You may eventually run into some complex situations when you won't want full-time IK, but for now make it a habit to enable it.

    You also have the option to set rotation limits for the selected item for the Heading, Pitch, and Bank axes. These limits tell the IK process that it can't rotate the selected item past the defined angles, and it will have to pass along any further rotation to another item in the IK hierarchy.

    Just for practice, let's set some rotation limits for the eye to keep this character from looking out the back of his head.

13. Click the Heading Limits check box, and set the Heading Minimum to -50 and Maximum to 50. Click on the Pitch Limits check box, and set the Pitch Minimum to -20 and Maximum to 40. Click the Bank Limits check box, and set the Bank Minimum to -0 and Maximum to 0. (You don't want the eyeball spinning around its pupil, do you?)

    These limits are just rough approximations. The limits you use will change depending on the shape of the character's face and the range of expression you need to animate.

14. Click Continue to save the change and close the panel.

15. Repeat steps 11 through 14 for the EYE.LWO(2) object.

    Now both eyeballs are set to follow whatever IK influences they inherit from the EyeNulls. The next step is to set the EyeNulls to look at the EyeTarget.

16. Select EyeNullLeft from the Selected Item drop-down list. Click the IK Options button at the lower right of the Layout window to call up the Inverse Kinematics Options Panel.

17. Click the Full-time IK check box at the upper left. Pull down the Goal Object list at the top of the panel and select EyeTarget.

    This tells the IK routine that you want the EyeNullLeft object to constantly track the EyeTarget and drag along any Parent objects.

18. You don't need to set any rotation limits for the nulls. Click Continue to save the change, close the panel, and return to Layout.

19. Repeat steps 16 through 18 for EyeNullRight.

20. Click the Create Key button at the bottom of the screen. When the Create Motion Key Panel appears, choose the All Items option; make sure the frame is set to 0, and click OK to create the keyframe and close the panel.

21. To test the IK, select the EyeTarget null and move it around in all three axes. The eyeballs should rotate to look at the null.

22. Save the scene under a new name.

If all went well, you now have a head with eyes that are much easier to animate. You can animate the EyeTarget like any other object, and the eyes will follow along. You can use the EyeTarget to rotate the eyes along slaloms more easily and quickly than by setting separate sets of keyframes.

It is also much easier to mimic realistic eye movement. Researchers have compiled a lot of data about how humans and animals move their eyes in different circumstances and environments. One branch of this research is "eye gaze tracking." Figure 4-28 is from one of the most often cited sources in this field, Alfred L. Yarbus's 1967 book, *Eye Movements and Vision*. You can find out more by looking it up on the Web or in your local library.

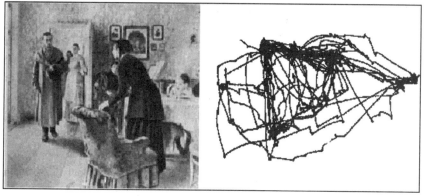

Figure 4-28: Test image and resulting eye gaze track.

The eye gaze track on the right represents three minutes' examination of the picture on the left. If you duplicated this eye gaze track in a series of EyeTarget keyframes during a three-minute animation, and positioned the test image at the appropriate distance in front of the face, you could accurately mimic the original subject's perusal of the image. Why you'd want to, I don't know, but the point is that you could.

From this and related research data, we can extract a few general guidelines that are useful in character animation.

When confronting a new situation, such as entering an unfamiliar room, the eyes "case" the area. This probably evolved as a survival trait: the first caveman to spot the bear tended to get out of the cave alive. What first attracts the eye is motion, especially of a living creature. If nothing is moving, the eye tends to explore the lighter areas first, looking at TV screens, windows, and lamps. After that, the eye examines the darker areas of the scene.

If the roving eye finds a living creature, the first reaction is to look at the creature's eyes. From there, the eye's path depends on the type of creature. If it is armed, the eye is drawn to the immediate threat, whether gun, knife, fang, claw, or tentacle. If the creature appears unarmed and has an expressive face, the eye tends to rove between the hands and face, cross-checking and corroborating information gathered from both areas.

Please note that these are gross generalizations, and there are always exceptions and modifications depending on the situation. We all know people who would overlook a bus unless it hit them, and others who would ignore a roomful of purple baboons for the television set in the corner. Part of your job as a character animator is to expose and accentuate those differences to show your audience, via animated eye movement, what your character is thinking about and what their likes, dislikes, and habits are.

Exercise 4-5: A Reading Test

Use a copy of the scene you created in Exercise 4-4 to animate the character reading an invisible page of text.

The EyeTarget should move left-to-right along the width of a printed line, at a reasonable reading distance for the character, then zip right-to-left and down a little to the beginning of the next line.

If you'd like to add a little personality, insert keyframe pauses into the middle of lines, as if the character is having trouble reading.

You can leave the head immobile, pitch it down slightly to follow the eyes down the page, or combine Pitch and Heading so the head follows along with each line. Moving the head more nearly matching the eyes conveys the laborious reading of a semi-literate character, while a minimal Pitch and no Heading changes at all convey the actions of a speed-reader.

Other Techniques for Animating Eyes

Parented eyeballs and IK goals are my personal preference for animating eye movements, but there are other methods that are appropriate for different circumstances.

For realistic animation you should mimic the actual physiological structure of the creature's eyes as closely as possible. You can adapt the exercises you just completed for most of these situations; dealing with the exceptions requires the modeling skills detailed in Part II.

For cartoon or caricature animation, all bets are off. Extreme caricature animation calls for squashing, stretching, and generally distorting the eyes, demands that pretty much rule out the nice, neat Parent
and IK approaches.

If you can get away with an iris and pupil that don't distort much,
you can use a fixed sclera, or white, that is part of the head object,
then simply animate the pupil and iris as a separate or Parented
object. You may even be able to use IK goals if the eyeball won't
change its curvature much. If the eye will be distorting a lot, this
approach can be more trouble than it's worth, since precisely matching the iris to the surface of a distorted eyeball can be tedious and
time-consuming.

One way to overcome the problems of a grossly distorted eyeball is
to use an image or image sequence to map the iris and pupil. This is
definitely not interactive and requires about the same level of preplanning as lip sync. Refer to Exercise 13-7 for details.

If the eyes need a lot more flexibility—especially if you are trying
to imitate the style of Tex Avery—I recommend that you treat them as
any other object to be animated using replacement or displacement
methods.

Replacement animation of eyes is very straightforward, using the
techniques you learned in Chapter 3. For most normal actions, you
can probably get along with a metamorphosis target library of a
dozen or so eyes. If you build them properly, you should be able to
use one set for both left and right eyes. Simply model (or have your
TD model) the baseline eye with the iris and pupil in the middle of
the sclera. Make sure the edges of the iris and pupil have enough
vertices to avoid showing straight edges, even in close shots.

Save a duplicate of the eye. Select and move the vertices defining the
iris and pupil so the iris's rim is tangent to one edge of the sclera. Save
this as one of your metamorphosis targets. Repeat this for each target
object, moving the iris and pupil to another point along the edge of the
sclera. I recommend building the up, down, left, and right models first,
then continuing to split the angles between targets until you are satisfied you can animate a morph to any required eye position.

You can set up an eye animation in advance, using an ObjList text
file or a duplicate series of numbered object files, just as in Exercises
3-3 or 3-2. Alternatively, you can load the whole Metamorph object
library as an MTSE sequence, as in Exercise 3-5, and tweak the animation interactively using the Envelope controls.

A Lot O' Blinkin' Good This Is!

Unless you are animating a zombie movie, your characters need to blink. Blinks are one of the unconscious signals that can help convince your audience that a character is alive.

Blinks are especially important for three-dimensional CGI character animation. One of the problems of this medium is that an absolute hold, where all movement stops, immediately destroys the illusion of life. This is not true for other animation media, in fact limited animation and camera-motion animation can get by with almost no in-screen movement.

If a character needs to pause for a moment, to remain believable it must do so in a *moving hold*. This is a hold as a human actor might perform it, with all the tiny motions of breathing, muscular twinges, nervous tics, shifting weight—and the occasional blink.

The mechanics of a blink are deceptively simple. The upper eyelid closes until it meets the lower lid, then rises again to its normal position. The pupil should also follow the lower edge of the lid as it closes, and follow it up again as it opens.

Ah, but how fast? For how long? Timing—both its placement within the longer sequence and the speed of the blink itself—makes a great deal of difference in how a blink helps or hinders the credibility of the character.

Then, too, the blink must relate to the animation of the eyes, the face, and the rest of the character. A random blink in the middle of a staring match destroys the tension, while a quick blink at a sudden action can really "sell" the shot. Remember, your audience will watch your character's eyes more than any other part of the scene.

Your character should blink quickly when alert, slowly when sleepy or stupid, repeatedly when surprised, and partially or fully, depending on speed, when the head changes direction. Chapter 11, "Facial Animation," includes more examples.

Exercise 4-6: Winkin', Blinkin' & Nod

If you have completed all the exercises so far, you should have learned to use the slalom path, linear and interpolated motion graphs, Parented eyes and eyelids, and Inverse Kinematics (IK) goals. Now you'll have a chance to put them all together.

Rather than a step-by-step set of instructions, this exercise is more like the assignments you'll get as a professional character animator. All you will get is a brief description of the action for a single shot, and it's up to you to interpret it.

The character you've been working with is asleep, head nodding forward. He is startled and wakes suddenly. His eyes blink rapidly as his eyes roam, looking for the source of the disturbance.

His eyes lock onto the source of the noise: a fly! (Don't worry, it's invisible, you don't have to animate it.) He stares at it intently, in a moving hold.

The fly takes off, and the character tracks it with his eyes and, with less accuracy, his head. The fly swoops and circles erratically, getting closer to the character's face with each pass.

Finally, the fly swoops in and lands—on the character's nose! He goes cross-eyed trying to see the fly, and blinks repeatedly in disbelief.

He shakes his head violently, apparently dislodging the fly.

Now, how would you end the sequence? Would he fall back to sleep? Just sit there blinking? Keep looking for the fly? You decide! Animate the whole shot, and keep the results in a safe place for future reference.

How did you decide on the timing for the blinks? What effect would it have on the whole piece if you put the blink keyframes closer together, or spaced them farther apart?

Did you remember to move the head and eyes on slaloms? Did the eyes always lead the head? Did you keep the eyelids lined up with the iris of each eye?

Was the action convincing? Did you believe in the character? Did he seem alive?

This is the kind of short exercise that you will want to revisit as your animation skills improve. With each new tool you learn, you will probably think of an embellishment or refinement you'd like to add. It's exactly this kind of practice that will hone your skills and help you become a better character animator.

Moving On

If you've completed all the exercises in this chapter, you now have a solid grounding in mimicking lifelike head and eye movement. Now that you've got the movement under control, the next step is to develop your timing.

This chapter barely touched on the subject of timing. The next chapter goes into much more depth, encouraging you to test the limits of pacing and emphasis, and develop your own sense of timing for animation.

Timing Is Everything

Timing makes or breaks character animation. A single frame is often the difference between an action that works and one that doesn't. To paraphrase Mark Twain, "The difference between the right timing and the almost right timing is the difference between lightning and a lightning bug."

In the preceding chapters, you learned to use LightWave 3D functions to move and deform objects. This chapter shows you how to set the timing of those movements to get exactly the effect you want.

CGI Timing: The Basics

The basic unit of timing is the frame. The *frame rate* is measured in frames per second or fps. Feature films are projected at 24 fps and NTSC video at 29.97 fps, usually rounded up to 30 fps for convenience. The high cost of transferring animation to film means that you will most likely be working in video formats for your first few projects. With that in mind, I have designed the exercises in this book for 30 fps. With experience, you will be able to pick out a single frame's difference in an animation. You may start off being able to judge only a quarter-second or more, but with practice you will learn to estimate and work with a thirtieth of a second.

The smoothest, most realistic animation is shot "on ones"; that is, each image is shown for only one frame. This is sometimes referred to as *full animation*. Shooting on ones is also the most expensive form of animation. More often, animation is shot on twos, where a single image is held for two frames. This cuts the cost of animation in half, as only 15 images are required for 30 frames worth of projection time.

To save money, *limited animation* is often shot on fours; even shooting on sixes is not unheard of when a budget is tight. Other "cheap" tricks include animating only part of a character, while the rest of the scene is untouched; animating camera moves over still images; and reusing image sequences of standard actions such as walks and gestures.

3D animation can't use most of the shortcuts employed in limited animation. Audiences seem more tolerant of such tricks when the animation is drawn, but when the images are three-dimensional, the audience becomes critical of anything not animated on ones. This is true of both puppet animation and CGI: animating on twos produces a jerky strobing effect that destroys any illusion of life. Fortunately, 3D CGI animation has a few advantages of its own.

There are two major approaches to animation. The simplest, most improvisational approach is *straight-ahead*. This means just what it sounds like: the animator starts with the first frame of the animation, poses the character, and then moves on to the next frame. Straight-ahead animation is mostly used in 2D drawn animation, but has a lot in common with puppet animation, too. You can improvise, exercise an intuitive grasp of timing and posing, work with a minimum of paperwork and planning—and lose lots of work with a single mistake. It's definitely not a technique for beginners.

The drawback of straight-ahead animation for CGI character work is that you create so many keyframes—one per animated variable per frame—that it is almost impossible to go back and correct errors. It is easier to simply junk an entire sequence and start over from the last good frame.

The other major approach is *pose-to-pose*. This is the approach used in most 2D animation productions. It is also much more forgiving for the beginner, although it does require more planning.

An animated character's actions are defined by its *key poses*. A key pose is where an action changes speed or direction. Filling in from one key pose to the next are *inbetweens*; these frames show the incre-

> The drawback to straight-ahead animation for CGI character work is that you create so many keyframes—one per animated variable per frame—that it is almost impossible to go back and correct errors.

mental changes between the key poses. In traditional 2D animation, key poses are drawn by a senior artist, and each inbetween is drawn by a junior artist known as an *inbetweener*. Computers can sometimes perform the inbetweener's job in 2D drawn animation.

The great advantage of CGI animation is that the computer generates every inbetween. The animator creates the key poses, ranging anywhere from every frame (for fast, complex action) to fewer than one in 30 (for slow or repetitive actions). The rest of the frames are interpolated and rendered automatically. This is a huge savings in the most expensive production commodity—the animator's time. If the computer system is powerful enough, the animator can tweak a key pose and generate a new *pencil test* sequence faster than a skilled traditional animator could draw one.

CGI pose-to-pose animations can also be revised piecemeal, without starting over and losing everything as in traditional cel or clay animation. A skeleton of Bones or Parent/Child objects can be animated one layer at a time, perfecting hip action, for instance, before you invest any time in animating the rest of the legs. Also, you can save each revision of an animation as you work, and reload it if something goes wrong with a later version. This "safety net" encourages animators to experiment—to try different compositions, actions, and timing. This is one reason CGI animation is more forgiving of, and easier for, the beginning animator.

A number of elements contribute to good timing. To be a competent character animator, you need to learn them all. You also need to learn how to apply them to each animation so they work in harmony.

The following exercises introduce one element at a time and build up to an exercise that ties them all together.

Mass & Energy

To appear real, CGI objects must move in ways that simulate the mass and energy of the real-world.

CGI objects have no mass or energy of their own. They are simply illusions displayed on your computer screen. To appear real in an animation, CGI objects must move in ways that simulate the mass and energy of the real-world materials they represent.

The mass of an object limits how fast it can be moved by a given amount of energy. A beach ball, for example, has very little mass, so a small amount of energy—a finger snap—can move it rapidly. The same amount of energy applied to a bowling ball would produce a much slower movement. Energy can be expended to change an object's speed, direction, or shape. This energy can come from out-side—another character's action, the wind, an Acme falling anvil—or inside—from the character's own muscles.

Gravity, for all practical purposes related to character animation, is a form of energy that constantly tries to force objects towards the largest mass in the neighborhood, typically the ground. (This defini-tion is not scientifically correct, but this is not a physics textbook.)

The behavior of an object is also governed by *inertia*, the tendency of objects to keep doing what they've been doing. If a large rock is just sitting there, it will continue to sit there until some other object acts to change it, perhaps by levering it over, dragging it away, or even shattering it into smaller rocks.

You can mimic all of this behavior simply by controlling the timing of the action. For example, let's look at one of the simplest actions, an inanimate object—a rock, let's say—falling to the ground. The rock is initially at rest, with no velocity relative to the ground. You can imag-ine a character holding it up, if you like. When the character releases the rock, it stays in midair for a tiny fraction of a second. This is due to inertia. The rock was motionless; inertia says it will remain motion-less until something else acts on it.

That something else is gravity. Immediately, gravity overcomes inertia by pushing the rock toward the ground at an acceleration of 9.8 meters per second, per second. This doesn't mean the rock is falling at 9.8 meters per second; this means 9.8 mps is added to the rock's down-ward speed for every second that it falls. Given the constant accelera-tion due to gravity, and leaving out any other influences such as updrafts or a character's intervention, you can figure the exact position of the rock for each fraction of a second. The equation is:

$$Y=Y_s-(1/2gt^2)$$

where Y is the Y-axis height in meters, Y_s is the original Y-axis height in meters at the start of the drop, g is the constant of acceleration for gravity of 9.8, and t is the time in seconds since the start of the drop. In simpler form, it reads:

$$Y=Y_s-(4.9t^2)$$

If you calculate the distance for each thirtieth of a second, you have the positions of the rock for each frame of a second of animation.

If you now create an animation of a rock object, starting it at frame 0 with no velocity in any direction, you can set the rock's position in each frame to mimic the fall of the real rock (see Figure 5-1). The rendered animation shows the rock object falling with a realistic acceleration.

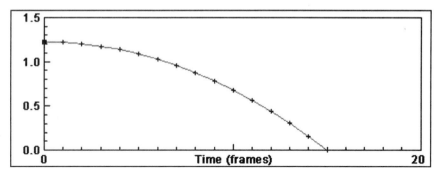

Figure 5-1: The simple timing of a falling rock.

See Table 5-1 for the distances for the first half-second, or 15 frames, of a standard fall.

Table Head	
FRAME	DISTANCE
:00	0.000
:01	0.005
:02	0.022
:03	0.049
:04	0.087
:05	0.136
:06	0.196
:07	0.267
:08	0.348
:09	0.441
:10	0.544
:11	0.659
:12	0.784
:13	0.920
:14	1.067
:15	1.225

Table 5-1: Distances for the first 15 frames of a standard fall.

This table is provided as a guide to get you started. You should not type in a calculated value for every keyframe of an animation, especially for a simple action like this. There's no art or human judgment involved in that approach, and you could easily be replaced by a piece of software. Your animations will look like it, too.

If you plan to animate simulations of real-world physics, I recommend buying Dynamic Realities' Impact plug-in. It simulates gravity, collision detection, and a lot of other useful behaviors that are tedious or difficult to set up by hand. No sense reinventing the wheel, right?

A slightly more complicated motion that you should be able to animate is the *parabola*, the arc followed by a projectile. Parabolas define the movement of a character in midleap, as well as the flight paths of cannonballs and hurled anvils.

A parabola is just like the acceleration curve of a falling rock, except there are two of them, connected at the top and spread apart at the base. The horizontal distance between the starting and ending points of the parabola depends on how much energy the projectile has and at what angle it is launched.

A thrown rock moves up at the reverse of the rate it would fall, starting off fast and slowing down until it reaches zero vertical velocity at the peak of the parabola. Then it falls, following the same acceleration path as if it had simply been dropped from that peak's height (Figure 5-2). The horizontal velocity of the projectile remains the same throughout the parabola; only the vertical velocity changes.

Setting up a parabola using keyframes is simple; it only requires attention to detail and basic arithmetic.

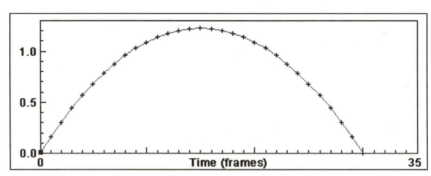

Figure 5-2: A parabola defining the path of a thrown rock.

Setting up a parabola using keyframes is relatively simple; it only requires attention to detail and a little basic arithmetic.

Exercise 5-1: Keyframing a Parabola

This exercise shows you how to keyframe a standard parabola for Earth's gravity.

1. Calculate the Y-positions for the keyframes of a straight fall beginning at the height of the parabola's peak.

    If the parabola is the exact height of one of the distances in the table above, you can copy the values from the table. (Hint, hint.)

2. Open the EXER0501.LWS scene file, located in the Chapter 5 directory of the Companion CD-ROM. Select the BBALL.LWO object and open the Motion Graph Panel.

3. In the Motion Graph Panel, select the Y-axis Position graph and make keyframes for the parabola.

4. Type in the calculated values for the appropriate Y-axis keyframes. Start at the peak of the parabola and proceed down the right-hand leg as in Figure 5-3.

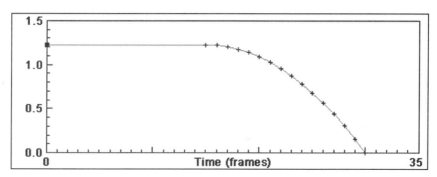

Figure 5-3: First leg of parabola defined by calculated keyframes.

5. Copy the values from each calculated keyframe to the corresponding keyframe on the left side of the parabola, as shown in Figure 5-4.

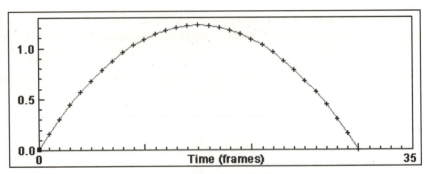

Figure 5-4: Second leg of parabola defined by duplicated keyframes.

Presto! You have created a parabolic motion graph! Save the Motion as PARA0501.MOT. Save the scene file, too, as EXER0502.LWS. You'll use it in the next exercise.

The constraints of mass, inertia, and gravity apply to animated characters as well as inanimate objects. Once a character leaves the ground, (also known as *going ballistic*) the path they follow is a parabola. Their limbs may thrash or make gestures, but their *center of gravity* (CG) must remain on the parabola (see Figure 5-5).

Figure 5-5: Character tumbling along a parabola.

If you animate a Parent null for position and rotation, you won't disturb the keyframes used to pose the character.

You can create this type of action most easily by adding a null object to the scene and animating the null along a parabola. Parent the character to the null object and position the character so its CG is centered on the null. This enables you to rotate either the null or the character for a tumbling motion. If you animate the null for both position and rotation, you have the advantage of not disturbing the keyframes used to pose the character.

Exercise 5-2: Beach or Bowling Alley?

This exercise shows you how to create a series of diminishing parabolas, first for a very bouncy object, a beach ball, then for a heavier object, a bowling ball.

1. Open the EXER0502.LWS scene file you just saved, or load the prebuilt version located in the Chapter 5 directory of the Companion CD-ROM.

2. Select the BBALL.LWO object and open the Motion Graph Panel.

3. Load the motion file PARA0501.MOT that you saved from the previous exercise. This creates the first bounce of the beach ball object.

    Since each bounce of the ball will be a little shorter than the one before, you need to accurately model the shrinking parabolas. Fortunately, there is a quick-and-dirty way to do this without recalculating and typing a bunch of Y-coordinates. The Y-coordinates of every gravity-based parabola are identical near the peak. The only differences are in the length of the legs. Therefore, you can cut and paste the top of a parabola to create shorter ones.

    This creates an automatic diminishing bounce. The only choice you have to make is how many keyframes you cut off the bottom of the preceding bounce. If you cut off more frames, you create the appearance of a heavier, less bouncy object. This is like setting the *modulus of elasticity* for the object's material. It should not vary within the same action (except for comic effect), so keep track of the number of frames you delete and be sure to use the same number for each bounce.

    You need to be careful to cut off one more frame on the trailing (lower frame number) side of the parabola than on the leading side. The last frame of the preceding parabola will become the first frame of the new one.

4. Click Copy/Paste Keys. In Low Frame, enter 3. In High Frame, enter the keyframe number two frames back from the end of the parabola, in this case frame 28. Leave the default of 31 for the value of Paste at Frame. Press Enter or click OK to accept the values and close the panel.

These settings trim only two keyframes off the bottom of the next bounce. This makes the ball very bouncy, so it appears light and resilient in the finished animation.

The duplicated frames are pasted in place at their original Y-axis values. You need to shift them vertically so the last keyframe is at 0 on the Y-axis.

5. Go to the last keyframe of the new parabola. Make a note of its Y-axis value.

6. Click Shift Keys. Enter 31 for Low Frame, and the number of the last keyframe for High Frame. Enter the last keyframe's value in the Shift Values by Field, and make it negative (i.e., 0.659 becomes -0.659). Press Enter or click OK to accept the values and close the Shift Keys Panel.

The new parabola is shifted to rest on the Y-axis, Figure 5-6.

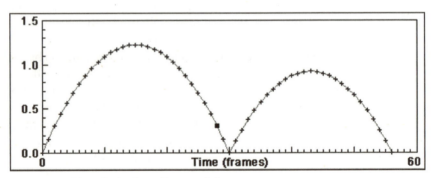

Figure 5-6: First derived smaller parabola.

If you like, you can make and play a preview to see how the bounce looks.

7. Repeat steps 4, 5, and 6 until the progressively smaller bounces fill the motion graph to frame 90. Edit the graph as necessary to make sure the last keyframe Y-coordinate is zero, to match the first keyframe. Save the scene under a new name.

You should end up with a motion graph like the one shown in Figure 5-7.

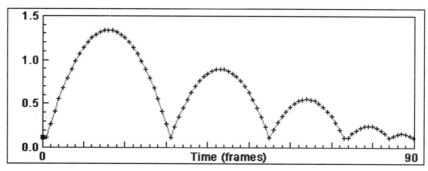

Figure 5-7: Beach ball motion graph.

8. Load another copy of the beach ball. In frame 0, position it a couple of diameters along the X-axis to one side of the other ball, so you can see it clearly. Create a keyframe for the ball.

9. Repeat steps 2 through 7 for the duplicate ball. This time, chop off more keyframes to make the bounces even shorter. Try to make a motion graph like Figure 5-8. This is more like a bowling ball than a beach ball, wouldn't you say?

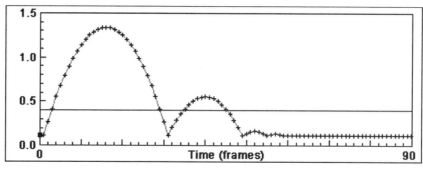

Figure 5-8: Bowling ball motion graph.

10. Make and play a preview.

Photographers sometimes capture a complex motion by leaving the camera shutter open and using a high-speed flash to illuminate the action many times per second; this technique is called *stroboscopic* photography. It is useful for showing a series of actions within a single image. I use LightWave 3D to simulate this effect for several figures in this book. If you tracked the camera during a stroboscopic rendering of this animation, you might get a final image like Figure 5-9.

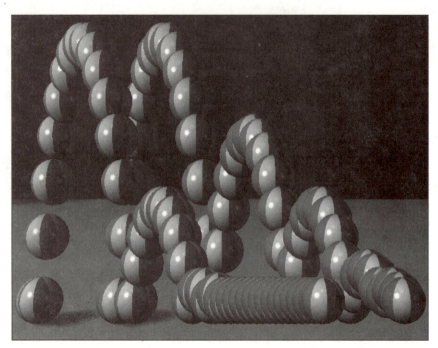

Figure 5-9: Stroboscopic image of bouncing different masses.

Shaping Motion Graphs With Spline Control Tools

You can mimic acceleration and parabolas by precalculating coordinates for the object for each frame, or you can use LightWave 3D's built-in Spline Control Tools to automate most of the work.

The Bias control pushes the bulge of the spline to one side of the selected keyframe, as shown in Figure 5-10. A negative value pushes the curve back, and a positive value pushes it forward.

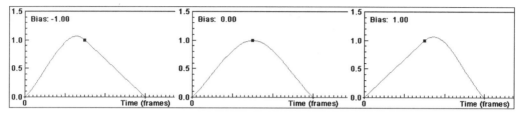

Figure 5-10: -1, 0, and +1 values for Bias.

Tension controls the apparent speed or rate of change of an object in the vicinity of the keyframe (see Figure 5-11). Higher tension bunches up the adjoining frames, bringing their values closer to the keyframe. There is less change between these frames, so the motion appears slower. A lower tension has the opposite effect; objects appear to move more rapidly near the keyframe.

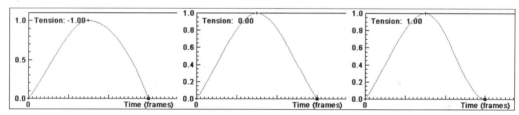

Figure 5-11: -1, 0, and +1 values for Tension.

Continuity controls the curvature of the spline as it passes through the selected keyframe (see Figure 5-12). A negative value takes away all curvature, making the spline cut a sharp corner. A zero value pushes the curvature of the spline outward so it is nearly flat as it passes through the keyframe. A positive value pushes the spline into inverted entry and exit curves around the keyframe.

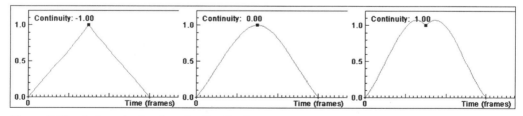

Figure 5-12: -1, 0, and +1 values for Continuity.

Exercise 5-3: Curves Ahead

This exercise shows you how to duplicate the realistic bouncing motion from Exercise 5-1 by using fewer keyframes combined with the Spline Control Tools.

1. Open the finished scene file from Exercise 5-1.

2. Load a second copy of the beach ball object. In frame 0, position it a couple of diameters on the X-axis to one side of the other ball, so you can see it clearly. Create a keyframe for the ball.

3. Open the Motion Graph Panel. Create two more keyframes for Y-axis position for the new object. You are trying to duplicate the original parabola, so create the new keys at the beginning, peak, and end frames. For example, if the parabola looks like Figure 5-4, the keyframes are 0, 15, and 30.

4. Set the three keyframe values by the numbers, the same as the equivalent keyframes in Exercise 5-1.

5. Using the Spline Control Tools, try to duplicate the shape of the parabola from Figure 5-4. Adjust the Continuity for the peak keyframe. Adjust the Tension for the start and end keyframes.

    You may have to add keyframes between 0 and 15 and between 15 and 30 to get a better parabola. Keyframes for splines work best when placed where there is the most change in direction. Instead of choosing frames 7 and 22, exactly halfway, try frames 10 and 20, where the curve is stronger.

    If you are using the calculated keyframe values from the table, the Spline Control settings are a no-brainer. All three keyframes have a zero Bias value, since the parabola is symmetric. The beginning and ending keyframes have a -1 Continuity, and the center keyframe has a +1 Continuity. This makes the bottom of the bounce a sharp corner, and the peak of the parabola nearly flat. The Tension settings are the same as Continuity in order to slow the motion near the peak keyframe and accelerate it near the bottom keyframes.

6. Make and play a preview. Compare the first bounce from Exercise 5-1 to the one you just created. If they are not an exact match, go back to step 5 and try again.

7. You should end up with a parabola like the one in Figure 5-13. When you are satisfied with the Spline Control bounce, save the motion as PARA0503.MOT. You may find a use for it later.

Keyframes for splines work best when placed where there is the most change in direction.

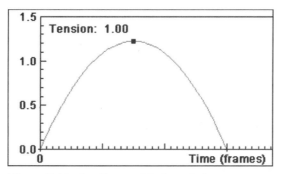

Figure 5-13: A spline-modeled parabola.

Squash, Stretch & Motion Blur

Squash is used to show the effects of rapid deceleration and of energy expended to compress the shape of an object (see Figure 5-14).

Figure 5-14: Squash frame from a bounce cycle.

Stretch is used to show the effects of rapid acceleration and of energy expended to lengthen the shape of an object (see Figure 5-15).

Figure 5-15: Stretch frame from a bounce cycle.

To maintain the visual volume of an object, squash-and-stretch is usually synchronized on tangent axes.

To maintain the visual volume of an object, squash-and-stretch is usually synchronized on tangent axes. That is, if an object stretches in one axis, it must also squash in the other axes to maintain its original volume. This particular rule can be broken for extreme cartoon-style effects, but is usually more effective when simply exaggerated. If you intend to break this rule for comic effect, you should establish the rule very firmly before you break it; the sudden, unexpected change in the rules is the source of the humor.

2D traditions use stretch to prevent *strobing*, changes between frames that are too extreme, catch the audience's eye, and destroy the illusion of smooth movement. The CGI artist can use *motion blur* instead of stretch to maintain visual continuity and prevent strobing.

Motion blur occurs when an action is faster than a camera's shutter speed; the action appears blurred between the beginning and ending positions of the moving objects. LightWave 3D simulates motion blur by interpolating and rendering extra frames in between the actual numbered frames. LightWave 3D then composites these extra images together with a slight transparency. Anything that moves has a number of "ghost" images that combine to create a blur.

Exercise 5-4: One Standard Bounce, Please

The first part of this exercise shows you how to add stretch to the animation of a bouncing ball to prevent strobing.

1. Load the EXER0504.LWS scene file located in the Chapter 5 directory of the Companion CD-ROM.

2. Select the BBALL.LWO object. Open the Motion Graph Panel.

3. Rotate the ball's Bank Angle at the keyframes to align it with the parabola. Set Bank Angle to -90 degrees for the peak frame, and whatever looks good for the rest. I used 0, -10, -70, -90, -160, -170, -180.

4. Add stretch to the ball for the up and down legs of the parabola, frames 1-8 and 23-31. Increase the Y-axis size to 1.5, and reduce the size proportionally for the Z- and X-axes. I used 0.75. Leave the ball's proportions normal at the peak frame.

5. Add squash to the hit frames, the beginning and end of the parabola. Decrease the Y-axis size and increase the size proportionally for the Z- and X-axes.

6. Close the Motion Graph Panel. Save the file under a new name.

7. Render an AVI. Play back the AVI.

You should get an animation like Figure 5-16.

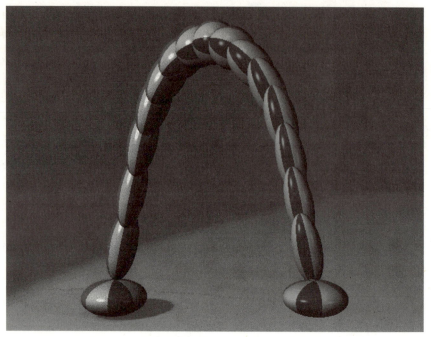

Figure 5-16: Bouncing ball with stretch and squash. Note the overlap of stretched ball images which prevents strobing.

Now try the same effect, using motion blur instead of stretch.

1. Reload the scene file you just saved.

2. Select the BBALL.LWO object. Open the Motion Graph Panel.

3. Remove the stretch from the ball along the up and down legs of the parabola, leaving the ball's proportions normal at the peak frame and along each leg. Only the squash at the beginning and ending frames should remain. Close the Motion Graph Panel.

4. Open the Camera Panel. Turn on antialiasing to at least Low (motion blur is disabled when antialiasing is off) and increase the Motion Blur setting to 100%. Close the Camera Panel.

5. Render an AVI. Play back the AVI.

You should get an animation like Figure 5-17.

Compare the effect of motion blur to the effect of stretch. Which animation would you prefer to watch? Which looks more realistic?

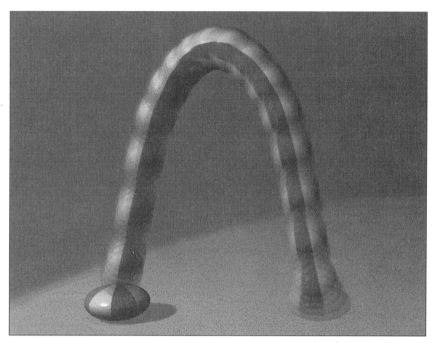

Figure 5-17: Bouncing ball with motion blur. No stretch is necessary. Squash is still used to show deformation of the ball against the floor.

Motion blur is almost always better than stretch for smoothing rapid motion.

Motion blur is almost always better than stretch for smoothing rapid motion. It is more realistic, and LightWave 3D renders it automatically, so it is easier for the animator. Stretch is still useful, but mostly for exaggerated action.

Squash-and-stretch tells the audience a lot about the material of an object. Different parts of a character should have different amounts of squash-and-stretch; a hard wingtip shoe, for instance, should not squash or stretch nearly as much as a flabby pot-belly.

Squash-and-stretch can also be very effective in showing a character's internal energy, as shown in Exercises 5-8 and 5-9.

Ease-in, Ease-out

Objects in the real world can't abruptly change from standing still to moving very fast. Any object that has mass needs a little time to get up to speed; the more mass, the longer the acceleration, or the more energy is required. The same is true for slowing down, changing direction, or distorting the object's shape.

In animation, a gradual change that leads into an action is called an *ease-in*. Coming out of an action gradually is called an *ease-out*. The precise timing of an ease tells the audience just how massive the object is, and how much energy it is using to perform the action.

The quickest way to understand ease and how to apply it is to study and experiment with one of LightWave 3D's motion graphs.

Figure 5-18 shows two motion graphs. One shows a constant speed between the start and end positions and the other shows an acceleration curve, or ease-in, at the beginning, and an ease-out, or deceleration, at the end. Note that the object still moves from the first position to the second in the same amount of time; it just moves faster in the middle, and slower on each end.

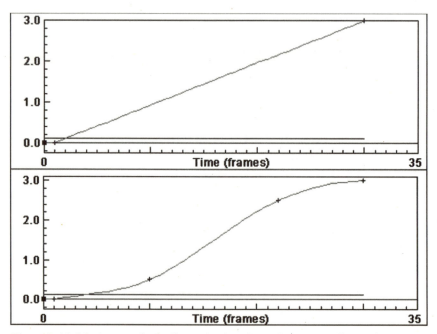

Figure 5-18: Motion graphs for linear (top) and ease-in/ease-out (bottom) motion.

Exercise 5-5: Get the Ball Rolling

1. Load the EXER0501.LWS scene file.

2. Select the BBALL.LWO object and open the Motion Graph Panel.

3. Create keyframes at 0, 1, 20, and 40.

4. Set X-Position values for the new keyframes.

   The ball is to start from a standstill at frame 1, then ease in to its maximum speed at frame 20, and roll off-screen in three complete rotations to frame 60. The ball is 0.111 units in radius, which means that it can travel 0.6974 units (2Xr=2 x 3.1416 x 0.111) for each complete rotation. That's a total of 2.092 units to travel.

   Let's start the ball off at -0.5 on the X-axis for both frames 0 and 1, pass through 0 at frame 20, and roll right to 1.592 in frame 60.

5. Adjust the Spline Control settings for each keyframe.

   You want the last section, between frames 20 and 60, to be at the maximum speed, a constant. You can turn on the Linear option in the Spline Control Panel for frame 60 to make the spline a straight line between frames 20 and 60.

   Adjust the Tension and Continuity values for frames 1 and 20 so the end of the curve nearest frame 20 closely matches the slope of the line from 20 to 60. If the slope changes abruptly at frame 20, the ball will jerk noticeably at that frame. See Figure 5-19 for one possible solution.

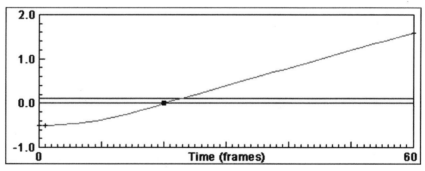

Figure 5-19: X-Position motion graph for rolling ball's ease-in.

6. Set the Bank Angle keyframe values.

   You want the ball to start off at 0 degrees and make three full rotations by frame 60, a total of 1080 degrees. Frame 60 should therefore be set to -1080 degrees (Bank Angles are negative for a forward roll with this object's orientation), and frame 0 and 1 left at 0 degrees.

   Determining a value for frame 20 is a little more of a challenge. The distance from 1 to 20 is 0.5 units; the total distance from 1 to 60 is 2.092, a ratio of 0.239. Multiply that by the total of degrees rotated and you get 258.12, the number of Bank Angle degrees to set for frame 20. Don't forget to make it a negative rotation.

7. Click Use Motion to save the settings and close the Motion Graph Panel.

8. Save the scene under a new name.

9. Make and play a preview.

   Your results should look something like Figure 5-20.

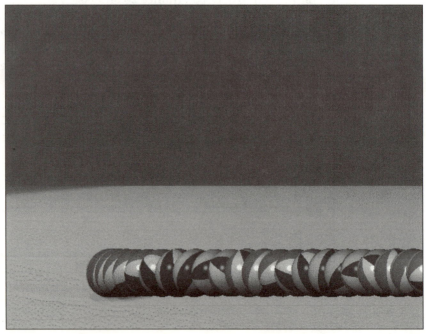

Figure 5-20: Stroboscopic rendering of ease-in for a rolling ball.

Exercise 5-6: Easy Does It

1. Reload the scene file you saved from Exercise 5-5.

2. Select the BBALL.LWO object and open the Motion Graph Panel.

3. Shift keyframe 1 to frame 10.
   This compresses the ease-in into half the time, making the acceleration much more sudden.

4. Revise the Tension and Continuity values for frames 1 and 20 so the end of the curve nearest frame 20 closely matches the slope of the line from 20 to 60.
   As noted in the previous exercise, if the slope changes abruptly at frame 20, the ball will jerk noticeably at that frame.

5. Click Use Motion to save the settings and close the Motion Graph Panel.

6. Save the scene under a new name.

7. Make and play a preview.

   Your results should look something like Figure 5-21.

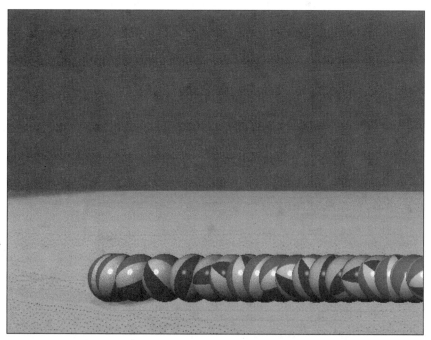

Figure 5-21: Stroboscopic rendering of faster ease-in for a rolling ball.

Notice how the different rates of ease made the ball seem to roll itself forward with greater energy. This is an example of how a frame or two difference in timing can have a great effect on the animation.

Snap

Don't overdo the ease-in and ease-out. It is tempting to use motion graph splines to make the whole action a smooth curve, like a lazy integral sign (see Figure 5-22).

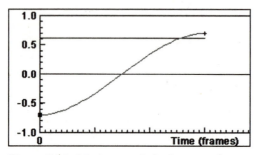

Figure 5-22: Motion graph for lazy, mushy movement.

Spline interpolation is a wonderful tool. It's unique to computer animation and can save you a lot of effort if you use it properly. But if you overuse it, your animations will look just like all the other beginners' out there. Motion graphs like this give you soft, mushy actions, as if the characters are moving underwater.

Snap is the animator's term for action that is quick, lively, and full of energy. To create an action with more snap, use motion graphs like the one in Figure 5-23.

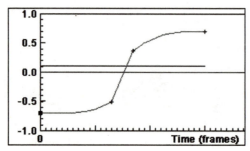

Figure 5-23: Motion graph for snappy movement.

Remember that it takes more energy to accelerate and decelerate an object quickly. To have more snap, the ease-in and ease-out curves of a motion graph should be shorter and sharper.

CD-ROM

Take a look at animation file EXER0507.AVI located in the Chapter 5 directory of the Companion CD-ROM. The upper ball has a motion graph like Figure 5-22; the lower ball has a motion graph like Figure 5-23.

Compare the motions of the lower ball and the upper ball (see Figure 5-24). Which looks more lively? Which looks more sluggish? Which one has more personality, and which one looks like a computer animated it?

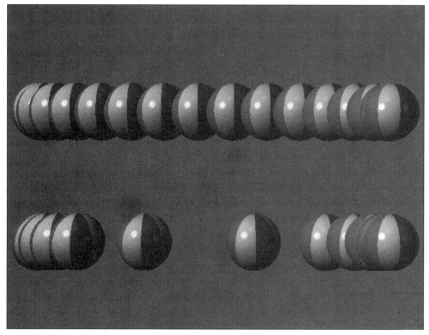

Figure 5-24: Stroboscopic image from EXER0507.AVI.

Judging the balance between ease and snap takes practice. Take advantage of every opportunity you can to play with the motion graphs, testing trade-offs and noting what values work for specific situations and moods. There are no hard and fast rules for this aspect of timing; you have to develop your own judgment.

Anticipation

Anticipation is an action in one direction intended to prepare the audience for a much larger action in the opposite direction. A baseball pitcher's windup is an example of anticipation.

You anticipate every time you prepare to take a step. Try this: stand with your weight balanced evenly on both feet. While concentrating on your posture and balance, take one slow step forward. If you pay attention, you'll notice that you lean back and to one side as you raise your foot, then lean forward and to the other side as you put your foot down. That is an anticipation and action: you moved backward a little, in order to move forward even more.

Exercise 5-7: Roll 'Em Again

This exercise shows you how to apply anticipation to the rolling beach ball.

1. Reload the scene file you saved from Exercise 5-5.

2. Select the BBALL.LWO object and open the Motion Graph Panel.

3. Shift keyframes 1 through 60 by 10 frames, leaving frame 0 intact.
    This adds 10 frames of no action onto the front of the animation, since frame 0 is still nailing down the initial X-axis position and Bank Angle of the ball.

4. Create a new key at frame 5. Move it to -0.557 on the X-axis.
    This is an appropriate distance for an anticipation movement. You could push it farther for an exaggerated move, or make it more subtle for a realistic move. This is somewhere in between.

You can find appropriate values for an anticipation by moving to the symmetrical frame on the other side of the motion's origin.

You can find appropriate values for an anticipation by moving to the symmetrical frame on the other side of the motion's origin.

For example, this motion begins at -0.5 X at frame 0. The ball is located at -0.5 X again as it passes frame 11, after the anticipation. The anticipation is centered on frame 5. Frame 11 is six frames after frame 5, so move to six frames further along after frame 11, to frame 17. Make a note of the Bank Angle and X-axis Position values at frame 17—in this case, 29.4 degrees and -0.443.

Note that these values will not be accurate if you have the Bias spline control set to anything but zero for any of these frames. You can use Bias settings later, but at this time you need the spline segments to be evenly balanced between the keyframes.

The X-axis position is (0.500-0.443), or 0.057. Subtract this from the resting X-axis position of -0.5 to get -0.557.

The Bank Angle at frame 17 is -29.4. All this requires is a change of sign, as the ball is rolling in the opposite direction.

5. Set the Bank Angle for keyframe 5 to 29.4 degrees.

Keyframe 5 should now have the correct position and rotation values. The only remaining tweak is to smooth out the acceleration curves, to create the proper ease-in.

6. Revise the Tension, Bias, and Continuity values for frames 0, 5, 11, and 30 so the anticipation is smooth. The end of the curve nearest frame 30 must closely match the slope of the line from 30 to 70.

As noted earlier, if the slope of the motion graph changes abruptly at any keyframe, the ball will jerk noticeably at that frame. You should end up with a motion graph like Figure 5-25.

If the slope of the motion graph changes abruptly at any keyframe, the object will jerk noticeably at that frame.

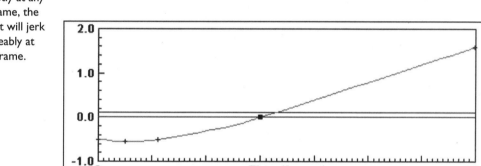

Figure 5-25: Motion graph showing anticipation.

7. Click Use Motion to save the settings and close the Motion Graph Panel.

8. Save the scene under a new name.

9. Make and play a preview.

Your results should look something like Figure 5-26.

Figure 5-26: Ball anticipates, then rolls.

Exercise 5-8: It Lives!

So far, all the animations have given the impression that some invisible hand, or maybe the wind, moved the ball. The ball itself seemed inert, as if it were being acted upon by outside forces but not taking any action of its own.

Now let's try combining anticipation with squash-and-stretch to make the beach ball seem alive and capable of moving itself.

1. Load the EXER0508.LWS scene file located in the Chapter 5 directory of the Companion CD-ROM.

    This is the same as the file you saved from Exercise 5-7 except the beach ball now has a single Bone. The Bone is set up to stretch the upper part of the ball as shown in Figure 5-27.

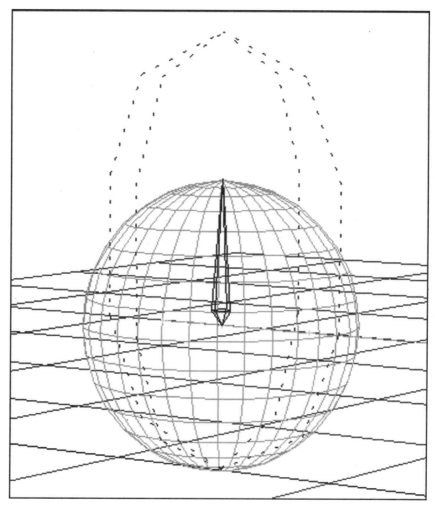

Figure 5-27: Bone placement in BBALL.LWO.

2. Set the Bone's keyframes to stretch the beach ball upward during anticipation, then squash down and stretch forward during the start of the forward roll, then return to normal as the top of the ball reaches the ground. See Figure 5-28 for examples.

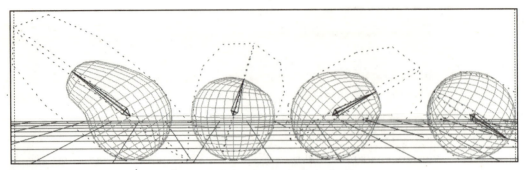

Figure 5-28: Bone distortions during anticipation and start of roll.

Your Pitch Angle and Z-Scale motion graph for the Bone should look something like Figure 5-29.

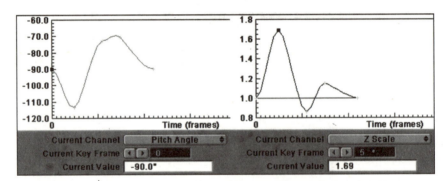

Figure 5-29: Bone Z-Scale and Pitch Angle motion graph for beach ball.

3. Save the scene under a new name.

4. Make and play a preview. Your results should look something like Figure 5-30.

Figure 5-30: Ball appears to motivate its own anticipation and roll.

This shows how a very minor change in an animation can make the difference between an object that is animated and one that has the illusion of life.

Follow-through

Follow-through is almost exactly like anticipation, but on the other end of the action. You already acted out an anticipation. Let's do it again, but instead of starting a walk, let's stop one. Take a couple of steps, just enough to get up some momentum. Stop suddenly.

Did you notice how your body swayed forward a bit, until your muscles could bring you to a complete stop? Did you rise up on your toes a little or have to brace one foot ahead of the other? Either of these actions would be a shock absorber, dissipating some of your forward motion.

You can watch another example of follow-through if you repeat that walk-and-stop exercise while carrying a cup of liquid. Not hot coffee, you don't want to scald yourself! Watch the liquid when you stop suddenly. That slop-up-and-fall-back is a contest between inertia, gravity, and the extra energy you put into your stopping action.

Your animated characters have to perform the same kind of actions. If they stop dead, they have to look weightless and artificial. If they appear to have mass, they must overshoot their goal a little, then bounce back to it. These actions are called *follow-through*.

If your characters are to appear to have mass, they must overshoot the goal a little, then bounce back to it.

Exercise 5-9: Whoa, Nellie!

By this time you should have had enough practice modifying motion graphs that you don't need step-by-step directions. The goal of this exercise is to create a complete set of motion graphs for anticipation, stretch, ease-in, snap, ease-out, squash, and follow-through.

1. Load the EXER0509.LWS scene file.

   This file is similar to the earlier ones in this chapter, but the keyframe settings have been deleted. The keyframes are all there, but you will have to set the values to create the timing for this animation.

   The goal for this shot is to make the ball roll backward and stretch in anticipation, then squash and ease-in to a forward roll with plenty of snap, ease-out to a stretch in follow-through, then squash back to a hold position.

   As a guide, Figure 5-31 contains the motion graphs used to make one version of this animation. You don't need to duplicate these graphs exactly. It's a better exercise if you create a different timing that still achieves the goal of the shot.

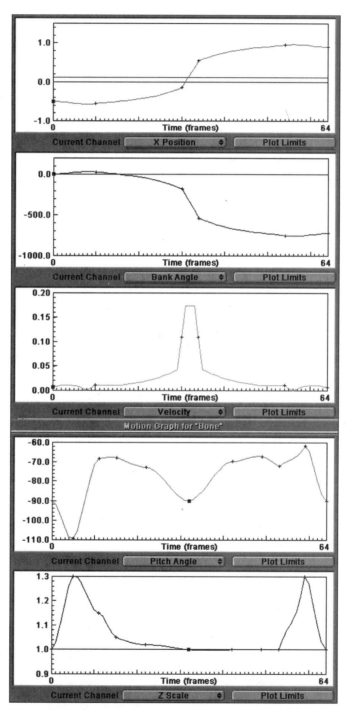

Figure 5-31: Motion graphs for one version of this animation.

2. Select the BBALL.LWO object. Open the Motion Graph Panel.

3. Choose the X-Position graph. Set the ball to move across the Camera's view, making at least two full revolutions. Start at frame 0 with the ball at rest position, then move it left in anticipation, then forward again. Make sure you put some snap in the middle of the motion. Finish it by easing-out past the final hold position in a follow-through, then sliding back to the hold.

    You might end up with something like the X-Position graph in Figure 5-31, but then again, feel free to make up your own interpretation. Remember that the ball is 0.6974 units in circumference; if you want to match its movement to a particular number of rotations, the ball has to rotate 516.18 degrees for every unit traveled.

4. Choose the Bank Angle graph. Set angles for the keyframes so the ball rolls in contact with the ground, not sliding or spinning. Don't forget the reverse rotations for the anticipation at the beginning and the follow-through at the end. Again, you can refer to Figure 5-31 for one possible solution.

5. Click Use Motion to save the new settings and close the Motion Graph Panel. Make a preview to check the motion so far.

    You can tweak the X-Position and Bank Angle at the keyframes, if you find it easier to work this way rather than in the Motion Graph Panel.

6. Click Bones in the Edit area. The single Bone in the BBALL.LWO object is highlighted. Open the Motion Graph Panel.

7. Choose the Pitch Angle graph. Pitch the Bone forward or back, as appropriate, to accentuate the anticipation and follow through motions. See Figure 5-31 for an example.

8. Choose the Z-Scale graph. Vary the Z-axis of the Bone to stretch and squash the ball during the anticipation, ease, and follow-through. Figure 5-31 shows one possible interpretation.

9. Click Use Motion to save the new settings and close the Motion Graph Panel. Make a preview to check the motion again.

You can also tweak the Bone Pitch and Z-Scale at the keyframes if you find it easier to work this way rather than in the Motion Graph Panel. I personally prefer to tweak squash-and-stretch in close-up views to get the best "feel" for the amount of distortion.

When you are satisfied with your timings, save the scene file under a new name and render the animation. Your results may look something like EXER0509.AVI from the Companion CD-ROM or Figure 5-32.

Figure 5-32: Ball rolls, then follows-through with ease-in, ease-out, stretch, and squash.

Moving Holds

You should create a *moving hold* to keep the character alive.

As I mentioned earlier, a 3D character cannot hold still for very many frames before it loses the illusion of life. If the character must stay in one place or position for a number of frames, you should create a *moving hold* to keep the character alive.

A moving hold is a series of tiny, almost imperceptible motions that mimic the behavior of a real living creature. Your audience perceives these clues unconsciously and accepts the illusion that the animated character is alive.

For example, most creatures breathe. You can imitate this subtle movement for a moving hold by stretching and squashing the character's torso (or whatever it uses for a lung casing) in the appropriate rhythm. Eyelid blinks, shifting of weight from one foot to the other, and small twitches of the hands are other useful pieces you can add to a moving hold. If the scene setup permits, you can even create a slightly modified copy of the entire character, and create a moving hold by performing repeated Metamorphosis changes between the original and the copy.

Exercise 5-10: Move That Hold

This exercise shows you how to add subtle motions to an object to create a moving hold.

1. Reload the scene file you saved from Exercise 5-9. Select the Bone and open the Motion Graph Panel.

2. Add four new Bone keyframes at 65, 80, 95, and 110.

3. Choose the Z-Scale. Animate a slight swell-and-shrink of the beach ball that peaks at frames 80 and 100 and drops at 65 and 95, as if the beach ball is breathing.

4. Make and play a preview.

5. Critique the action and make revisions to the breathing action until you are satisfied with it.

   You may want to render the animation so you can evaluate the subtlety of the breathing motion more easily.

6. Animate a very slight forward-and-back wobble for frames 65 through 100, rotating the upper surface of the ball about 5 degrees on the Bone Pitch axis, as if the beach ball is preparing to roll again.

7. Make and play a preview.

8. Critique the action, then make revisions to the timing and amplitude of the wobble until you are satisfied with it.

You can generally add moving holds to a sequence after the main action is complete. If a moving hold requires special setups or models, you need to layout the moving holds in your storyboards and all the ensuing design processes, just like any other action. In this example, you could just as easily have used the Object scale and rotation graphs to achieve a similar effect.

You can generally add moving holds to a sequence after the main action is complete.

Exercise 5-11: Show a Little Character

This exercise shows you how to apply all the timing elements covered so far to animate the desk lamp hopping. This exercise is patterned after John Lasseter's exposition of Luxo Jr.'s hop, in the 1987 SIGGRAPH paper referenced in the Bibliography.

1. Load the EXER0511.LWS scene file from the Chapter 5 directory on the Companion CD-ROM. This scene file is identical to the results of Exercise 3-5, except for the modified Camera position.

2. Select the REPLAC00.LWO lamp object. Open the Motion Graph Panel.

    The lamp's base is very heavy. The lamp can only lift it with a strong, quick jerk, so the base will leave the ground with no ease-in at all. For the same reason, the base falls back to the ground very quickly and does not rebound at all; it behaves like a solid, heavy, rigid piece of metal.

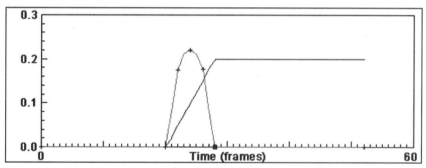

Figure 5-33: Y-Position motion graph for hopping lamp.

3. Add and drag keyframes to create a motion graph like Figure 5-33 for the lamp to make it move in a parabola on the Y-axis. Turn the Linear spline control on for the motion keyframes at the takeoff (frame 20) and ending (frame 60) keys for the Y-axis, so that the lamp base leaps up and slams down abruptly. Adjust the motion graph for the X-axis so it is straight throughout.

    Note that the lamp is only airborne for 8 frames, just over a quarter-second. If you keep the core of the action short and fast, the overall action usually has more snap.

> If you keep the core of the action short and fast, the overall action usually has more snap.

4. Create Pitch axis keyframes to rotate the base during the lamp's hop. Use ease-in and ease-out so the hop starts toe-last and ends heel-first. Make the lamp base flush to the ground, with zero pitch, at both the takeoff and landing keyframes. The maximum pitch angles should be just before and just after the peak of the hop, as in Figure 5-34.

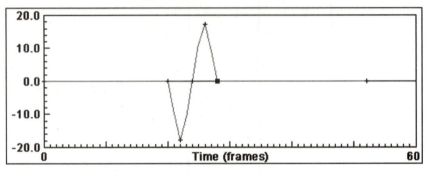

Figure 5-34: Motion graph for lamp's rotation on the Pitch axis.

5. Close the Motion Graph Panel and return to Layout. Press p to call up the Objects Panel and click the Envelope button next to MTSE in the middle of the panel.

   The MTSE sequence for the REPLACXX objects controls the amount of bend in the lamp's neck. A zero MTSE percentage stretches out the lamp neck, while a 600 percent setting bends the neck so the shade nearly touches the base. Three hundred percent, reasonably enough, is the middle or "rest" position for the lamp.

   You already set the movement and rotation values, so the lamp should be going where you want it to. The challenging part of this exercise is to use the MTSE sequence to give the lamp the illusion of life.

6. Create and modify MTSE keyframes so the lamp bends (squashes) in anticipation, stretches out just before the takeoff keyframe, returns to rest position in midhop, compresses immediately after landing in follow-through, and vibrates slightly in a moving hold to the end of the animation. You should end up with something like Figure 5-35.

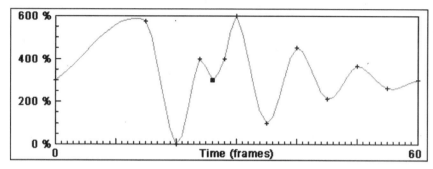

Figure 5-35: MTSE envelope for lamp hop.

7. Create keyframes for the Camera to line up with the lamp at the beginning and end frames of the animation. This makes the animation *hook up* for a seamless repeating cycle.

8. Make and play a preview.

You can modify the timing of the MTSE and motion graphs to change the character of the lamp. Drag out the number of frames between hops to make a more tired or melancholy lamp, or scale down the interval and the hop itself for a more energetic lamp. Save your results to use with the next exercise.

Drag out the number of frames between hops to make a more tired or melancholy lamp, or scale it down for a more energetic lamp.

Overlapping Action

When a character has loose parts, or appendages that are not held rigidly to the main body, these parts must demonstrate to the audience that they also have mass and energy of their own. A hound's floppy ears, for example, will continue to drag behind after the dog begins to run; and after the dog stops, the ears will flop forward under their own inertia. The ears' motion is an *overlapping action*.

The usual guidelines for ease, squash-and-stretch, and anticipation apply to overlapping action just as to the main action.

Up to this point you've been animating objects with only one part, or with parts firmly fixed. Now let's try something just a little more loosely constructed.

Exercise 5-12: Overlapping the Lamp

This exercise shows you how to add a loosely attached object to your main object and animate the additional part using overlapping action.

1. Open the scene saved from the preceding exercise or use the EXER0512.LWS scene file from the Companion CD-ROM.

2. Open the Objects Panel. Load the TAGRING.LWO and PRICETAG.LWO objects from the Chapter 5 directory of the Companion CD-ROM. Close the Objects Panel.

    The TAGRING object is modeled after the flexible plastic O-rings sometimes used to attach tags, and the tag is modeled after a very common retail sales tag profile. I could have modeled a loop of string instead of the O-ring, but the string's flexibility would have required Bones or MTSE animation techniques, and the extra complexity might have distracted you from the point of this exercise. If you want to try that approach on your own, please do so; it's an excellent practical exercise in both modeling and animation.

3. Select the TAGRING.LWO object. Parent it to the REPLAC00.LWO object.

4. Move the TAGRING.LWO object to 0, 0.077, 0, change its heading to 90 degrees, and create a key at frame 0. You won't be moving or rotating the O-ring again, so turn off all the options in the Mouse area.

    You want the price tag and O-ring to remain visibly attached to the lamp, but you also need as much space as possible for the price tag to move. These coordinates position the O-ring near the base of the lamp's neck, where any gaps caused by the neck's bending will be small and less noticeable.

5. Parent the PRICETAG.LWO object to the TAGRING.LWO object. Match the tag to the O-ring by moving the tag to coordinates 0.0015, -0.0004, -0.01, changing Bank to 5 degrees, and creating a key at frame 0.

    You should have a scene like Figure 5-36, with the price tag hanging naturally off the loop in the plastic O-ring.

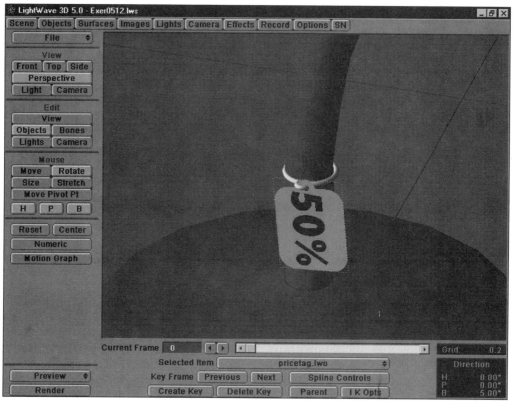

Figure 5-36: TAGRING.LWO and PRICETAG.LWO objects loaded, Parented, and positioned.

This arrangement of the tag and O-ring enables you to animate the price tag using only the Bank, Pitch, and Heading settings. The pivot point of the tag is inside the loop of the O-ring, so pivoting the tag simulates the constraints of a real tag. If you want to push the simulation further, you can reposition the tag anywhere along the O-ring's loop, as long as you keep the tag's pivot point within the loop and keep the tag from penetrating the lamp or O-ring.

Note the Bank Angle of the scene in Figure 5-36. The thickness of the O-ring loop and the profile of the paper tag prevent the tag from hanging straight down. The tag can never be rotated to less than 5 degrees of Bank Angle without penetrating the O-ring. The allowable range of motion for the tag is 5 to 165 degrees Bank, 45 to -4 degrees Pitch, and 30 to -30 degrees Heading. Any angle exceeding these limits will probably push the tag into the O-ring, the lamp itself, or both.

6. Make a series of keyframes for the PRICETAG.LWO object. Rotate the tag around the Heading, Pitch, and Bank axes to create overlapping actions.

    The tag has no motivation or "life" of its own. Any movement of the tag must be initiated by the lamp or an outside force such as wind or gravity.

    You need to keep four factors in mind when animating the price tag's overlapping action: lamp motion, inertia, gravity, and air resistance:

    - Lamp motion is the prime mover for the tag. The tag goes along, willy-nilly, following the lamp's position changes. The tag does not, however, react to the lamp's MTSE changes. This helps you choose where to set keyframes for the tag; one at each of the lamp's Position keyframes is a good start.

    - Inertia takes over when the lamp is not actively dragging the tag. At the top of the lamp's parabola, for instance, the tag changes from following the lamp's lead to following its own parabola. Since the center of gravity (CG) of the tag is below its pivot point, the tag shows inertia by swinging up toward the direction it had been traveling.

    - Gravity pulls the tag down whenever the lamp motion and the tag's inertia are not strong enough to resist it. At rest, gravity keeps the tag firmly resting at 5 degrees of Bank, as noted earlier.

    - Air resistance is a factor due to the low mass and relatively large surface area of the tag. As the tag moves under the influence of the three preceding factors, it should also appear to be pushed around by the resistance of the air it passes through. For example, if the tag is descending under the influence of gravity (rotating in the Bank axis), the tag may wobble in the Heading and/or Pitch axes.

If you are eyeballing the angles, it's much easier to work in the Perspective view with the Center and OpenGL options turned on, as in Figure 5-36. Adjust the Zoom Factor and Rotate settings to give you a clear view of the tag's edges, and where they may be intersecting other objects. Figure 5-37 shows one possible solution for the price tag's overlapping action.

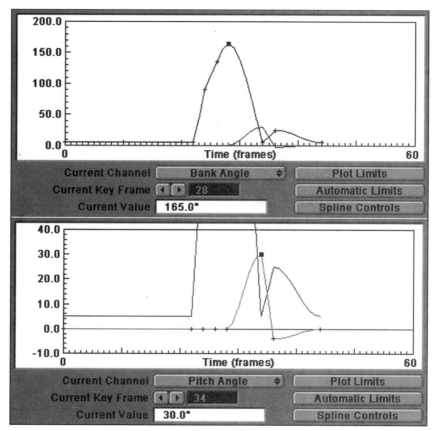

Figure 5-37: Heading, Pitch, and Bank Angles for the price tag's overlapping action.

7. Make and play a preview.

You should end up with an animation similar to Figure 5-38 or the EXER0512.AVI animation located in the Chapter 5 directory of the Companion CD-ROM.

Figure 5-38: Secondary action of a pivoting price tag.

8. Critique your animation.

Bones techniques are especially useful when parts of a seamless character object must overlap the main action.

Does the tag move lightly enough in comparison to the lamp? Does the lamp seem heavy, and the tag lighter? Does the tag flutter enough to give the impression of a loose joint, or does it seem to be rigidly hinged? If the answers aren't what you intended, go back and revise the angles and timings for the tag (and perhaps the lamp as well) until you are satisfied.

Overlapping action can be animated with just about every tool you learned in Chapter 3. Bones techniques are especially useful when parts of a seamless character object must overlap the main action.

Don't Stop Now!

Practice, practice, practice! Try every example with variations in timing. Note what works and what is communicated differently with each change.

A piece of advice I have heard quoted by several traditional artists is: "Everyone has a hundred thousand bad drawings inside them. The sooner you get them out of your system, the better." I'd like to extend the spirit of that quote to CGI character animation. I believe knocking out a hundred thousand keyframes (not just rendered frames!) should be enough experience to make you a really good character animator.

X-Sheet Practice

Most of the preceding exercises have included some initial timings, or at least a hint or two about the appropriate range of timings. As a professional animator, you need to be able to write up actions on an exposure sheet (an "x-sheet") without mocking them up in LightWave 3D first. This is both for your own development and discipline, and so you can communicate effectively with other pro- duction team members.

X-sheet shorthand varies from studio to studio, and even from animator to animator, but there are a few general conventions. The start or stop of an action is usually marked with an X, especially if it must match a "hit" on the sound track. A hold is marked with a straight line between the Xs. An action is represented by a curve, and an anticipation before an action is a loop. A repeated action such as a walk or run is drawn as a series of curves connecting Xs located in each heel-strike frame.

Exercise 5-13: Write It Up

This exercise gives you some practice in writing an x-sheet.

1. Make a lot of copies of the blank x-sheet from Appendix F.

2. For each exercise in this chapter, write up x-sheets for the differ- ent timings you used. It is not necessary to mark each keyframe. The start, stop, anticipation, follow-through, and a brief written description of each action are adequate.

3. Critique your x-sheets. Could you recreate the animation from just the exposure sheets and a sketch of a keyframe in the sequence? That's pretty much what you're expected to do as an animator, working from an x-sheet and a story sketch or two.

It's a good idea to keep practicing x-sheet markup as you work through the following chapters. X-sheet shorthand should be second nature by the time you're done.

Moving On

At this point you should have a basic understanding of the elements of timing. You have practiced with some basic objects and found you can create a sense of life and character with a minimal amount of complexity.

In the next chapter you'll apply the tools you've learned to a more complex character. From the single joint of the desk lamp, you'll be stepping up to animating 14 or more for a bipedal walk.

Take a Walk

This chapter concentrates on the animation of basic walks for bipedal characters of humanoid proportions. Later chapters will explore runs, other gaits, and nonhuman and caricatured motion cycles. This chapter also introduces the concept of the animation hierarchy, the division of the character into levels of a hierarchy for the creation of keyframes.

Step by Step

A *motion cycle* is an action that you can repeat by connecting duplicates end-to-end—for example, walking, running, hammering a nail, or any other repetitive action. Cycles require special attention to the *hookup*, the matching of beginning and ending frames to eliminate jerks or strobing when you loop the action, or play it repeatedly. You generally use cycles in what is referred to as *transportation animation*, walking or other means of moving the character around within the shot.

Walk cycles are a core requirement for character animation.

Walk and run cycles are not difficult to animate once you understand the basics, but they are a core requirement for character animation. A prospective employer may even ask you to animate a simple walk (along with the classic bouncing ball exercise), just to ensure that you know what you're doing. It may be to your advantage to practice the following exercises until you can do a simple walk by reflex, and an emotional or characteristic walk with a minimum of thought.

Animation Hierarchy

The *animation hierarchy* does not refer to the hierarchical organization of parts to form a Boned or Parented character. The animation hierarchy refers to the division of the character into levels of a hierarchy for the creation of keyframes.

This concept is unique to CGI character animation. In cel and puppet animation, the entire character is posed completely for every frame of film, then the pose is modified as a whole for the next frame. No matter how many layers of cels are used for different character parts, or how many replacement parts are socketed into a puppet, the complete character has to be assembled in front of the camera for every frame of film exposed. At the most basic physical level, every frame is a key frame for cel and puppet animation.

LightWave 3D enables you to set a different sequence of keyframes for each object and Bone in a character. You can use as few as one or two keyframes to move the hierarchical root, the character's CG (center of gravity), along a shallow slalom. In the same shot, you can keyframe a part in the lowest level of the hierarchy (perhaps the character's toes) a dozen times, none of them on the same keyframe as the CG. This enables you to move, rotate, and scale each part of a character along its own slalom, creating smooth action with the absolute minimum of keyframes.

So what's the advantage of a hierarchy? Think about this: every part of a character is a dependent of the hierarchy, right back to the CG. If a part moves, every part below it in the hierarchy moves along. If a part above it moves, it has to move along. Each part of the character also has to interact with the character's world. Feet must contact the ground properly, hands must grasp and move objects, and so on.

So what happens if you spend hours posing a character's hands just right, setting dozens of keyframes to make precise contacts—then discover you didn't pose the hips correctly, and the whole figure must be reposed? Short of hiring another animator to do the shot over, you have to chuck out all your work on the hands and start from scratch. Discouraging. Not to mention costly, especially if you are on a tight deadline or budget. On the other hand (pun intended), if you had animated according to the character's animation hierarchy, you would have found the error in the hips before you even started on the hands.

So how do you use the animation hierarchy? Very simple: start at the root, and animate each level of the hierarchy completely before going down to the next level. For most characters, this means you start with the CG. You need to plan where you want the character to travel, and then keyframe the CG to follow that *slalom*, the feedback curve that describes all natural, directed motion.

Start at the root, and completely animate each level before going on to the next.

Walking has been described as a fall interrupted by the interposing of a limb. This observation has a special significance for CGI animation. You have already learned how to animate a fall using a spline-based parabola; you can use the same parabola, slightly modified, to describe the repeated falls of a walking character's body.

The first step (oh, the puns never end!) is to determine how high and low the character's CG will move, and the distance between the ends of the parabola. To calculate these distances, you need to understand the key poses for a walking character.

Best Foot Forward

There are only three basic key poses in a walk: *heel strike*, *squash*, and *passing*. These poses are repeated in sequence for each side, to give a total of six key poses for a complete bipedal walking cycle.

The heel strike, shown in Figure 6-1, is the primary pose for the walk. The leading leg is straight, the ankle joint holds the foot at nearly a right angle to the leg, the trailing foot is solidly planted and flat to the ground, and the character's CG is evenly balanced between the feet. The arms are also at the limit of their forward and backward slaloms, balancing the opposite legs. For a natural walk, the heel strike is the low point in the CG's parabola.

The heel strike is kind of like a pole vault, converting the forward inertia of the body into an upward arc, with the straight leg defining the arc's radius. The heel strike pose also determines the stride length for the character's walk, that is, the distance the character travels with each step. This is the distance between the ends of the CG's parabola. If you want the character to travel a specific distance in a certain number of frames, you must pay close attention to stride length when planning the animation.

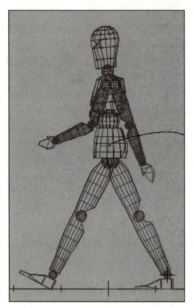

Figure 6-1: Heel strike pose.

The squash pose, shown in Figure 6-2, is just what it sounds like: the leading leg bends at the knee, squashing slightly to absorb the impact of the heel strike. If you didn't include the squash pose, and kept the leg straight from heel strike to passing, the character would walk very stiffly, like an extra from a bad monster movie.

Figure 6-2: Squash pose.

In the squash pose, the trailing foot's toes barely touch the ground, with none of the character's weight on them, and the sole of the trailing foot is angled 70 degrees or more to the ground. This pose is the prime candidate for exaggeration in a caricatured walk, as detailed in Chapter 8. Cartoon squash positions are often the CG's low point, giving the walk much more bounce between heel strike and passing poses.

Passing pose, shown in Figure 6-3, is where the leading leg straightens out again, boosting the CG to its highest position. The passing CG height is the peak of the CG's parabola. The trailing leg is bent at nearly its sharpest angle, raising the foot high enough that the toes clear the ground as the leg rotates forward.

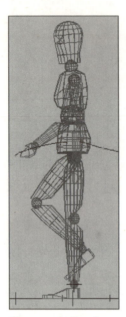

Figure 6-3: Passing pose.

Simply copying these basic poses onto a series of keyframes does not produce a natural-looking walk. The results will be stiff, artificial, and lifeless. Look at the 6EXAMPL1.AVI animation file, located in the Chapter 6 directory of the Companion CD-ROM. This animation has only six keyframes, one for each of the basic poses for left and right sides. This is obviously not enough detail for either a realistic or caricatured motion.

Compare 6EXAMPL1.AVI to the 6EXAMPL2.AVI animation, which has more keyframes but is still derived from the basic three poses. To produce these results, you need to set the timing and spline controls for each object in the character's hierarchy, using anticipation, ease-in, snap, ease-out, and follow-through.

The following exercises lead to the goal of a natural-looking humanoid walk cycle as shown in the 6EXAMPL2.AVI animation. Along the way, you'll learn to apply the concepts introduced in Chapter 5 to a more complex action.

A Few Words About Our Star

The Puppet used in the preceding figures and in the following exercises, shown in Figure 6-4, was originally modeled by Jim Pomeroy of Arlington, Texas, in December of 1991, and released by him into the public domain. Thanks, Jim!

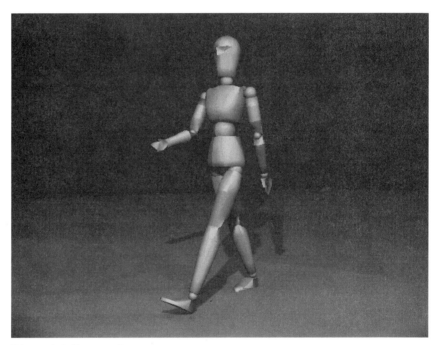

Figure 6-4: Puppet character.

I've made just a few modifications, mostly scaling the Puppet up to more average human dimensions and tweaking a few Pivot placements. This Puppet is about as simple as you can get within the limits of human proportions and joint structure. It uses only 15 small objects and two nulls in a Parented hierarchy, and no Bones at all. There are several reasons to use such a simple model:

- Screen redraw is a lot faster than if you had the same objects animated by Bones. Redraw times with hierarchical characters can quickly get out of hand, especially when you are down to trial-and-error tweaking of fine detail. You will be more productive, and learn more easily, if you can minimize your waiting time.

❧ This Puppet can be loaded by just about any system that can run LightWave 3D. The polygon count is very low, and the memory requirements are minimal. This also translates into faster redraws, less waiting, and more effective learning.

❧ There are fewer distractions in a simple character. If the Puppet had bandoleers, fighting knives, and Uzis dangling off a combat harness, you could spend all your time just animating the overlapping action of the bells and whistles. Keep it simple, and concentrate on the lesson at hand. When you've mastered the animation of a simple character, you can apply the same principles to a complex one—then spend extra time on the frills and gewgaws.

❧ This Puppet is also easier to keep track of than a more complex or Boned object. The Parented joints clearly show the physical limits of their rotations; the shin should obviously Pitch no more than 110 degrees relative to the thigh, and so on. The necessary notes a TD might deliver with this character are relatively brief.

There are a few disadvantages to this Puppet. It has no fingers or toes, so subtler gestures or a more refined heel-and-toe stride aren't possible. The low polygon count and minimal structure mean that there is no provision for object-level squash-and-stretch deformation; any squash or stretch must be animated by posing the joints. If you squash-and-stretch a bit of geometry that has too few polygons, you end up with non planar polygons (and therefore rendering errors) at worst; at best, the shape won't deform at all. The Puppet also lacks some crucial joints for expressive characters, as it has no independent shoulder joints and therefore can't even shrug without literally coming apart at the seams.

TD Character Notes: Puppet

These character notes are intended to help you pose the Puppet in simple walk and run cycles. The recommendations for joint constraints and usage may not be appropriate for animating other actions.

All surfaces are set to the default material. This is a simple Parented hierarchy of objects; there are no Bones, Metamorph, or other enhancements.

Note: Nulls are nonrendering objects that are used as pivots for objects or groups of objects.

First Level of the Animation Hierarchy

The Puppet_Ground_Null and Puppet_CG_Null are the root, or first, level of the animation hierarchy, and they should be animated for almost any action. You may find it helpful to think of the Puppet_Ground_Null as a support rod for the Puppet, and the Puppet_CG_Null as a clamp that can only travel up and down the rod.

※ Puppet_Ground_Null: This null controls the position of the character in the X-Z plane. Always position the Puppet_Ground_Null at ground level, and on uneven terrain you should position it at the height of the grounded foot or other grounded body part. This null is separate from the Puppet_CG_Null so you can animate the vertical and horizontal components of the character's movement on different keyframes. You should not rotate or scale this object.

※ Puppet_CG_Null: This null controls the Y-Position and attitude (Heading, Pitch, and Bank) of the character as a whole. It is located at the approximate center of gravity of an equivalent real-life human. You can animate this null in the Y-axis to keep the contact foot (or other contact body part) on the ground, and rotate it on the appropriate axes for free-fall tumbling. If you need to rotate the character while it is in contact with the ground, rotate the Hips object.

Second Level of the Animation Hierarchy

※ Hips: This object includes the lower abdomen, the ball joint that forms the pivot for the Chest object, and the ball joints of the two Thigh pivots. This is the Parent object of the character's body. This is the second level of the animation hierarchy, and you should animate it immediately after the CG and Ground nulls for almost any action. The Pivot point is located at the center of gravity (CG). You can rotate this object a few degrees on the Bank and Heading axes to enhance leg motions, but anything more than that will look really strange.

Third Level of the Animation Hierarchy

◈ Chest: This object includes the ribcage, the ball joint for the Head object, and the two ball joints for the UpArm objects. This is the Parent for the upper half of the body. You should animate the Chest's action completely and to your satisfaction before beginning on the head or arms. You can animate the Chest to Pitch nearly 60 degrees, as for a deep bow, and Bank 40 or so. You should not animate Heading more than 30 degrees without some complementary action of the Hips.

Fourth Level of the Animation Hierarchy

◈ Head: Generally, you can animate the Heading, Pitch, and Bank of the Head with the inverse values (–3.4=3.4, etc.) of the same axes of rotation of the Chest, simply to keep the Head level and pointed in the original direction. Since the Head tends to follow the eyes, in more complex actions the Head is a good candidate for IK and Tracking setups as explained in Chapter 4.

◈ LUpArm, RUpArm: You can animate the upper arm objects' Headings with the inverse Heading value of the Chest to keep the arms pointing in the right direction. You should keep Pitch values between –160 and 70, and Bank values between –30 and 135 degrees.

◈ LThigh, RThigh: You can animate the thighs' Headings with the inverse Heading and Bank values of the Hips to keep the legs pointing in the right direction. You should keep Pitch values between –120 and 45, and Bank values between –20 and 45 degrees, unless you are animating a gymnast.

Fifth Level of the Animation Hierarchy

◈ LLowArm, RLowArm: The fifth level of the animation hierarchy includes the lower arms and lower legs. These joints are simple hinges, and you should animate them only in the Pitch axis. You should animate other rotations using the hand or upper arm objects. The lower arm objects can Pitch between 0 and –120 degrees relative to the upper arm objects.

❧ LShin, RShin: You should animate the shins between 0 and 110 on the Pitch axis, relative to the thigh objects. Animate the feet or thigh objects for other rotations.

Sixth Level of the Animation Hierarchy

❧ LHand, RHand: For these exercises, you only need to animate the hands through small angles on the Pitch axis as overlapping action to the swing of the arms. The hands are set to 15 degrees Bank rotation to give them a more natural line with the rest of the body. The Pitch limits are –60 to 60, but 5 to 10 degrees are enough for the overlapping action. Since the fingers and toes for this character are not articulated, the hands and feet represent the sixth and last level of the animation hierarchy.

❧ LFoot, RFoot: You can reasonably animate the feet from –45 to 70 degrees on the Pitch axis, but much shallower angles are sufficient for these exercises. You should not use Heading and Bank rotations unless they are necessary to match the feet to odd terrain angles. Keyframing the foot rotations should be your next-to-last step in posing the hierarchy, as any change in higher layers will change the alignment to the ground. Generally, you should align the feet by eye with the ground surface, and keyframe them as often as necessary to keep them from penetrating or floating over the ground. Keyframes for a foot that is not in contact with the ground can be spaced as for overlapping action, as in the rotation of hands using Pitch.

Steppin' Time

The following exercise is longer than previous ones but all the explanatory notes about walks in general are inserted between the steps. Take your time, think about the notes, and save your work every now and then.

To set each motion's timing appropriately, you need to understand the *dynamics* of a walk, the motions that connect each key pose. Different parts move at different rates, accelerating and decelerating in a complex balancing act that you must learn to mimic.

It's useful to divide a character's motions among as many objects as possible.

It's often useful when using LightWave 3D to divide the motions of a character among as many different objects as possible. The Puppet uses one null as its CG, which is Parented to a second null at ground level. This enables you to animate the height of the Puppet above the ground by changing the CG's Y-Position, then animate the figure's travel along the ground by moving the Ground Level null. Keeping the two motions separate gives you more control over where you put your keyframes and how you set the tension, continuity, and bias for each motion graph.

For a simple walk, you can determine the position of the CG by the geometry of the legs and hips relative to the ground. Since the character geometry is fixed, it is possible to set the height of the Puppet_CG_Null in advance, with a fair degree of accuracy, for the entire walk cycle.

When I need to measure anything in Layout, I move an extra null object to the positions to be measured and note the XYZ coordinates from the Status window in the lower right corner of the Layout screen. This enables me to measure to a surface or particular point of an object, rather than just the Pivot position that the Status window displays for the selected object.

In the heel strike pose, the legs form an equilateral triangle with the CG at the apex. This height is one keyframe for the Puppet_CG_Null. According to my measurements for the heel strike pose in Figure 6-1, the vertical (Y-axis) distance from the sole of the Puppet's foot to its CG is 0.867, and the stride length is approximately 0.75. The distance traveled in a full two-step walk cycle is therefore 1.5. A deeper or shallower pose would give different numbers, but let's stick with the example for now. Measurement of the other poses gives 0.954 for the CG height at Passing, and 0.913 at Squash.

Exercise 6-1: Animating a Basic Walk

1. Open the scene file EXER0601.LWS, which you can find in the Chapter 6 directory of the Companion CD-ROM.

   This scene file includes the complete Puppet character, Parented, lighted, and ready to animate.

2. Select the Puppet_Ground_Null object. Set the null's X-Position to 1.5 at frames 0 and 1, and 0.0 at frame 33. Set the Spline Controls to Linear at frame 33.

These keyframes will make the Puppet_Ground_Null object travel 1.5 units over the 33 frames of the walk cycle. This is a very mechanical approximation of the motion for the finished walk, with no anticipation, ease, or follow-through. You'll refine it later, to precisely match the finished foot positions to fixed locations on the ground.

It is generally not an effective approach to try to pose the entire character in precise relation to the ground. Every little tweak, from the CG on down, changes the position of the feet relative to the ground. You'll find it much more productive to tweak the character's CG position at the end, after you have finalized all the other adjustments.

The three basic key poses for this walk cycle are each mirrored—used on both the right and left sides of the character—once, for a total of six key poses. The spacing for these poses is:

- Heel Strike Left: frame 1

- Squash Left: frame 6

- Passing Left: frame 11

- Heel Strike Right: frame 17

- Squash Right: frame 22

- Passing Right: frame 27

- Heel Strike Left: frame 33 (duplicated from frame 1 to produce an accurate hookup)

Later in this chapter, we'll explore how you can vary the spacing of the key poses to change the character of the walk. The spacing used in this exercise produces an ordinary brisk walk when played back at 30 fps.

3. Select the Puppet_CG_Null object. Set the object's Y-Position as follows:

- 0.867 in frames 0, 1, 17, and 33, the heel strike keyframes.

- 0.913 in the squash frames, 6 and 22.

- 0.954 in the passing frames, 11 and 27.

You should end up with a motion graph like Figure 6-5.

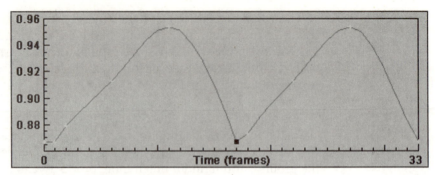

Figure 6-5: Y-Position motion graph.

You may have to adjust the tension, especially at the peaks and valleys. I set the tension to 1.0 in frames 11 and 27, and –1.0 in frame 17. In the Perspective view, the scene should now resemble Figure 6-6, with the white line representing the motion of the Puppet.

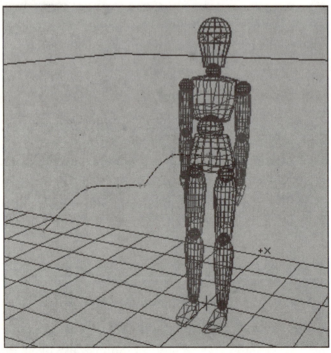

Figure 6-6: Puppet with keyframes set for Puppet_CG_Null and Puppet_Ground_Null objects.

4. Make a preview, from the Camera, Perspective, or Front view. Play the preview. Look at the motion of the hips, chest, and head. Does the bouncing action seem appropriate for a walking character?

    It's a little distracting to have the figure's arms and legs dragging along before they are posed. Let's limit the view to just the parts you're actually working on.

5. Click the Scene button to open the Scene Panel. Choose Hide | All Objects, then manually reselect the CG and Ground Nulls and the Hips, Chest, and Head objects to Show as Full Wireframes (or whatever mode you prefer). You should end up with something like Figure 6-7.

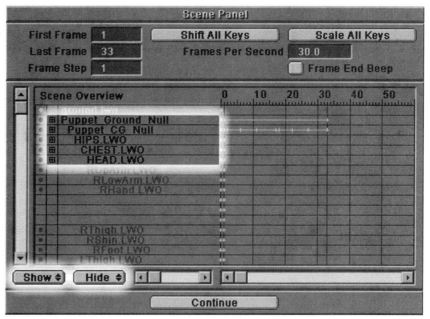

Figure 6-7: Scene Panel after hiding the lower levels of the animation hierarchy.

6. Make and play another preview. You should get something like Figure 6-8.

Figure 6-8: Frame 1 of the preview animation after hiding the lower levels of the animation hierarchy.

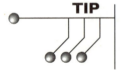

TIP

It's a lot easier to evaluate an action when just the pertinent parts are visible, isn't it? Keep this in mind, and hide or show objects as appropriate.

You should animate each level of the hierarchy so it reads perfectly before you begin to animate the next lower level. If you don't remember this rule, you will waste a lot of time revising poses you shouldn't have been animating in the first place.

The second level in the animation hierarchy includes the hips and chest. Before you go any further, save the scene under a new name. You should develop the habit of saving the scene file every time you make significant changes to a motion.

The hips are the driving force behind walks and runs. Just try walking without using your hips, sometime. If you manage to stay on your feet, you'll look like an arthritic penguin. Be sure to send the tape to "America's Funniest Home Videos."

The hips rotate around the CG. At the heel strike poses, the hips rotate on the Heading axis, effectively giving a little more length to the stride by pushing the leading leg forward and the trailing leg backward. At the passing poses, the hips Bank to raise the trailing leg slightly, giving it more ground clearance as it swings forward. The hips can also rotate on the Pitch axis to give a forward lean to the character, especially when it is moving quickly.

All these movements should be kept as subtle as possible. Each of these rotations acts from the center of the character, and can therefore have a disproportionate effect on the extremities. A single degree of Pitch in the hips, for example, can move the feet several centimeters.

7. Select the Hips object. Make keyframes at frames 6, 11, 17, 22, 27, and 33. Set the Hips to Bank at the passing poses, 3 degrees at frame 11, –3 degrees at frame 27. Set the other frames to Bank 0, and set Spline Controls to Linear for frames 22 and 6 to keep the Bank flat for the other poses. You should get a motion graph like Figure 6-9.

    The Linear settings are needed to flatten out the motion graph between frames 1–6 and 17–22, because that's where the feet are on the ground. The hip action is a smooth slalom during the passing pose, then—Boom!—the heel strike literally stops it flat.

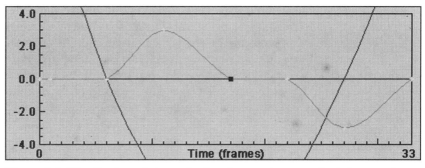

Figure 6-9: Hips Bank motion graph, showing maximum and minimum values for passing poses.

8. Set the Hips Heading to help lengthen the stride by rotating 10 degrees at the left heel strike frames 0, 1, and 33, and –10 degrees at right heel strike frame 17. Drag the intervening keyframes to make a smooth slalom, as in Figure 6-10.

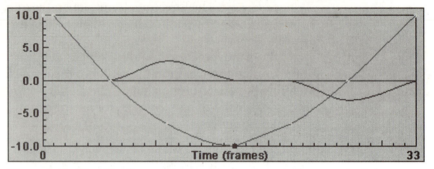

Figure 6-10: Hips Heading motion graph, showing maximum and minimum values for heel strike poses.

9. Set the Hips Pitch to 5 degrees for each keyframe. This tilts the figure forward, to lean into the walk. A slower walk could use a smaller angle, a faster walk needs a larger one.

10. Make and play a preview. How does the hip action look? Does it seem natural? Try a different view. You can try changing the peak Bank values a degree or two in either direction. More Bank tends to produce a more feminine walk, while less Bank makes it more robotic. Reducing the Heading values makes the character walk like a wind-up toy, while increasing them stretches the stride as if in preparation for a run.

Hip action can be the toughest part of animating a character. It is usually very subtle, and attempts to analyze it from life seem prone to trigger all sorts of bizarre reactions from informal test subjects. Whenever possible, study your own actions, then try to find confirmation of your conclusions in film or video motion studies. Good hip action can be a matter of a fraction of a degree, so still photos or video sequences that you can rerun and study in detail are an extremely valuable tool.

Once the hips are animated to your satisfaction, the Chest is relatively easy. You can animate the Chest by using the Hips settings as a guide to setting up a *dynamic balance*.

During a walk, the upper and lower parts of the body are in dynamic balance—the combination of mass, inertia, and energy in the lower body is equaled by the mass, inertia, and energy in the upper body, so the body as a whole is in balance. This is different from *static balance*, in which opposing parts are in balance at rest; dynamic balance means the parts are constantly changing and reacting to change to actively maintain the balance.

For this exercise, dynamic balance means that for every clockwise Heading rotation of the hips, the Chest Heading must rotate counter-clockwise. It's pretty simple, really. You need to keep in mind that the Chest rotations are measured from the Hips, the Chest's Parent, so you need to double the angle in reverse to get the same effect. That is, if the Hips are at Heading 10 degrees, and you set the Chest to Heading –10 degrees, the Chest will just be facing straight ahead again. Set the Chest Heading to –20, and the Chest will rotate as far to one side as the Hips do to the other.

11. Select the Chest object. Set each Heading keyframe to twice the negative value of each corresponding Hips Heading keyframe. You should end up with a motion graph like Figure 6-11.

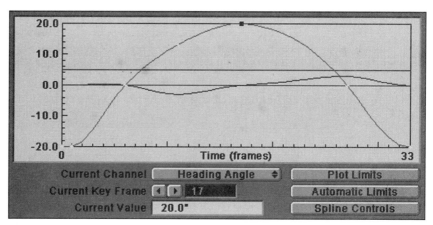

Figure 6-11: Chest Heading motion graph.

12. Set each Chest Bank keyframe to the exact negative value of each corresponding Hips Bank keyframe. This keeps the shoulders level. Keep the Pitch keyframes set to 0. You should end up with a motion graph like Figure 6-12.

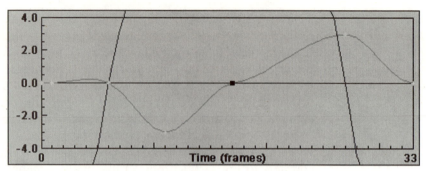

Figure 6-12: Chest Bank motion graph.

13. Make and play a preview. Do the Hips and Chest rotate properly? Does the motion seem natural? Does the action look alive, or is it mechanical and dead? Are the upper and lower body in dynamic balance? If the animation is working, you should be able to visualize arms and legs following the motions of the hips and shoulders.

    Save the scene file again, if you haven't already. You've completed level 2 of the animation hierarchy for the Puppet. The next level includes the Head, Upper Arms, and Thighs.

    The Head is already visible, so let's start there. The Head is a hierarchical dead end, since it isn't a Parent to any other objects and it doesn't have to align or make contact with any other parts of the scene. For a simple walk, all the Head has to do is look straight ahead until animated to do otherwise.

14. Select the Head object. Set each Heading keyframe for the Head to the exact negative value of each corresponding Chest Heading keyframe. This keeps the Head pointing in the direction of the Puppet's travel. You can set the Pitch keyframes to the negative of the Hips Pitch if you want the Puppet to walk with its head up. You can leave the Bank keyframes set to 0. You should end up with a motion graph like Figure 6-13.

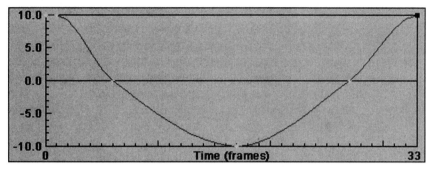

Figure 6-13: Heading motion graph for puppet's head.

15. Make and play a preview. Does the Head remain looking forward, counterbalancing the motions of the Chest and Hips?

    After this point, the X-Position animation of the Puppet_Ground_Null is more trouble than it's worth. You will find it easier to compare poses and analyze motion if the Puppet remains centered in all the views. To do this, you need to change the Puppet_Ground_Null's keyframes to a constant value.

16. Select Puppet_Ground_Null. Change its X-Position to 0.0 at keyframes 0, 1, and 33. Whenever you make and play a preview, the Puppet will now appear to be walking in place. Later, we'll restore and fine-tune the Puppet_Ground_Null's motion graph.

    Now for the fun part! Animating the Thighs is nearly as hard as animating the Hips, although it usually requires less judgment. Most of the Thigh animation is dictated by the Hips, another fraction is guided by the three key poses, and the rest depends on you to add anticipation, ease, snap, and follow-through.

17. Open the Scene Panel again, and set RThigh and LThigh to show as Full Wireframes. Close the Scene Panel.

18. Set the Heading and Bank rotations of RThigh and LThigh to counter the Heading and Bank angles of the Hips in each keyframe. You don't need to set the Linear option for any Bank keyframes as you did for the Hips, since the Thighs' motion should have more ease. You should get Heading motion graphs like Figure 6-14, and Bank motion graphs like Figure 6-15.

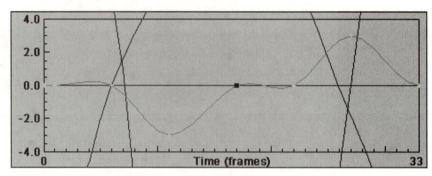

Figure 6-14: Heading motion graph for RThigh and LThigh.

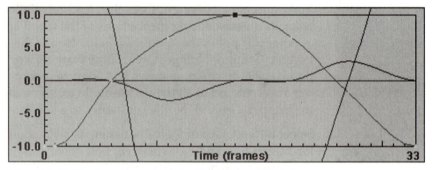

Figure 6-15: Bank motion graph for RThigh and LThigh.

This just gets you back to zero with the Thighs. Entering inverse angles like this is probably the most noncreative part of character animation, but it beats mousing everything around by hand and eyeballing poses that would probably become glaring errors in the finished animation. When you can get away with animating "by the numbers," it's smart to take advantage of it.

The Thighs must be Heading in the direction of travel, or the character will appear to waddle. The combined Bank angle of Hips and Thighs should be near 0, or the character may appear knock-kneed, bowlegged, or listing to one side. This would be good for caricature (again, see Chapter 8), but is not so good for a normal, plain-vanilla walk.

19. Make and play a preview. Do the Thighs head and bank properly? If not, go back and compare the motion graphs. Did you forget something?

The next step in posing RThigh and LThigh is to set the Pitch angles for the heel strike, squash, and passing poses. Since the poses are repeated exactly on the left and right sides, you only have to create one side's poses and copy those settings to the other side's corresponding keyframes.

20. Adjust RThigh's Pitch in keyframe 17 to match the leading Thigh's angle in Figure 6-1, the heel strike pose. I used an angle of about -26.5 degrees, but your results may vary. Set LThigh to the negative of RThigh's Pitch. Both Thighs should have the same amount of Pitch in the heel strike poses. When you are satisfied with your results, copy the Pitch values to the opposite Thighs in keyframes 0, 1, and 33.

21. Adjust RThigh's Pitch in keyframe 11 to match the lifted thigh's angle in Figure 6-3, the passing pose. I used an angle of about –39 degrees. When you are satisfied with your results, copy the Pitch value to keyframe 27 for LThigh. The opposite Thighs in both keyframes 11 and 27 are easy ones: set their Pitch to 0.

22. Adjust RThigh's Pitch in keyframe 6 to match the leading thigh's angle in Figure 6-2, the squash pose. I used an angle of about 9.5 degrees. Adjust LThigh's Pitch in keyframe 6 to match the trailing thigh's angle in Figure 6-2. I used -24.8 degrees. When you are satisfied with your results, copy the Pitch values to the opposite Thighs in keyframe 22. You should end up with Pitch motion graphs like Figures 6-16 and 6-17.

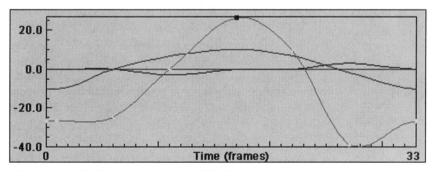

Figure 6-16: Pitch motion graph for LThigh.

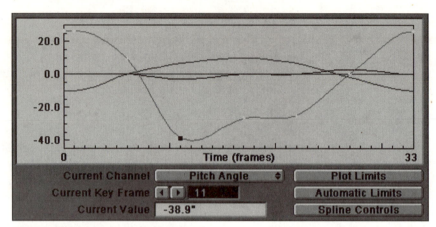

Figure 6-17: Pitch motion graph for RThigh.

Note the shape of the RThigh graph. Frame 1 shows the Thigh trailing as the opposite heel strikes. RThigh eases-in to frame 6, where it reaches maximum velocity; it passes through frame 11 as it begins to ease-out, then follows through to the heel strike pose at frame 17. The sharper curves between frames 1–6 and 11–17, and the relatively straighter segment between frames 6–11, give the action a fair amount of snap. This gives the impression of a quick, energetic movement; the heavy muscles of the upper leg are only moving themselves, and don't have to support the body's weight or accelerate its larger mass.

The motion graph for the rest of the cycle is the other side of the story. The thigh is now the prime mover for accelerating the whole body. It's hard work to move all that mass, so the thigh rotates in a smooth, efficient acceleration curve, close to a 45 degree angle, between frames 22 and 33.

The timing and control of each Thigh Pitch keyframe can make the difference between a stroll, strut, march, and many other types of walk. You could also change the walk dramatically by leaving each key value right where it is, but edit the tension, bias, and continuity of each keyframe to smooth out these curves. This approach would give you the typically over-interpolated, mushy, boring action that just screams, "The computer animated this!"

23. Make and play a preview. Do the Thighs pitch properly? Do they ease-in and ease-out at acceptable rates? Is there enough snap in the motion?

When you are satisfied with the motion of the Thighs, it's time to move on to the last parts of the animation hierarchy's fourth level, the upper arms. Save the scene again before proceeding with the next step.

24. Open the Scene Panel again and set RUpArm and LUpArm to show as Full Wireframes. Close the Scene Panel.

25. Set the Heading rotations of RUpArm and LUpArm to counter the Heading angles of the Chest in each keyframe. You should get Heading motion graphs like Figure 6-18. This rotates the UpArms's Headings back to zero, relative to the overall position of the Puppet. The UpArms should usually be Heading in the direction of travel, but when you are animating an energetic walk you may want them to head slightly inward for balance.

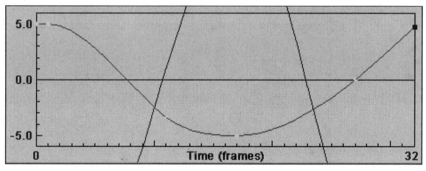

Figure 6-18: Heading motion graph for RUpArm and LUpArm.

26. Make and play a preview. Do the UpArms have appropriate Headings?

27. Pitch RUpArm and LUpArm according to the three key poses in Figures 6-1, 6-2, and 6-3.

How would you set the ease-in, snap, ease-out, and follow-through of the upper arms? These limbs do not have to carry any weight other than their own, and are much more like ideal pendulums swinging to counterweight the legs. If you reasoned that RUpArm and LUpArm should move in near-perfect slaloms, you should have come up with motion graphs like Figures 6-19 and 6-20.

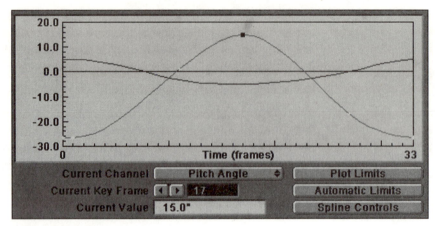

Figure 6-19: Pitch motion graph for RUpArm.

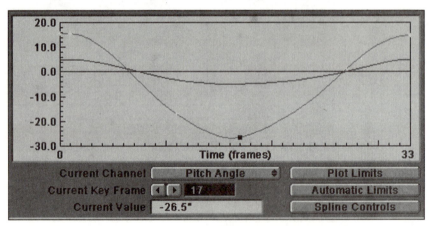

Figure 6-20: Pitch motion graph for LUpArm.

At this point, you have a torso with one level of stump for each limb, the Head included.

28. Make and play a preview. Look very closely at this preview; make more previews, from each principal view and whatever perspective angles and zoom factors you find useful. You want to make absolutely sure that the action so far is to your liking; changing your mind later is a good way to waste time and effort, not to mention your patience.

When you are satisfied with the action, save the scene again and proceed to the fifth animation hierarchy level, the Shins and Lower Arms.

29. Open the Scene Panel again, and set RLowArm and LLowArm to show as Full Wireframes. Close the Scene Panel. The lower arm joint—the elbow—is a simple hinge, and can only rotate in the Pitch axis. This level of the animation hierarchy is a piece of cake!

30. Pitch RLowArm and LLowArm according to the three key poses in Figures 6-1, 6-2, and 6-3. As with the upper arms, you can animate these objects in near-perfect slaloms, to result in motion graphs like Figures 6-21 and 6-22.

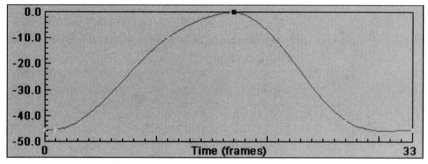

Figure 6-21: Pitch motion graph for RLowArm.

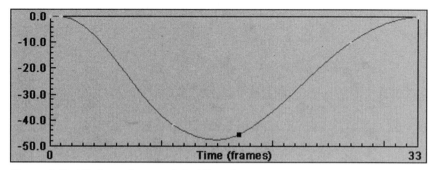

Figure 6-22: Pitch motion graph for LLowArm.

31. Make and play a preview. How does the full arm motion look? You have plenty of leeway with the timing of the arm swings; you can tweak the Spline Control Tools a lot, as long as the arm positions match the three key poses.

    This is a good place to introduce another phrase borrowed from traditional animation, *successive breaking of joints*. This technique is a little like overlapping action, but it applies specifically to the hierarchy of joints in a character. Basically, when a higher joint starts to rotate, there should be a slight lag before the lower joints start to rotate as part of the same action. In practical terms, this means the rotation of a child object should begin, peak, and end some time after the Parent performs the same actions.

    There is a very easy way to do this in LightWave 3D. Simply pose the "successive joint," the next Child down the hierarchy, the exact keyframes as its Parent object. When you have completely animated the action, use the Shift Keyframe function in the Motion Graph Panel to delay the child's rotation a frame or two behind the Parent's. The rotations of each joint will break in succession, down through the animation hierarchy.

32. Shift all the keyframes for the RLowArm and LLowArm back (toward frame 33) by one frame. Make and play the preview again. What difference did the successive breaking of joints make? Try shifting the LowArm keyframes back another frame or two. Increase and decrease the shift until you get a feel for timing this technique. When you have a timing you like, save the scene again and proceed to pose the Shins.

33. Open the Scene Panel again, and set RShin and LShin to show as Full Wireframes. Close the Scene Panel.

    The shin joint—the knee—normally moves as a simple hinge, and can only rotate in the Pitch axis. This action is relatively easy to animate, but you have to pay extra attention to the timing of the heel strike-to-squash transition. This is supposed to be a reaction to the mass of the Puppet striking the ground, and the Shin and Thigh squash to cushion the impact. The squash should be a little faster than the rebound.

34. Pitch RShin and LShin according to the three key poses in Figures 6-1, 6-2, and 6-3. You should end up with motion graphs like Figures 6-23 and 6-24.

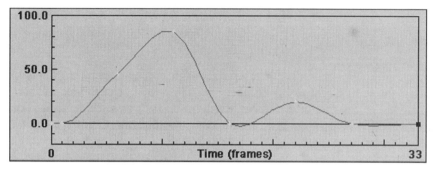

Figure 6-23: Pitch motion graph for RShin.

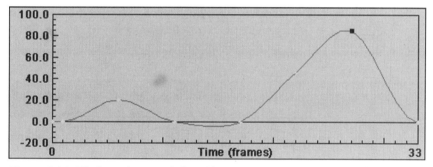

Figure 6-24: Pitch motion graph for LShin.

35. Make and play a preview. How does the full arm motion look? Is there enough snap to the forward motion, leading into the heel strike?

    You must hold the straight leg of the heel strike (the shin's zero-degree Pitch angle) long enough for it to register visually with the audience, or the adjoining poses (preheel strike and squash) will blur together and the step will appear mushy. It's a good idea to keep the leg straight for at least two or three frames.

    This is one of the critical parts of a walk; a mushy heel strike looks tired or lazy, while a very sharp snap can define a march or strut. The depth and snap of the squash also say a lot about the amount of muscle tone and tension in the leg, and the character as a whole.

A mushy heel strike looks lazy; a sharp snap can define a march or strut.

When you are satisfied with the action, save the scene again and proceed to the sixth and last animation hierarchy level, the Hands and Feet.

36. Open the Scene Panel again, and set RHand and LHand to show as Full Wireframes. Close the Scene Panel. The wrist is a universal joint and can rotate in both Pitch and Heading. For this exercise you only need to use the Pitch axis.

37. Pitch the RHand and LHand according to the three key poses in Figures 6-1, 6-2, and 6-3. As with the upper and lower arms, there are no critical alignments to the ground or other objects. Since this is the end of the hierarchy, there are no dependent actions to plan for, either. You can animate these objects in near-perfect slaloms with very few keyframes, and use successive breaking of joints just as you did for the lower arms.

38. Shift the Hand rotation keyframes down a frame or two, for successive breaking of joints.

39. Make and play a preview. How does the timing look? Try shifting the keyframes back and forth a few frames, and compare the effect of each shift on the overall action. This is a relatively loose and free-swinging action, so you do not need to add much snap to the Hands' extremes. You should end up with motion graphs like Figures 6-25 and 6-26.

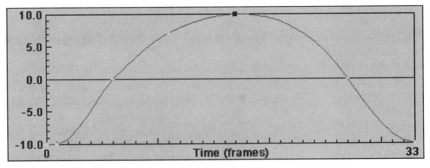

Figure 6-25: Pitch motion graph for RHand.

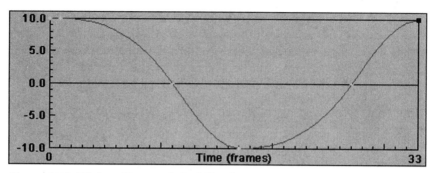

Figure 6-26: Pitch motion graph for LHand.

40. When you are satisfied with the Hand rotations, save the scene file again.

    You're almost done! Just the feet are left to pose, then you can make the final tweaks to polish off the action.

41. Open the Scene Panel again and set RFoot and LFoot to show as Full Wireframes. Close the Scene Panel. The ankle is also a universal joint, and can rotate in both Pitch and Bank axes, but for this exercise you only need to use the Pitch axis.

42. Pitch RFoot and LFoot according to the ground and the three key poses in Figures 6-1, 6-2, and 6-3.

    For keyframes where the foot is on the ground, it's more important to match the foot to the angle of the ground than to the precise angle of the pictured poses (this prevents a large discrepancy at the foot, in the event that your pose is slightly different than the pictured poses).

    Flatten the foot to the ground immediately after the heel strike pose, so the joint appears flexible and lifelike. If the foot is held at an angle to the ground after the heel strike, the ankle joint appears stiff and unnatural. Just try walking that way once, you'll feel what I mean. The muscles that run up the front of your shin act as shock absorbers when you run or walk. Holding a bent ankle after a heel strike will quickly exhaust them, and the lack of shock absorption will pass a lot more heel-strike shock to the rest of your body.

43. Make and play a preview. How does the timing look? Do you get a sense of the mass of the Puppet and the springiness of the leg muscles? You may want to go back and tweak the entire Thighs, Shins, and Feet hierarchy to get better leg motion.

    You'll probably have to add a number of keyframes to keep the feet level to the ground. Whenever the feet are lifted free of the ground, you can use fewer keyframes and create smoother sla-loms, but matching feet to the ground tends to produce motion graphs like Figures 6-27 and 6-28.

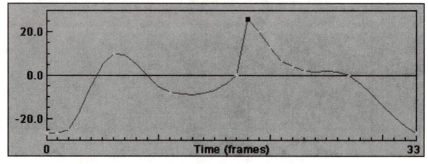

Figure 6-27: Pitch motion graph for RFoot.

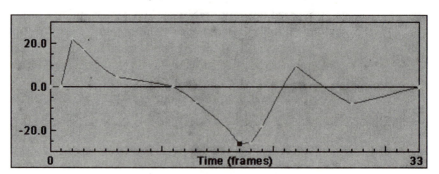

Figure 6-28: Pitch motion graph for LFoot.

44. When you are satisfied with the Foot rotations, save the scene file again.

    You've just finished the overall motion for the Puppet hierarchy. Congratulations!

No Skating Allowed

Now it's time to go back and tweak the position of the roots of the hierarchy, to keep the Puppet lined up properly with its environment.

One of the major problems with CGI character animation is keeping the feet aligned with fixed points on the ground. If this is not done precisely, the figure can appear to skate—slip the foot forward—or moonwalk—slip the foot backward, while the character moves as if walking normally. Even the best animators occasionally make a mistake on foot slippage. There is even one example in *Toy Story*, where Bo Peep is walking away from Woody and her foot slides a bit. Nobody's perfect.

In stand-alone LightWave 3D, your best defense against foot slippage is a lot of keyframes. The combined Hips-Thighs-Shins-Feet hierarchy produces an undulating Y-Position sequence that is difficult to match with a simple motion graph spline. This complex movement for the Puppet_CG_Null's Y-axis is loaded on top of the Puppet_Ground_Null's Z- and X-axes, which makes it even harder to match Puppet_Ground_Null's motions to a simple spline. The brute-force solution is a lot of keyframes.

45. Go to frame 0. Select RFoot. Turn on the Center option, and use the Front view. Change the Zoom Factor to 20 or so, and turn off the Center option. Select Puppet_CG_Null. You should have a view like Figure 6-29.

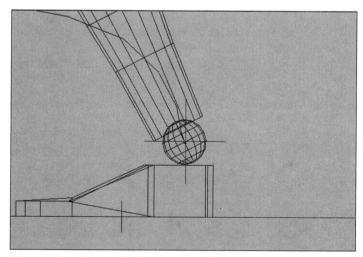

Figure 6-29: Zoomed-in Front view for tweaking Foot/Ground match.

46. Modify the Y-Position of Puppet_CG_Null only; leave the X- and Z-Move buttons turned off. Drag the null up or down until the sole of RFoot is level with the ground. When you have an exact alignment, save the keyframe.

47. Repeat step 46 for all the existing keyframes where RFoot is on the ground.

48. Step through each frame, starting at frame 0. Locate the biggest discrepancies, and try using Spline Tools on the nearest keyframes to smooth out the problems.

49. For large alignment problems that you can't fix with Spline Controls, add a new keyframe in the middle of the problem area, as close to halfway between adjoining keyframes as you can get. Adjust the new keyframe to fix the problem.

50. For any frames where there is still noticeable bouncing, try turning on the Linear option between closely spaced keyframes.

51. As a last resort, keep adding keyframes as necessary, up to every frame being a key.

52. Turn the Center option back on, and select LFoot. Go to the first frame (probably frame 3) where LFoot is planted. Turn off the Center option, and select Puppet_CG_Null.

53. Repeat steps 46 through 51 for LFoot. Tweak, tweak, tweak. Gee, this is fun. Not!

54. When you are satisfied with the Y-Position motion, save the scene. You should end up with a motion like Figure 6-30, but you may have more or fewer keyframes.

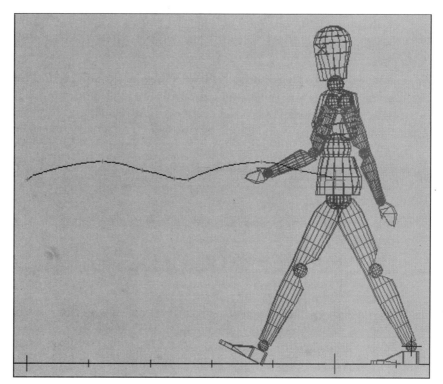

Figure 6-30: Tweaked motion for Puppet_CG_Null object.

You should now have a Puppet that only walks on the top of the ground, not bouncing over or wading through it. But it still skates and moonwalks a bit. On to the Puppet_Ground_Null! When you tweak the Puppet_Ground_Null, you move it in both X- and Z-axes. To make it easier to judge the alignment, you can position another null object at a consistent point for both Front and Side views, and flip back and forth between them.

55. Go to frame 0. Select RFoot. Turn on the Center option, and use the Front or Side view. Change the Zoom Factor to 20 or so, and turn off the Center option. Add another Null object, or use the Measuring_Null. Position the null, in both Front and Side views, in the center of the ankle sphere. Make a keyframe for the null.

Technically, you could also use the Top view, but it's pretty cluttered for most of the frames and you'd have to hide the rest of the Puppet hierarchy.

56. Go to frame 3 and use the same procedure to reposition the null in the center of the LFoot ankle sphere, in both Front and Side views. Make a keyframe for the null.

57. Repeat step 56 for each frame where the ground foot changes, and for the frame before it. My keyframes are 1, 2, 3, 17, 18, and 33, as shown in Figure 6-31. Yours may be slightly different. Turn on the Linear option for each keyframe to make the null snap directly to the next position without any interpolated movement.

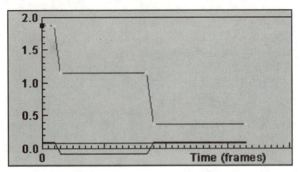

Figure 6-31: X-Position motion graph for Measuring_Null, tracking the ankle joint.

Your next step is to drag the Puppet_Ground_Null around to align the Measuring_Null with the center of the ankle sphere in each frame. This is just like steps 46 through 54, but this time the positioning is in two axes.

58. For each keyframe, drag the Puppet_Ground_Null around in the X- and Z-axes to align the Measuring_Null with the center of the grounded foot's ankle sphere, as in Figure 6-32.

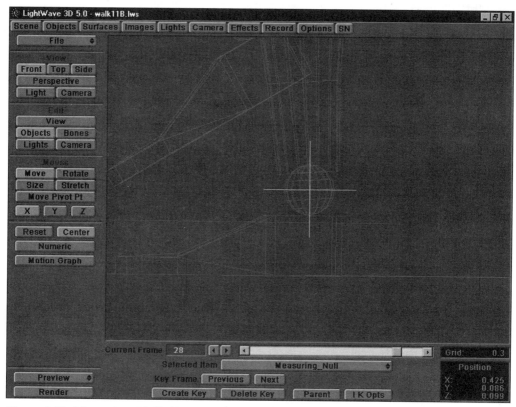

Figure 6-32: Measuring_Null aligned with ankle sphere.

59. Use the procedures in steps 46 to 54, to gradually refine the Puppet_Ground_Null's movement and eliminate the Puppet's skating and moonwalking.

    You can try adjusting both the X- and Z-values at the same time, flipping between Front and Top or Side views, or do all the Xs and then all the Zs. Whatever you prefer.

    You're trying to define a slalom to match the combined effects of all the joint rotations back through Shin, Thigh, and Hip, in Pitch, Bank, and Heading axes. Don't feel discouraged if you need to keyframe every frame for most of the action—it's just the nature of the beast. You may end up with motion graphs like Figures 6-33 and 6-34.

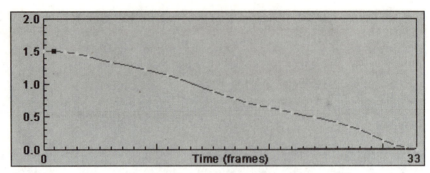

Figure 6-33: X-Position motion graph for Puppet_Ground_Null.

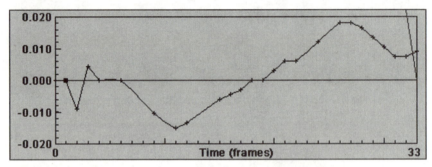

Figure 6-34: Z-Position motion graph for Puppet_Ground_Null.

60. Make and play a preview. Critique the finished walk. You shouldn't have to make major changes at this point. If you have to go back and tweak anything you don't like, start with the root of the problem and follow the corrections down through the animation hierarchy. You'd most likely have to revise at least the keyframes for every object lower in the hierarchy, and certainly for the Puppet_Ground_Null and Puppet_CG_Null.

Now you need to tweak the hookup frame. You'll have noticed that frames 1 and 33 are identical at this point. If you rendered an animation from 1 to 33 and looped it, the animation would stutter at the 1-33 hookup, because the same pose would appear for two successive frames. What you need to do now is delete either frame 1 or frame 33 for a seamless hookup. Deleting frame 1 is probably a bad idea, as you don't know what LightWave 3D's automatic interpolation between frame 0 and frame 2 will look like. It's easier to delete frame 33.

61. Go to frame 32. Select the Puppet_Ground_Null object. Click Create Key. In the Create Motion Key Panel, Click Selected Item and Descendants. Click OK.

    Most of the objects in the Puppet had interpolated values for frame 32. This step makes those interpolated values into keyframes, which means their values will not change when you delete frame 33 in the next step.

62. Go to frame 33. Click Delete Key. In the Delete Motion Key Panel, click Selected Item and Descendants. Click OK.

63. Open the Scene Panel. Change the Last Frame to 32. Click Continue. The animation now runs from frame 1 to frame 32, and the hookup should play back without a stutter.

64. Make and play a preview. This should be the finished walk cycle. How does it look?

Looping the Loop

When you are satisfied with the walk cycle, save the scene file again. Save the motion graphs for the Puppet_CG_Null and Puppet_Ground_Null, too; you'll be deleting them for the next exercise, and you may want to be able to reload them for reference.

65. Select Puppet_CG_Null. Open the Motion Graph Panel, and click Save Motion. Save the motion file with a name like WALKY01.MOT, so you can figure out what it means later. Close the Motion Graph Panel. Repeat for the Puppet_Ground_Null's motion.

    The last step in building a motion cycle is making it cyclical. LightWave 3D has a set of options in the Motion Graph Panel that govern the End Behavior of motions. You can set a motion to Stop and hold at the last value of the graph, Reset to the first value of the graph, or Repeat the entire graph endlessly for the entire scene. In this case, you want each part of the Puppet to Repeat its actions.

66. Select the Hips object. Open the Motion Graph Panel. Select Repeat from the list of End Behavior options. Click Use Motion to save your changes and close the Motion Graph Panel.

67. Repeat step 66 for each object in the Puppet hierarchy. When you're finished, save the scene again. With every object in the Puppet hierarchy set to Repeat, the Puppet will continue to execute the walk cycle for an animation of any length. Try it!

68. Make and play a preview of frames 1 to 64. You'll note that the lateral and vertical motions of the Puppet did not repeat. The rotations of the various objects were designed to be looped, but the XYZ motions of the nulls were designed for just one linear motion (the Puppet is moving forward, not back and forth, and you can't loop an action that doesn't return to the starting point). If you want to use them as well, try the Copy/Paste and Shift Values functions in the Motion Graph Panel to assemble longer, repeating versions of these motions.

You can use this scene as a stock action scene. Document it and file it away. Whenever you need a walk cycle, just use Load From Scene to bring in the Puppet hierarchy and all its motions. It's good animation practice, and a basic test of a new character, to create and save a variety of walk cycles for every character you build.

Create and save a variety of walk cycles for every character you build.

It was a long exercise, but I hope you got a lot out of it. Now let's look at a way you could have cut it short, and saved yourself quite a bit of effort.

There's Gotta Be a Better Way: Using the Lock & Key Plug-in

In traditional puppet animation, the figures are held in place during walk cycles by a *tie-down*. This is usually a threaded rod with a keyed head that locks into the bottom of the character's foot. The animator passes the rod through a hole in the stage and tightens it down with a wingnut, securing the puppet in place. The animator can pose the rest of the puppet as needed, and the secured foot remains in place. For each step, the animator transfers the tie-down to the other foot and a matching hole in the stage. This is usually much easier than trying to conceal a support rod and maintain vertical and horizontal alignments to keep the feet from skating or moonwalking.

There is a motion plug-in available for LightWave 3D that emulates the traditional puppet tie-down, among other functions. It's called Lock & Key, and is produced by Meme-X and distributed by Dynamic Realities. You can see some of their work and find more information in the DYNAREAL directory of the Companion CD-ROM.

CD-ROM

This is an extraordinarily useful plug-in for character animation with LightWave 3D. I highly recommend that you buy it. You will need it for the following exercise; if you don't have it, read through the exercise anyway (so you know what you're missing!).

Lock & Key can Parent almost any combination of Bones, objects, lights, and Camera, and change that Parenting from frame to frame within an animation. Lock & Key can also Parent a hierarchy to another item by using the Offset of any part of the hierarchy. For example, the following exercise Parents the Puppet to a null near the ground, using the Offset of the Foot objects. The result is that the entire Puppet moves in relation to the Foot and null.

This capability would have enabled you to skip steps 45 through 65 in the preceding exercise, the most tedious part of the whole chapter. Clearly, Lock & Key is a desirable tool for animating a character to interact with its environment.

Lock & Key uses a few terms:

❧ A Key is the object to be moved or rotated by the plug-in.

❧ A Lock is another item.

❧ A Combination, or Combo for short, is a pairing of a Key with a Lock.

Once the Combo is set, the plug-in moves and/or rotates the Key to fit the Lock. Easy enough to remember, a key belongs in a lock, right? And a key is a lot lighter and more movable, so it makes sense that the Lock stays put and the Key is drawn to it.

Exercise 6-2: Replacing CG & Ground keyframes With Lock & Key Combos

1. Load a copy of the last Puppet animation you saved.

2. You can use the Measuring_Null from the preceding exercise as the Lock. If you haven't already done so, position the Measuring_Null to match the coordinates of the center of the grounded ankle sphere for the entire walk cycle.

   A quick way to check the Measuring_Null alignment is to select the null, go to the Front view, turn on the Center option, and make a preview. As long as the ankle sphere is centered in every frame of the preview, you're all set.

3. Make a note of the frames when Measuring_Null changes position, and when it moves from RFoot to LFoot. These are the end and beginning frames of the Lock & Key Combos. I ended up with coordinates for RFoot at frames 1-2, 18-32, and for LFoot at frames 3-17.

4. Lock & Key must work with the root of a hierarchy. Since Lock & Key replaces the function of the Puppet_Ground_Null, you can delete Puppet_Ground_Null from the Objects Panel. Be sure you don't delete its descendants as well! You want to clear the motion of the Puppet_CG_Null too, but keep the null itself as the root of the Puppet hierarchy.

5. Select the Puppet_CG_Null and press m to open the Motion Graph Panel. Clear the motion. Restore the null's Heading to −90 degrees at frame 0, and click Use Motion to save the changes and close the Motion Graph Panel. This keeps the Puppet rotated to the original Heading, but leaves all the movement to the Lock & Key Combos.

6. Select the Key object, Puppet_CG_Null. Open the Motion Graph Panel.

7. Click Motion Plug-ins to open the Motion Plug-ins Panel. Select Lock & Key from the pull-down list. Click Options to call up the Lock & Key List Editor Panel, Figure 6-35.

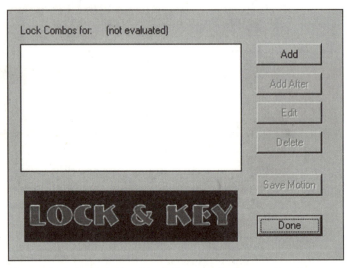

Figure 6-35: Lock & Key List Editor, ready for new Combos.

8. Click Add. The Combo Editor Panel appears. The Puppet_CG_Null is the key. Now you want to set the Measuring_Null as the Lock, and the frames when Combo should be in effect.

9. Set the Range from 0 to 2. Choose Measuring_Null from the Lock Item pull-down list. The Use Offset Item area of the panel is grayed out, as in Figure 6-36. Lock & Key needs LightWave 3D to pass it some plug-in data, and that won't happen until the changes have been saved through the Motion Graph Panel. This just means you have to save the settings, close all the panels, and reopen them.

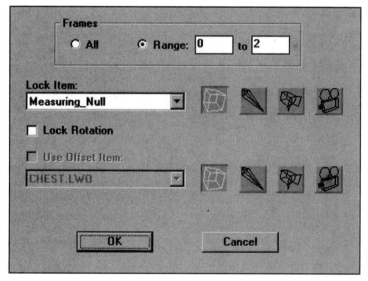

Figure 6-36: Lock & Key Combo Editor.

10. Click OK to close the Combo Editor. Click Done to close the List Editor, Continue to close the Motion Plug-in Panel, and Use Motion to close the Motion Graph Panel. An error message appears. Don't panic, this is normal. Again, Lock & Key is waiting for LightWave 3D to pass it some plug-in data, and the first time you set up a Combo that data is not available.

11. Reopen the Motion Graph Panel, the Motion Plug-ins Panel, and the Lock & Key List Editor. Click Edit. Now the Combo Editor allows you to select an Offset Item.

12. Click the Use Offset Item check box. Choose RFoot.LWO from the Use Offset Item list. Click OK.

13. Click Add After. Set the Range from 3 to 17, Lock Item as Measuring_Null, and Offset Item as LFoot.LWO. The Combo Editor Panel should look like Figure 6-37. Click OK.

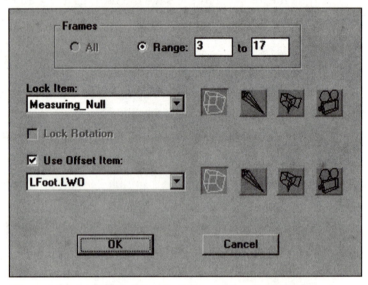

Figure 6-37: Lock & Key Combo Editor with second Combo set.

14. Click Add After again. Set Range from 18 to 32, Lock Item as Measuring_Null, and Offset Item as RFoot.LWO. Click OK. The List Editor should look like Figure 6-38.

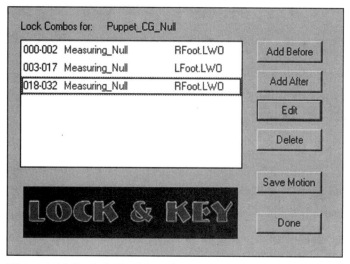

Figure 6-38: Lock & Key List Editor with all three Combos set.

15. Click Done to close the List Editor, Continue to close the Motion Plug-in Panel, and Use Motion to close the Motion Graph Panel.

16. Make and play a preview.

That's it. You just got the same action with a lot less work. Plus, you can tweak the Puppet's poses all you want, and the feet will stay in place. Lock & Key sure beats setting about three zillion keyframes, doesn't it?

Some Important Extras

If you're going to make a character walk, you'd better know how to make it start and stop, too. Unless, of course, you have an idea for an animated film that's nothing but walking. (Never mind, it's been done: Ryan Larkin's *Walking*, the definitive work on the subject.)

Starting a walk means accelerating all the Puppet's parts from a standstill to full walking speed. To start the forward movement, you must anticipate by leaning the Puppet back, then forward into the first fall, and bring the leading leg forward as if from a passing pose. Accelerate the body forward into the first step by rotating the trailing arm forcefully to the rear, and continue into a normal heel strike position. You can proceed from there with a normal walk cycle.

Exercise 6-3: Starting Out

1. Load your best walking cycle. You need to add 20 frames onto the beginning of the cycle, to give you time to move the Puppet from standing still into the walk.

2. Open the Scene Panel. Click Shift All Keys. Shift all keyframes by 20 frames. Close the Scene Panel. Since you shifted the original starting frame, you need to create a new start at frame 1.

3. Go to frame zero. Select the root object of the Puppet hierarchy, either Puppet_Ground_Null (unless of course you have deleted it, as per the last example) or Puppet_CG_Null, depending on whether you are using a scene from Exercise 6-1 or 6-2. Click Create Key, and create the new keyframe for Selected Item and Descendants in frame 1. This duplicates the Puppet hierarchy keyframes from frame 0 to frame 1.

   Set up the default standing position for the Puppet. This was designed to be simple: just set all the objects in the hierarchy from the Hips on down to 0, 0, 0 rotation.

4. Go to frame 1. Set all rotations for the Puppet hierarchy to zero at frame 1, for a pose like Figure 6-39.

Figure 6-39: Puppet in standing pose, before beginning walk.

5. Duplicate the Puppet keyframes from frame 1 to frame 14. Go to frame 14 and pose the Puppet as shown in Figure 6-40.

   Duplicating the nearest pose can save you effort in posing, as some of the objects' rotations will stay the same from one keyframe to the next. Frame 14 is the anticipation key pose that precedes the fall into the walk. The hips tilt back, shifting the Puppet's balance and enabling the leading leg to come up and slightly forward. The opposite arm also comes forward, preparing for the forward shift in balance of the next key pose. The same-side arm comes forward slightly less, preparing for an energetic backward swing.

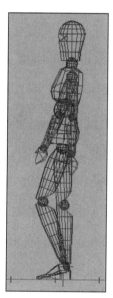

Figure 6-40: Puppet in anticipation pose, just beginning walk.

6. Duplicate the Puppet keyframes from frame 14 to frame 18. Go to frame 18, and pose the Puppet as shown in Figure 6-41. Frame 18 is the falling key pose. The hips have come back to level, the leading leg and arm are more fully advanced toward the heel strike pose, and the trailing arm is strongly thrust back to add more forward acceleration.

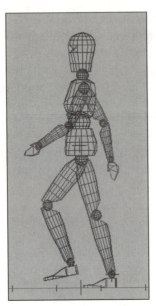

Figure 6-41: Puppet falling forward, leading to first heel strike position.

7. Tweak the splines to get the appropriate ease-in, snap, and ease-out for the motions leading into the first heel strike. The trailing arm is especially important if the start is a rapid one. The backward swing of the arm helps push the upper body forward, accelerating it to a walking pace. You may want to shift the keyframes for the arm, and pay special attention to the ease-in and -out in the motion graph. One possible solution is shown in Figure 6-42.

Frame 21 is the heel strike, the transition to a normal walk cycle, which you can leave as is.

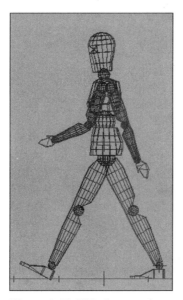

Figure 6-42: LUpArm motion graph, showing anticipation and quick accelera-tion into the first step.

8. Edit the first squash pose, frame 26, to bend a little deeper. Change the leading foot, shin, and thigh Pitch angles. You may have to adjust the trailing leg's shin just to keep the trailing toes above the ground.

   This cushions the first heel strike impact and provides more visual bounce to the first full stride. A change of gait like this— from standing still to a walk—is visually jarring to your audience; make sure you anticipate, follow through, and generally make the action as easy to read as possible.

   If the timing seems a little off, try shifting the anticipation or falling keyframes. The procedures for tweaking the Puppet_CG_Null and Puppet_Ground_Null positions to elimi-nate foot slippage are the same as in Exercises 6-1 and 6-2.

9. Save the finished scene under a new name. You'll be using it for the next exercise.

Exercise 6-4: Somebody Stop Me!

Stopping a walk means decelerating all the Puppet's parts from full walking speed to a standstill. Stopping forward motion requires you to make the squash position deeper, using the Thigh and Shin as a spring to absorb most of the Puppet's forward inertia.

Since the Puppet is not continuing into another step, you should bring the trailing leg only up to level with the leading leg, not past it. You should also reduce the forward rotation of both arms, and exaggerate their backward rotations.

Keep the upper body leaning backwards against the Puppet's forward inertia until the character is nearly at a full stop, then Pitch it forward slightly in follow-through.

If the walk is an especially vigorous one, or the stop very sudden, you might pose the Puppet to rise up on its toes before settling back into the hold, the standing pose. Keep the Puppet's CG behind its toes at all times, to maintain the appearance of balance.

1. Reload the scene file you saved at the end of Exercise 6-3. Go to frame 26. This is the squash pose for the leading left leg, which is close enough to the stopping squash pose that using a duplicate can save some posing.

2. Select the Puppet_CG_Null. Click Create Key. In the Create Motion Key Panel, Click Selected Item and Descendants. Change the frame number to 57, and press Enter to close the panel and create the new keyframe. This creates a duplicate of frame 26 at frame 57, adding a squash pose to the heel strike pose at frame 52.

3. Go to frame 1. Select the Puppet_CG_Null. Click Create Key. In the Create Motion Key Panel, Click Selected Item and Descendants. Change the frame number to 67, and press Enter to close the panel and create the new keyframe.

   This creates a duplicate of frame 1 at frame 67, the default standing pose for the Puppet. You now have a smooth default interpolation from the heel strike at frame 52 to the standing pose at frame 67, as shown in Figure 6-43. Your next task is to modify that interpolation to make a more realistic stop from a walk cycle.

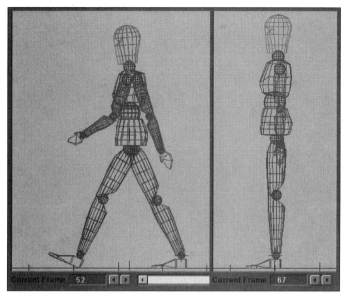

Figure 6-43: Heel Strike, frame 52, and Standing, frame 67.

4. Go to frame 53. Select the LFoot, and Pitch it level with the ground. The foot still has to flatten to the ground immediately after the heel strike, but if you simply duplicated frame 27 it would introduce a lot of other keyframes that you don't need.

5. Go to frame 56. Create a Pitch keyframe for the Hips of –5 degrees, shifting the mass of the upper body backwards to help the Puppet slow down. The Hips don't need another keyframe until frame 67, although you should tweak the Spline Controls a bit to get a smooth deceleration. Pitch RThigh so it continues to swing forward, and Pitch RShin so RFoot clears the ground, as in Figure 6-44.

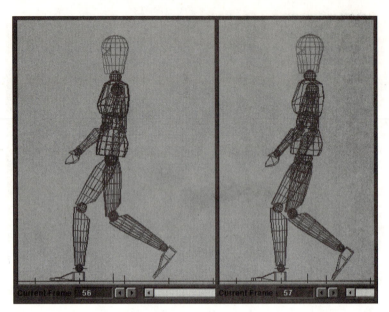

Figure 6-44: Frames 56 and 57 Puppet poses.

6. Go to frame 57. Create a Pitch keyframe so LShin reaches its maximum pitch of about 32 degrees. This makes the squash pose deeper to absorb some of the Puppet's forward inertia, slowing it down (Figure 6-44). From about -25 degrees at this frame, LThigh should change Pitch almost linearly to 0 degrees at keyframe 65.

7. Go to frame 60. RThigh should already nearly match LThigh, but you need to create a Pitch keyframe for RShin so RFoot still clears the ground. Pitch both arms so they are nearly aligned. They should be moving backwards, as in Figure 6-45, to counterbalance the rise of the Hips and upper body from the squash position of frame 57.

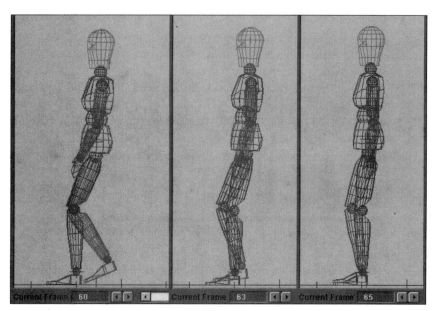

Figure 6-45: Frames 60, 63, and 65 Puppet poses.

8. Go to frame 63. Create a Pitch keyframe for RShin so RFoot clears the ground. This is the peak Pitch for RShin; after this frame you will be lowering the foot to flat contact with the ground.

9. Go to frame 65. Create Pitch keyframes for RThigh, RShin, and RFoot so RFoot is parallel to the ground, and moving down towards flat contact with the ground.

10. Create follow-through and hold keyframes between frames 67 and 75, to soften the rigid "attention" pose of the Puppet.

11. Make and play a preview.

   You will probably note some uneven decelerations between keyframes. Go through each object, and take a look at its motion graph for Pitch Angle. Use the Tension, Continuity, and Bias controls to smooth out the graphs, but make sure you leave a little snap, a short, sharp curve, near the last frames. It'll make the Puppet "snap" to attention.

If the timing seems a little off, try shifting the follow-through or deceleration keyframes for different objects, keeping in mind the guidelines for overlapping action and successive breaking of joints. The procedures for tweaking the Puppet_CG_Null and Puppet_Ground_Null positions to eliminate foot slippage are the same as in Exercises 6-1 and 6-2.

 When you're done tweaking, you should have an animation something like EXER0604.AVI, which you can find in the Chapter 6 directory of the Companion CD-ROM.

Got a Bone to Pick?

As I noted earlier, the redraw times for complex Boned characters can quickly get out of hand, especially if you are running on a slow machine. If this becomes a production problem, you may be able to save time in the animation end of the process by doing a little more work in the modeling end.

When an action requires a lot of tweaking, substitute the stand-in.

Once you (or your TD) have the complete Boned version of a character finalized and tested, make a Parented hierarchy that exactly duplicates the location, alignment, and range of motion of the Bones that control skeletal joints. You don't need to duplicate Bones designed only to deform surfaces. Make sure the surfaces that interact with the environment—hands, soles of feet, eyes—are accurately replicated. This hierarchy will act as a stand-in for the Boned object.

Whenever an action requires a lot of experimenting and tweaking, substitute the stand-in. When you finish animating the action, save each hierarchical object's motion from the Motion Graph Panel. In the case of the Puppet, that would be 15 motion files.

Any nulls used for position and rotation can remain in the scene, as long as the Pivot for the Boned object is compatible with the root object of the Parented hierarchy. For example, a Boned version of the Puppet would have its Pivot positioned and rotated to match the Pivot of the Hips object.

The next step is to load the Boned object from its default scene. Parent it to the same null as the stand-in. Select each Bone in turn, and use the Motion Graph Panel to load the corresponding motion file you saved from the stand-in. When you've loaded all the motion files, the action of the Boned character should exactly match the Parented stand-in. When the match is complete, clear the stand-in.

If you are using motion plug-ins like Lock & Key, you will also have to change the Combos from the stand-in objects to the character's Bones.

This workaround won't save you much time on short sequences; you'd spend as much time saving and loading motion files as you would have spent waiting for screen redraws. On longer animations, the time spent copying the motion files can be a very small fraction of the total animation time, and a great deal less than the total of screen redraws.

With time, improvements to LightWave 3D and faster, cheaper computers will make this workaround unnecessary. Until then, it may save you some valuable time.

Moving On

By working through this chapter, you've mastered the basic principles of hierarchical animation, dynamic motion, motion cycle construction, and starting and stopping an action. With all that under your belt, you're ready to tackle the more challenging actions detailed in the next chapter.

Getting the Lead Out

Runs,
Other Gaits &
Motion Studies

This chapter shows you how to apply the principles you used for walk cycles in Chapter 6 to animating run cycles, animal gaits, and simple clothing. This chapter also provides a guide to materials that can help you develop skills for analyzing and reproducing motion, and resources for animal and human motion studies.

Run for It

The two major differences between walks and runs are foot contact with the ground and the strength of the poses. Walkers, by definition, always have at least one foot on the ground. Runners may have both feet off the ground for the majority of the run cycle. This midair time, and the actions required to produce it, are the key poses of run cycles. Run poses are also much stronger visually than walk poses; both cycles show the same actions, but almost every joint rotation is more extreme in a run.

The run cycle starts off just like the walk, with a fall forward. Instead of simply rotating one leg forward to stop the fall, a running character must also thrust upward by flexing the trailing leg and foot, as in Figure 7-1. Note the bends in the trailing leg and foot, which straighten to propel the runner forward faster than a simple fall. This is the thrust, or push-off, pose of the run cycle.

Figure 7-1: Thrust pose of a run cycle.

Instead of falling back to a more upright posture after the cycle is started, a running character must maintain a forward lean during the entire run cycle. A faster run requires the character to lean forward farther, pushing the upper body ahead of the center of gravity (CG). This continuous "fall" helps convert the thrust of the driving leg from vertical to horizontal movement. It's also the reason running is more hazardous than walking: if a runner stops suddenly, he has to quickly get his feet under his CG, or he falls down. A walker is stable at every heel strike position; there are no stable poses in a run cycle.

The result of the thrust pose is the midair pose, as shown in Figure 7-2. Both feet are well off the ground, and the character is "ballistic." From the time the trailing foot leaves the ground until the leading foot makes contact, the running character is following a parabola.

The height and width of the parabola can say a lot about the character. A short, broad parabola is the mark of a serious runner or sprinter, who converts most of his or her energy into forward motion. A high, narrow parabola shows the character is very springy, spending more energy on moving up than moving forward.

You can exaggerate this to create a very lively, bouncy character (see the following chapter for details). The up-and-down motion of the walk cycle is limited by the arc of the character's pivoting legs; the only limit for a run cycle's vertical motion is the amount of energy you allocate your character. Just make sure that any extra energy you animate into a thrust pose is balanced by an extra-deep squash on the other end of the parabola. What goes up, must come down.

The midair pose makes your job of animating a running character a little harder, as you can't rely on foot placement to keep the character properly positioned in the scene. For the midair part of the run cycle, you'll have to figure the trajectory of the character just as you did for the falling objects in Chapter 3. The pose itself is a simple extrapolation from the preceding thrust pose to the following squash pose. The trailing leg recoils from the full extension of the thrust and starts to bend forward again. The leading leg stretches out toward the ground, remaining slightly bent to absorb the anticipated impact.

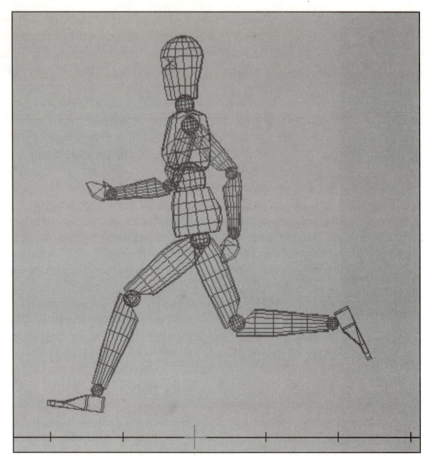

Figure 7-2: Midair pose of a run cycle.

The third pose is the squash (see Figure 7-3). Since everything happens faster in a run, several of the walk poses are compressed into one run pose. The important elements of the walk cycle's passing position, heel strike, and squash poses all happen at once in the run cycle squash pose. The leading foot makes ground contact and bends to absorb the impact, and the trailing leg folds so the foot clears the ground as it kicks forward to pass the leading leg.

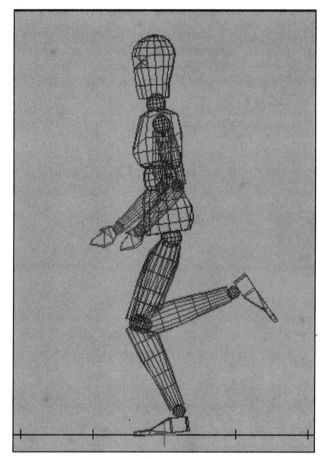

Figure 7-3: Squash pose of a run cycle.

The runner's foot can make contact either heel-first, as in the walk, or on the ball of the foot. The faster the run, the more likely the character is to run on the balls of his or her feet. If the character heel-strikes, you should put a little extra deceleration in the forward motion; the jar of the heel strike slows a runner down perceptibly. When a running character brakes to a stop, he literally dig in his heels. You might try to animate this, based on the stopping and starting exercises in the last chapter.

A running character's arms make pretty much the same motions as a walking character's. The difference is a matter of degree; the runner's extremes are a little farther out, and the speed of transition between extremes is faster. A runner does not move faster by throwing his arms out wider; instead, a runner keeps his arms folded more closely, making them shorter and easier to move, and moves them more rapidly. A short arm can dynamically balance a longer, heavier leg by moving faster. When you animate a runner's arms, use all the snap you can; avoid ease-in and -out like poison, for it will surely kill your character.

Exercise 7-1: Animate a Running Puppet

1. Open the scene file EXER0701.LWS, which you can find in the Chapter 7 directory of the Companion CD-ROM. This scene file includes the complete Puppet character, Parented, lighted, and ready to animate, just as you used it in Chapter 6.

2. Follow the procedures you learned in Chapter 6 to pose the Puppet to match the key running poses in Figures 7-1, 7-2, and 7-3. Repeat the poses for the opposite side, making six keyframes in all.

    This is where you really start developing your judgment. How far apart should you place your key poses? Try the Scale Keys functions in the Scene Panel to slide your key poses around. Experiment, and keep notes on what works best for you.

3. Look at the motion graphs for each object. Look for patterns, especially for patterns that need a little help.

    You should be developing a sense of what a motion graph should look like for a sharp, snappy motion versus a gradual, smooth one. You should also be developing your judgment of when each type of motion is appropriate.

4. Calculate and set keyframes for the Puppet_CG_Null and Puppet_Ground_Null objects to define the parabola the Puppet travels during the midair part of the run cycle. Remember, the Puppet's CG should follow a parabola precisely, no matter what the rest of the character is doing.

5. Starting at the root of the animation hierarchy, tweak the motion of each object to make the run cycle more lifelike. Follow the usual procedure of rendering previews to check your progress.

    Look very closely at the hip and chest action before you jump to any conclusions. As I pointed out in the last chapter, the hip and chest rotations are among the smallest in the whole Puppet, but they affect everything else and are a real pain to revise. Keep to the animation hierarchy and most of your mistakes will be small.

One of the noticeable differences in timing between walks and runs is the kick forward of the trailing leg. In a run, this kick is very fast, with a lot of snap. You might try a straight linear transition over two or three frames, just to see how extreme you can get before the Puppet starts moving like he sat on a high-voltage line. On the other hand, the thrust pose is accelerating the entire body weight up and forward, so there's a lot of effort to move a large mass. A more gradual acceleration for the trailing leg's extension, with more ease-in, is appropriate here. The same goes for the squash position; the idea is to absorb the impact gradually, using the leading leg as a spring to ease-in to the flexed pose, then straighten again in an ease-out to the thrust position.

There are some considerations for the runner's attitude, as well. If the character's head is kept high, looking ahead rather than at his path, the usual perception is that the runner has plenty of energy and is nowhere near his limits. If the runner's head is low, he is more likely to be going all-out, or near exhaustion. Then again, maybe he is just watching for loose change on the sidewalk.

6. When you've got a run cycle you are happy with, save the scene under a new name. You'll probably find other uses for it.

If you're feeling adventurous, you can animate the Puppet through a running jump by exaggerating the leg compression of the thrust pose, stretching out the midair pose (make it follow a larger parabola), and exaggerating the compression of the squash pose at the landing. The same exaggeration principles apply to running hurdles and stairs, too.

Seeing Is Believing

A recurring question for character animators is, "How does a creature to be animated move?" The answer is sometimes found in a book or journal, often on file footage, recently even on CD-ROM, but always in nature. If you start building and animating a creature without studying it live, if you trust your assumptions and preconceptions, you will most assuredly end up scrapping most of your work. If you don't like wasting time and effort, do a little research before you start pushing pixels. And when you need the real data, go back to the source.

There are two broad categories for the information you need: anatomy and kinesiology—the studies of creatures' physical structure and the ways they move. You can get a lot of anatomical information from zoology and comparative anatomy textbooks, which any good library or bookstore should be able to find for you. I keep a few general zoological references around, but when I'm working on a new creature I usually head to a library and research it from the most up-to-date sources.

- The kinesiology information is a little harder to come by. Most of the research is done on humans or on "economically significant" animals. The best sources of information are films and videotapes of animals and humans performing a variety of actions against measurable backgrounds, called *motion studies*.

- Still images of the same subjects are second best, but when collected in books like Eadweard Muybridge's (see the Bibliography), have the advantages of portability and independence from viewing equipment.

- A distant third in usability are the scholarly analyses, derivations, and explanations published in the scientific literature; most of these studies ignore or omit at least some of the raw data necessary to the animator. Even if someone ran a study on the creature you're working on, there's no guarantee he or she gathered or published the data you need.

The ideal study would include (at least) three-axis position data for each joint in a fully articulated skeleton, plus a complete analysis of muscle, fat, and ligament arrangements and their effect on surface appearances. In reality, what you're likely to find are very crude profile views of the creature, with the approximate locations of the major joints marked inconsistently between successive frames.

Until recently, access to most of this information was limited to people who could use film libraries or visit a zoo. The availability of consumer videotape players, and the production of nature videotapes by organizations like the National Geographic Society, have put the study of animal and human motion within reach of any aspiring animator. The development of the computer as a mass-market educational tool has also expanded the motion study resources you can acquire.

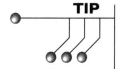

TIP

My favorite motion study materials include the classic works by Eadweard Muybridge, a variety of National Geographic videotapes, several Discovery Channel videotapes, the other books on animal motion listed in the Bibliography, and an excellent CD-ROM, "How Animals Move," authored by R. McNeill Alexander and distributed by Maris Multimedia and The Discovery Channel.

I recommend that you invest in a laserdisc player, one with a digital freeze frame. You can use this to view motion studies repeatedly, single-framing and looping segments without damaging either your player or a tape (the Muybridge work is available on laserdisc from Voyager).

If you can't get a laserdisc player, a video digitizer board for your computer can be the next best thing. Digitize clips of your favorite animation or nature videotapes, and loop them to play back on your computer. As long as this is for private, educational use, it's within the fair use limits of copyright. Just don't do something ill-advised like posting the clips on the Internet. It's illegal and it's disrespectful to the people who produced the video in the first place.

If you get into digitizing reference material, sooner or later you are going to be tempted to try a process called *rotoscoping*. This is really easy to do with LightWave 3D—you just load the clip as an image sequence and assign it as a Background layer in the Effects Panel. Add and Bone an object that matches the one in the background, pose the object to match each frame of the background, and presto, you have a rotoscoped "animation." Only it isn't character animation, and it produces really crummy-looking action. Anybody who's watched a little animation can tell when something's been rotoscoped. Most professional animators hate it.

I mention rotoscoping only as a learning tool. One of the longer learning processes in CGI character animation is the interpretation of motion graphs. An experienced animator can read them like large print, having the experience to know when a graph isn't showing enough snap, ease, or whatever. If you are just starting out in CGI animation, you need all the help you can get for learning to read and analyze motion graphs. If you digitize some of your favorite animated or live-action clips, and rotoscope the Puppet or other characters over them, you can build yourself a set of motion graphs to study and learn from.

While I'm on the subject, I'd like to put in a few words about *motion capture*, aka *mocap*: it's not character animation, it almost always looks like a guy in a rubber suit, you can't do really exaggerated actions because they'd kill the actor, the raw data is a horrendous mess to try to edit into something usable, and it is neither cheaper nor faster than full animation, assuming the same level of finished quality. The basic principle of motion capture is to collect streams of real-time data during a performance. The basic principle of character animation is to deliberately plan, create, and revise a sequence of poses. The two approaches are antithetical at best. Three professional animators, Jeff Hayes, Steph Greenberg, and Ken Cope, have named motion capture "Satan's Rotoscope" due to the insidious way mocap vendors are trying to market it as a replacement for trained animators. There are historical parallels between mocap and the Rotoscope process patented by the Fleischers: both have been touted as a replacement for skilled animators, produced lousy results that stuck out like a sore thumb when combined with traditional animation, produced disasters at the box office, and offended animators forced to work with them. Rotoscoping eventually died out of feature film production, once it was obvious the audience could tell the difference; mocap may go the same route. Satan's Rotoscope doesn't even have the advantage of enabling you to capture classic 2D animation the way rotoscoping does. Mocap is a legitimate tool that supports the nature of other art forms: performance capture for dance and virtual filmmaking, yes; digital puppeteering and animatronic programming, sure; character animation, absolutely not. Maybe someday the technology will evolve to be a useful adjunct to character animation, but for now I advise you to just say no.

When in doubt, act it out.

If all these sources on motion studies don't help, you can always fall back on real-life simulation. When in doubt, act it out. You will find it easier to animate actions if you first act them out yourself. Get in the habit of walking through an action, testing the different approaches a character might take. If you feel silly at first, get over it. Professional animators at the major studios do this all the time. Jumping on and off desks and walking around with a board nailed to your sneakers seem to be normal, acceptable behavior for character animators. Wearing a tie to work, however, can get you blacklisted.

On All Fours

Aside from bipedal humanoids, the largest class of creatures you are likely to animate are the four-legged variety. They present some interesting problems for character animators: creating motions contrary to bipedal intuitions, visualizing actions you are unable to act out accurately, keeping twice as many legs locked to the ground, and animating a lot more gaits than you'd use for we two-legged critters.

Basic anatomy accounts for the first two problems. Humans walk on the equivalent of the palms of their hands, on the metatarsal bones that form the arch of the foot. Many quadrupeds, in contrast, move on the equivalent of their toes. Cows, deer, and other hoofed animals actually walk around on tiptoe. Dogs and many other mammals walk on the balls of their feet, with the digits spread for balance. You can come close to emulating this without joining the ballet; just stand barefoot and lift both heels off the ground at once. This feels very awkward, but the change in tendon and muscle layout makes trotting and running more efficient for the animals.

When it comes to preventing moonwalking or skating, the solution for four legs is the same as for two: tweak, tweak, tweak. Or buy Lock & Key.

The gait "problem" isn't really a problem; you just need to know what's available and what's reasonable in certain circumstances for certain creatures. There are six different four-legged gaits: walk, pace, trot, canter, transverse gallop, and rotary gallop.

- The quadruped walk is similar to the human walk in that each foot is grounded for more than half the cycle. The usual order of foot placement is left fore, right hind, right fore, left hind.

- The pace is an odd gait used naturally only by camels and some breeds of dog; it can also be taught to other animals. In the pace, the legs move together on each side—that is, both left feet move forward together, then both right feet. This produces a unique rocking motion.

- The trot, canter, and gallop are similar to the human run, in which each foot is grounded for less than half the cycle. The feet move in diagonal pairs in the trot, left fore with right hind, and right fore with left hind. In the gallop, the fore and hind feet move separately; that is, if the forefeet are grounded, the hind feet are in motion, so the spine can bend and add longer reach and more muscle to the stride. The canter is like a slow gallop crossed with a trot, in which the grounding of the fore and hind pairs overlaps.

◈ The rotary gallop is the fast gait of cats and some other animals, in which the spine curls up and stretches out to lengthen the stride and increase the animal's speed.

The exact sequence and range of motion for each gait varies according to the animal. If you have to animate one of these gaits, your best bet is to observe or acquire photos of an animal similar to the one you are animating and work out the poses from the above guidelines and the creature's individual proportions.

Exercise 7-2: Animate a Walking Cow

This exercise uses the cow object included on the LightWave 3D CD-ROM. I've set up a very basic arrangement of the minimum Bones necessary to animate a four-legged walk or other simple gait. The Bone names are fairly self-explanatory. All the Bones have been laid out to animate only in the Pitch axis; this is not perfectly anatomically correct, but it's good enough for this exercise. The Bones have also been laid out in order, shoulder to hoof, then the next leg, so navigating through the Skeleton with the arrow keys should be relatively easy.

1. In Layout, load scene file EXER0702.LWS from the Chapter 7 directory of the Companion CD-ROM. The scene file looks in the default NEWTEK\OBJECTS\ANIMALS for the cow object; if it is not there, you will have to specify the correct path and directory.

2. Set keyframes for the entire cow and all dependent items at frames 0, 1, 13, 17, and 21. The first two frames are a baseline reference; the last three are the minimum keyframes for the walk cycle.

3. Pose the cow in frame 13 to match Figure 7-4. This is the heel-strike pose for the front feet.

Figure 7-4: Heel-strike pose for walking cow.

4. Pose the cow in frame 17 to match Figure 7-5. This is the squash pose for the front feet. Most of the shock-absorbing squash is accomplished by rotating Bones that are concealed in the shoulder of the cow. This makes pose details hard to see in the rendered animation, but they're there.

5. Pose the cow in frame 21 to match Figure 7-6. This is the passing pose for the front feet.

Figure 7-5: Squash pose for walking cow.

Figure 7-6: Passing pose for walking cow.

Now for the fun part. This particular motion repeats on a 20-frame cycle; that is, the left front hoof's setting in frame 13 is identical to that of the right front hoof's setting in frame 33. Also, the entire animation is designed to loop after frame 40, so you can "wrap around" keyframes that go over 40.

6. Duplicate the settings of the left front leg in frame 13 for the right front leg in frame 33. Repeat this alternating duplication of settings for the rest of the animation. For frame 21, duplicate the settings to frame 1 (21+20=41, 41-40=1).

   When you're finished, you should have a decent approximation of the original walk cycle. Unfortunately, there's no easy solution to this object's difficulty with coordinating rear and front pairs; that requires full spine, pelvic, and shoulder skeletons to mimic whole-body flexibility. This means the vertical and lateral movements of the cow object will not match the original's, so you can expect the foot placement not to match the ground, either.

   Don't be discouraged if the cow doesn't walk the way you wanted it to. Coordinating the fore and hind legs of an object like this is a difficult job, as the next exercise illustrates.

Exercise 7-3: Try to Tune Up a Rotoscoped Cow

This exercise presents you with a partially completed walk cycle for a cow, rotoscoped from one of the motion study sources mentioned earlier in the chapter. The front legs seem to be animating all right, as shown in the animation file Front.AVI, which you can locate in the Chapter 7 directory of the Companion CD-ROM.

CD-ROM

1. Load the Front.AVI file and play it. It isn't the greatest—it could use some more stabilizing Bones to smooth out the muscle action—but it works. More importantly, the feet lock to the ground and don't skate all over. The down side to this setup becomes obvious when you look at the rest of the cow.

2. Load the Whole.AVI file and play it. Yuck! What is going on with the back legs? Both the front and back leg Bones were rotoscoped to motion capture footage on four-frame key intervals, and are fairly reliable. The difficulty seems to be that there is no provision for spine or pelvic movement, the body of the object is just a rigid block. Even a seemingly rigid creature flexes its spine and pelvis when moving, especially if it is as heavy as a cow. If the pelvis and spine moved accurately, the rear legs might be correct as is.

Possible approaches to repairing this animation include:

❀ Add Bones to emulate the pelvis and spine, then manipulate the rear legs of the object to coordinate with the front legs.

❀ Tweak the existing Bones in the rear legs to match the front legs, and just forget about matching the rotoscope footage exactly.

If you'd like to give it a try, load EXER0703.LWS into Layout, and give it your best shot.

Advanced Exercise 7-4: Animate a Cat's Rotary Gallop

Arguably the toughest character animation job is to animate a feline. Most other animals have a fairly rigid bone structure, but cats are extraordinarily flexible. They have only a vestigial collarbone, and their forelegs simply attach to an overlapping nest of muscles. Their spines are only a little less flexible than a snake's, enabling them to face 180 degrees from the direction of their hind feet. They also have the most extreme of rotary gallops, with the spine alternating convex to concave on each stride.

If you'd like to try this project from scratch, here are a few guidelines:

1. Research your subject. Start with the appropriate references in the Bibliography, and see where they lead you. One additional reference you may want to check is an article by John T. Manter in the *Journal of Experimental Biology*, volume 15, number 4 (1938), "The Dynamics of Quadruped Walking." This report includes X–Y plane data for a domestic cat's legs during a walk, plus a lot of other information about force analysis. Unfortunately, it completely ignores lateral displacement, so it's only about half the data you need for a complete animation.

2. Narrowly define your goal. One complete stride of a domestic cat's legs is plenty. You don't even need to do the whole cat.

3. Keep it simple. Use something like the Puppet to start with; once you've got a clear idea of the skeletal measurements, you can model an object and use Bones to animate it more smoothly.

Animating Clothing

You have had a fair amount of practice animating overlapping action and follow-through by now. Those are the most important principles of animation if you are trying to do realistic clothing. Fabrics are tedious to animate, and it is nearly impossible to hand-animate a surface to precisely mimic the behavior of cloth. This exercise is included so you will be familiar with the problems, but this approach is not intended to be used for production work.

The following exercise is designed around the simplest example of clothing that still demonstrates the principles, a very basic kilt for the Puppet character. The kilt object and the scene that contains the Bone structure to animate it were built from the directions in Exercise 14-5.

Exercise 7-5: Animate Clothing on Puppet

1. In Layout, load scene file EXER0705.LWS. This is essentially the same as the file you saved at the end of Chapter 6. The Puppet character is set up to walk across the scene.

2. In the Object Panel, click Load From Scene. Select KILTBONE.LWS. This scene contains the kilt object, its Bones, and a series of control Nulls, as shown in Figure 7-7.

Figure 7-7: Kilt object with Bone effect envelopes showing.

The kilt object alone has 64 Bones, 16 Nulls (the control handles for the kilt's Bone chains), and one object. You can animate the kilt by moving one of the Nulls (named Dangle 1 through 16) along the X- and Z-axes to change the angle of the Bone chain running from the Null to the kilt's waistband. Alternately, you can turn off the IK goals setting for each chain and pose each chain manually.

3. Parent the Kilt04 object to the Hips object, then move the kilt model to coordinates 0, 0.01, 0 to prevent the Hips from showing through the kilt object. You should end up with a scene like Figure 7-8.

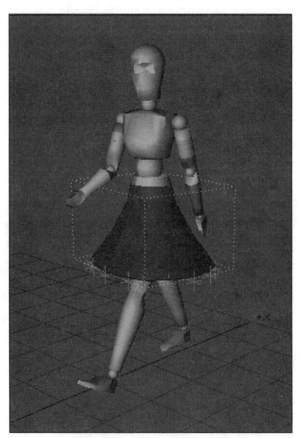

Figure 7-8: Puppet with kilt object Parented properly.

4. Animate the kilt from rest, through beginning and sustaining the walk, to slowing and stopping. Make sure the underlying figure never passes through the kilt surface, and that the kilt appears to be resting on the surface at appropriate times. Create the illusion that the kilt has weight, using overlapping action and follow-through.

When you have animated several key poses, you may want to consider using Save Transformed to create Metamorph target objects for the kilt. If you will be using the Puppet's action cycle in other situations, you may want to set up a Parented MTSE chain with the appropriate kilt objects.

Exercise 7-6: Animate Puppet Changing Gaits

In the last exercise in Chapter 6, you animated the Puppet character to accelerate, walk, and stop. In this exercise, you animate the Puppet to change from a walking gait to a fast run.

1. Load EXER0705.LWS just as you did for Exercise 7-5.

2. Go to the heel-strike position for the second step of the cycle. Modify it to have a deeper bend and forward lean to match the squash position of Figure 7-3.

3. Continue with the remaining key poses for a fast run, as in Exercise 7-1. If you want to animate a fast run, make sure the Puppet runs on its toes, the heel never makes contact with the ground, and the Hips are Pitched at a more extreme angle.

Moving On

You now have a better understanding of how to create walk and run cycles for a variety of creatures, and where you can find information to help you mimic other natural actions. You also have some idea of how difficult manually animating clothing can be. The next chapter expands your character animation skills to caricature action.

How Would the Chicken Cross the Road?

Caricature Action

Your goal in this chapter is to learn how to extrapolate your observations of natural motion to create caricatured animation. Along the way, exercises show you how to animate actions from the repertoire of classic cartoon animation, including takes, sneaks, staggers, and zips. You'll also learn the concept of staging for foreshadowing action.

An Art of Essences

The art of character animation is not the literal reproduction of realistic movement. Simple reproduction can be automated, and anything that can be automated is not an art. The basic art of character animation is the same, whether expressed in CGI, clay, or cel. It is distilling the essence of movement, then creating it again in a new form, obviously different and just as obviously true in essence.

The first step, then, is to observe. As explained in Chapter 7, you must observe in detail exactly how an action is performed in real life before you can understand it well enough to recreate it as an animation. You must understand the forces acting on each part of the character, the mass, inertia, and energy that are expressed in acceleration, deceleration, and deformation.

"The continuous detailed analysis of all kinds of motion is basic to any animator's ability to recreate it or, better still, to transform it for his or her own purposes."
Steven S. Wilson, *Puppets and People*

Develop the habit of watching people and animals move. Anywhere you go, there are lessons to be learned about movement. Keep your eyes open, and when you notice an especially fine movement (incredible grace running for the bus, a particularly elegant gesture in conversation), try to figure out why it was so good. Make notes, and try to animate the Puppet to achieve the same effect.

This is part of training yourself to really see. Your brain is very good at categorizing information as it comes in, pigeonholing it into classifications like "dangerous," "familiar," "food," and so on. This enables you to walk through a crowded shopping mall without having a nervous breakdown; most of the flood of information is immediately classified as unimportant noise, so you can ignore it all and carry on a conversation with your companion.

The downside to this sorting process is that you miss a lot of the details in everyday life. You need to retrain your brain to sort information about human and animal movement into a "pay attention and analyze this" pigeonhole. With practice, you can watch a person walk, and be able to reproduce the exact amount of knee flex for the squash, the precise speed of the kick forward to the heel strike, even the extent of the counterbalancing shoulder action. This analysis is the essence of mimicry, and the beginning of animation.

What Makes a Chicken a Chicken?

Once you can analyze and reproduce movement, you are halfway to caricaturing it. The idea of caricature is to make something more like itself. In caricaturing movement, this means exaggeration of not just the individual key poses but also the acceleration, deceleration, and deformation that connect the poses. If a character walks with a certain amount of knee bend in squash, a caricatured version will bend the knee even farther, making the squash deeper.

The real art to caricature is the judgment of what is essential and what is not.

The real art to caricature is the judgment of what is essential and what is not. The heart of an action may not be the broadest movement, the largest change, or the most visible deformation; it may be the smallest nuance that defines that action. For example, let's take a look at a basic emotional transition, from a pose of neutrality—simply standing, relaxed but alert—to a pose of aggressive anger, almost a boxer's stance. Act this transition out yourself; create your own interpretation, and analyze the changes between the neutral and anger poses.

You probably raised your arms, bringing your hands up in front of your body, and clenched your fists. You may have also taken a half step forward, shifting your balance into a stronger stance, and perhaps pitched your head forward so you would glare at your opponent from lowered brows. This would be a typical "looking for a fight" pose.

So, what's the most important part? Which of these changes is the essence of "anger"? The motion of the arms is certainly the largest angular change, over 90 degrees to bring the hands up to waist level. The change in stance would probably be second, for the smaller angular changes of both legs plus the resulting forward movement of the body add up to a large perceived motion. Possibly the smallest motions are the forward pitch of the head and the closing of the hands into fists.

Guess what? The hands and head are the essential, defining motions for "anger." How to prove this? Drop back to the neutral pose, and use just the head pitch and glare. Not quite anger, but maybe severe annoyance? Now clench your fists, but keep them at your sides. Bingo! If you took this pose in a bar, either your friends would try to calm you down or the person you were facing would be getting ready to rumble. This is repressed anger, a version of anger that minimizes the grosser body movements, but communicates almost the same information. Pure aggressive anger is being ready to throw a punch; repressed anger is aggressive anger restrained—just barely—by better judgment, but still ready to explode at the next provocation.

But the grosser body pose still has something to say, doesn't it? Try this: assume the aggressive anger pose, then open your hands so your palms face your imaginary opponent, and pitch your head level or a little bit back, so you are looking straight at him or her. It's the same body pose—just the hands and head are different, but it's the difference between starting a fight and trying to stop one.

You have to look at the gestalt of the movement first, then start picking apart the individual elements.

The point to this exercise is that you can't assume any part of a movement is the essence. You have to look at the gestalt of the movement first, then start picking apart the individual elements. Until you develop the judgment that comes with experience, you would do well to analyze every element of every pose you look at, and compare them to similar elements of other poses as we just did with anger, neutrality, and placation.

"In the fields of observation, chance favors only the mind that is prepared."
Louis Pasteur

Try varying one element, one variable, at a time (using the ol' scientific method again) and evaluating the change in expression. Like most forms of systematic research, this can be slow going, but when you eliminate all the wrong answers, you are left with the right ones. Also, when you are forced to work through every possible permutation, you often stumble across valuable information that you weren't even looking for. Keep your eyes and mind open.

Mountains From Molehills

Once you have identified the essence of a movement, the remaining question is how to exaggerate it. This breaks down naturally into two parts: the key pose and the transition. The key pose can be caricatured as if it were a drawing, so you can apply the guidelines used by artists working in 2D media to create a stronger pose, a more expressive silhouette, a smoother line of action, and a clearer definition of character. The next chapter explains the application of these concepts in more detail; for now, just try to make a key pose look even more like itself.

The caricature of a transition is a matter of timing and emphasis. This is another area where the importance of experience, judgment, and inspiration define animation as an art, not a science. You can exaggerate each of the principles of movement you learned in earlier chapters to create a caricature movement. You can push anticipation farther away from the main action, deform squash-and-stretch even further, delay overlapping action keys farther from the main action, and shorten snap to fewer frames.

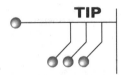

TIP

The only principle you usually shouldn't exaggerate is ease; caricatures look best when they are very snappy—the antithesis of ease. Too much ease makes an animation floaty, as if the character is performing underwater.

Subtlety is for live action; if you want an action to read well as a caricature, exaggerate more than you think you should. You learn from your mistakes, if you're smart. This is a time when you can learn most rapidly by deliberately making mistakes. Push the exaggeration of an action to a really outrageous extreme, both in key pose and transition. Try to do it wrong, to exaggerate too much. Examine each element of the action, and push it to the virtual limits of the character. If a part of the character is supposed to squash, mash it flat; if part is to stretch, draw it out to a needle shape; if a joint is to bend, fold it as far as it will go; if the joint is to extend, make it perfectly straight; shorten each snap to a linear transition across a single frame.

When you're done exaggerating this action, it should be so extreme that even Tex Avery would disown it. So what's the point? This is an investigation, a search for the right amount of exaggeration. The low end is perfectly natural movement, the kind you could rotoscope or motion capture straight from life. You know you don't want to go any further in that direction. When you animate an action that is too exaggerated, you establish a high end. Together, the high and low ends define the limits of your search, which is the first step in the process of solving the problem.

You may find it's not possible to exaggerate an action too much. That's the fun part of cartoon-style animation: sometimes the absolute virtual limit is the exact effect you want. Sometimes the antagonist does end up as a perfectly flat grease spot on the wall; sometimes the protagonist does stretch clear across the screen in a zip exit.

This is another time a laserdisc player can come in handy. Rent or buy laserdiscs of classic Warner Brothers cartoons, and single-frame through the most extreme actions. It's amazing what you can get away with in a cartoon.

A Caricature Walk

You can thoroughly caricature an action the same way you originally animated it, starting at the root of the animation hierarchy and proceeding through the layers, exaggerating as you go. If you've already worked through the exercises in Chapters 6 and 7, you should be comfortably familiar with the key poses and transitions of walks, runs, and other motion cycles. Let's see how you might exaggerate a normal walk cycle to create a caricature walk.

The easiest key pose to exaggerate is the squash. The limits to this pose are defined by the structure of the character: no squash at all is just a character walking with straight legs (Thud! Thud! Thud!), and maximum squash doubles up the knee joint so the character's hips are nearly on the ground. The variations on squash are mostly in the timing: how fast and far is the snap to the ease-in, how slow is the ease-in to full squash, and how fast is the snap out of full squash?

Almost all the exaggeration in the squash is concentrated in the knee joint, as the hips are nearly level and the foot is constrained to be flat on the ground.

The passing position uses the Banked hips to help increase ground clearance for the trailing foot, so the hip is eligible for exaggeration as well. You can exaggerate the normal passing position to elevate the character in a bounce. You can also exaggerate both knees to a deeply flexed position, and coordinate the rotations of the knees, thighs, and hips to maintain a constant distance between the hips' pivot and the ground. This will remove any up-and-down motion from the character's CG, mimicking a waddling duck-walk.

The heel strike provides lots of opportunities for exaggeration, but must also be handled more carefully to produce the right effect. The heel strike is the result of a fast forward rotation of the trailing upper leg, with the trailing lower leg folded at least high enough that the foot clears the ground during the upper leg's forward rotation. This enables you to exaggerate the speed and angle of the hip, the speed and angle of the upper leg, the speed and angle of the lower leg, and the speed and angle of the foot, all in the same motion.

For example, you could rotate the upper leg very quickly up past the final heel-strike angle, whipping the lower leg out straight at the same time, and point the toe at the leg's maximum extension. Hold that pose for a frame or three while the rest of the body continues to lean forward, then rotate the upper leg down rapidly to slap the foot flat on the ground. That's basically a goose-step. Ugly, inefficient, and stupid, but it makes a loud noise.

Exercise 8-1: Animate the Puppet Doing a Caricature March

1. Load scene file EXER0801.LWS from the Chapter 8 directory of the Companion CD-ROM. This is a default walking scene file for the Puppet character, including lights and ground. It's basically the same type of walk you created in Chapter 6, so you may want to substitute your own walk cycle.

2. Exaggerate the key poses and transitions to animate the Puppet doing a caricature march. Here are a few guidelines, which you should supplement by acting out a marching action yourself—or perhaps watching the Rose Bowl parade—and trying to analyze what's going on:

    ◈ The trailing leg should move rapidly through the passing position and kick out straight before the heel strike.

❧ The foot should form a right angle, or even pull the toes back toward the knee a bit, until the heel hits the ground. This exaggerates the slap of the foot flattening to the ground immediately following the heel strike.

❧ Lean the hips and chest back a few degrees.

❧ Keep the Puppet's head high, or even Pitched back a bit.

❧ Pose the arms to keep the hands high, the elbows out, and the arms pumping vigorously, with plenty of snap to balance the motions of the legs.

You might put some John Philip Sousa on the CD player while you work on this, just to put yourself in the mood.

Exercise 8-2: Animate the Puppet Doing a Caricature Sad Walk

1. Reload the basic walk scene you used to start the preceding exercise.

2. Exaggerate the key poses and transitions to animate the Puppet doing a caricature sad walk:

   ❧ Pitch the Hips back a few degrees and the Chest forward a few degrees, effectively curving the spine and making the Puppet slump.

   ❧ Pitch the Head forward, and keep the eyes tracking on the ground.

   ❧ Keep the arms limp and without volition. Animate them using overlapping action, as if they were a pair of scarves tacked to the shoulders.

   ❧ Lift the legs as little as possible, and make the stride very slow and short. Either keep the feet nearly parallel to the ground and shuffle them, or drag the toes along the ground through each passing position.

   ❧ The feet should be very close to the angle of the ground at the heel-strike position so that there is very little distance for the foot to slap down.

   ❧ Use longer, more gradual anticipations and ease-ins, but shorten the ease-outs as if the character is too exhausted to effectively absorb the impact of the action.

Advanced Exercise 8-3: Sync Caricature Action to a Soundtrack

The goal of this exercise is to match a caricatured walk to sound effects and to a piece of music composed and mixed especially for it. The music is the opening sequence of "Easy Come, Easy Go," the film used as an example throughout this book.

1. Following the procedures detailed in Chapter 19, analyze the sound clip 00-00-00.WAV from the Appendix E directory of the Companion CD-ROM, and transcribe it to exposure sheets. Pay special attention to marking hits for the sound of footsteps. Use the appropriate slip so the finished action will read well with the soundtrack.

2. Animate a sad, slow walk, as in the previous exercise, but match the footstep hits in the exposure sheet. Refer to the script in Appendix D and the storyboards in Appendix E for guidelines on camera angles and shot composition.

   You may find it helpful to play the WAV sample while watching a LightWave 3D Preview. Set both Preview and WAV to loop playback, then just toggle the Pause control of one or the other until they are in pretty close sync. This is a little awkward, but less trouble than doing the entire dub for a test.

   If you are using Adobe Premiere or another AV editor that lets you save a project, you can set up a dub project where the WAV file is in place, and an image sequence prefixed "TEST_" is in the first video track. Just render your wireframes or other quick tests to overwrite the original TEST_ files, and you can load and run the project file to automatically dub the test animation. A little slower than the Preview, but you'll have more accurate sync and you can save your work.

3. When you are satisfied with the animation, render it.

4. Using the AV editor of your choice, dub the sound file over your animation.

   If you match the first footstep, and your track analysis was accurate, all the other footsteps should match as well.

Sneaks

The sneak is a time-honored part of the repertoire of any classically trained animator. What fun would an animated story be if no character snuck up on another? The comic potential for consequences befalling the sneaker or the intended victim are so rich, a sneak practically guarantees your audience's full attention.

There are two basic classes of sneak: fast and slow.

The Fast Sneak

The fast sneak is essentially a compressed, fast walk on tiptoes. The hips and chest are pitched toward each other, as in the sad pose described earlier, to curve the spine and compress the body; the sneaker is trying to look as small as possible. The head is angled forward, and the eyes should either fixate on the intended victim or rove the scene nervously with the head following the eyes' lead.

The legs are bent throughout the sneak; if the sneaker straightened his legs, he would be a larger target. The stride is very short, with the thighs and knees rotating as little as possible. The feet are pitched downward so only the toes make contact with the ground, and are also picked up higher than a standard walk, as if to avoid tripping over something.

The short stride, bent posture, and quick movement contribute a greater amount of up-and-down movement to the fast sneak, so the sneaker often appears to bob rapidly. The arms are carried high and the elbows are held close to the body; the arms do not swing to balance leg movement, but are instead held ready to pounce.

Exercise 8-4: Animate the Puppet Doing a Fast Sneak

1. Load scene file EXER0804.LWS from the Chapter 8 directory of the Companion CD-ROM. This scene contains only the Puppet character, with no motions loaded. The sneaks are different enough from normal or caricature walks that you are probably better off starting from scratch than trying to adapt a dissimilar action.

2. Create a fast sneak passing pose at frame 1. The lifted foot should be level with the opposite knee, and the character's CG should be directly above or slightly in front of the grounded toes. The lifted thigh can be horizontal or slightly above it, for a really exaggerated sneak.

3. Create a fast sneak heel-strike pose at frame 7. The toe should be planted slowly, not just slapped down, and the sneaker should immediately lean forward to move the CG toward the leading foot.

4. Create a fast sneak squash pose at frame 15. As the CG moves over the leading foot, the leading knee must bend more to absorb the weight without being forced to drop the heel. The trailing foot lifts off the floor, again easing slowly (to avoid creaking floorboards).

5. Make and play a preview. Ignore the default interpolation for now; how does the timing of the key poses look? Are the keys too close together, or too far apart? Use the Scene Panel Shift All Keys function to adjust the key poses' intervals.

6. Add keyframes and adjust the motion graphs to add snap, anticipation, overlapping action, and follow-through to the sneak, just as you did for the walks and runs in Chapters 6 and 7.

7. When you are satisfied with the animation, save it under a new name.

The Slow Sneak

The slow sneak is an elongated, slower walk, only partially on tiptoes. The action is a more rolling, fluid gait, with the intent being to cover as much ground as possible as smoothly and quietly as possible. The hips and chest are pitched toward each other, and the head is angled forward in the squash position, to curve the spine and compress the body. In the heel-strike position—actually a toe strike, but let's not quibble—the angles are reversed to make the entire body a convex arc from head to leading toe.

The eyes, again, should either fixate on the intended victim or rove the scene nervously with the head following the eyes' lead. The legs range from a compressed pose as the trailing leg squashes, to a full extension as the lead toe stretches toward the next footstep. The stride is quite long, at least equal to the normal walking stride. The feet are picked up higher in passing position than a standard walk to avoid tripping. The long stride and slower movement smooth out the movement, but the deeper squash position still exaggerates vertical motion.

Exercise 8-5: Animate the Puppet Doing a Slow Sneak

1. Reload scene file EXER0804.LWS.

2. Create a slow sneak passing pose at frame 1. The lifted foot should be level with the opposite knee, and the character's CG should be directly above or slightly in front of the grounded foot, which is flat on the ground. The lifted thigh is not quite horizontal. The body should be nearly vertical, making the transition from the forward to the backward lean.

3. Create a slow sneak heel-strike pose at frame 15, and supporting keys immediately following. The toe should be planted slowly, as if testing the floor for creaks. The body is leaning backward at full extension, counterbalancing the extended leg. After contact, the foot should be rolled slowly to make full sole contact with the ground. As the leading heel touches the ground, the sneaker begins to lean forward to move the CG toward the leading foot.

4. Create a slow sneak squash pose at frame 30. As the sneaker leans fully forward and the CG moves over the leading foot, the leading knee must bend more to absorb the weight. The trailing foot lifts off the floor, again easing slowly (to avoid creaking floorboards).

5. Make and play a preview. How does the timing of the key poses look? Are the keys too close together, or too far apart? Use the Scene Panel Shift All Keys function to adjust the key poses' intervals.

6. Add key frames and adjust the motion graphs to add snap, anticipation, overlapping action, and follow-through to the sneak, just as you did for the walks and runs in Chapters 6 and 7.

7. When you are satisfied with the animation, save it under a new name.

Staging

Staging is the posing of a small action to foreshadow the character's next major action, preparing the audience to read it. Examples of staging are looking intently at the object of the action; pointing the hands toward the object, as if "targeting" it; and aligning the body to face the direction of the action. In real life, people tend to unconsciously stage their actions. Good negotiators and salespeople know this; you put your hands in your pockets when you really want something, to hide their involuntary twitching toward the object of your desire.

In animation, you should make your characters look at or point toward the object of the foreshadowed action in the reverse of the usual animation hierarchy order: Eyes, Head, Hands, Limbs, Torso. You should also vary the lead timing of the eyes, depending on the nature of the following action. The more violent the action, the faster (shorter) you should make the staging.

Exercise 8-6: Staging a Reach

Stage the Puppet leaning on a street lamp.

1. Load scene file EXER0806.LWS from the Chapter 8 directory of the Companion CD-ROM. This scene contains the Puppet character and a street scene, including a street lamp.

2. Pose the Puppet beside the street lamp at easy arm's-length leaning distance.

3. Animate the eyes first, to glance toward the street lamp.

4. Follow the motion of the eyes with a slight head turn.

5. Animate the hand nearest the street lamp to lift from the wrist, pointing the fingertips toward the post.

6. Animate the nearer arm to lift, and the Puppet's body to lean toward the street lamp. Maintain the angle of the hand until the palm is parallel to the street lamp's surface.

7. Continue the Puppet's lean until the palm makes contact with the street lamp. Complete the leaning action with an elbow bend for squash, follow-through and rebound to a moving hold.

8. Animate the eyes and head to face the Camera again.

9. Experiment with the timing and transitions for each key pose until you are satisfied with the animation.

Do you see how staging an action can help "sell" a shot? The audience will read it better if they are prepared by a character's foreshadowing of the next action.

Balance & Mass

Balance and mass, which we discussed in Chapter 5, are closely related, but you must handle them in completely different ways. You must animate balance with realism; mass requires some of the most extreme exaggeration. Your characters must always keep their visible supports under their CG, or the audience will wonder why they don't fall over. When a character's CG shifts, as when he or she picks up a heavy object, you must pose the character to place his or her feet under the new center of gravity.

Mass, on the other hand, simply begs for exaggeration. If you want to animate a character struggling with a heavy load, you can use every trick in the book: bent posture, squash-and-stretch arms, exaggerated anticipation, very slow accelerations upward, and dangerously fast ones downward, just to name a few. The comic uses of differential application are fun to play with, too. Cool characters can appear to lift anything effortlessly; uncool characters can get squashed flat trying to move those same items.

Exercise 8-7: Animate the Puppet Picking Up Objects

1. Load scene file EXER0807.LWS from the Chapter 8 directory of the Companion CD-ROM. This scene contains the Puppet character and a variety of objects.

2. Animate the Puppet picking up objects and moving them to different parts of the scene.

    Assign any mass you like to the different objects, but be consistent. A small object can be very heavy (plutonium is apparently easy to come by in cartoon-land), but it must remain heavy for the entire animation.

Pay attention to staging, shifting CG, and appropriate posing of legs and arms to brace the masses and maintain balance. Don't forget to add anticipation, overlapping action, follow-through, and especially squash-and-stretch.

You can use a variety of techniques to keep another object aligned with the Puppet's hand. I prefer Lock & Key, but you can use Object Replacement, Parenting, and ParentBone as well, depending on the character you are animating and the requirements of the shot.

Takes, Double-Takes & Extreme Takes

A *take* is a character's overreaction to a surprise. The nature of the surprise determines the appropriate extent or type of take, and the shot composition determines whether you need to animate a full-body take or just a head take.

There are three key poses for all takes: the normal pose, the squash pose, and the stretch pose. Some takes require special inbetweens, but they all use the same key poses:

◈ A standard take starts out with a *normal* pose—the default, natural, or rest post of a character.

◈ The character presumably sees something to induce surprise; this causes the *squash* pose. The character's eyes squeeze shut as if to block out the sight, and the head and possibly the entire character recoils from the source of the surprise. Depending on the animation style and the construction of the character, this can be a literal squash.

◈ The next pose is the *stretch*, the reaction to the squash position. The character stretches out, eyes wide—just the opposite of the squash—commonly with an extremely surprised expression.

◈ The last part of the take is a return to the *normal* pose.

Anticipation is very important to a take. For every action in a take, there should be a very pronounced anticipation in the opposite direction.

Exercise 8-8: Animate the Puppet Doing a Take

1. Load scene file EXER0808.LWS from the Chapter 8 directory of the Companion CD-ROM.

2. From frame 1, set a key for all items at frames 4, 8, and 13.

3. Leave frame 1 as the normal pose. In frame 4, squash the character for a full-body take, or just the head for a head take. Close the eyelids tightly. Throw the arms out to the sides in a wild gesture of surprise. Make a keyframe to save the changes.

4. In frame 8, invert all the changes you made to frame 4, doubled. Stretch out everything you squashed, and open the eyelids wide. Bring the arms back in, close to the body. Save the changes.

5. Leave frame 13 alone as the return to the normal pose. Make and play a preview.

You should experiment with the timing of the key poses and the motion graphs connecting them. Try different amounts of snap in the transitions; how briefly can you hold a pose, before the audience can't read it? How long can you hold a key pose, and what's the minimum animation needed in a moving hold, to keep the character from going dead?

Exercise 8-9: Animate the Puppet Doing a Double-Take

A *double-take* is a regular take with a head shake between the squash and the stretch, as if the character is trying to deny what he or she sees.

1. Use the Scene Panel to shift all the keyframes from the stretch pose down about 15 frames, to give you room to insert a head shake.

2. Insert a head shake between the squash pose and the stretch pose. Make the shake very abrupt and snappy, with very little ease.

If you'd like a little more of a challenge, you can set up the street scene with the Fred character, and animate the double-take depicted in Shot 4 of the storyboards in Appendix E.

Exercise 8-10: Animate the Puppet Doing an Extreme Take

This should be fun.

1. Load scene file EXER0810.LWS from the Chapter 8 directory of the Companion CD-ROM.

2. Given the Bones available in this character, see how close you can come to duplicating the extreme stretch pose of the take depicted in Shot 15 of the storyboards. Just how much stretch can you use before the character comes apart?

3. Try to create a matching squash pose.

Staggers

In animation, a *stagger* is when a character or object oscillates rapidly between two extreme poses, often in alternating frames, to give the appearance of vibrating from a shock or other overwhelming force. If one part of the character is affected more strongly by the impact, the remaining parts can be animated in overlapping action to emphasize the stagger. Stagger techniques can be very effective, and like takes and sneaks, are borrowed from classic cartoon animation.

There are several ways to create staggers in LightWave 3D. You could simply move the staggered object on alternating frames, using linear interpolation, gradually diminishing the distance the object is displaced as the stagger tapers off. This should work well, as long as Motion Blur is turned off or the percentage is set low enough that the key poses are visible.

If you want more detailed differences between the staggered poses, you could create separate extreme key poses on two successive frames, one odd, the other even; then duplicate each pose to alternating frames, keeping one pose on odd frames and the other on evens. When all the stagger poses have been duplicated, you work down the keyframes, incrementally reducing the extreme poses toward the "normal" pose at the end of the stagger. This is probably the most tedious method, but it does give very precise control; you can even animate gestures and lip sync during the course of the stagger.

You could also create two extreme key poses, then use the Save Transformed function in the Objects Panel to create three objects with the two extreme poses plus a normal pose. If you set the objects up in an MTSE chain with the normal pose as the baseline, you could simply edit the MTSE Envelope to create any sort of stagger pattern you wanted. One drawback to this technique is that MTSE requires straight-line transitions; any difference in the poses that required a rotation or bend is going to look really bad in the MTSE chain.

Exercise 8-11: Animate the Puppet Staggering

1. Refer to Shot 11 from the storyboards in Appendix E, where Fred gets hit by a windblown $1,000 bill.

2. Load scene file EXER0811.LWS from the Chapter 8 directory of the Companion CD-ROM.

3. Choose one of the above methods for creating a stagger, and try to animate an action like that depicted in Shot 11 as applied to the Puppet character.

Zip Pans

A *zip pan* is exactly like a stagger, except the Camera gets oscillated instead of the character. This is very effective for animating earthquakes or high-speed character impacts with immovable objects. To create one in LightWave 3D, simply open the motion graph for the Camera, and create a single-framed zigzag line in the axis of the Camera's vibration.

Exercise 8-12: Animate the Puppet Hitting a Wall

1. Load scene file EXER0812.LWS from the Chapter 8 directory of the Companion CD-ROM.

2. Animate the Puppet hitting the wall, from extreme squash-and-stretch and rebound to moving hold. Make sure you include the overlapping action of the arms and legs, as they would rebound faster and flop around while the main body was still stuck to the wall.

3. Animate a zip pan of the Camera, synchronized to the impact of the Puppet against the wall.

4. Experiment with the timing and duration of the zip pan to discover what works for you.

Sorting Out the Animation Hierarchy

The animation hierarchy is not always going to start with the hips, the CG, or even the body of a character. Sometimes the center of a composition is one of the extremities. In cases like this, the center of the composition temporarily becomes the root of the character's hierarchy. Reasoning from the earlier chapters' statements about animating from the root of the hierarchy outwards, it seems logical to pose models in the current order of importance. The root of the animation hierarchy can change, even within a single shot. If the character's hand is the center of the composition, you should pose the hand first and make the rest of the figure follow naturally from the hand.

Get Unreal!

One of the most challenging fields in CGI character animation is motion picture special effects. Creatures like *Dragonheart*'s Draco, *Jurassic Park*'s dinosaurs, and *Arrival*'s aliens represent the state of the art in fantastic creature creation and character animation. In each case, the goal was to make the audience believe that the creatures on the screen were (or had been) alive. To achieve this, the character designers had to work out all the details of anatomy and kinesiology that would affect how the creatures looked and acted. In the case of *Jurassic Park*, they were able to extrapolate from the work of generations of paleontologists; for the other two, sheer fantasy was to be brought to life.

If you want to do the same, you need to study anatomy, physiology, zoology, anthropometry, kinesiology, and a host of other disciplines. Not enough to get a degree, mind you, just enough to soak up the basic principles and learn where the really good references are. You can always look up the details of the orbicularis oculi; but at least you'll know what to ask for. Once you understand how the underlying structure, the muscles, tendons, and other tissues all contribute to the way a creature looks and moves, devising a realistic-looking simulation of a completely unreal character does not seem so impossible.

Moving On

If you've worked through all the exercises thus far, you understand how to use the animator's tools, the individual parts of characterization. Now, how will you use them to affect your audience? That's what you will learn in the next two chapters, "Getting Your Point Across: Composing Shots for Effect," and "Getting Your Point Across II: Acting by Proxy."

Getting Your Point Across

Composing Shots for Effect

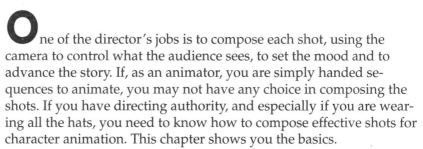

One of the director's jobs is to compose each shot, using the camera to control what the audience sees, to set the mood and to advance the story. If, as an animator, you are simply handed sequences to animate, you may not have any choice in composing the shots. If you have directing authority, and especially if you are wearing all the hats, you need to know how to compose effective shots for character animation. This chapter shows you the basics.

Shot composition shows off one of CGI animation's major advantages over other cinematic forms: you have absolute control over your camera. You are not limited by the physical size and weight of a camera, nor by the tracks, dollies, and cranes required to move one. You can choose any lens you like, move the camera in any fashion and at any speed you desire, and generally indulge your creative whims without paying the exorbitant costs of more traditional cinematography.

This is not to say you should do all those things, at least not if your purpose is to tell a story using character animation. For each camera move, ask yourself: does it advance the story? Does it help develop the character? Does it distract the audience from the focus of this shot? Your audience is used to a more limited range of cinematography, so going to extremes with the camera may distract them from the story and characters. Keep it simple.

Keeping Your Distance

The first choice in composing a shot is the distance from the camera to the object, or central character, of the shot. This distance affects how much information falls within the frame, how much of the frame the character occupies, and the emotional impact of any actions on your audience. Let's take a look at some of the stock distances used in traditional cinematography and note how they affect these three variables.

Figure 9-1: Long shot.

The Long Shot

A *long shot* contains a great deal of information (see Figure 9-1). It includes the complete central character of the shot, plus a good bit of the environment surrounding the character. This is especially useful for an *establishing shot*, which shows the audience the general environment in which the action will take place.

The long shot has the greatest emotional detachment from the audience. Any action composed at this distance will generally have much less impact than a closer shot. Also, minor actions will be so small a part of the screen that your audience will probably overlook them. A long shot is not a good choice for showing subtle emotional transitions or actions.

Exercise 9-1: Composing a Long Shot

1. Load the EXER0901.LWS scene. Click Camera in the Edit area at the left of the screen.

2. Click Move in the Mouse area. Press n to call up the Camera Position Panel. Change the Camera position to 8.0, 1.75, -9.5. Click OK or press Enter.

3. Click Rotate in the Mouse area. Press n to call up the Numeric Rotate Panel. Change the Camera Heading to -48, Pitch to 3, and leave the Bank setting at 0. Click OK or press Enter.

4. Set a keyframe at frame 0.

5. Render an image of frame 0 at whatever resolution and antialiasing you prefer. You should get something like Figure 9-1.

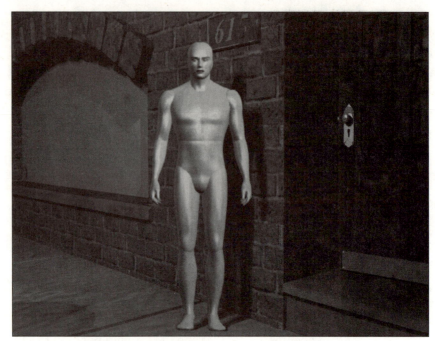

Figure 9-2: Full shot, including feet.

The Full Shot

The *full shot* is an emotional step closer than the long shot (see Figure 9-2). Any action shot at this distance will have a greater impact, since the audience will feel closer to it. The audience can also see more clearly the posture and the grosser expressions of the character, so you have a greater practical dramatic range for character animation.

The full shot conveys less information about the character's surroundings, but can add details that are lost at the greater distance. The full shot is a good choice for establishing the character's general appearance, including props and clothing that have a bearing on the story. A long shot might show only the profile of a character in front of a building; a full shot will reveal the six-gun on his hip, the silver star pinned to his vest, and the lettering over the building's doorway reading "Sheriff."

You can compose a full shot of the provided set by changing the Camera position to 1.34, 1.3, -3.44.

A full shot must always include the character's feet. If you frame the character as cut off at the ankles, you will not get a pleasing composition.

This brings us to the concept of *cutting heights*. Since most films are about people, you can usefully describe shot compositions in relation to the human body. Over the years, directors and cinematographers have developed a set of empirical rules for composing shots relative to the actor. The standard cutting heights are under the armpits, under the ribcage, under the waist, across the upper thigh, and under the knees. If a script or director uses a term like *waist shot*, they mean a composition that ends just below the feature described.

The Medium Shot

The *medium shot* brings the audience another emotional step closer to the action (see Figure 9-3). From a character's point of view (POV), this is only a couple of steps away, just beyond arm's reach. All but the most subtle facial expressions can be read by the audience, and any body language expressed using the legs is, of course, lost off-screen.

Figure 9-3: Medium shot, upper thigh.

The audience can still pick up information about the character's immediate surroundings, but most of the screen is now occupied by the character and the audience's attention will generally be focused there.

You can compose a medium shot of the provided set by changing the Camera position to -0.1, 1.6, -2.34.

The Close Shot

The *close shot* focuses the audience's attention on the head and upper body of the character, which occupy most of the screen (see Figure 9-4). This composition shows just enough of the character's body for the audience to readily perceive shrugs and general body posture. The emotional distance is arms' length, a conversational distance, so any action will have a fairly strong impact on your audience.

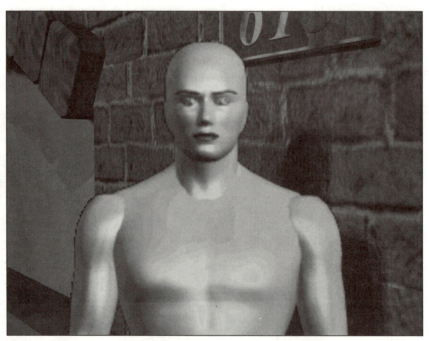

Figure 9-4: Close shot, through ribcage.

It will be difficult for your audience to absorb any information from the background, as most of their attention will be drawn to and held by the foreground character. Conversely, any information conveyed by the character will be that much easier for the audience to read.

You can compose a close shot of the provided set by changing the Camera position to -0.59, 1.8, -1.87.

The Specific Close Shot

The next closer distance is the *specific close shot*. The example in Figure 9-5 shows a Close Shot Head, but descriptions such as Close Shot Hand, Close Shot Window, and so on are also used. The composition is generally interpreted as including the specified object and a visual border around the object. Again referring to Figure 9-5, the head is shown with a visual border beginning well above the head and extending below the chin. The specified object occupies the entire action area of the screen.

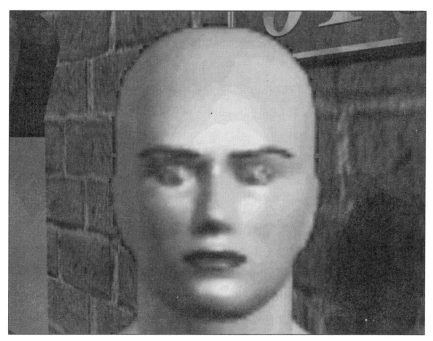

Figure 9-5: Close shot head.

This composition is very strong emotionally. The nuances of facial expressions are easy for the audience to read, and there is almost no chance of a distraction from the background. The only information the audience can observe is that expressed by the character. From a character's POV, this is a very intimate distance used only between friends, or when one character is violating the other's personal space.

You can compose a specific close shot of the provided set by changing the Camera position to -1.11, 1.93, -1.44.

The Extreme Close Shot

The composition shown in Figure 9-6 is literally in your face. The audience is being force-fed the information, whether they want it or not. The audience can't see anything but the object of the shot.

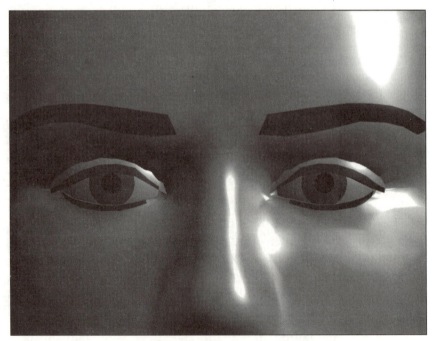

Figure 9-6: Extreme close shot eyes.

Emotionally, this composition can be so strong as to be overwhelming, especially on a large screen. You should be careful not to overuse it and to keep extreme shots like this as short as possible. The emotional intensity is difficult to sustain, and you risk boring your audience with an overly close, overly simple composition. Give them enough time to absorb the emotional impact, then move back to a more distant shot.

You can compose an extreme close shot of the provided set by changing the Camera position to -1.32, 1.9, -1.24.

Pick a Lens, Any Lens

The exact position coordinates you use for the Camera in LightWave 3D's Layout depend on the lens equivalent you select in the Camera Panel. The default Zoom Factor of 3.2 was used for each of the exercises above. A higher Zoom value would require more distance between the character and the Camera to achieve the same composition, and vice versa.

Depth of field is one more variable you need to keep in mind when setting the distance for a shot. Unlike real-world cameras, LightWave 3D by default has infinite depth of field, so all objects are in perfect focus. If you want to simulate the focal behavior of a real-world camera, you need to use the Camera Panel's Depth of Field function. When activated, this feature determines what is in focus at different distances from the Camera. Objects at the exact focal distance from the Camera are in sharpest focus, while those closer or farther are progressively out of focus.

You can use the Depth of Field function to minimize distractions for your audience. You can make backgrounds (or foregrounds) so blurry and out of focus that the audience ignores them. You can even set the Focal Distance and F-Stop so everything but the central character is out of focus. You can also animate these settings with their respective Envelopes, to shift the audience's attention without moving the Camera.

Exercise 9-2: Blurry, Blurry Night

This exercise shows you how to set up an extreme depth of field for a medium shot of the Character object.

1. Load scene EXER0902.LWS.

2. Click on the Camera button at the top of the screen to open the Camera Panel.

3. Set Antialiasing to Medium or higher. The Depth of Field option does not work with lower antialiasing settings.

4. Click on the Depth of Field button at the lower left of the panel.

5. Set Focal Distance to 3.0. This is the distance between the Camera and the object, CHARACTR.LWO, you want to be in sharpest focus.

6. Set Lens F-Stop to 0.5. This setting specifies a very shallow depth of field, producing a large amount of blurring in the foreground and background.

7. Click on Continue.

8. Render frame 0. You should get an image like Figure 9-7.

Figure 9-7: Shallow depth of field.

Note how the character in Figure 9-7 is still in sharp focus, but the background is blurred and much less of a distraction.

If you need to match the depth of field of a shot to live action, the Film Size feature in the Camera Panel can automatically emulate the settings for several real-world film and video formats.

What's Your Angle?

The second part of composing a shot is selecting the camera angle. The basic criteria for selecting camera angles are the same as for setting the distance. You want the angle to help control what the audience sees, set the mood, and advance the story.

The most common camera setup is probably the *omniscient observer*, a camera positioned and angled as if it were another character in the scene. The POV is usually near or below the other character's eye levels, so the Pitch angle of the Camera is nearly zero.

The Heading angle varies, but is rarely close to the cardinal points (0, 90, 180, 270). These angles would give head-on, perfect profile, and rear views that would read as flat and artificial, since you rarely get a view like that in real life. It is usually better to keep the Heading at a more natural angle, at least five degrees away from any cardinal point.

If you consistently use omniscient observer camera angles, your shot compositions will quickly become boring. If you want to keep your audience's attention, you need to spice up the mix a little with more dramatic camera angles.

Try using higher and lower camera positions, with corresponding Pitch angles. There are no absolute rules governing the emotional impact of camera angles, but here are some useful rules of thumb.

High angles, where the camera is above the character and looking down, tend to give the audience a literally lower view of the character. The character is perceived as smaller, weaker, of less importance, or even as being threatened. Subtlety counts for this type of composition; an extreme high angle loses the audience simply by being extreme. A relatively small high angle has the desired emotional effect without tipping off the audience.

Low angles, reasonably enough, tend to give the audience a higher view of the character. The character is perceived as larger, stronger, of greater importance, and in closer shots can readily be perceived as threatening. Again, subtlety counts; a worm's-eye view will lose the audience, but a more subtle angle will have the desired effect.

It's generally a bad idea to bank the camera.

You may have noticed I didn't mention camera angles using the third axis, bank. That's because it's generally a bad idea to bank the camera at all, unless you are going for a very specific type of effect. Bank angles have the effect of tilting the horizontal edges of the screen frame, relative to the sets and characters. This "off-kilter" view can be very disturbing to the audience, and is rarely used apart from action sequences or psychological thrillers.

The action shot can justify banking the camera if the character's POV is actually going through a bank angle, as in a car turning over or an aircraft doing a barrel roll. This is consistent with the action expected by the audience and will not have a strong effect—other than making the audience unconsciously lean into the angle!

The psycho thriller uses of the bank angle are more disturbing. The basic technique is to compose a more normal shot, then slightly bank the camera to skew the composition. If done subtly enough, the audience may never notice the angle. They will, however, become emotionally tense, sensing that something is not right. A variation on this technique is used to underscore a progressively more unbalanced character or setting. If you gradually increase the bank angle of any shot from their POV or that includes them, the audience will sense that the psychosis is becoming worse.

Keep it simple.

The best rule for camera angles in character animation is, keep it simple. Barraging your audience with lots of odd camera angles is confusing and can get in the way of telling your story. The audience will spend too much time adjusting to the new POV, and miss whatever you are trying to communicate through the character. Using the same angle in several shots gives your audience a POV they can identify quickly, so they can concentrate on the character's actions. Try to find a balance between standard shots and more unconventional compositions. Choose your camera angles to emphasize and work with, not against, the current action.

Continuity

You also need to keep continuity in mind. Look at the shot compositions you have planned to precede and follow the current one. You need to match screen position, onscreen movement, and sight lines between successive shots or you will lose continuity.

Screen position means keeping the character in the same approximate relation to the screen frame. If the character appears on the left of the screen in one shot, he should not appear on the right in the next shot.

Matching movement means you should keep the character moving in the same direction in successive shots. If the character is walking left-to-right in one shot, he should also be walking left-to-right in the next. If the character is to change direction (Oops! Forgot something, I'll be right back!), you need to show that change of direction within a single shot.

Matching sight lines means the characters should be looking in the same direction. If a character is looking out a window in one shot, the following shot should not show him staring at the tabletop. As with direction of movement, if a change is necessary you need to show that change within a single shot. In this case, an insert shot of the character's head swiveling from the window sight line to the tabletop sight line would bridge the change nicely.

Finally, it is best to keep the camera on the same side of the action throughout a sequence. The main action should be following a slalom, as discussed in Chapter 3. You can use this slalom as a spatial dividing line for the sequence, sometimes referred to as the *line of action*. Keep the camera positioned on one side of this divider; if you jump from one side to the other, your audience will become disoriented. If you shift the camera from one side to the other at the end of a sequence, hold the first shot a little longer to give the audience time to adjust.

Animating the Camera

You can animate the camera in a number of ways to connect shots in a sequence. There are two major divisions of camera animation in CGI, the move and the cut. Moves are continuous transitions from one position, attitude, and lens setting to another, while cuts are abrupt changes between one frame and the next. In traditional cinematography cuts are accomplished by editing. In CGI, since you are free of the constraints of a physical camera, you can make a cut within the animation.

Camera animation should be treated as any other technique—used only to tell the story. Inappropriate use distracts the audience and detracts from your story, and is the mark of an amateur still infatuated with technological toys.

It's Your Move

A camera move is generally one of several stock types, or a combination of more than one. The stock moves are pan, tilt, dolly, tracking, zoom, rack focus, and copter. The following exercises show you how to set up each of these stock moves.

Exercise 9-3: Pan Camera Move

1. Load the EXER0903.LWS scene. Click Camera in the Edit area at the left of the screen.

2. Click Rotate in the Mouse area. Press n to call up the Numeric Rotate Panel. Change the Camera Heading to -15. Leave the Pitch and Bank settings as they are. Click OK or press Enter.

3. Set a keyframe at frame 0. Go to frame 30.

4. Click Rotate in the Mouse area, if it is not already selected. Press n to call up the Numeric Rotate Panel. Change the Camera Heading to 15. Leave the Pitch and Bank settings as they are. Click OK or press Enter.

5. Set a keyframe at frame 30.

6. Make and play a preview.

Figure 9-8: Beginning, middle, and end frames of a Camera pan.

The pan, shown in Figure 9-8, is one of the simplest and most often used moves, both in traditional cinematography and CGI. All you have to do is rotate the Camera.

Exercise 9-4: Tilt Camera Move

The tilt move is essentially identical to the pan, but on the Pitch rather than Heading axis.

1. Load the EXER0904.LWS scene. Click on Camera.

2. Click Rotate in the Mouse area. Press n to call up the Numeric Rotate Panel. Change the Camera Pitch to -5. Leave the Heading and Bank settings as they are. Click OK or press Enter.

3. Set a keyframe at frame 0. Go to frame 30.

4. Click Rotate in the Mouse area, if it is not already selected. Press n to call up the Numeric Rotate Panel. Change the Camera Pitch to 15. Leave the Heading and Bank settings as they are. Click OK or press Enter.

5. Set a keyframe at frame 30.

6. Make and play a preview. You should end up with something like Figure 9-9.

Figure 9-9: Beginning, middle, and end frames of a Camera tilt.

Exercise 9-5: Dolly Camera Move

1. Load the EXER0905.LWS scene. Click Camera.

2. Click Move in the Mouse area. Press n to call up the Camera Position Panel. Change the Camera position to -1.1, 1.64, -12.0. Click OK or press Enter.

3. Set a keyframe at frame 0. Go to frame 30.

4. Click Move in the Mouse area, if it is not already selected. Press n to call up the Camera Position Panel. Change the Camera X-coordinate to -7.0. Leave the Y- and Z-coordinates as they are. Click OK or press Enter.

5. Set a keyframe at frame 30.

6. Make and play a preview.

Figure 9-10: Beginning, middle, and end frames of a Camera dolly.

The dolly move, shown in Figure 9-10, mimics a traditional camera mounted on a wheeled dolly, moving down a track. You can combine the dolly move with a pan or tilt to produce a compound motion. The dolly move is also a part of the tracking and rack focus moves in the next exercises.

Exercise 9-6: Tracking Camera Move

The other camera moves are pretty much independent, although you should always animate them with an eye to framing the action. The tracking move, however, is intended to follow a particular object, character, or action exclusively. There are several ways to do this. The easiest is to simply Parent the camera to the object to be tracked, then position and rotate the Camera as appropriate.

1. Load the EXER0906.LWS scene. Click Camera.

2. Click Parent at the bottom of the screen. Select CHARSIDE.LWO from the pull-down. Click OK.

3. Create a keyframe for the Camera at frame 0.

4. Click Move in the Mouse area. Press n to call up the Camera Position Panel. Change the Camera position to 0, 1.4, -2.75. Click OK or press Enter.

5. Click Objects in the Edit area. Select CHARSIDE.LWO from the Selected Item list under the View window.

6. Click Move in the Mouse area, if it is not already selected. Press n to call up the Object Position Panel. Change the CHARSIDE.LWO position coordinates to -4, 0, -4. Click OK.

7. Set a keyframe for CHARSIDE.LWO at frame 0. Go to frame 30.

8. Click Move in the Mouse area if it is not already selected. Press n to call up the Object Position Panel. Change the CHARACTER X-coordinate to 1.0. Leave the Y- and Z-coordinates as they are. Click OK or press Enter.

9. Set a keyframe for CHARSIDE.LWO at frame 30.

    This makes the CHARSIDE.LWO object slide along the X-axis from -4 to 1. Since the Camera is Parented to CHARSIDE, it goes along for the ride.

10. Make and play a preview.

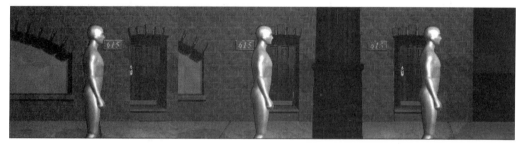

Figure 9-11: Beginning, middle, and end frames of a tracking shot.

The tracking move, shown in Figure 9-11, is especially useful for following transportation animations like walking, running, or moving vehicles.

Exercise 9-7: Zoom Camera Move

1. Load the EXER0907.LWS scene. Click Camera in the Edit area at the left of the screen.

2. Click the Camera button at the top of the screen to call up the Camera Panel.

3. Click on the E button next to Zoom Factor. This calls up the Zoom Factor Envelope Panel.

4. Create a new keyframe for the graph at frame 30. Set the Zoom Factor at frame 30 to 10. Close the panel. Close the Camera Panel.

5. Make and play a preview for frames 0 through 30.

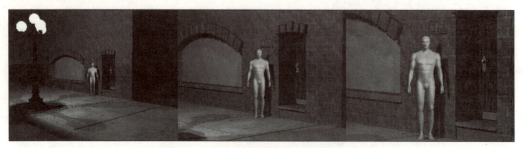

Figure 9-12: Beginning, middle, and end frames of a zoom.

The zoom move, shown in Figure 9-12, is another simple camera move that has been grossly overused. Avoid it wherever possible, using dolly moves or cuts instead. If you must use a zoom, keep it to a minimum and make sure it is essential to telling your story.

Exercise 9-8: Rack Focus Camera Move

The rack focus is a combination of zoom and dolly camera moves, registered to each other to maintain the position and focus of the central object while the rest of the frame changes.

1. Load the EXER0908.LWS scene. Click Camera.

2. Click Move in the Mouse area. Press n to call up the Camera Position Panel. Change the Camera position to -1.1, 1.1, -15.0. Click OK or press Enter.

3. Click Rotate in the Mouse area. Press n to call up the Camera Direction Panel. Make sure Heading, Pitch, and Bank are all set to zero. Click OK or press Enter.

4. Click the Camera button at the top of the screen to call up the Camera Panel.

5. Click the E button next to Zoom Factor to call up the Zoom Factor Envelope Panel.

6. Create a new keyframe for the envelope at frame 30. Set the Zoom Factor at frame 0 to 10, and at frame 30 to 3.2. Click Use Envelope to close the panel. Click on Continue to close the Camera Panel.

7. Go to frame 30.

8. Click Move in the Mouse area. Press n to call up the Camera Position Panel. Change the Camera Z-coordinate to -7.5. Leave the Y- and X-coordinates as they are. Click OK or press Enter.

   The distance between the Camera's first Z-coordinate and the second is the equivalent to the distance covered by the Zoom factor you set in step 6. This matches the distance the Camera travels to the distance the Camera lens zooms.

9. Set a keyframe for the Camera at frame 30.

10. Make and play a preview of frames 0 through 30.

Figure 9-13: First, middle, and last frames of Rack Focus.

The rack focus move, shown in Figure 9-13, produces a unique effect. The central object, located at the camera's focal distance, appears to remain in place and in focus. The background and foreground both appear to shift, producing a very strong disorienting effect.

This is another camera move that is prone to abuse, especially by amateurs. Use it only when it serves a valid dramatic purpose for your story, and otherwise leave it in your bag of tricks.

Exercise 9-9: Copter Camera Move

The copter move is a catch-all description of a style rather than a specific move. It was coined as a description of camera movement from a helicopter, an aerial platform capable of moving in almost any direction. The copter move, therefore, can move the camera in any direction, using any combination of pan, tilt, and dolly moves. The copter shot can also be a tracking shot, keeping the camera pointed at a particular object throughout the camera's travels.

1. Load the EXER0909.LWS scene. Click Camera.

2. Click Move in the Mouse area. Press n to call up the Camera Position Panel. Change the Camera position to -1.1, 1.1, -15.0. Click OK or press Enter.

3. Create a keyframe for the Camera at frame 0. Go to frame 30.

4. Click Move in the Mouse area if it is not already selected. Press n to call up the Camera Position Panel. Change the Camera coordinates to -0.66, 1.4, -1.14. Click OK or press Enter.

5. Set a keyframe at frame 30.

6. Click on the Motion Graph button at the lower left of the screen to call up the Motion Graph Panel.

7. Add a keyframe for the X-coordinate at frame 15, with a value of 2.05. Do the same for the Y-coordinate, with value 3.0. You should end up with graphs that look like Figure 9-14.

8. Close the Motion Graph Panel. In Layout, click the Objects button in the Edit area, then press p to call up the Objects Panel.
   Now you'll add an object for the Camera to look at as it moves.

9. Click on the Add Null Object button at the top right of the panel.

10. Click the Save Object button, then edit the name of the Null to "CamTarget" and close the Save Object Panel. This doesn't save the Null, it just changes its name. Click Continue.

11. Go to frame 0. Click Move in the Mouse area, if it is not already selected. Press n to call up the Object Position Panel. Make sure CamTarget is the item selected. Change the CamTarget position to -1.4, 2.4, -5.3. Click OK or press Enter.

12. Create a keyframe for the Camera at frame 0. Go to frame 30.

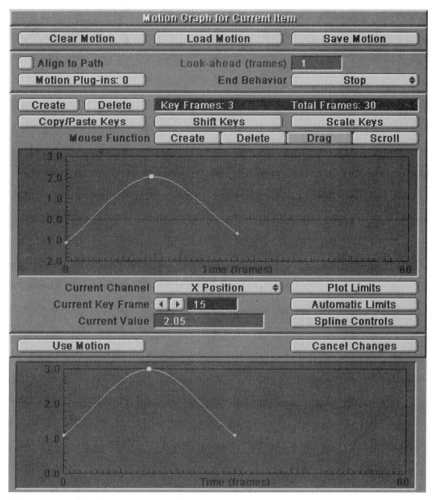

Figure 9-14: Motion graphs for Camera.

13. Press n to call up the Object Position Panel. Change the CamTarget coordinates to -0.83, 1.51, -0.3. Click OK or press Enter.

    This sets up the CamTarget null object to move from near the lamppost to near the doorknob. The next step is to Target the Camera to look at the null, keeping track of a moving target while it also moves.

14. Click on Camera.

15. Click the Target button. Select CamTarget from the Target Object pull-down. Close the Target Object Panel.

16. Make and play a preview.

Figure 9-15: Beginning, middle, and end frames from copter shot.

The copter move, shown in Figure 9-15, is generally used for flythroughs and other action sequences. If you use this shot in character animation it should either be a shot from inside a moving vehicle, or you should set up the motion path according to the "Characteristic Camera Movement" section later in this chapter.

Go Ahead & Cut

You may find it useful to think of a cut between shots as simply a move with zero frames between keys. The same guidelines for continuity still apply, you just have to pay a little more attention to some additional timing issues.

A cut that changes the volume of the shot or its contents creates a *visual jar* or disorientation for your audience. The *volume of the shot* is the space contained in the pyramid formed by the lens (the apex) and the four corners of the frame. The apparent volume of the shot ends at the central object or character.

A close shot of a character's head would enclose only a few cubic feet; a long shot of the Empire State Building might contain millions. A cut between these two shots would cause an extreme visual jar due to the difference between volumes. A series of intermediate cuts, bridging from close to medium to full to long shots, would soften that shock; the difference in volume between each cut would be much smaller.

Sometimes you will want to use the visual jar of a cut for dramatic reasons. Probably the most famous example of this is the shower scene from Alfred Hitchcock's *Psycho*, a series of such fast cuts between different contents (but nearly identical volumes) that the audience often "sees" what is not actually there.

More often, you need to make the cut to a shot that is simply a better composition for the following action, and your goal is just to get there as quickly as possible.

Cutting on the action is the technique of changing from one camera position to the next during the character's action. This timing of the cut relieves the visual jar, since the audience focuses it's attention on the action, not the shot composition.

You can also animate a character to presage a cut, warning the audience so they expect it, and so reduce the visual jar. Animate the character to reach for or look intently at something out of frame, in the direction of the cut. The audience will follow the look or the action with their eyes, and the subsequent cut will be "expected" and therefore less jarring. This is similar to the staging of action discussed in an earlier chapter.

Cutting between angles is another way of changing the shot composition without jarring your audience. Simply keep the distance between camera and object constant, and move the camera to a new angle. The audience only has to reorient itself to the new angle, as the volume and content of the shot is essentially unchanged.

You can also minimize visual jar for an entire sequence of shots by creating a *master shot*. The master shot establishes the entire environment of a sequence, laying out a visual map for the audience. When you intercut a tighter insert shot of some part of this environment, the audience can quickly orient itself from the master shot.

In live-action cinematography, directors often shoot "coverage," additional footage that gives them more editing options. This is almost unheard of in traditional animation, as each frame is expensive to produce. Ideally, a traditional animated production never throws away a single frame. All the editing is done at the storyboard stage, and the actual production of images is dictated by that blueprint.

Currently, the most economical approach for most LightWave 3D animators is to animate the Camera using linear interpolation between adjacent keyframes. This effectively duplicates the live-action technique called "cutting in the camera." This technique is practiced mostly by directors who don't want an editor to have any latitude in how the film is assembled. It doesn't do much for flexibility in editing your animation.

3D CGI animation has the potential to return to shooting coverage. The 3D part of the equation means that, within the constraints of shot composition, you can pick and choose any camera angle you like. Why not choose more than one? If (and this is a big "if") you can afford the extra image storage and rendering time, there is no reason why you can't render shots from more than one camera position, then edit together bits and pieces from each sequence. For that matter, as long as you are careful to save each scene file and its components, you can always go back and rerender a shot with a different composition.

Characteristic Camera Movement

You can animate the Camera as a character's point of view (POV). This makes the Camera an actor, giving it the ability to help tell a story.

You can use the procedure spelled out in the copter shot exercise to animate a Camera for a character's POV. This will give a very Steadicam-style movement. However, real people don't run around with a Steadicam for a neck. Neither should your LightWave 3D Camera.

Choosing an appropriate style of camera movement can add a great deal to your animations. For example, let's use a short involving two characters, one extremely active and zany (Speedy), and the other placid and lethargic (Sleepy).

When shooting from Speedy's point of view, you need to zip the Camera around much more rapidly and in more directions than when shooting from Sleepy's point of view. Otherwise, your audience will not be as quick to identify whose viewpoint they are sharing at a particular moment, and your story will not get across as effectively. Handled properly, character-based camera styles can be a major storytelling tool.

Character-based camera styles can be a major storytelling tool.

Even for something as basic as an architectural walkthrough, there are human perceptual factors you can use to make a stronger impact. The idea is to make the audience feel as though they are in the scene. If you run the Camera straight down the centerline of every hallway, do perfect 90-degree pans around every corner, and keep a dead-level line of sight, you won't do that. Instead, you'll make the audience feel they've been dumped on an amusement park ride with a hefty dose of Quaaludes.

So, how do you make the camera more human? Researchers in various branches of psychology and medicine have been developing tools for what they call "eye-gaze tracking," the mapping of the movements of the subject's eye. As mentioned in Chapter 4, following Exercise 4-4, the extensive body of work on the subject can be boiled down to a handful of general rules that are applicable to character animation.

Just as these rules can be used to animate the rotation of a character's eyeballs, they can be applied to the animation of the Camera. Keep in mind that these are generalizations and are not to be followed without judgment or exception.

If there is a person or creature in the scene, the character's first focus is the eyes, followed by the rest of the face. The hands are next, unless two or more people are facing each other. In that case, the scan typically goes back and forth between the faces, attempting to correlate their interaction before moving on to the rest of the scene.

After faces and hands, objects are examined in order of brightness and contrast. A bright object on a dark table top will attract the eye, as will an open window in a dim room. Television sets, brightly lit pictures on the walls, anything moving, and other details will attract attention for longer periods of time. Blank, unchanging areas will be dismissed with a quick glance. Lower-priority items with many details may be revisited later after other elements of the scene have been examined.

Finally, the eye roves to clues needed for navigation. Occasional glances at the floor, followed by slight corrections in the direction of travel, mimic the way people actually walk. These corrections are the defining points for slaloms, as discussed in Chapter 4.

If the camera is going to go through a door, the camera needs to dip to locate the knob or handle, then quickly return to nearly eye level as the door opens.

You shouldn't exactly mimic the rapid eye movement of a real person.

Keep in mind that you shouldn't exactly mimic the rapid eye movement of a real person, unless you want a particularly frantic and disorienting effect. Real eye movements can be very rapid without disorienting the observer, because the observer is in control of their own eyes and is expecting the rapid shifts. Your audience is not in control, and needs more time to recognize the character's surroundings. Instead of mimicking the quick, angular rotations of a real eye gaze track, you should animate your character POV tracks to be more gradual and rounded. You should also use a little ease-in and ease-out for all the major Camera moves for a character POV, and don't forget to use slaloms. LightWave 3D makes it very easy to animate the Camera in this way.

Exercise 9-10: Targeting the Camera for Character POV Animation

This exercise shows you how to set the Camera to follow a Target Null object, and how to animate that Target to mimic a character's point of view.

1. Load the EXER0910.LWS scene. Click Camera.

2. Click Move in the Mouse area. Press n to call up the Camera Position Panel. Change the Camera position to -9, 1.7, -2. Click OK or press Enter.

3. Create a keyframe for the Camera at frame 0. Go to frame 90.

4. Click Move in the Mouse area, if it is not already selected. Press n to call up the Camera Position Panel. Change the Camera coordinates to 1, 1.7, -2. Click OK or press Enter.

5. Set a keyframe at frame 90.
   This makes the Camera move smoothly down the sidewalk, at an appropriate height for an average human character.

6. Click the Objects button, then press p to call up the Objects Panel.
   Now you'll add a null object for the Camera to look at as it moves. This makes it much easier to control the Camera angle, rather than manually setting Heading, Pitch, and Bank values for each keyframe.

7. Click on the Add Null Object button at the top right of the panel.

8. Click on the Save Object button, then edit the name of the Null to "CamTarget" and close the Save Object Panel. This doesn't save the Null, just changes its name. Click Continue or press Enter.

9. Click Move in the Mouse area, if it is not already selected. Press n to call up the Object Position Panel. Make sure CamTarget is the item selected. Change the CamTarget position to 1, 0, -1. Click OK or press Enter.

10. Set a keyframe for the CamTarget null at frame 0.

11. Click Camera.

12. Click the Target button. Select CamTarget from the Target Item pull-down. Close the Target Panel. Save the scene under a new name.

At this point, you have a scene where the Camera travels at character eye level down the sidewalk, looking at a null object, CamTarget. In frame 0, the CamTarget is positioned to direct the Camera towards the sidewalk just past the doorway.

13. Render frame 0. You should get results like Figure 9-16.

Figure 9-16: Frame 0 of character POV animation.

Consider what details in this scene would attract the attention of the character during a 90-frame walk. Would he look at the ground? How about the lamppost? Perhaps the shop doorway?

14. Make a list of three to six points of interest for the character. Number them in the order the character would look at them.

15. How long (for how many frames) would the character look at each point of interest? Write this number on the list next to each point of interest.

16. Using a copy of the blank exposure sheet from Appendix F, write up the points of interest in order from first to last, spacing them according to the numbers you wrote in step 15.

17. Click the Objects button, then select the CamTarget from the Selected Item list under the View window.

18. Refer to the exposure sheet you just created. Each point of interest is going to be a keyframe. The first point of interest should be at frame 0. Click on the Move button in the Mouse area, and make sure the X, Y, and Z buttons are all active.

19. Use the mouse to drag the CamTarget null object to the point of interest. Make a keyframe for the current item at the current frame. Refer to the exposure sheet for the next point of interest.

20. Repeat step 19 for each point of interest on your exposure sheet. You should end up with a 90-frame animation of the Camera looking at several points of interest as it travels down the sidewalk.

21. Make and play a preview.

LightWave 3D automatically creates a slalom running through each of the keyframe null positions you set up, so you won't jerk the Camera around too sharply. You can use the Motion Graph Panel's Spline Control Tools to change the bias, tension, and continuity of each keyframe. You can make the slalom even smoother, or tighten it up to make the ride a little rougher.

This brings us to fine tuning. Just how rough is too rough? If you are animating a sedate walk down a corporate corridor, you want the movement to be just a little rougher than Steadicam style. If you are animating a character running down a flight of stairs, and want a real documentary feel to it, bang that Camera around a lot!

Exercise 9-11: It's a Dog's Life

1. Repeat the preceding exercise, but this time start the Camera at only 0.2 units above the sidewalk. Make up another point-of-interest list, but this time for a small dog.

2. Try to remember everything you have ever observed about a dog's behavior. In what are they most interested? How do they approach it? Do they follow a direct path, or a more roundabout, wandering path? How close do they get to what interests them? How much

time do they spend looking at (and sniffing) it? How do they move, and how does their POV change, while examining it?

3. Make up an exposure sheet that is at least three seconds (90 frames) long. This gives you a little more time to develop the character. Mark both the points of interest and the Camera positions on the exposure sheet. Make an effort to convey the character and behavior of the dog by the way the Camera and the CamTarget move.

4. Animate the Camera and CamTarget according to the exposure sheet.

5. Make and play a preview.

6. If you are not satisfied with the Camera's characterization of the dog, go back to your exposure sheet and tweak it a little. Try using the Motion Graph Panel's Spline Control Tools to change the bias, tension, and continuity of the keyframes, making the Camera or CamTarget slaloms smoother or rougher.

7. When you are satisfied with the preview, render the animation to an AVI file. Play back the animation.

Does the animation seem to be a dog's-eye view? Does this seem like the behavior of a dog? Ask someone else, preferably a dog owner, to look at the animation. What is their reaction? If you get a laugh, consider your animation a success!

Posing Characters Within the Shot

You can set up an acceptable Camera distance, angle, and movement, yet still have a composition that is boring or hard to read. The success of the shot's composition depends as much on the character's pose as on the Camera setup.

You should keep two concepts in mind when evaluating your character's poses: *line of action* and *twins*. Your key poses should always have a strong, clear line of action, and you should avoid twins like the plague.

Line of Action

Line of action is a pretty simple concept. The line of action should grow from the visual base of the character, up through its centerline, and out to the goal of the action. If this line is bent too sharply or in different directions, it is more difficult for your audience to read the pose, as in Figure 9-17.

Figure 9-17: A line of action splitting toward two goals is harder to read.
Copyright 1996 Mike Comet, from the game Vicious Circle, used with permission by Digital Storm.

Each part of a character's pose should add something to the main line of action. If part of the character is jutting out at an angle, that part breaks up the visual flow of the pose, as in Figure 9-18.

In 2D drawing, the line of action can be drawn first, and the character sketch built around the line. In 3D, the line of action is added afterwards, as an analysis and critique for making changes. Figure 9-19, below, is the result of an animator applying a line of action. Compare this to the two previous poses. The head and torso point toward the same goal as the arm. A much smoother arc can be drawn from the character's feet up through the body centerline and out through the arm.

Figure 9-18: A jagged pose with parts of the character interfering with the line of action. Copyright 1996 Mike Comet, from the game Vicious Circle, used with permission by Digital Storm.

Figure 9-19: A pose with a clearer line of action. Copyright 1996 Mike Comet, from the game Vicious Circle, used with permission by Digital Storm.

Twins

This is a label used to describe perfectly symmetric poses. Beginners often compose a character in a twins pose, lining up each joint as if the character were a soldier standing at attention.

Figure 9-20: Twins. Yuck! Copyright 1996 Mike Comet, from the game Vicious Circle, used with permission by Digital Storm.

A perfectly symmetric pose is highly unnatural and makes your character look boring, mechanical, and dead.

The first step to preventing twins is to avoid head-on camera angles. Even if a character is posed symmetrically, an angled camera shows enough variation between left and right that the pose will hold the audience's interest.

The second step is to make sure the left and right sides of your character are never perfectly matched. Even if a pose seems to require symmetry, make it just a little "off"—slide one foot forward a few centimeters, or tilt the hips and shoulders in alternate directions. Whatever is necessary, as long as the resulting pose looks imperfect enough to be natural.

Figure 9-21: A stronger pose, but still a touch of the twins. Copyright 1996 Mike
Comet, from the game Vicious Circle, used with permission by Digital Storm.

Figure 9-22: A much more dynamic pose, without a trace of the dreaded twins.
Copyright 1996 Mike Comet, from the game Vicious Circle, used with permission by Digital Storm.

Testing Poses in Silhouette

As you probably noticed, poses of complex or heavily textured characters are often hard to analyze. Camouflage still works, I guess. What you need is a tool that masks all that extraneous stuff and leaves just the pose itself. One such tool is the *silhouette*, a simple black-and-white outline or negative image of the character, with no details internal to the outline.

It's important to test your key poses in silhouette. If the action does not read well as an outline, your audience is probably going to have to rely on much more subtle clues to understand what the character is trying to do or say. That takes more time, makes your audience work harder, and is generally poor animation practice. On the other hand, an action that reads well in silhouette will only get better and stronger when you add color, depth, and surface details.

Figures 9-23, 9-24, and 9-25 are examples of the same pose considered in different Camera setups. The heavy texturing of the character makes the color images difficult to read, but the matching silhouettes are very easy to evaluate.

Figure 9-23: A very confusing pose. There's a lot of information inside this outline that you just can't see. Copyright 1996 Mike Comet, from the game Vicious Circle, used with permission by Digital Storm.

Figure 9-24: Better than the first pose, but still a little cluttered and confusing. Copyright 1996 Mike Comet, from the game Vicious Circle, used with permission by Digital Storm.

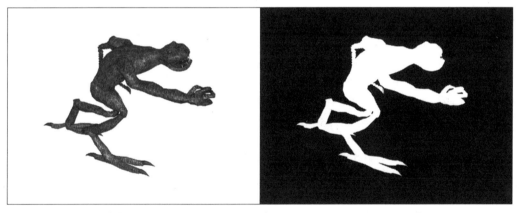

Figure 9-25: A much better pose, very easy to read. Copyright 1996 Mike Comet, from the game Vicious Circle, used with permission by Digital Storm.

In 2D drawing, testing in silhouette requires making another drawing or tracing of the pose in question, blocking out or omitting the details inside the character's outline. LightWave 3D enables you to do essentially the same thing, automatically, by rendering an alpha channel image.

Exercise 9-12: Making Pose Silhouettes With Alpha Channels

1. Load the scene you wish to analyze, or one you are working on.

2. Open the Record Panel by clicking the Record button. In the Record Panel, specify which Alpha Image format you prefer. Which format you choose isn't really crucial, as the files are only temporary.

3. Click Save Alpha Images. Choose a directory and a root filename. I generally use ALF. Click on Continue.

4. Render frame 0 just to save an alpha channel image.

5. Open the Images Panel. Click Load Sequence. Choose the alpha channel file you just rendered. Click Continue.

6. Open the Options Panel. In the Layout View layer, activate the Background Image feature by clicking the BG Image button, then click Continue.

7. Open the Effects Panel. In the Compositing layer, choose ALF from the drop-down list as the Background Image. Click Continue.

    The alpha channel image loads as a backdrop to the Layout view. How much of the image you can see depends on the complexity of the wireframes in your scene.

8. Whenever you need to check a silhouette, simply render the frame you want, then get an unobstructed view of the alpha channel image by opening the Scene Panel and choosing the Hide All Objects option.

Composing Shots for Multiple Characters

If you are animating a crowd scene, or the interaction between two or more characters, you should apply these principles of composition to the individuals and to the group as a whole.

Evaluating the distance, angle, depth of field, and movement of the camera, the characters' and groups' lines of action, and especially avoiding twins and checking silhouettes, are just as important for groups as for individuals. Animating a solo character is generally a piece of cake compared to coordinating a group.

For every important action, you need to clear enough space around the character that the action reads well in silhouette. The space between characters must be appropriate to the action, neither too far nor too close. If the characters take turns in leading the action, getting good poses can require a constant reshuffling of the composition. This is another instance where you will need to experiment a lot and develop your own judgment.

Composition for Direct Playback & Game Design

If you are animating for computer games, multimedia, or any other application that will play back through a computer, there are a few more factors you need to keep in mind.

At the current state of technology, most desktop computers can't play back full-frame video without skipping frames. The problem is that a computer can only push so much information through the system, and most video sequences contain much more information than a computer can handle at full speed.

There are several approaches to solving this problem. One is, of course, to get a faster computer. In time, this will be the solution for most people and this text will be obsolete. For now, other options are within the reach of more people.

There are several techniques for compressing a video or audio/video stream for computer playback. Three of the more common are MPEG, AVI, and QuickTime. Each has its advantages and disadvantages, zealots, and critics, but they all share a few important attributes.

The amount of information in an animation is not necessarily all the information about each pixel in each frame. That is what is called an uncompressed stream, and can run about 30 megabytes per second for a broadcast-quality image. Most compression techniques take advantage of the fact that most of the pixels in frame 1, for instance, will be identical to the corresponding pixels in frame 2. These duplicated pixels do not have to be recorded all over again, just their locations. The minority pixels, the ones that show a change, or delta, have to be recorded completely.

Do you see the implications? If a video clip has very low deltas, it can be compressed a great deal. If the deltas are high, the clip may be near its original, uncompressed size.

So how do you ensure low deltas? Simple: don't move the camera.

If a video clip has very low deltas, it can be compressed a great deal.

Ouch. No camera movement. No cuts or transitions, either. The whole screen is one big delta when you do that. This is why a lot of early computer animation was (and is) boring; the playback penalty simply ruled out any use of dramatic camera movement or cutting. This limitation just isn't acceptable any more. So what else can you do?

You can lower the size of the animation file by limiting the number of colors. If you cut a 24-bit video clip down to 8-bit, you just trimmed two-thirds of the file. The down side is that you will see *banding*, an abrupt borderline between adjacent color areas, because there are not enough different colors to seamlessly shade the borders.

You could cut back the frame rate, too; if you only have to display 15 frames per second instead of 30, you've cut the data stream in half again. The disadvantage is that motion starts to look choppy, and below about 10 frames per second you can do better with flip-books.

You can also reduce the resolution. Using 640x480 pixels takes up a lot of screen real estate; 320x240 is one-quarter the data, but still acceptable to most audiences. Even smaller resolutions are acceptable for animations designed to accompany text or occupy small screen windows in a computer game.

What it usually comes down to is a combination of all these techniques. If you need fast action, cut down the color depth and lock down the camera, but keep the frame rate high. If you want a "talking head" with good color reproduction, lock down the camera, lock down the subject, use a compromise frame rate, and boost the color palette back to 24-bit. If you want to move your camera or do a lot of cuts and edits, you'll have to sacrifice something else.

Moving On

If you have completed all the exercises in this chapter, you've got a practical selection of Camera setups and moves you can use to help tell your story. The next chapter shows you what to do with the character once it's in front of the Camera.

Getting Your Point Across II

Acting by Proxy

This chapter teaches acting technique as it applies to character animation, covering posing, gesture, mannerisms, and emphasis. Animating for emotional communication requires at least as good a sense of timing as stage acting. In fact, acting classes are a pretty good idea for an animator; they break down inhibitions about performing and can acquaint you with a lot of references on physical expression that apply to animation as well as to live action.

There are many resources available on acting technique. These resources can help you define a mood or attitude with a pose. The essential truths of acting, whether on stage or through character animation, are based on natural, observed behavior. If you want to become a better animator, study candid photos and films of people who are not acting, but reacting to real-world situations. I strongly encourage you to take movement classes of any kind, but acting or mime classes are generally best for animation purposes.

Show Some Character

"Get every-thing to read just in the acting, the pantomime, then when you stick the face on, it'll only plus that." — Pete Docter, *The Making of Toy Story*

A character is defined by its actions. To define a character, you have to animate some sequence of actions that tells your audience who this character is.

The basis of all action is posture, the broadest stroke of establishing mood. A change in posture, with all else remaining the same, can completely change the effect of a scene.

Posture can be defined as the line from the feet to the head, but I prefer to include the upper arms and sometimes the entire body, as well. The eyes always lead a change in posture, preparing the audience for the following action. If the character becomes sad, the eyes drop first; if happy, the eyes open wider and sparkle.

As you learned in earlier chapters, you must work to create consistently strong poses. You can judge this by testing them in silhouette, as described in Chapter 9. Make this testing a habitual part of your workflow, so it becomes second nature.

You must time transitions so the audience has a chance to read them, but not so long that the audience is bored and their attention wanders. Never start an action within the first quarter-second of a shot; you must allow your audience at least that much time to adjust to the new camera angle and contents of the scene before they are ready to read an action. If you start an action too early in the shot, your audience may miss it entirely.

If the TD has done a good job of scene setup, your job as animator will be much simpler. You can use the standard Front, Side, Top, and Perspective views to relate the character to its environment, and use the dedicated View Light views (see Chapter 15 for details) to see the close-ups you'll need when you pose the face or hands of a complex character.

Don't forget to follow the animation hierarchy when animating changes in posture, just as in Chapter 6. The same rules apply for saving time, effort, and aggravation, whether you're animating a simple walk cycle or a very complex dramatic performance.

Exercise 10-1: What a Moody Guy!

The goal of this exercise is to create a series of strong, dramatic poses.

1. Load scene file EXER1001.LWS from the Chapter 10 directory of the Companion CD-ROM.

    This scene file contains a posable character and default three-point lighting, as described in Chapter 17. Frame 1 shows the character in a normal posture.

2. From frame 1, create a keyframe for all objects at frame 30.

     Let's suppose the character starts off in a normal pose, then is given some very saddening news by an opponent we don't see. Suppose the opponent then threatens the character, frightening him. Next, the opponent ridicules the character, causing the character's fear to transition to anger. Finally, the character's anger causes the opponent to leave, and the character exults in his victory. That's four major emotional poses, sadness, fear, anger, and exultation.

3. Pose the character in frame 30 in an expression of sadness. Remember to pose the character in order, using the animation hierarchy. Set the hips first, then the chest, and so on.

     You have a number of options for figuring out what a "sad" posture looks like. You can find a full-length mirror and look at yourself while acting sad. You can find a movie or news video that shows a real person or a good actor acting sad. You can look for a sad pose from a traditional cartoon or comic strip. You can ask someone else to act sad for you. You can look up an example of a sad pose in one of the references cited earlier.

     If you can't find your own example of a sad posture, here are a few suggestions: slump the chest forward and tilt the hips back. For this character, this is the closest pose to curving the spine and slumping the shoulders. Make the arms hang straight down, as if the character has neither the energy nor the inclination to do anything else with them. Pitch the head forward, and track the character's eyes to look at the ground in front of him. It's difficult to avoid a twins pose when mimicking sadness; the general lack of energy in the character seems to preclude any difference between the sides. To avoid the appearance of twins, rely on three-quarter Camera angles for sad poses.

4. Make a key for the character at frame 30 to save the sad pose. Repeat step 2 to create a "normal" key at frame 60.

5. In frame 60, pose the character to express fear. Again, try to extract the essence of a fearful pose from your own observations.

     A fearful pose is a natural progression, both emotionally and physically, from the posture of sadness. The concave slump of hips and chest is held a little deeper, and the knees bend to lower the body even further. The arms are posed with the elbows held close to the body and bent sharply to bring the hands, open and palm-forward, in front of the chest as if to ward off an attack. A little jitter in the hands protecting the body will add to the expression.

The head is pitched back, looking up, and the eyes tracked to the object of the fear; in this case, pick a point where an opponent's face would be, a few steps in front of the character you are posing. To avoid a twins pose, tweak Bank and Heading to turn the head slightly away from the direction of the eyes, move one foot a little behind the other, and raise one hand slightly above the level of the other.

6. Make a key for the character at frame 60 to save the fearful pose. Repeat step 2 to create a "normal" key at frame 90.

7. In frame 90, pose the character to express anger.

   An angry pose is a very strong dramatic change, from a passive, weak pose that folds the character in on itself, to a strong, aggressive pose that extends the character to full height and toward the object of the anger. Straighten the alignment of the hips and chest, and pitch the hips forward so the entire character is leaning toward the imaginary character with a ramrod-straight spine.

   Trail one foot farther back and advance the other as if in the first step of an attack on the opponent, keeping the character's CG between the feet for proper balance. Rotate the arms to bring the hands down to waist level, and clench the hands into fists. Keep the eyes tracked on the opponent's face, but rotate the head to match the eyes' alignment, with a little extra Pitch to make the jaw jut out aggressively.

8. Make a key for the character at frame 90 to save the fearful pose. Repeat step 2 to create a "normal" key at frame 120.

9. In frame 120, pose the character to express exultation.

   You're on your own for this one. I'm sure you can come up with something.

10. Evaluate all four poses in silhouette. Look for strength, readability, and no twins. Tweak the poses as necessary.

11. When you are satisfied with the four dramatic poses, save the scene under a new name.

You've got a logical series of solid, dramatic poses. Now let's connect them with appropriate inbetweens and timing.

Exercise 10-2: Timing Transitions

1. Make a preview from the scene you animated in Exercise 10-1. Play the preview.

   LightWave 3D automatically creates smooth interpolations between the key poses you set. This action looks too smooth, more hydraulic than human or caricature. The changes all happen at the same time, too; there is no overlapping action, anticipation, or follow-through. You need to change that by setting more keyframes that add anticipation, snap, moving holds, overlapping action, and follow-through to the animation. These are the same procedures you learned in Chapters 5 and 6.

2. In the Scene Panel, hide all the objects except the Hips.

   You'll be using the animation hierarchy again, posing the root of the hierarchy throughout the animation before proceeding to the next level.

3. Add keyframes. Use the Spline Control Tools to animate a sharper snap between key poses and to add a very slight motion around each key pose to produce a moving hold.

   The largest part of the transition from one pose to the next should occur over just a few frames, starting with an abrupt change at the end of the preceding pose's moving hold. An ease to a moving hold should occupy the rest of the interval. Remember, if your character holds perfectly still for even a few frames, it loses the illusion of life and becomes dead.

   Consider how long the transition between two key poses should take. The transition between fear and anger, for example, should happen much faster than that between normal and sadness. How long does it take you to get angry, when someone plays a nasty trick on you? Use the Scene Panel Shift All Keys function if you want to relocate a key pose to shorten or lengthen a transition.

   Keep in mind that the root of the hierarchy carries the load of moving the entire character. The Pitch or Heading of the hips has to give the impression of driving the mass of the whole character, so don't use quite as much snap for the root of the hierarchy as you would for the higher, less massive levels.

4. Make and play a preview. Critique the animation of the Hips and make revisions until you are satisfied with this level of the animation hierarchy.

5. In the Scene Panel, make the next level of the hierarchy visible.

6. Repeat steps 3 and 4 for this level of the hierarchy.

    When you add keyframes, make sure they aren't all on the same frames as the keys for other parts of the character. Different parts of a character should reach their extreme poses at different times; if all the parts peak together, the animation loses continuity. Always keep some part of the character moving, especially during long moving holds.

    For each higher level of the animation hierarchy, make the snaps a little sharper, the eases a little shorter. Each level has less mass to move, and can therefore speed up and slow down faster. The higher levels of the animation hierarchy can also vary more during a moving hold; a 5-degree twitch in a finger is not nearly as noticeable as a 5-degree twitch in the chest.

7. Repeat step 5, then 3 and 4 again, for each level of the hierarchy.

8. When you are satisfied with the entire animation's timing and all the additional keyframes, save the scene under a new name.

You should end up with a series of dramatic transitions that have strong poses; read well; show appropriate anticipation, snap, overlapping action, and follow-through; and hold well without going dead. Don't be discouraged if your first try at this animation isn't as good as you hoped; timing emotional transitions well takes lots of practice. Make up other sequences of emotional transitions and animate them for practice. Pivotal scenes from plays or movies are excellent source material for animating emotional transitions.

Gestures & Mannerisms

Body language and hand gestures are an international language. Although some gestures have special meanings in certain countries or regions, there are many gestures that have almost universal meanings. Your characters will seem much more lively and self-motivated if they use gestures and body language to emphasize the message of their posture.

You can build up a repertoire of gestures by your own observation, but I recommend studying one or more of the available books on the subject. Desmond Morris's *Bodytalk* is one of the more accessible works on the subject, and includes notes on regional usage.

Mannerisms are a personal version of gestural communication. A particular motion, gesture, or posture may have a special meaning when expressed by one character, but not when used by another. Mannerisms are only effective in repetition; if one of your characters displays a mannerism, it will probably not be interpreted correctly by your audience the first time they see it. With repetition, the audience can associate the mannerism with the character and understand the intended message. Over time, a mannerism can become a character's identifying characteristic. One has only to think of the phrase, "What's up, Doc?" to realize how powerful a mannerism can become.

Both gestures and mannerisms should help to further define the character. Whenever you pose a character, ask yourself, "Could another character hold that pose to get that effect?" If the answer is yes, the pose doesn't help define the character; it's weak, and should be changed. A gesture, mannerism, or other action should specifically and exclusively define the character performing the action.

> The most important guideline for animating character hands is to avoid mittens.

The hands are a rich source of expression. Most gestures involve at least one hand, and many require both. The average character's hands have more joints than the rest of the body combined, even when using the classic three-fingered cartoon character gloves. The most important guideline for animating character hands is to avoid mittens, the tendency to clump all the fingers side-by-side in an undifferentiated lump. Even if an illustrated gesture shows the fingers aligned, it's a good idea to express some individuality by moving one of the fingers slightly out of line.

The hands are closely watched, ranking right behind the eyes and face in attracting your audience's attention. You should therefore practice animating hands, and pay at least as much attention to fine-tuning them as you do to the rest of the character's body. Also, try to keep the hands above the waist, unless you intend the character to look exhausted or sad.

Exercise 10-3: Get Over Here!

The goal of this exercise is to apply what you've learned about posture, gesture, and mannerisms to animate a unique performance for the character.

1. Load scene file EXER1001.LWS again. Frame 1 shows the character in a normal posture.

2. For the first keyframe, pose the character to show an imperious, pompous attitude.

   Use your imagination. I'm sure you can think of a suitable model.

3. Make additional keyframes at appropriate distances. Pose the character to summon another (unseen) character, using hand gestures and posture to communicate the action and define the character.

   Typical poses might include a forceful pointing movement with fully extended arm in the direction of the unseen character, a withdrawal of the extended arm, and a second forceful pointing movement down toward the pointing character's feet, as if to say, "You! Get over here!"

   Pay special attention to the nuances of the hand pose. Don't forget to stage the action by pointing the hand first, as in Chapter 8.

4. Animate the character waiting impatiently for the summoned character to respond.

   Animate whatever waiting twitches you prefer. Toe-tapping, clenched fists on hips, or crossed arms are all good indicators of impatience.

5. Animate the character directing the summoned character.

   Lots of pointing fingertip jabs should communicate the idea adequately.

6. Animate the character dismissing the summoned character.

   This is comparatively easy; you can use a backhanded flipping hand motion as dismissal, while the rest of the character is animated to be looking elsewhere, bored. Remember to keep an upright, imperious posture throughout the animation.

7. Make and play a preview. Tweak the moving holds, timing, and other settings as necessary. When you are satisfied with the animation, save the scene under a new name.

Exercise 10-4: Come Here, Please

1. Repeat Exercise 10-3, but this time create a more persuasive character.

   This is a variation on a theme: animate the character to summon, direct, and dismiss an unseen subject in a cajoling way. Spend more time on the directing part, using lots of encouraging and even imploring hand gestures.

2. Make and play a preview. Tweak the moving holds, timing, and other settings as necessary. When you are satisfied with the animation, save the scene under a new name.

Exercise 10-5: Would You Care to Step This Way?

1. Repeat Exercise 10-3 again, but this time create an extremely diplomatic and polite character.

   The character should spend a good amount of time bowing and making other polite, considerate gestures. The key pose groups might be described as invitation, ingratiation, negotiation, and farewell.

2. Make and play a preview. Tweak the moving holds, timing, and other settings as necessary. When you are satisfied with the animation, save the scene under a new name.

Timing Is Still Everything

Timing actions to emphasize lip sync dialog is the best way to sell a shot. If the action is timed well, even poor lip sync looks acceptable. If the action is not timed to emphasize the dialog properly, even excellent lip sync does not look very good.

When you are working with a lip sync exposure sheet, one approach to accents is to listen to the track and to mark each syllable that the voice talent emphasized. You can animate physical gestures like head nods to emphasize the dialog. These forms of emphasis always precede the actual syllable.

Try it yourself. Read a particularly dramatic bit of prose or poetry while watching yourself in the mirror and you will see that you nod or lift your head well before the sound you are accenting.

You probably need to experiment, but a good starting offset is three to six frames. Simply write the emphasis ("nod" or "lift") in the Action column of the exposure sheet, the desired number of frames in advance of the lip sync frames.

Exercise 10-6: A Dramatic Reading, Sans Mouth

1. Play back the Finest Hour WAV clip from the Companion CD-ROM. Note the emphasized syllables and mark them on the exposure sheet from Appendix F.

2. Transpose all the emphasis marks from three to six frames to allow for physical emphasis to precede the sound.

3. Load scene file EXER1001.LWS again.

4. Animate the character according to your modified exposure sheet. Since the character does not yet have a mouth, you need to convey the desired emphasis by head and body motions alone.

5. Using Adobe Premiere, or the editing software of your choice, dub the provided soundtrack over the rendered animation to check the sync.

6. When you are satisfied with the quality of the finished piece, save the file under a new name.

Moving On

Now that you've learned to animate the broader pantomime, let's follow Pete Docter's advice and add the face, the topic of the next chapter.

Stroboscopic rendering of the Puppet character doing a forward flip. Note that the character's center of gravity (CG) follows a parabola, even when its extremities change position.(Figure 5-5)

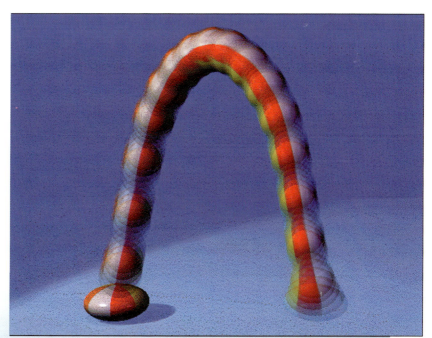

Stroboscopic rendering of a bouncing ball, using motion blur to replace stretch. (Figure 5-17)

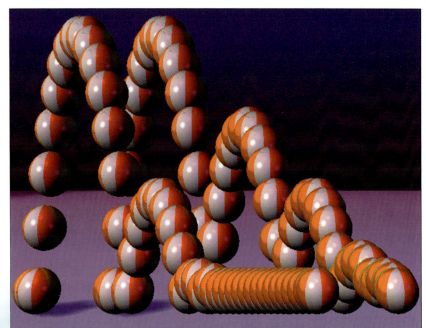

Stroboscopic rendering of two bouncing balls, simulating different masses and elasticities. (Figure 5-9)

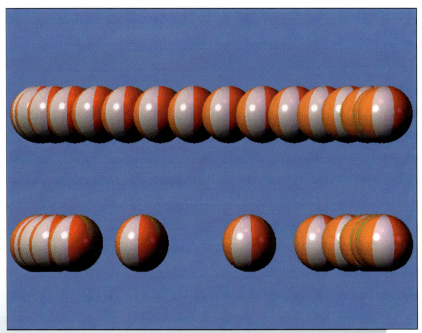

The upper ball moves smoothly, using LightWave 3D's automatic interpolation. The lower ball moves with more snap, as you can see when you play EXER0507.AVI. (Figure 5-24)

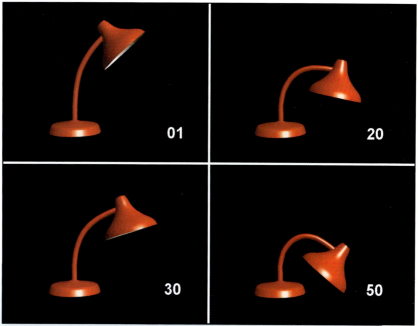

Frames from EXER030X.AVI, as the desklamp bends. (Figure 3-15)

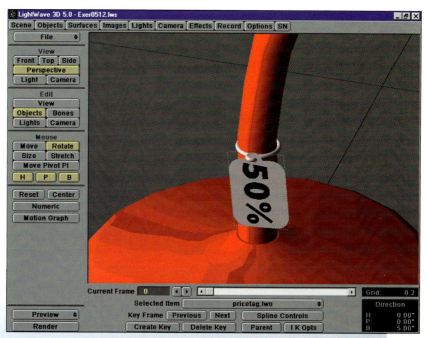

TAGRING.LWO and PRICETAG.LWO objects loaded, Parented, and positioned.
(Figure 5-36)

Creature posed without a clear line of action, confusing and hard to read. (Figure 9-17)

Creature posed with clear line of action, easy to read. (Figure 9-19)

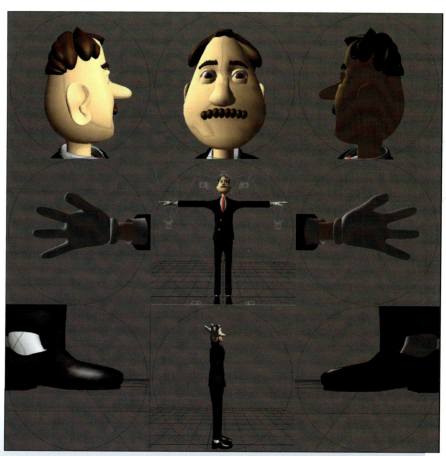

Nine posing views recommended for Lights Parented to a character. (Figure 15-1)

This creature was created with Bones. Copyright 1996 Mike Comet, from the game Vicious Circle, used with permission by Digital Storm.

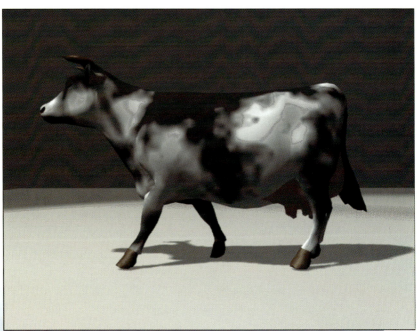

Heel strike position for left front leg of a cow. (Figure 7-4)

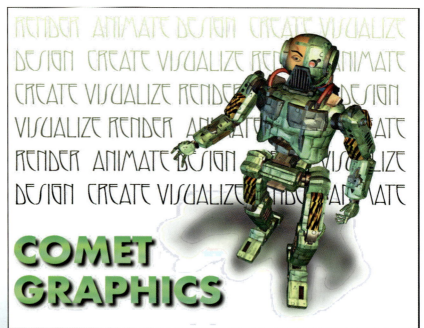

Copyright 1996 Mike Comet, from the game Vicious Circle, used with permission by Digital Storm.

Copyright 1996 Mike Comet, from the game Vicious Circle, used with permission by Digital Storm.

Face Facts

Character Facial Animation

This chapter is about the finishing touch, the last tweak to the animation that makes all the difference. The pantomime and composition may get your main point across, but it's the subtlety of the facial animation that really sells the shot to your audience. It's amazing what you can do with a well-arched eyebrow, instead of a whole-body shrug or gesture.

Lip Sync

It seems that everybody who learns character animation is initially excited about doing lip sync. OK, we'll work through lip sync first (animators have to know how to do it), then move on to more important things.

Why this attitude, you ask? Good question! Lip sync is arguably the least creative of character animation tasks. You are slavishly following the frame-by-frame timing of the voice talent, and have little leeway in which to be creative with the timing. Your audience, however, will be sensitive to glitches in lip sync and will often criticize an otherwise fine animation job based on a few mismatched frames.

Further, since the process is so closely coupled to the sound track, a lot of R&D work has been done recently on completely automating it. For example, the proprietary software used by Mainframe Entertainment to animate "Reboot" and "Beast Wars" uses a component called GRIN that automates lip sync. Other animation houses probably have similar software in use or development. The CGI software industry has typically added new functions to desktop software within a few years of their high-end proprietary development. My advice, therefore, is not to spend a lot of time mastering lip sync. It most likely will be automated by a LightWave 3D plug-in very soon.

This is not to say you shouldn't work through the exercises in this chapter. At the least, you'll understand what the "old hands "are talking about when they complain about doing lip sync the old-fashioned way.

Plans & Maps

Lip sync starts, as does everything else in animation, with a lot of foresight and planning. You don't even need to think about animating for lip sync until the script and storyboards are finalized, the voice talent has recorded all their tracks, and the director and editor have pieced together the takes they want for the final soundtrack. Once the soundtrack is locked, at least as far as the dialog is concerned, the track can be analyzed and the exposure sheets written up (see Chapter 19 for details of these processes).

What you typically see on the exposure sheets is a frame-by-frame phonetic breakdown of the vocal track, along with all the other information about action, camera directions, and so on (see Figure 11-1). For this set of exercises you can ignore everything but the phonetic breakdown.

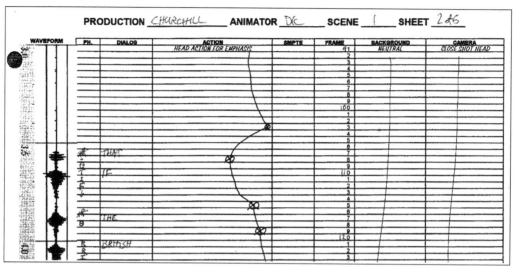

Figure 11-1: Example exposure sheet.

Lip sync is one of the skills that transfers directly from traditional stop-motion or cel animation to CGI. There is a 70-year body of work on synchronizing sound to animation, most of it already available to the animator in book or video form. There is little call for cut-and-try experimenting when it comes to lip sync.

Just about every book on cel or cartoon animation has a section on lip sync, usually including a model sheet of basic drawings for the mouth. These drawings can be adapted directly as image maps for the following exercises. The image maps reproduced in Figure 11-2 are provided with the Magpie track analysis software described in Appendix H.

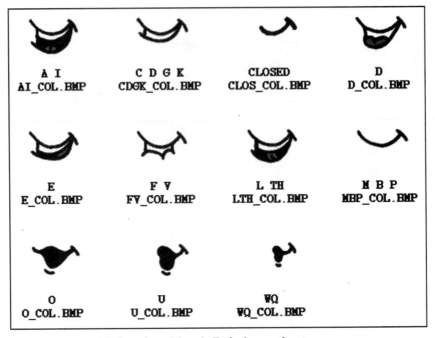

Figure 11-2: Model sheet from Magpie Default mouth set.

If your TD has not already made up a phonetic map library, or you are doing everything yourself, you can either use the map library provided on the Companion CD-ROM or create your own maps. If you choose to roll your own, refer to Exercises 14-1, 14-2, and 14-3 for details on their construction and application.

The first exercises explain how you can use image sequences to animate the phonetic mouth shapes, painting the mouth as you might paint an Easter egg. This is the easiest way to do facial animation, but it is not without drawbacks.

Animating with image sequences generally provides the lowest level of realism in animation. Stylistically, this method lends itself to a number of different approaches. The burden of realism or style is lifted from the TD or sculptor building the objects and transferred to the artist drawing the maps. The map artist can therefore employ almost any drawing style, ranging from the harshest minimalist abstractions to the softest, most realistic textures possible. With the right image processing software and a good deal of patience it is possible for a talented graphic artist to turn a primitive egg shape into a photorealistic human face and head.

That goal is beyond the purpose of these exercises. We'll concentrate on a very simple approach—the standard cartoon mouth shapes applied to the Head object you animated in Chapter 4.

You can use the color image sequence to change the surface colors of the object, "painting on" the mouth shapes. If the background of the color maps is not the exact shade of the object, you must apply matching alpha maps to make the background of the color maps transparent.

These image sequences can be used alone if it suits the style of the animation. This is the simplest approach, but it does not change the profile or give any impression of a third dimension to the mouth. Also, any specularity or diffusion spot will continue to reflect from the open mouth, spoiling the effect as in Figure 11-3.

Figure 11-3: Head with color and alpha mouth image maps applied.

The next step in complexity, a precisely matched bump or displacement image sequence, gives the lips the appearance of some depth. A bump map permits the use of a simpler object, but does not alter the profile of the object and is less realistic. If you use a displacement image sequence, it will alter the profile of the object. The tradeoff is that the object must have a finely divided geometry in the area to be mapped, or the mouth appears to have unsightly jags. With the combination of color, alpha, and either bump or displacement image sequences, any specularity or diffusion spot will still reflect from the open mouth (see Figure 11-4).

Figure 11-4: Head with color, alpha, and bump mouth image maps applied.

The last level of image sequence mapping is the addition of a matched clip image sequence. The clip map cuts away the surface of the object where the mouth is open, to reveal the teeth, tongue, and inner mouth surfaces (see Figure 11-5).

Figure 11-5: Head with color, alpha, bump, and clip mouth image maps applied.

Obviously, the border between the inner edge of the lips and the opening of the mouth must be carefully drawn, or the lips appear jagged or uneven (see Figure 11-6). While it is possible to dither and otherwise "cheat" the resolution of both color and bump images, the clip images should be the highest resolution consistent with memory resources.

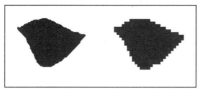

Figure 11-6: Adequate and jagged clip map resolutions.

With the clip image sequence, the highest level of mapped realism is possible. If the bump or displacement map is drawn correctly, the clip should occur exactly where the surface is distorted to a 90 degree angle, and the clipping will take effect exactly where the surface would disappear if it were modeled in three dimensions. The only giveaways will be at this abrupt edge of the lips. If the camera is positioned at an angle approximately tangent to the lips, the inner surface of the object's face may be visible. You should avoid these camera angles if you use clip mapping.

You pays your money and you takes your choice; every cheat and trick used in animation has its down side. Your challenge as an animator or TD is to make those choices depending on the demands of the job at hand.

Timing for Lip Sync

Timing good lip sync isn't just a matter of sticking an "a" map in the frame where the exposure sheet is marked "a." Different phonemes are held for different lengths of time and transition to and from other phonemes in different ways. Here are a few rules to keep in mind:

- **Snap open, close slow.** The mouth should snap open quickly in a single frame, two at the most, to full extension for vowels. It should close much more slowly to hold the vowel.

- **Hold for emphasis.** Hold important or emphasized vowels longer, just as you hold an important pose.

- **Shut up with inbetweens.** Use transition or inbetween maps when closing the mouth slowly from a held phoneme.

- **Explosive plosives.** Ts, Ds, Bs, and Ps cannot be held. Snap them out in a frame or two, or your character will look mush-mouthed.

- **Speed kills.** Don't try to keep up with a very fast speaker— your audience won't catch it. If the mouth actions become too frenetic, use inbetweens rather than full poses for alternating mouth actions.

- **Watch yourself.** Just as discussed in the preceding chapter, you are your own best model. Keep a mirror handy; most professional animators keep a nice-sized one propped right next to their monitors when doing facial animation. When in doubt about a mouth action, pronounce it yourself and observe what your face does.

With all these guides firmly in mind, let's move on to the real thing: animating lip sync.

Fortunately for this approach LightWave 3D doesn't require you to specify a map for each frame in a sequence; it holds the last used map until the next higher number in the sequence is reached. For example, if the file order is:

1, 2, 5, 10, 11

the displayed file sequence will actually be:

1, 2, 2, 2, 5, 5, 5, 5, 5, 10, 11

Obviously, this can save you a great deal of work in laying out a lip sync image sequence. You only have to specify the changes, not the holds.

The approach we're going to use is simple, albeit tedious at times. Since there are only a handful of phoneme image maps to choose from, we'll simply make a bunch of copies of these image files, numbered in the order we want them to appear. For example, if the phoneme image for "o" appears in the exposure sheet at frames 5, 18, and 24, we make three copies of the file O_COL.BMP, renamed LIPC0005.BMP, LIPC0018.BMP, and LIPC0024.BMP. When LightWave 3D loads the images from the sequence for frames 5, 18, and 24, the "o" phoneme map copies will be loaded.

One more drawback of this approach should now be obvious. If you've got a long shot, with a lot of speaking, the number of copied files is going to get very large very quickly and demand a lot of hard disk space. If this becomes a problem, you may have to render the shot in segments, limited by how many phoneme image maps you can store at one time.

While not exactly a drawback, it is especially important with this approach to keep your files organized. If you mess up a directory name, you could end up with one character lip synching another's lines. Comical, sure; but the audience will be laughing at you, not your animation!

Exercise 11-1: Cooking Up a Batch

This exercise shows you how to create batch files to make the image sequence mapping process easier.

1. Set up a directory for the shot named SHOT0065, if you haven't already. (It's a good idea to keep copies of every file you need for a shot in the shot's own directory.) Create a subdirectory for the character, SHOT0065\WINSTON. Create four subdirectories

within the character directory, \COLOR, \BUMP or \DISPLACE, \CLIP, and \ALFA.

Creating separate subdirectories is an easy way to manage more than one character in a shot; you don't have to worry about overwriting or deleting map or object files that are needed for another character.

2. Copy the color, bump or displacement, clip, and alpha channel map libraries for the character to the new character directory. For this exercise, use the map library located in the directory CH11\MOUTHS on the Companion CD-ROM.

These maps are derived from the Default mouth set bundled with the Magpie track analysis software described in Appendix H.

3. Get the shot's exposure sheet from your director, or if you are doing it yourself, follow the breakdown procedures outlined in Chapter 19. For this exercise, we'll work from the six-page sample exposure sheet provided in Appendix F.

The exposure sheet contains the analysis of a phrase from one of Winston Churchill's more famous speeches. The words of the quote are: "So bear ourselves that if the British Empire and its Commonwealth last for a thousand years, men will still say, this was their finest hour."

4. Starting with the first phoneme color map in the library, count how many times it is called for in the exposure sheet and list or mark each starting frame number. Repeat this process for each phoneme color map; some may not be used, especially in a brief shot.

5. Using Windows Write or another text editor, create a new batch file named for the shot and character (WINS0065.BAT) and save it in the shot\character subdirectory, SHOT0065\WINSTON.

6. The first marked frame of the sample exposure sheet, frame 30, calls for the phoneme "s." According to the MAGPIE.INI file, the "s" phoneme is represented by the image file labeled CDGK. This is kind of a catch-all mouth shape for most of the consonants. Edit the first line of the batch file to read:

```
COPY CDGK_COL.BMP COLOR\LIPC0030.BMP
```

This command duplicates the "s" color image into the Color subdirectory. This means the phoneme color map for the "s" sound will be applied to the character in frame 30 of the animation.

7. Select the first line (including the carriage return), copy it, and paste it as many times as the first map is called for. You should end up with something like this:

```
COPY CDGK_COL.BMP COLOR\LIPC0030.BMP
COPY CDGK_COL.BMP COLOR\LIPC0030.BMP
COPY CDGK_COL.BMP COLOR\LIPC0030.BMP
COPY CDGK_COL.BMP COLOR\LIPC0030.BMP
COPY CDGK_COL.BMP COLOR\LIPC0030.BMP
COPY CDGK_COL.BMP COLOR\LIPC0030.BMP
COPY CDGK_COL.BMP COLOR\LIPC0030.BMP
COPY CDGK_COL.BMP COLOR\LIPC0030.BMP
COPY CDGK_COL.BMP COLOR\LIPC0030.BMP
```

8. Select the number part of the new filename in the second line. Type the number of the next start frame for this phoneme map:

```
COPY CDGK_COL.BMP COLOR\LIPC0030.BMP
COPY CDGK_COL.BMP COLOR\LIPC0065.BMP
```

9. Repeat the number editing for the rest of this phoneme map's frames:

```
COPY CDGK_COL.BMP COLOR\LIPC0030.BMP
COPY CDGK_COL.BMP COLOR\LIPC0065.BMP
COPY CDGK_COL.BMP COLOR\LIPC0072.BMP
COPY CDGK_COL.BMP COLOR\LIPC0179.BMP
COPY CDGK_COL.BMP COLOR\LIPC0239.BMP
COPY CDGK_COL.BMP COLOR\LIPC0265.BMP
COPY CDGK_COL.BMP COLOR\LIPC0279.BMP
COPY CDGK_COL.BMP COLOR\LIPC0326.BMP
COPY CDGK_COL.BMP COLOR\LIPC0340.BMP
COPY CDGK_COL.BMP COLOR\LIPC0403.BMP
COPY CDGK_COL.BMP COLOR\LIPC0438.BMP
COPY CDGK_COL.BMP COLOR\LIPC0460.BMP...
```

10. Repeat these steps for the rest of the phoneme color maps. When you're finished you should have a fairly lengthy list of files to be copied. Save the batch file.

11. You really don't want to go through this whole process again to match up the clip and bump or displacement maps. Here's the easy way to do it: save the batch file again under a new name. The exact name isn't important; this is only a temporary file. Use

the Replace function in the temporary file to replace LIPC with LIPB and _COL. with BUMP. (or DISP.). Note the period included in the search term; if you leave it off, you'll end up with a lot of lines looking like:

```
COPY CDGK_BUMP.BMP BUMPO\LIPB0030.BMP
COPY CDGK_BUMP.BMP BUMPOR\LIPB0065.BMP
COPY CDGK_BUMP.BMP BUMPOR\LIPB0072.BMP
COPY CDGK_BUMP.BMP BUMPOR\LIPB0179.BMP...
```

12. Use the Replace function again, but replace COLOR\ with BUMP\. Save the file in case you need it again.

13. Select All and Copy. Reopen the original batch file, go to the end of the file, and Paste.

    You should now have two sections of batch file, the first copying all the color maps and the second copying the corresponding bump or displacement maps:

```
COPY CDGK_COL.BMP COLOR\LIPC0030.BMP
COPY CDGK_COL.BMP COLOR\LIPC0065.BMP
COPY CDGK_COL.BMP COLOR\LIPC0072.BMP
COPY CDGK_COL.BMP COLOR\LIPC0179.BMP...
COPY CDGK_BUMP.BMP BUMP\LIPB0030.BMP
COPY CDGK_BUMP.BMP BUMP\LIPB0065.BMP
COPY CDGK_BUMP.BMP BUMP\LIPB0072.BMP
COPY CDGK_BUMP.BMP BUMP\LIPB0179.BMP...
```

14. Repeat the preceding steps, replacing LIPC, BUMP., and BUMP\ in the temporary file with LIPP, CLIP., and CLIP\, respectively. Copy the revised section and paste it to the end of the batch file. Repeat again, replacing LIPC, BUMP., and BUMP\ in the temporary file with LIPA, ALFA., and ALFA\, respectively.

    Now you have all the copy instructions for every phoneme map you want to use in this shot:

```
COPY CDGK_COL.BMP COLOR\LIPC0030.BMP
COPY CDGK_COL.BMP COLOR\LIPC0065.BMP
COPY CDGK_COL.BMP COLOR\LIPC0072.BMP
COPY CDGK_COL.BMP COLOR\LIPC0179.BMP...
COPY CDGKBUMP.BMP BUMP\LIPB0030.BMP
COPY CDGKBUMP.BMP BUMP\LIPB0065.BMP
COPY CDGKBUMP.BMP BUMP\LIPB0072.BMP
COPY CDGKBUMP.BMP BUMP\LIPB0179.BMP...
```

```
COPY CDGKCLIP.BMP CLIP\LIPP0030.BMP
COPY CDGKCLIP.BMP CLIP\LIPP0065.BMP
COPY CDGKCLIP.BMP CLIP\LIPP0072.BMP
COPY CDGKCLIP.BMP CLIP\LIPP0179.BMP...
COPY CDGK_ALF.BMP ALFA\LIPP0030.BMP
COPY CDGK_ALF.BMP ALFA\LIPP0065.BMP
COPY CDGK_ALF.BMP ALFA\LIPP0072.BMP
COPY CDGK_ALF.BMP ALFA\LIPP0179.BMP...
```

15. Make a backup copy of this batch file! It's fairly easy to rebuild the directory structure if you accidentally delete some files, but if you lose this batch file you'll have to go back to the exposure sheet and start all over.

16. Make sure you've got plenty of disk space available. Multiply the number of lines in your batch file by the size of the largest file you are duplicating to get an upper-limit estimate of the total storage required. When you are ready, execute the batch file.

    If all goes well, the batch file makes copies of the appropriate color, alpha, bump, and clip maps and places them in their respective subdirectories, one of each type for each phoneme keyframe numbered in the batch file.

17. Now you get to do some preemptive quality control. Browse the subdirectories in the shot directory. Did the files end up where you expected them to? Open up a few files from each directory as a spot check, and compare them with the exposure sheet. It's much better to catch any mistakes now than after rendering the entire shot.

18. In LightWave 3D Layout, load the SHOT0065.LWS scene file from the CH11 directory of the Companion CD-ROM.

19. Click the Images button at the top of the screen to call up the Images Panel. Click Load Sequence to call up the Load Image Sequence file dialog. From this dialog, select the first numbered color map file, LIPC0030.BMP. Press Enter or click Open to confirm your selection and close the dialog.

20. Click Load Sequence again. Select the first numbered alpha map file, LIPA0030.BMP. Press Enter or click Open to close the dialog.

21. Click Load Sequence again. Select the first numbered bump map file, LIPB0030.BMP. Press Enter or click Open.

22. One more time, click Load Sequence. Select the first numbered clip map file, LIPP0030.BMP. Press Enter or click Open.

23. Click Continue or press Enter to close the Images Panel and return to Layout.

    You now have all four matching image sequences loaded and ready to apply.

24. Click Object in the Edit area at the left of the Layout screen. Select the HEAD0065.LWO object from the Current Item pull-down list.

25. Click Surfaces at the top of the screen to call up the Surfaces Panel. In the Surfaces Panel, choose Head from the Current Surface drop-down list.

    This surface covers the entire head, except for the eyes, lids, or ears.

26. Click the T button for Surface Color to open the Color Texture Panel.

27. Choose LIPC(sequence) from the Texture Image pull-down list. This is the sequence of color maps.

28. Choose LIPA(sequence) from the Texture Alpha pull-down list. Click the Negative Alpha check box under the Alpha thumbnail window in the middle of the panel.

    This sets the black of the alpha image to cover the object with the color map, and sets the white areas of the alpha image to let the object color show through (see Figure 11-7).

29. Set Texture Type to Planar Image Map, set Texture Opacity to 100 percent, turn on Texture Antialiasing and Pixel Blending, and turn off Width and Height Repeat.

30. Set Texture Size to 1, 1, 1, Texture Axis to Z, Texture Center to X=0, Y=-0.15, Z=-0.42, and Texture Falloff to 300 on the Z-axis. Click Use Texture to accept the new settings and close the Texture Panel.

Figure 11-7: Color and Alpha maps applied to Head object.

This centers the texture below the nose, at the surface of the mouth area, and limits the texture's size. The Falloff setting limits the penetration of the map so it doesn't color the back of the Head. I used trial and error to find the 300 value for this exercise; you'll have to test different values to fit your own objects. Remember, all these settings are made relative to the Head's local coordinates; make sure the World Coordinates button is not active!

Now make the matching settings for the bump map sequence.

31. Click the Smoothing check box in the bump map section near the bottom of the Surfaces Panel. Click Bump Map T in the center of this section to call up the Bump Map Panel.

32. In the Bump Map Panel, choose LIPB(sequence) from the Texture Image pull-down list. This is the sequence of bump maps.

33. Set Texture Type to Planar Image Map, set Texture Opacity to 100 percent, turn on Texture Antialiasing and Pixel Blending, and turn off Width and Height Repeat.

34. Set Texture Size to 1, 1, 1, Texture Axis to Z, Texture Center to X=0, Y=-0.15, Z=-0.42, Texture Falloff to 300 on the Z-axis, and Texture Amplitude to 70 percent. Click Use Texture to accept the new settings and close the Texture Panel.

35. Click Continue to close the Surfaces Panel and return to Layout.

    Last but not least, make the matching settings for the clip map sequence that "cuts out" the opening of the mouth. You access these settings from the Objects Panel rather than the Surfaces Panel.

36. Press p to call up the Objects Panel. Click the T button next to the words Clip Map to open the Clip Map Panel.

37. Choose LIPP(sequence) from the Texture Image pull-down list. Click the Negative Image check box under the image thumbnail window.

    This sets the black areas of the clip image to make those parts of the object invisible and transparent to shadows, and sets the white areas of the clip image to have no effect on the object.

38. Set Texture Type to Planar Image Map, set Texture Opacity to 100 percent, turn on Pixel Blending, and turn off Texture Antialiasing and Width and Height Repeat.

39. Set Texture Size to 1, 1, 1, Texture Axis to Z, Texture Center to X=0, Y=-0.15, Z=-0.42, and Texture Falloff to 300 on the Z-axis.

    As before, this centers the texture below the nose, at the surface of the mouth area, and limits the texture's size. In this case, the Falloff setting limits the penetration of the clipping so it doesn't make a hole in the back of the Head. If you use clip maps, the background of the scene shows through the clipped area unless you either turn on the Double Sided option for the Head object, or model another object as a lining for the mouth.

    Click Use Texture to close the Clip Map Panel. Click Continue or press Enter.

40. Test render a few frames at a high enough resolution that you can check for map misalignments. Compare the maps in the rendered frames to the exposure sheet callouts to make sure they match.

If your Head object's teeth are very close to the surface of the face, the clip map may cut into them. If you can't reposition the teeth, you may have to redesign the teeth as a separate object, Parented to the head. You can match the lower teeth to the JawBone's movement by animating the JawBone first, then copying the JawBone's motion graph to the LowerTeethBone.

41. If all the spot checks are OK, test render the entire shot in 1/4 screen resolution, with anti aliasing disabled, using Quickshade, and save the animation in AVI format.

    This is for the next step in checking, before you commit the time to rendering at full resolution and antialiasing.

42. Open Premiere, or whatever other editing software you are using. Load the rendered AVI file, and dub the lip sync WAV file over it. Save the results to a new AVI file.

43. Play back the dubbed file to see if the lip sync reads accurately. Make sure the playback is locked to the frame rate at which you animated it in Layout.

If you have to revise just a few of the maps' timing, you can edit the batch file manually. Just make sure you change all four file types to the same frame numbers, or the maps won't match up! You should also delete the old duplicate image files manually, as the new numbers will be different and some of the older files would probably not be overwritten by the new set.

If you have to slip the entire shot, use the Offset function in Layout. Click Images to open the Images Panel. The Frame Offset box is just below the center of the panel.

Using a positive Frame Offset value is like slipping the image sequence ahead. Add an Offset of 5, and the sequence image for frame 15 will be used in frame 10 of the animation. Conversely, using a negative Offset value is like retarding the image sequence; a value of -5 means frame 15 of the sequence will be used for frame 20 of the animation.

Usually, you want to push the image sequence ahead, so the screen has a chance to show the lip image before the audience hears the phoneme. Some animation houses slip the images ahead of the audio track three or four frames as a matter of standard procedure. Nobody seems to know why, but it works for the audience.

If you have to slip large sequences, but not the entire shot, you are probably better off deleting the alpha, bump, and clip sections of the batch file, editing the color section, then repeating Steps 11 through 14.

Usually, you want to push the image sequence ahead, so the screen has a chance to show the lip image before the audience hears the phoneme.

This may seem tedious the first couple of times you try it, but with a little practice it becomes second nature. This is one of the first jobs you can hand off to an assistant. It's a no-brainer after the first few iterations, but the quality control in the last steps trains the eye to spot details.

You might have noticed another advantage of this process. If a set of maps needs to be changed for any reason, it is relatively easy, right up to final rendering. Just delete the duplicate maps from the four map subdirectories, replace the master maps in the character directory with the updated maps, and reexecute the batch file. No problem. Just make sure the person who requested the changes thinks you sweated blood to make them!

You should now have a solid grasp of the principles of lip sync. Play around with the Head a little more, making it say anything you like. Follow the procedures in Chapter 19 to break out your own exposure sheets from digitized sound samples, and Chapter 14 to create additional mouth maps for caricatured mouth actions.

As with most skills in character animation, you can learn the basics of lip sync very quickly, but honing and polishing your timing and caricature skills is a lifetime pursuit.

Lip sync for either replacement or displacement animation uses the same principles. Each has the advantage of providing its own inbetweens, which means you only have to model or pose the actual keyframes. If you really like doing lip sync, you can repeat Exercise 11-1 using these techniques.

For now, let's leave lip sync and use facial expression exercises to learn about other facial animation techniques.

Facial Expression

Animating facial expressions makes lip sync look like a walk in the park. Conveying emotions, especially complex transitions and slow, subtle changes, is a much tougher proposition. As I stated in Chapter 10, animating for emotional communication requires at least as much judgment and sense of timing as acting on the stage.

While you can animate emotions using layers of image sequences, this requires such a large number of inbetween maps and such care in their timing that you will lose most of mapping's usual production advantage. As both morphing and Bones techniques create inbetweens automatically and with finer control, they give you a significant advantage when you animate emotional transitions.

The human face is covered with many layers of muscle and other tissues, overlapping in different directions and bridging attachment points from the shoulders to the top of the skull. The goal of character facial animation is not to realistically simulate every one of these muscles, but to mimic the surface appearance produced by their combined actions well enough to tell the story. Refer to Chapter 13 if you want more detail on how to model an expressive face. For the purposes of this chapter, I'm just going to summarize the functions a LightWave 3D face has to emulate.

Most of a human face attaches closely to the underlying bone structure. The cheeks and lips have a great deal of freedom because they are only attached to bone at their outer edges, and their muscles and skin are flexible and elastic. Other areas of the face can't move as freely because they are on a shorter leash, so to speak. The jaw and the skull proper are the two major divisions for animating the human face. The face from the upper lip upwards is mostly attached to the skull; from the lower lip downwards and back to the angle of the jaw, the face is attached to the jawbone. This is a good start for defining the animation hierarchy for the face; the skull is the root, the jawbone is the second layer, and all other animation controls will be attached to either the skull directly or through the jawbone.

The visible function of most facial muscles is pushing skin around, changing the shape of the face in small increments. The jaw and eyeball muscles are notable exceptions, since they rotate through comparatively large angles. To animate skin deformation in LightWave 3D, you can either use a lot of overlapping Bones to deform the object, or model the changes in a series of objects and use object replacement techniques to animate them. The following exercises show you how to animate facial expressions using both approaches.

The Sample Face

In the Chapter 11 directory of the Companion CD-ROM you'll find a sample object and scene of a basic articulated head, EXER1102.LWS. This scene is the bare minimum necessary to create most facial expressions. Even so, the number of Bones required may significantly slow down screen redraw if your system's CPU is running much below 100MHz. Figure 11-8 is a screen shot of frame 3 of EXER1102.LWS with all Bones made visible.

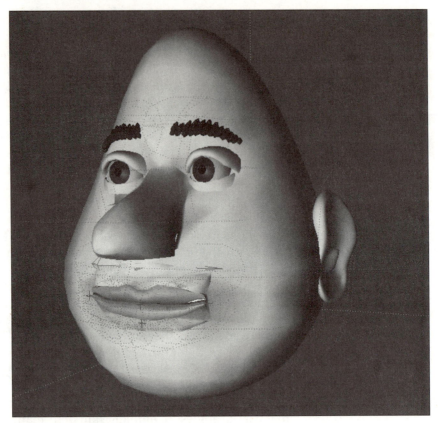

Figure 11-8: Bones in example face scene.

Here is a brief description of the animation controls and limits for this scene. As an animator, you should get similar summaries from the TD or setup person with every character you animate. Animating can be a lot easier if you understand where each control for a character is located and what it was designed to do.

There is only one light in the scene, a spot aimed at the character's face and Parented to the head. This enables you to switch Views to Light and always have a consistent, face-on view of the character. When you animate a full character, you may prefer to have more lights preset for other useful views; refer to Chapter 15 for details.

The scene uses a combination of nulls and Bones to control the shape of the Head object. The nulls are used as IK targets for multiple chains of Bones, so instead of having to pose four or eight Bones you can just move a null and the associated Bones will follow along. All poseable nulls and Bones are Parented to the head, so you can create keyframes using the Selected Item and Descendants option to save an entire facial expression. You can also create keyframes for the MouthUp and MouthLow Bones and the MouthParentNull and their descendants to keyframe the mouth and leave the rest of the face alone.

I automated the eyes as much as possible. The eyeballs are IK targeted on a null, which can be moved as described in Chapters 4 and 9 to animate most eye movements. The eyelids are also IK targeted to the same null, but with Pitch Limits for realistic action; limited Pitch rotation and no rotation at all on Heading or Bank axes. This means you just move the null, and the eyeballs and eyelids follow along. When you need to change the angle of the eyelids, Pitch the LUpEyeLidHandle and RUpEyeLidHandle +20 degrees for a wide-eyed expression, -25 degrees for a sleepy or drunk expression, and -55 degrees for fully closed, as in a blink or wink. Return the UpEyeLidHandles to 0 degrees Pitch to resume normal IK tracking.

The eyebrows are very simple—just two Bones each. The inner Bone is the Parent, so you can move it along the Y-axis to move the entire eyebrow. For this object, I recommend no more than 0.015 up on the Y-axis and rather less than that down. Since the forehead and brow ridge for this character have pronounced slopes, you need to bring the eyebrows forward as well as down for some expressions, or the eyebrows will disappear inside the head. Changing the Pitch of the outer Bone bends the eyebrow; simple, but adequate for most eyebrow actions. I'd keep the Pitch angle within 80 degrees of the outer Bone's rest direction.

The left ear has a Hinge Bone, which can change Heading to flap the ear. This is silly, but useful as an example in Chapter 13. If you're feeling ambitious by then, you might set up similar Bones for the right ear.

The JawBone is Parent to the face below the lower lip. You can Pitch the JawBone about -30 degrees before you start getting gross distortions, but -5 to -10 degrees is plenty for most expressions. Reset the JawBone to 0 degrees Pitch to close the mouth. The JawBone controls the lower half of the cheeks, as well; when the jaw gapes, the polygons along the border between JawBone and HeadRoot stretch out to bridge the distance. A more advanced face would have additional Bones placed to puff the cheeks out or bulge the cheekbones under the eyes; as I stated earlier, this scene is the simplest I could design consistent with full expressive range.

MouthUp is the Parent Bone for the upper lip Bones. MouthLow is the equivalent for the lower lip Bones. The upper teeth are fixed to the skull, and the lower teeth are fixed to the JawBone. The controls for the lips are evenly divided between nulls and Bones; there is a null at the left and right corners of the mouth, and one null each at the midpoint of the upper and lower lips. One Bone is positioned between each of these nulls, in the middle of the top left (LipUpLeft), top right (LipUpRight), lower left (LipLowLeft), and lower right (LipLowRight) quadrants of the mouth.

These Bones and nulls are visible, but there are another 16 hidden Bones that actually control the shape of the lips. The visible lip Bones are the Parents of two separate chains, and each chain is IK targeted at one of the adjoining nulls. The effect is, move a null, and the hidden Bones keep the nearest section of lip lined up toward the null. Move a Bone, same thing. So by animating 8 control nodes, (4 Bones, 4 nulls) you're controlling twice that many Bones.

Keep the changes small to start with. Most of the nulls and Bones around the mouth can only move 0.02 units along the Y axis before serious rendering errors appear. It doesn't require much movement to create a convincing expression. You can also Pitch the four Lip Bones to suck in or push out the lips, which is useful when you try to pose an F or V for a lip sync sequence.

Obviously, this object has room for improvement; both mouth corners should be remodeled so the upper and lower lips share a common point, to keep the corner from pulling apart when the JawBone is at full gape. The area around the lips is not subdivided enough, or in the right pattern, to deform without rendering artifacts. In a real animation production house this character would have been sent back to the TD or setup person for repairs. It's good enough for these exercises, though, and if you like you can repair this object when you work through Chapter 13.

Creating & Reusing Facial Poses

The human face has an enormous dramatic range, with nearly infinite gradations of expression. To attempt even a brief summary of facial expression in this space would be futile. Instead, I recommend that you consult one of the facial expression works listed in the Bibliography. And as I've noted before, one of your most useful study guides is a mirror beside your monitor; when you want to create an expression, act it out and observe yourself.

Even though the full range of human facial expression is too large to catalog, there are a relatively small number of types or classes of emotional expression: sadness, anger, joy, fear, disgust, and surprise are the basics. You may find it useful to create one facial pose of each type, then experiment with variations between the poses to create a library with more dramatic range.

Keep in mind that a library of "standard" emotional poses is only the starting point for developing a character's expressions. You shouldn't use the same expression on any two characters; they should have idiosyncrasies, minor variations on the common pattern that make each expression uniquely suited to one character.

You can reuse poses if you create them in "stock" scenes, collections of poses you can add to a scene with the Load From Scene function in the Objects Panel. As long as all the posing controls are Parented to or Boned in the object, you can copy or delete a pose using the Selected Items and Descendants keyframe option. To do this for lip sync, you should set up the first 11 frames (after the three-frame setup discussed in Chapter 13) in lip sync poses like those pictured in Figure 11-2. You can then make an entire lip sync sequence by copying the appropriate keyframe poses to the keyframes called out on the x-sheet, very much like you did in Exercise 11-1 with the image map sequence.

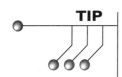

TIP

If you render 128x128 thumbnail images of the 11 lip sync poses, you can use the thumbnails with Magpie (see Appendix H) to do lip sync track analysis.

Exercise 11-2: It's the Moody Guy Again

This exercise is an extension of Exercise 10-1, but for the face rather than the entire body.

1. Load scene file EXER1102.LWS from the Chapter 11 directory of the Companion CD-ROM.

To review from Chapter 10, let's suppose the character starts off in a normal pose, then is given some very saddening news by an opponent we don't see. Suppose the opponent then threatens the character, frightening him. Next, the opponent ridicules the character, causing the character's fear to transition to anger. Finally, the character's anger causes the opponent to leave, and the character exults in his victory. That's four major emotional poses: sadness, fear, anger, and exultation.

2. Using the Bones and Null controls for the sample Head object, animate the character from normal through sadness, fear, a quick burst into anger, and finally a victorious exultation. The following four Figures, 11-9 through 11-12, may give you some ideas for what poses to use.

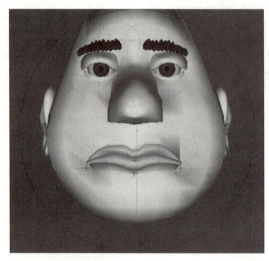

Figure 11-9: Key pose for sad.

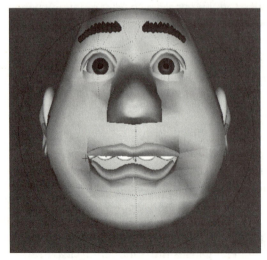

Figure 11-10: Key pose for fear.

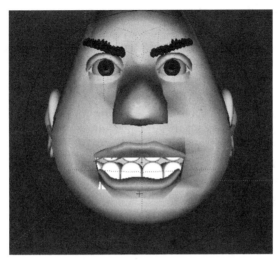

Figure 11-11: Key pose for anger.

Figure 11-12: Key pose for exultation.

3. Experiment with the timing and spline controls (tension, continuity, and bias) for each transition and observe the overall effect. Which transitions do you have to stretch out? Which work better when shortened?

4. When you're satisfied with the timing of each transition, save the scene file under a new name.

Timing is still everything. When you set the timing for an emotional transition, you must hold each stage in the transition just long enough for the audience to read it, and no longer. The best acting job in the world is useless if it flashes by so quickly the audience can't see it, or drags on so long the audience is bored and their attention wanders. The timing of a transition alone can make a big difference in how your audience perceives a character. Imagine a character taking several seconds for a transition from confusion to comprehension. You might think this character is a little slow. On the other hand, compress this same transition to a half-dozen frames, and the character appears to be very bright, even inspired. Timing emotional transitions is another skill that takes time and practice to develop. Experiment, practice, and experiment some more; you can never have too much experience in timing character animation.

Avoid twins in posing the face, just as you would for the character's body.

Avoid twins in posing the face, just as you would for the character's body. A perfectly symmetric face is rarely found in nature, and few human expressions are balanced. The smirk, sneer, lopsided grin, and wink are just a few of the stronger examples of one-sided facial expressions. Even blinks can be slightly offset to good effect, as you might observe in the early parts of *Toy Story*.

The principle of overlapping action applies to emotional transitions, too. You should offset the keyframes of each facial feature. If the eyes, mouth, and other features all peak at the same frame, the transition will look artificial. The action of the eyes generally leads the transition, just as it leads other actions, with the mouth following last. The mouth is controlled less by reflex and instinct than by volition, so while the eyes immediately react to a situation, it takes a conscious decision by the character to move the mouth. This is why a surprised person's mouth may hang open; they simply don't think about doing something with it. Therefore, keep the eyes under tight control. The eyes should be the first part of the face to animate, and even in extreme situations the eyes are the last part of the face to lose control—eyes rolling up in the head as the character loses consciousness, for example. The mouth lags behind and represents conscious decisions rather than reflexes. The mouth can lie more easily, but is often betrayed by the more truthful actions of the eyes.

A facial pose should precede the sound or phoneme the action is supposed to emphasize. In lip sync, for example, the lower lip should curl under the upper teeth several frames before the "F" sound occurs. The lead time for emotional transitions is even longer. If a head movement or facial expression is intended to emphasize a word, the entire action should end just when the word begins.

A good rule of
thumb is,
"Deeds before
words."

For example, look at the x-sheets in Appendix F while listening to the FINESTHR.WAV sound clip. The word "this" has a strong vocal emphasis. You might choose to emphasize this word with a strong facial expression as well, and perhaps a nod of the head. This visual emphasis should completely precede the sound. The nod and the facial transition to a strong key pose should end just at the first frame of the "th" phoneme, at which time the lip sync poses should dominate. If you lap the action over the sound, the action will look stilted and poorly rehearsed. If you run the action and sound at the same time, it will look out of sync. If you run the action after the sound, it will look like a first reading by a very poor actor. When you are animating for lip sync or emotional transitions synched to a soundtrack, a good rule of thumb is, "Deeds before words."

Be selective in what you empasize. If you bob the character's head at every lip synched syllable, they'll look spastic. When you first look at a lip sync x-sheet, look for the emotional or dramatic high and low points of the passage, and start off with just those for emphasis. If you need emphasis, you can add poses to support the major points; but it's better to start off with too few emphases in the action than too many.

Exercise 11-3: Lip Sync Using Bones

1. Reload scene file EXER1102.LWS again.

2. Create a series of 11 poses, comparable to the images in Figure 11-2, in frames 4 through 15.

3. Save the modified scene file as PHONEME1.LWS.

4. Using the lip sync poses you just created and the x-sheets from Exercise 11-1, lip sync the Finest Hour sound clip with a dramatic reading. The easiest way to do this is select the Head object, move to the first lip sync pose frame, and create a keyframe for Selected Item and Descendants for each keyframe called for in the x-sheets. This, however, creates lots of unnecessary keyframes for the eyes and other parts of the objects that are not involved with lip sync. A more careful procedure is to create the keyframes for the MouthParentNull, MouthUp, and JawBone. This is, of course, slightly more work.

5. Add eye and head movements to the animation, as discussed in Chapter 4.

6. Save the scene file under a new name.

7. Set the beginning frame of the animation to frame 16, the first frame of the actual lip sync. Render an animation, from frame 16 to the last frame of the lip sync.

8. Dub the FINESTHR.WAV file over the rendered animation. How did you do? Is the emphasis on the correct frame for each action?

Exercise 11-4: MTSE Revisited

If you haven't figured it out already, you can use the Save Transformed function to create a series of Metamorph target objects from a Boned head animation. If standard poses are acceptable, it's much easier to experiment with timing transitions using an MTSE Envelope than individual Bone motion graphs.

1. Reload the scene file you saved from Exercise 11-2. Select the Head object.

2. Go to the first key pose, normal, and open the Objects Panel.

3. Click Save Transformed and save the object as NORMAL1.LWO.

4. Close the Objects Panel.

5. Go to the next key pose and repeat steps 2, 3, and 4 for the remaining key poses. You should end up with objects for normal, sad, fear, anger, and exultation.

6. Reload the final scene file you saved from Exercise 10-2.

7. In the Objects Panel, replace the existing head with the NORMAL1.LWO object. You may have to adjust the Y-axis offset; I suggest shifting the entire Y-axis motion graph up 0.1, to preserve whatever keyframes you made for the original head.

8. Follow the procedures you learned in Chapter 3 to set up an MTSE sequence, with NORMAL1.LWO as the base object and the sad, fear, anger, and exultation objects as the targets.

9. Edit the MTSE envelope to vary the timing for each key pose and observe the overall effect. How well can you match the MTSE sequence to the body animation you created in Exercise 10-2? How much does the face add to the emotional message of the animation?

10. Save the finished scene file under a new name.

Note that by using MTSE objects for the whole head, you can vary the timing only for the entire expression, rather than the individual Bone control poses, and that the eyes are locked in position and no longer tracking a Null. If you plan to create MTSE objects, you may want to use Parented eyeballs and eyelids that will not be included by the Save Transformed function.

If you want the convenience and speed of animating a Boned face separately, but still want the flexibility to tweak it along with the entire body, you can use the Load From Scene function to merge two or more complete animations. This enables you to create a separate animation for each Bone Child object—for example, the head and each hand—then merge them with the body animation.

Exercise 11-5: Pull Yourself Together

This exercise shows you how to merge Boned animation sequences from different scene files.

1. Reload the final scene file you saved from Exercise 11-4.

2. In the Objects Panel, delete all the MTSE target objects, but leave NORMAL1.LWO. Close the panel.

3. Make a note of the Parent assignment for NORMAL1.LWO.

4. With NORMAL1.LWO selected, open the Motion Graph Panel. Save the motion graph as HEAD1105.MOT. Close the panel.

5. Open the Scene Panel. Shift all keyframes 15 frames. This creates space at the beginning of the scene for the setup frames of the scene you created in Exercise 11-2, which you are about to merge into this scene.

6. Open the Objects Panel again. Clear NORMAL1.LWO.

7. Click Load From Scene. Select the scene file you saved at the end of Exercise 11-2. Close the panel.

8. Select the Head object you just merged into this scene. Assign it to the same Parent as NORMAL1.LWO.

9. With the new head selected, open the Motion Graph Panel. Load the HEAD1105.MOT motion file you saved in step 4. Close the panel.

If all went well, you now have a Boned face Parented to the body you animated in Exercise 10-2, with all the appropriate motions. At this point, the entire animation for body and head is accessible for tweaking; you still have complete control. Unfortunately, the screen redraw times and the length of Selected Item and Scene Panel lists are rather unwieldy. Again, character animation with LightWave 3D is a matter of choosing your trade-offs.

A hybrid Boned/Image Mapped head can be much simpler to set up and a great deal faster to animate.

In some situations, you may be able to combine Bone or Metamorph animation of a head object with image sequences for the mouth. This hybrid approach allows a greater dramatic range and more interactive control for the rest of the face, while making it easier for you to coordinate lip sync. You can set up the image map sequence at the beginning, as soon as you have an x-sheet, and animate the character's face to match the maps. Since most of the controls for a fully-boned face are around the mouth, a hybrid head can be much simpler to set up and a great deal faster to animate, especially on slower computers. The disadvantage of this approach is that the character's style must be compatible with a painted-on mouth, as shown in the first part of this chapter.

If they are appropriate for your character, bump maps to add wrinkles can be a nice finishing touch to smiles and other expressions that crinkle up parts of the face. The only method currently available in LightWave 3D for animating bump maps is as an image sequence, so you are better off adding the wrinkle maps at the very end, after the action has been finalized. At that time, you can add wrinkle notes to the x-sheet, specifying the depth of the wrinkles at particular frames. With these notes, you can create a batch file to duplicate bump maps of different wrinkle depths, following the procedures in Exercise 14-4. This is just like lip sync; maybe we should call it "crinkle sync."

Morph Gizmo

At the time of this writing, NewTek is still developing a plug-in known as Morph Gizmo. If development goes according to schedule, Morph Gizmo should be available soon after this book is published. I don't have any reliable screen shots, but the anticipated features of this plug-in are worth mentioning.

Morph Gizmo is an extension to the concept behind MTSE. You can load several metamorph objects in a chain and control how much each object is weighted for each frame. The great leap forward for Morph Gizmo over MTSE is that the new plug-in automatically detects what part of an object is different from the base object, and only acts on those points. For example, suppose you raised the left eyebrow of a character and used Save Transformed to create a new object, then did the same for the right eyebrow, and loaded both modified objects into Morph Gizmo with the original object. Morph Gizmo would enable you to control the percentage of change between the base object and either or both new raised-eyebrow objects. The rest of the character would not change, because only the eyebrow points were different from the base object.

Presumably, you would create a library of objects that each contain a single facial feature at an extreme pose. Combined in Morph Gizmo, this would give you completely independent, highly interactive control over every facial feature of a character. The user interface for Morph Gizmo may be markedly different at release, but at the time of this writing the morph percentage for each target could be set interactively using a slider control. If all goes well, Morph Gizmo will be a major new character animation tool for LightWave 3D animators.

I'll be writing more about Morph Gizmo as the information becomes available. For the latest information, new files, and exercises, check out Ventana's Online Updates web page (see Appendix B for details).

Moving On

This wraps up the animator part of this book. If you have completed all the exercises and continue to practice, you should be able to adequately animate any character a TD sets up for you. Part II, "The Technical Director," shows you how to create your own characters from scratch, and set them up so you can animate them as easily as possible.

The Technical Director

The seven chapters of this section describe the responsibilities of the technical director (TD). The TD is the CGI counterpart of most of the skilled trades that support traditional cel or clay animation. Even if you are only interested in animating, you should read and work through these chapters. Understanding the TD's job can make you a better animator, because it gives you a better understanding of how your tools and materials are made. If you aren't sure whether you want to be an animator or a TD, working through these exercises should help you make up your mind. If you have more fun or success with this part of the book, you may want to consider working as a TD. If you like both parts equally, you may want to find a shop that lets TDs animate.

The exact duties of a TD vary from studio to studio. As a TD, you may be responsible for modeling, shading, lighting, and other technical parts of the character animation process. Studios usually look for TDs with strong backgrounds in computer graphics theory. If the studio uses LightWave 3D, they will also want you to be familiar with LightWave 3D and the operating system and hardware used to run it. Don't neglect your programming skills, either, as you may be called on to write custom shaders or other plug-ins.

TDs often work closely with animators and other members of the production team to solve problems. As a technical director, you may have final responsibility for the working character models. If there is a problem in animating the character, you will be called on to fix it, or perhaps simply to make an awkward setup easier for the animator to work with. You may also be responsible for the lighting, texturing, and other factors that affect the final look of the animation. Even if these responsibilities fall to an art director or lighting designer, you may be called on to help them solve technical problems.

On Being a TD

Try to maintain a sense of humor. A large part of a TD's job is fixing problems, so you are more likely to hear complaints than compliments. This is not a reflection on your work; if you do your job well, the animators are too busy animating to thank you.

Never stop learning. No matter how much you know, there's always more to discover, and lots of other TDs and researchers are constantly pushing the state of the CGI art. At the least, you need to keep up on hardware and software developments, known bugs, and workarounds, just to keep your own systems humming along. Keep your eyes and ears open!

"I have one piece of advice for all senior technical directors. Make certain you are at least two steps ahead of anything being taught in a school." — Steph Greenberg

You need to know enough about your hardware and operating system software to keep things running, but don't spend more than 10 percent of your time on it or you'll get pegged as a network wrangler. Stay creative!

You should subscribe to and read *Transactions on Graphics* and other ACM SIGGRAPH publications referenced in the Bibliography. This is where many new techniques first appear in public. Techniques and algorithms published here tend to show up in desktop CGI software within a few years. The most useful algorithms show up in proprietary animation studio software as soon as the TDs can figure out how to implement them. Join ACM, and if there is a SIGGRAPH chapter near you, see if you can learn anything useful from their meetings. If not, go once in a while anyway, just to network.

Go to SIGGRAPH every year. Take it out of your personal vacation time if you have to, but twist your employer's arm to send you as a legitimate "continuing education" business expense. Go to the classes and sessions, talk to your professional colleagues, network at the parties. Buy the *Proceedings* and read them when you get home. You can learn more in one conversation with the right person at SIGGRAPH than in most of the technical sessions. If you've never gone to SIGGRAPH, don't make the mistake of trying to fit it all in one day. I've always gone for every exhibit day, and usually the pre- and post-exhibit sessions if I can, and I've never managed to see everything and everyone I wanted to.

There is little enough published specifically on LightWave 3D that I recommend you buy it all. There aren't many books; the few available titles are inexpensive, and most of them have something useful to offer. Subscriptions to *VTU* and *LightWavePro* magazines are dirt cheap compared to other product-centered journals, and their quality is better than fair by industry standards. I also highly recommend you subscribe to *3D Artist* magazine for its tutorials. If you feel like following industry news, read *Computer Graphics World* magazine. Read other trade magazines if you find them useful to your job; I've found most of them either too heavy on industry news or too light on LightWave 3D information.

As regular practice to hone your skills, make sure you can duplicate a popular piece of TD work at least as well as the original, preferably better. The lag time inherent in getting a piece of animation to public display is sometimes enough for the rest of the industry to catch up on a technique, and a popular piece tends to make clients ask for something like it. Even if you don't use it for a client job, it's something to put on your demo reel.

Even though you should strive for perfection, remember that true realism is a chimera. There is no such thing as a perfectly realistic CGI rendering, especially since most "real" shots in the mass media are now retouched or edited in some way. Learn how to fake reality enough to satisfy clients and to judge where you can afford to cut corners.

Learn everything you can from traditional methods and sources. The sources cited in the Bibliography are just a start. Hollywood, Broadway, and Madison Avenue have been refining lighting design, set design, special effects, cinematography, and other CGI-related arts for the better part of a century, and the basic principles don't change. You can learn a lot of the basics from inexpensive books. For the technical scoop on current film special effects, I like *Cinefex* magazine. Most of the behind-the-scenes material is on mechanical and optical effects, but more of the reporting has been on CGI lately, and you never know where you'll pick up a useful idea.

Advanced Modeling for Character Design

This chapter discusses the TD's contribution to a typical character design process. The exercises show you Modeler and Layout techniques for both Parented and Boned limbs, including Joint Compensation, Muscle Flexing, and a complete cartoon-style hand. Along the way you'll learn about tricks, tools, and resources to help you build characters that are efficient and easy to animate.

The Typical Character Design Process

As a technical director you work with a variety of people to design the characters the animators use. You have to cope with suggestions and direction from just about everybody—from the director, layout artist, animator, and sometimes, it seems, the janitor. Everybody has a different idea of how the character should look and work. The final responsibility for the working models, however, is all yours.

Whenever you discuss character design you should keep a few critical factors in mind. These factors determine the levels of detail, flexibility, and versatility you must build into the character (and its object, motion, and map libraries). They may not make a lot of difference to the rest of the production team, but they can make or break your end of the project. These factors are:

◈ **Distance.** How far will this character be from the camera? How much screen space will it actually occupy in its closest shot? If the character is just an extra, seen only in the distance and occupying only a few dozen pixels of screen resolution, you can cut all kinds of corners, save lots of time and effort, and the finished product will look just as good. If the character will appear in several extreme close shots, you must plan for more detailed modeling, higher resolution maps, and more subtle animation controls in the face.

◈ **Speed.** If the character is to move very fast, you can rely on motion blur to obscure any minor flaws or crudeness in the character design for the faster sequences, and focus your resources on more detailed modeling for the slower intervals. A character who always runs at top speed, for example, requires little more for those sequences than a detailed anticipation pose, a follow-through pose for stopping, and a run pose that looks good in motion blur (perhaps with multiple legs in different positions).

◈ **Style.** Is the character to have a very abstract style, or does the director favor photorealism? Can you get by with a simple surface color, or do you need to plan more complex models and layers of maps to get a realistic skin appearance? Can the surfaces remain relatively rigid and look artificial, or must you build them to be fully animated and appear organic?

◈ **Range of movement.** Ideally, every character you build should have at least the range of movement of the equivalent real creature or person. Practically, building such characters would break every deadline and budget you ever come up against. You must make every possible compromise in the construction of the character, without affecting the quality of the finished image.

If the storyboards never show the character raising its arms above shoulder level, you may not have to build that range of motion into the character. If the character is written as surly and nasty, you will probably not have to build its face to express benevolence or compassion. On the other hand, if the character is extraordinarily flexible or mutable (a classic cartoon wiseguy, for example), you can plan on creating several times the usual number of objects, animation controls, and maps.

Your performance in design meetings is just as important as your performance with LightWave 3D.

As a team member, your performance in design meetings is just as important as your performance with LightWave 3D's Modeler. You can exercise and develop your sense of tact by carefully questioning parts of the proposed script, storyboard, or layout that have a disproportionate effect on your workload.

For example, suppose the storyboard calls for a character to reach into a trouser pocket, extract a key, open the door with it, and the camera then cuts to the next shot, where the character drops the key on the entryway table. Nowhere else does the character pull anything out of that pocket, nor do the key or lock have any further effect on the story. It's a throw-away and should be discarded if possible.

You might propose that the character stage the action of reaching into its pocket, then cut on that action to an interior shot of the door, with the sound of the key going into the lock and turning. The rest of the shot is just as before. This approach saves all the expense of modeling and animating the trouser pocket and the complex arm-and-hand movement of fishing for the key.

Always try to have a better idea to suggest before you criticize or complain about something, and if you must complain, state your reasons for doing so in as productive and team-spirited a way as possible. You're much more likely to "get your way" if you point out where a change will save money, effort, or time for others as well as yourself. Keeping a positive tone doesn't cost you a thing, and keeping a production team's morale up through a long project is a lot more important than saving a couple of hours' work on a one-shot model.

Looks a Little Sketchy to Me

The usual tool for discussing character design is the sketch. Even if you are a lightning-fast modeler, anyone deserving the word "artist" in their job title will be able to sketch a figure faster than you can model it. Get used to pencils and paper, if you aren't already. And don't be shy about not being able to draw, if you come from the "propeller-head" side of computer graphics. I rarely attempt anything more character-oriented than a stick figure, myself, and there are plenty of working CGI professionals who could say the same.

The obvious advantage of pencil sketching is that it's cheap; you don't need a computer, everybody in a meeting can have one, it's easy to make revisions. You can start with a fairly light, hesitant line and firm it up or change it as the discussion progresses, and the product is easy to reproduce, fax, or digitize.

The disadvantage to pencil sketching is that it's not a 3D medium, so something that looks good on paper can turn out to be completely worthless in the computer. Caveat emptor.

While you have your four or so factors firmly in mind, the other members of the design team have their own ideas and concerns. The character usually evolves with a lot of pushing and grinding: everybody pushes their own agendas and grinds their own axes. If things go well, the character develops toward a design that helps tell the story, is economical to model, and is reasonably easy to animate. Sometimes the end design is rather far from the first concept, and sometimes it's pretty close to the original.

Figure 12-1: Early character sketch for "Easy Come, Easy Go."
Copyright 1996 Mike Comet.

Figure 12-1 is one of the earliest character sketches for Fred, the lead character of the example script in Appendix D. This was drawn by the film's technical director, Mike Comet, based on some verbal descriptions and a really simple stick-figure of my own, which I won't inflict on you. Even a simple figure like this can communicate the actions that define a character.

Figure 12-2: Section of storyboard sketch for "Easy Come, Easy Go."

Figure 12-2 is another step in Fred's evolution, as drawn by storyboard artist Brian Kelly. Again, the drawing captures an action that defines the character. At this point, the drawings also refine the surface appearances and ranges of motion that the TD will be called on to create.

Figure 12-3: Collage of early character objects.

Figure 12-3 is a collage of various stages in the modeling process. Mike roughed out the head first (inset left), and I ran some animation tests on it and came back with some suggestions. In between that we discussed body proportions and clothing (center), and Mike ran range-of-motion experiments on Fred's knee, hip, shoulder, and elbow joints. Finally, Mike put together all the changes and modeled the head's details (inset right): glasses, hat, hair, and mustache.

This is not too far from the finished version of Fred and is certainly good enough for more detailed animation and layout tests. If we had tried to jump straight from the script or storyboards to modeling and animating Fred, I don't think we would have ever gotten this far.

Once you start putting models into the computer, there is a very strong temptation to leave them alone. The pencil-sketch design process is cheap enough that it enables you to go back and revise or throw out materials without cutting out that "pound of flesh nearest one's heart."

Once you start putting models into the computer, there is a very strong temptation to leave them alone.

Nuts & Bolts

There are four general approaches in LightWave 3D to modeling an animated character: Parented, Bones, Metamorphosis, and Replacement.

Parented object hierarchies are relatively easy to model, and are fast and simple to animate as well. The individual objects don't have to be designed to deform; the animator simply moves and rotates the objects "as is."

Unfortunately, the joints between Parented objects are difficult to conceal, and they destroy the illusion of life unless the character is supposed to have visible seams. Parented hierarchies are best suited for puppets, robots, machines, and creatures with external skeletons like insects, arachnids, and silly English kinniggits.

Boned hierarchies work well for characters with internal skeletons and more flexible exteriors, and even invertebrates and squashy characters like classic cartoons. Bones enable the animator to pose a seamless object, eliminating the gaps and breaks in surfaces typical of Parented objects. A Boned character eliminates the management headaches of large object libraries, too, since one object is simply re-posed for every action.

Bones are especially useful for actions that require motion through long arcs, which require a lot of intermediary objects for both Metamorphosis and Replacement techniques. Since most creatures with a skeleton tend to make at least a few long-arc motions, Bones is a popular approach for character animation. For hips, knees, shoulders, elbows, and the like, it's hard to beat.

The down side to Boned characters is the relative imprecision of building the character in the first place. With other techniques, the available range of animation for a character is pretty cut-and-dried from the modeling side. Parented joints will go no farther than the joint is designed, Replacement models have no leeway at all, and even Metamorphosis objects have a limited envelope that the animator can completely anticipate by referring to a thumbnail sheet.

In contrast, you must first model a Boned character in LightWave 3D's Modeler, then load it into Layout to add the Bones. You're not quite sure how strong an effect the Bones will have, or exactly where they will affect the object's mesh until you try it out. Character design with Bones requires much more trial and error than the other techniques.

Metamorphosis is an animation technique for characters—or parts of them—that have a lot of detail, that repeatedly perform similar or derivative actions, and that would be a real headache to animate using Bones. In other words, this technique shoves a large load of the animator's work onto the TD.

Modeling characters for Metamorph animation is a balance of modeling constraints and benefits. On the one hand, Metamorph is very picky about point and polygon counts, and you can ruin an object by accidentally deleting a single point. On the other hand, Metamorph lets you use just about every tool in Layout that modifies the object, plus most of the useful tools for organic work in Modeler. Metamorph animation excels at heads and hands, items that you can fill libraries with, reuse, and add to every time you animate them.

Pure Replacement characters require a new object for each pose or change in the character. This is usually the most labor-intensive approach and provides the least flexibility for the animator. In special circumstances it can be more cost-effective to use pure Replacement.

One example would be a group of walking or running characters, critical as a group but not individually important or central to the shot. You could create a library of models for a single character, one for each pose in the motion cycle. Using procedures detailed later in this chapter, you could then generate a larger library of derivative objects. By writing an ObjList script for each character, you could easily create a whole crowd of unique characters designed to execute similar actions.

The disadvantage, obviously, is that the number of objects to be tracked quickly gets out of hand. The advantage is that you can use any modeling technique you like, because the object replacement functions in LightWave 3D do not require consistent point and polygon counts or distribution.

Have You Done Your Homework?

I have to assume that you are already familiar with the basic modeling tools for LightWave 3D, both in Modeler and Layout. If I tried to review every modeling tool you might use for character design, I'd have to duplicate most of NewTek's manuals, and there would be no room left for the animation exercises! If you have not already done so, you should work through the Modeler tutorials in the LightWave 3D User Guide.

A Look at the Seamy Side: Joint Design for Parented Objects

The tools for building an object for a Parented hierarchy are so basic that I won't go into a step-by-step tutorial describing them. Essentially, you can create the sliding surface of any rotating joint by using the Lathe tool, or create a round primitive and modify it as necessary.

There are three basic joint types for character animation: the hinge, the universal joint, and the ball and socket joint.

The simplest is the *hinge*, a joint with a single degree of freedom. That is, it can only rotate around one axis. The human knee and elbow are examples of hinge joints, for while they can move slightly in other axes, this is a strain on the joint and is more a matter of slop than design.

You can model a hinge with a simple cylinder. The socket, the hollow part of the joint, must be cut away enough to allow the pin, the cylindrical center, to rotate through the intended range of motion. For example, a hinged knee requires that the thigh and shin objects be cut away at the back, so the calf of the lower leg does not overlap the back of the thigh when the knee is bent. Look at the objects in the Puppet character from Chapter 6 for other examples of hinge joint cutaways.

The next joint type is the *universal joint*, or U-joint, which has two degrees of freedom. The wrist and shoulder are universal joints. The wrist can rotate the hand up and down and side to side, but twisting is a job for the forearm. The shoulder can rotate the arm to the side, on LightWave 3D's Z-axis, and forward and back on the X-axis.

You can model a universal joint with two interdependent hinge joints, but I recommend skipping straight to a spherical socket. It's much simpler. If you really want to do a universal joint, take a look at a marine gimbal or a car's driveshaft U-joint.

Despite the apparent flexibility of the shoulder's combination of motions, it is not a true *ball and socket joint* like the hip. The hip has three degrees of freedom; it can rotate both forward and to the side, and also twist around the long axis of the upper leg.

Modeling the ball and socket joint is nearly self-explanatory. Create a spherical cap for one object, usually the Child. Use the spherical part of the object as a Boolean tool to carve a matching cavity in the Parent object. That's it; you have a ball and socket joint.

Incidentally, any joint with more degrees of freedom can substitute for lower-order joints. You can animate a ball and socket as any of the three types, and a universal joint can move as itself and as a hinge, but the hinge construction can only move as a hinge. I prefer to build ball and socket joints for everything, just in case the character is called on to perform an action the joints weren't designed for.

To help align the objects in Layout, I like to mark the center of a joint's rotation with a 3D crosshair. I put one of these in a Parent object wherever a Child object will be attached. You can build a crosshair by adding six vertices in three perpendicular pairs, one pair each on the X-, Y-, and Z-axes. Space the points just far enough apart that you will be able to see them, but try to keep them inside the Parent object. This forms a 3D crosshair like a toy jack, which is much easier to work with in Layout than a single reference point.

Exercise 12-1: Is There an Entomologist in the House? (Optional)

If you're really eager for some practice at constructing Parented object hierarchies, try building a bug. Insect, lobster, arachnid, whatever; just make sure it's got an external skeleton.

Check out a book on comparative entomology from your local library. I like Fox and Fox, *Introduction to Comparative Entomology,* for its line drawings, but a volume with more photographs would probably be more helpful. For range of motion and other constraints, you should refer to the Chapter 7 section on animation guidelines for multilegged critters.

Failing that, get down to your nearest seafood restaurant and buy a lobster or crab dinner, and insist they bring out the whole thing. Hang out by the tank for a while and watch how the lobsters move, too. Take your study model apart carefully when you eat, and bring the shell home in a doggy bag for closer study. If you can't finish your model in a couple of days, you need to make sure the shell is completely clean!

Rollin' the Bones

Designing for Boned animation is one of the easier modeling tasks. Bones are relatively tolerant of your modeling procedures and they don't care much what order you created the points they will be pushing around. Your biggest challenge in modeling for Bones is planning an object that the Bones won't warp into garbage and that can reach the range of motions the animator needs without using umpty-zillion Bones to do it.

Designing for a joint's range of motion is a matter of balancing the overlapping influence of the adjoining Bones so the result looks plausible.

Note that I did not say realistic, just plausible. LightWave 3D's Bones are useful and powerful tools, but I don't know anybody patient enough to animate the handful of controls you'd need to realistically emulate every perceptible muscle in the human body. If you want photorealism, you are better off trying Replacement animation with a whole lot of very detailed sculpting.

Probably the most popular use of Bones is in the animation of skeletal joints. The nice people at NewTek have even come up with some extra functions specifically to help you do this: Joint Compensation and Muscle Flexing.

Joint Compensation is intended to reposition the cross sections of a joint as it flexes, trying to maintain its internal volume and avoid the appearance of a kinked hose.

Muscle Flexing simulates the bulging of muscles on the inward surfaces of the joint's Parent and Child Bones when the Child Bone rotates on its Pitch axis. This is a handy function with lots of other uses, as well.

Sound interesting, useful even? Then let's move right in to learning how to build Bones skeletal joints.

Exercise 12-2: Create a Boned Joint for an Elbow

This exercise walks you through the procedure for building a Boned hinge joint. It covers range of motion, Joint Compensation, and Muscle Flexing.

1. Open scene file EXER1202.LWS, which you can find in the Chapter 12 directory of the Companion CD-ROM. This scene has an Arm object already loaded, a cylinder with a subdivided middle section. Select the Arm object. Click the Bones button. Press p to open the Skeleton Panel.

2. Click Add Bone. Rename the Bone to UpperArmBone.

3. Set the Rest Length to 4.0, turn on Scale Strength by Rest Length, and leave Strength at the default of 100%.

4. Turn on Limited Range and set Minimum and Maximum to 1.0.
   These are the default settings for the upper arm bone of the arm you are building. They set the area of influence for the Bone, that is, how far away this Bone can exert an influence to move a point.

5. Click Add Child Bone. Rename the new Bone to LowerArmBone.
   When you create a Child Bone, it automatically inherits the Skeleton Panel settings of its Parent Bone. LowerArmBone now has the same settings as UpperArmBone, as shown in Figure 12-4.

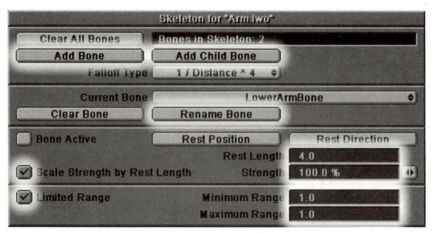

Figure 12-4: Skeleton Panel with initial settings for LowerArmBone.

6. Click Continue to close the Skeleton Panel.

7. Select the UpperArmBone. Move it to 0, 0, -4. Make a keyframe for this item, then press r to set this as the rest position and rotation for the Bone, and to make the Bone active.
   A dotted outline appears at the maximum effective radius of the Bone, telling you the Bone is active.

8. Select the LowerArmBone. It's already in the position you want, with its pivot in the center of the Arm object. Make a keyframe for this item, then press r to set the rest position and rotation and activate the Bone.

9. Select the UpperArmBone. Click Create Key, click Selected Item and Descendants, and click OK. Create another key at frame 30.
   This sets the baseline position and rotation for both Bones. These are very simple default settings, nothing fancy.

10. Go to frame 15. Select LowerArmBone. Change the Bone's Pitch to -135 and create a key at frame 15. Open the Motion Graph Panel and use the Spline Controls to make a graph like Figure 12-5. When you are finished, click Use Motion to close the Motion Graph Panel.

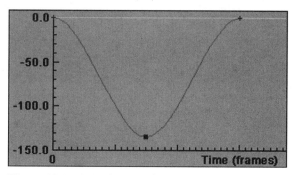

Figure 12-5: A motion graph to loop the flexing of the Boned arm.

This motion graph loops smoothly, with ease-in and -out at the extremes of the motion, making it easier for you to study.

11. Make a preview. Play the preview, at 6 fps if necessary so you can study the Bones' deformation of the arm object.
    Note the folding of the arm near the LowerArmBone pivot (see Figure 12-6). This doesn't look very good unless you are animating a garden hose.

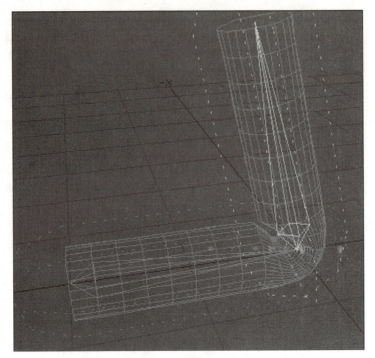

Figure 12-6: Kink in the flexing of the Boned arm.

Let's see how we can fix this problem, using Joint Compensation.

12. Open the Skeleton Panel again. Select LowerArmBone. Turn on the Joint Compensation and Joint Compensation for Parent options. Close the panel.

    You can choose to only use Joint Compensation on one side of a joint, but you generally get better results using both sides. You can also experiment with the percentages; a negative setting will actually exaggerate the kink we're trying to fix.

13. Make another preview. In the Side view, frame 7 should look like Figure 12-7.

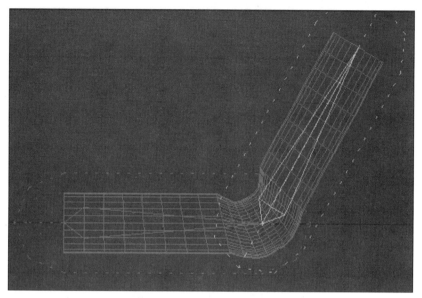

Figure 12-7: Flexing of the Boned arm with Joint Compensation on both sides at 100 percent.

This is much better, but what's with that bulge under the elbow at frame 7? Let's try nailing that down with another Bone.

14. Open the Skeleton Panel again. Select UpperArmBone. Click Add Child Bone. Rename the new Bone to ElbowBone.

    As noted earlier, a Child inherits the Parent Bone's settings. You need to change those settings since this Bone is supposed to have a much smaller influence.

15. Turn off Bone Active. Change Rest Length to 1.7, set the Minimum Range to 0.8, and close the panel.

16. Move the ElbowBone to the bottom center of the arm, 0, -0.6, 3.75, and flip it to 180 degrees Pitch so its pivot is near the elbow area. Press r to set the rest position and rotation. Create a key at frame 0 for this Bone.

    These settings place the Bone where its smaller area of influence will counteract the movement of the LowerArmBone. Take a look at frame 7 again. You should have something like Figure 12-8. Much better, isn't it?

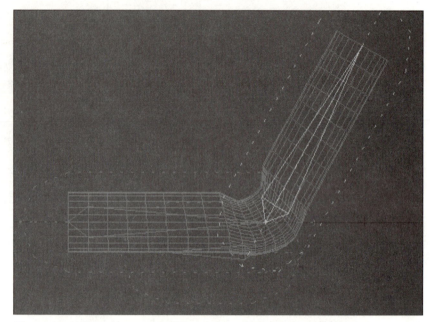

Figure 12-8: Flexed arm with Elbow Bone retarding unwanted bulge.

The last step in setting up a character's skeletal joint is turning on Muscle Compensation. This is a function designed to mimic the bulging of muscles as a joint rotates towards them. This is especially suited to joints like the elbow where opposing muscles tend to bunch up by compression.

17. Open the Skeleton Panel again. Select LowerArmBone. Turn on Muscle Flexing and Muscle Flexing for Parent. Close the panel.

    As with Joint Compensation, you can choose to use Muscle Flexing on only one side of a joint, but you generally get better results using both sides. You can also experiment with the percentages; a negative setting will make the "muscle" dimple rather than swell. Note that these effects only work with Bone rotation on the Pitch axis, so you'll have to align the Bones to Pitch in the direction you want the swells.

18. Make a preview. If you like your results, make an animation. You should end up with something like Figure 12-9 or EXER1202.AVI, which you can find in the Chapter 12 directory of the Companion CD-ROM.

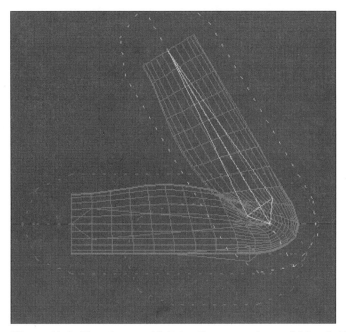

Figure 12-9: Flexed arm with Joint Compensation and Muscle Flexing.

You can use Muscle Flexing for some interesting special effects. The Child Bone that controls the flexing doesn't have to affect any points of its own. This enables you to set tiny Bones under the skin of a character, and use larger Child Bones as "handles" to control Muscle Flexing that distorts the skin. This can be a lot easier and faster to control than hunting around for and trying to accurately scale the smaller Bones.

Pinch an Inch

Bones can also be used to animate loose flesh or slack muscle, which is especially useful for overlapping action (see Chapter 5). The wider the interval between minimum and maximum Limited Range, the flabbier the behavior of the points affected by the Bones.

For especially loose masses you can borrow the motion files from the character's CG and delay it a few frames to create a first approximation of overlapping action.

Your concerns as TD are to make sure the object has enough points in the affected areas and that the Bones have the necessary position and settings. You also need to run a few basic tests, and document the results to hand over to the animator.

Let's try an example. The exercises in Chapter 6 resulted in a walk cycle with enough bounce to produce overlapping action in a more heavyset character. The Puppet character doesn't fit the bill, but maybe we can make a few changes.

Exercise 12-3: Create Boned Masses for Overlapping Action

1. Open the Modeler. Load the CHEST.LWO object from the Chapter 12 directory of the Companion CD-ROM.

2. Select the bottom polygons of the object and move them down to create an abdomen for the Puppet. Select the front polygons of the abdomen and subdivide them as in Figure 12-10.

   You need to make sure there are enough points for a smooth distortion of the belly by one or more Bones. When in doubt, more is usually better, as long as you don't run out of memory.

3. Save the object as BELLY01.LWO. Close the Modeler and open Layout.

4. Load scene EXER1203.LWS from the Chapter 12 directory of the Companion CD-ROM.

   This scene is essentially a duplicate of the last exercise in Chapter 6. It's a complete walk cycle, including starting and stopping, and has plenty of opportunities for overlapping action.

5. Select the Chest object. Open the Objects Panel and replace the Chest with the Belly object you just saved. Close the Objects Panel.

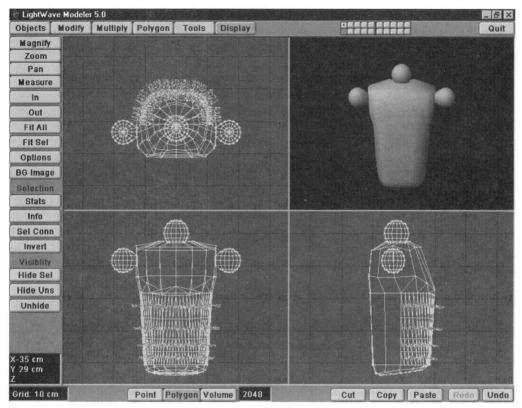

Figure 12-10: Stretched and subdivided torso for Puppet.

6. Open the Scene Panel. Hide all the objects and show the Belly object as a full wireframe. Close the Scene Panel.

7. Select the Belly object. Turn on the Center option, and arrange the views and Zoom Factor to give you a clear view of the object.

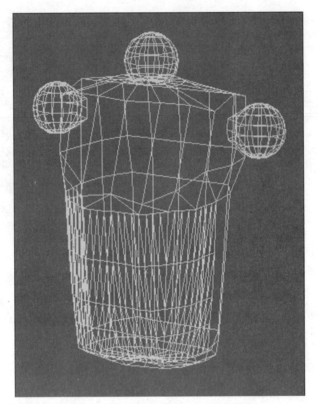

Figure 12-11: Belly object substituted for Chest.

8. Click on Bones in the Edit area and press p to open the Skeleton Panel.

9. Click Add Bone. Rename the Bone to BellyBone. You want the Bone to fit in the belly cavity of the character, so a fairly small Rest Length is needed. Set the Rest Length to 0.2, just for starters.

10. You want a fair amount of slack behavior for the Boned points, so set the Minimum for Limited Range to 0.01 and the Maximum to 0.15. Close the Skeleton Panel.

11. Keep the Bone in the middle of the subdivided area, with the Bone's pivot at the Belly object's pivot. When you're satisfied with the position, press r to set this as the Bone's rest position and activate the Bone. Make a keyframe for the Bone.

As it is, the Puppet appears to have a nice washboard set of abs. That just isn't funny. If you want to get a laugh, you'll have to give him a bit of a potbelly.

12. Move the Bone to about 0.05 on the Z-axis. You should end up with something like Figure 12-12.

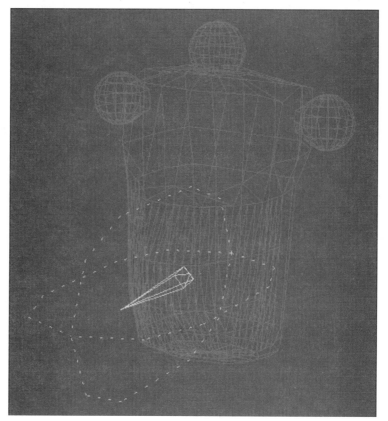

Figure 12-12: BellyBone positioned, set, and then moved to create a potbelly.

At this point you are ready to run some tests. Use whatever views give you a clear look at the BellyBone and Belly object, and experiment with moving and rotating the Bone. Push it until the object deforms enough to create rendering errors, and make notes about the limits. These notes should be given to the animator when the character is delivered, so he knows what can and can't be done with it.

In this case, the subdivisions of the belly give it a pretty good range of motion. You will probably run into grossly improbable (or just plain gross) poses before you actually see rendering errors.

If you'd like to play around with animating the BellyBone, try borrowing the motion of the Puppet_CG_Null and tweaking it a bit. The Y-Position motion graph for the CG_Null looks like Figure 12-13.

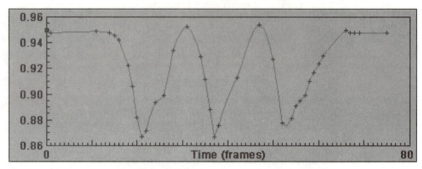

Figure 12-13: Puppet_CG_Null Y-Position motion graph from scene EXER1203.LWS.

You can save this motion, then select the BellyBone and load the motion. Shift frames 1 through 69 down about 5 frames, and the motion of the BellyBone will lag behind the rest of the Puppet enough to simulate a slack potbelly.

Shift the values for the graph up a bit, as well; the bottom of the BellyBone motion should probably be around -.07 or so, but the CG_Null drops a lot farther than that. You may end up with a motion graph like Figure 12-14.

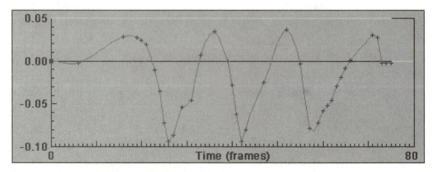

Figure 12-14: Modified BellyBone Y-Position motion graph.

You'll also need to shift the Heading values to get the BellyBone lined up facing forward again.

When you've tweaked it enough, try rendering an animation. Silly, isn't it?

Point & Polygon Density & Placement

No matter how powerful your computer, you will always be negotiating a balance between rendering speed, level of detail, hard drive space, and memory requirements. As the old joke goes, if you're not running out of memory, your scene isn't complicated enough.

Part of that balancing act is determining how many polygons you need and how many you can afford. More polygons generally respond to Bones' influence with better interpolation, and also render curves more smoothly. Fewer polygons redraw faster, use less memory, and are easier to edit when necessary.

One way to control the complexity of a character's objects is to place the polygons exactly where you need them. Some parts of a character need very few polygons and other areas need more. Shoes, mid-sleeves, or mid-legs with little or no motion or deformation can get by with fewer polygons, while joints and flexible masses of soft tissue require more subdivisions.

It's a good idea to plan for joint placement from the start of the modeling process, but not everything can be charted out in advance. Bone placement and range is especially tricky, and almost never exactly what you expect. Therefore, it's important that you develop the tools and skills to modify an object after you've made the first Bone assignments.

The first step in getting it right is to figure out what's wrong. Sometimes that's difficult, especially with a complex object or a very convoluted surface. Even front wireframe views can be misleading at times. Mapping a standard black grid onto the object is generally confusing, because once you zoom in you have no idea how the visible area relates to the rest of the object.

One of my favorite diagnostic tools is a simple color map (see Figure 12-15). With the colors running a continuous spectrum along one axis and hues ranging from saturation to gray along the other, you can instantly tell exactly where you are, even at high magnification. The regular gridlines give you a better indication of local distortions than the color gradations alone. I chose the white grid rather than black because I think it's less obtrusive when you're trying to evaluate the object's shape, but that's just my opinion.

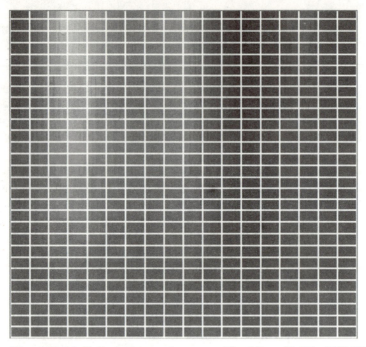

Figure 12-15. Full spectrum color map with white grid. File COLORS.TGA in the Chapter 12 directory of the Companion CD-ROM.

If you don't like this map, creating your own is fairly easy. I took a screen shot of the standard Windows color picker, with my display set to 24-bit color mode. I then used Adobe Photoshop to composite a white grid over it, being careful to match up the left and right borders.

You can apply this image to almost any object to get a better picture of how Bones, displacement maps, or other LightWave 3D functions are deforming it. I prefer to use Flat Planar mapping, as in Figure 12-16, but sometimes other mapping patterns are of use.

With that in mind, this color map is designed to tile horizontally so you can use it for cylindrical or spherical mapping, as shown in Figure 12-17. If you want it to tile in the other direction, rotate it 90 degrees and save it again, using whatever image editing application you prefer.

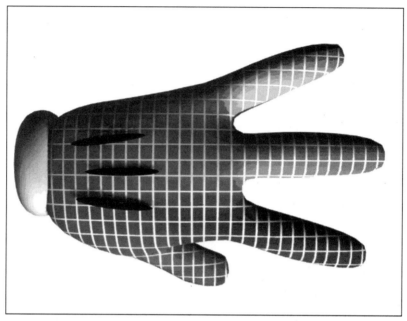

Figure 12-16: Color grid map applied to Hand object with Flat Planar mapping.

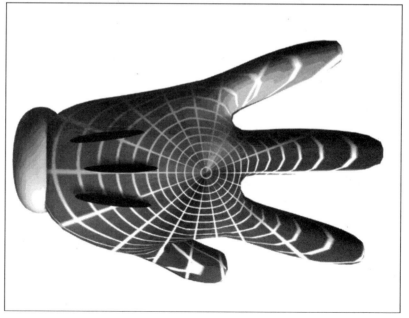

Figure 12-17: Color grid map applied to Hand object with spherical mapping.

Once you apply an appropriate reference grid map, you will get a much better picture of what's going on with your object's deformation and where you should be making revisions. For example, Figure 12-18 shows the point distribution and Bone placement of a character's hand.

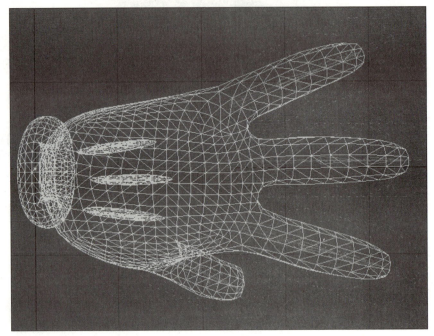

Figure 12-18: Character's hand object with Bones placed and active.

This is the same hand shown in Figure 12-16. The next figure, 12-19, shows the hand after the fingers are posed using Bones rotation.

Note the disproportionate stretching of some areas of the grid, especially directly behind each flexed knuckle. These areas are obviously being stretched more than they should, while adjoining areas are remaining almost untouched.

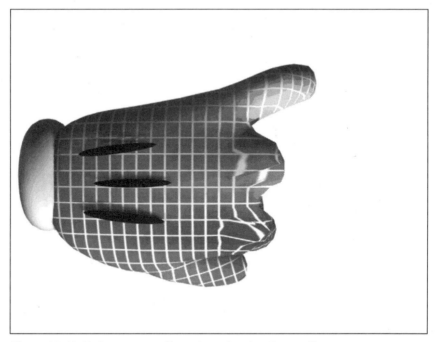

Figure 12-19: Reference map distortions showing Bones effects.

There are two operations that can repair this problem. One, increase the polygon count in the stretched area. Two, modify the Bone's Limited Range settings to spread the Bone's influence out more evenly.

Exercise 12-4: Subdividing Near a Bone

1. Create hard copies of screen shots and rendered images to act as guides for the following steps.

   Digging into a complex modeling operation without a map is like, well, getting into something complex without a map. Whatever your object is, you should have both a screenshot or rendered wireframe view and a rendered image of the object with a reference grid mapped onto it. Make sure both images are from the same angle; ideally, you should be able to hold them up to a light together and match them point for point.

2. Use the Volume selection tools to pick out the area of highest distortion, as in Figure 12-20.

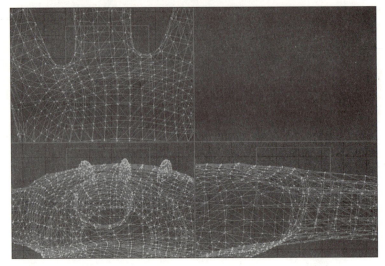

Figure 12-20: Volume selection of knuckle area to be subdivided.

For the example of the hand, the distorted area is immediately surrounding the knuckle, directly above the Bone's pivot. The selection area stops at the same level as the distortion of the reference grid. Wherever the grid lines are straight, there is no influence of the Bone, and any extra polygons would be wasted.

3. Change to Polygon mode. Choose the Subdivide tool. In the Subdivide Polygons Panel, select Smooth and click OK.

   The Subdivide operation should split each edge of the polygons in the selected volume in half, multiplying the points and polygons available for the Bone to deform.

4. Save the modified object under a new name.

   It's always best to keep the original object, just in case.

5. Return to Layout, open the Objects Panel, and replace the original object with the subdivided one.

   For the Hand, the scene looked like Figure 12-21 after the replacement.

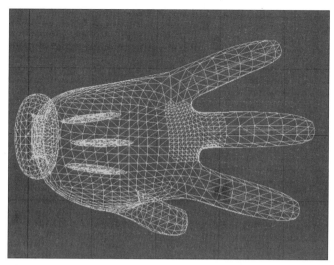

Figure 12-21: New Hand object with subdivided middle knuckle.

Let's take a look at what the subdivision does for the distortion pattern. Rendering the same frame with the bent-knuckle Bones pose as Figure 12-19 gives us Figure 12-22.

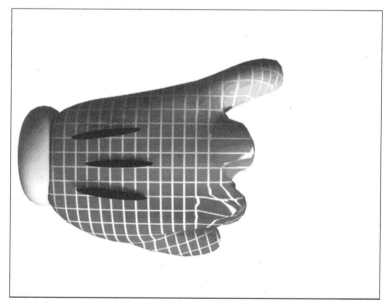

Figure 12-22: Subdivided Hand object after Bones distortion.

Uh oh. This isn't any better. There's less distortion in the back of the hand, but the distortion on the knuckle itself is even worse. An even smaller polygon has been stretched out by the Bone, to cover the same area as the larger one from the original object.

The remaining problem is the Bone's Limited Range setting. If you set the Limited Range minimum and maximum very close together, you don't give the Bone any space to perform a smooth deformation. It still comes down to which side of the border a point is on, there's no gray area; a point either moves completely along with the Bone, or it doesn't move at all.

In this case, the original Bone was set to a minimum range of .18, and a maximum of .20. Just .02 of a unit isn't very much for a smooth Bone deformation. Resetting the Limited Range to minimum .1 and maximum .2 gives a much better result, as shown in Figure 12-23.

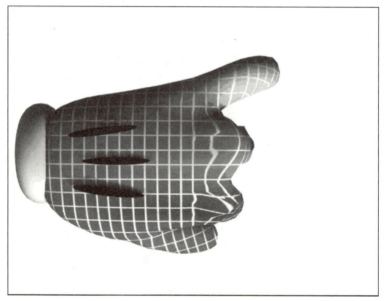

Figure 12-23: Subdivided Hand object after Bones Limited Range adjustments.

This moves some of the points within the Bone's range a little bit, others a lot, and out on the fringes it barely moves them at all. The result is a much more gradual distortion of the object, as shown by the reduced smearing of the grid lines and the more even distribution of stretching.

The point of this exercise is to demonstrate that, no matter how much you plan for Bones deformation, you will probably still have to do some tweaking to get just the right effect. It's not that difficult, just something you need to plan for if time estimates are important to your work.

Building Butterflies: Design for Metamorphosis

Modeling for Metamorph and MTSE animation is possibly the most restrictive task a LightWave 3D TD has to perform. The rigid requirements of identical point and polygon count and distribution automatically exclude most of your modeling tools.

If you make a mistake and add or delete a point, the difficulty of rematching the point order pretty much guarantees that you've ruined the object. You should therefore limit your modeling operations to tools that move points without adding or deleting them.

You can safely use all the Modify Panel functions in Modeler: Move, Rotate, Size, Stretch, Drag, Shear, Twist, Taper 1 and 2, Bend, Magnet, Vortex, and Pole 1 and 2.

If you are careful and consistent in setting them up, you can get away with using Patch, Skin, Morph, and other functions in the Multiply Panel. Be warned, any change in the settings produces an object with incompatible point and polygon counts and ordering.

You can also use MetaNURBS, if the source object and the Freeze Polygonal Detail settings remain the same.

One advantage Metamorph modeling has over other forms is that you get to use Layout tools as well. The Save Transformed function will save a copy of the currently selected object from the current frame, including all position, attitude, size, Metamorph, Bones deformation, and displacement map changes to the object's geometry.

This means you can use nearly any Layout function to modify an object, then save those changes in a permanent "snapshot" that will Metamorph perfectly with the original object. This opens up a lot of opportunities that would be difficult or nearly impossible in Modeler.

Before you get too excited, there is a drawback to using Layout for creating model libraries. The UV mapping coordinates are not saved with the same deformations. If you apply a map to an object, deform that object with Bones or other Layout tools, and save it in its deformed state, the map will not match the original. Figure 12-24 is a model that was Saved Transformed from Figure 12-23; compare the difference in mapping patterns.

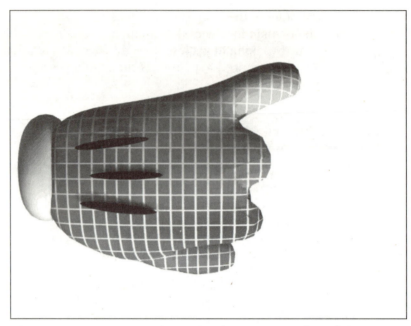

Figure 12-24: Mapping coordinates lost for a Save Transformed object.

The only available work-around is to use the original object as the root of the MTSE or Metamorph chain. Since the mapping coordinates and other surface parameters are not transformed, the mapping and surfaces of the rest of the object libraries don't matter.

This makes it doubly important that you keep a clean copy of the original object somewhere safe. You will be using working copies all the time to create new objects, and it's entirely too easy to inadvertently save over the original. There's nothing like trying to reconstruct an original from a lot of transformed copies to remind you to be more careful.

Unfortunately, the original-object work-around doesn't work for Replacement animation. One more strike against Replacement, I guess.

On the other hand, sometimes it's useful to deform an object, save it as transformed, then apply a map, and transform it back. This can give you a different picture of the deformation process, as in Figure 12-25.

This is the same object as Figure 12-24, just mapped and transformed in reverse. Note the density and pattern of the deformation over the knuckles; this helped me plan the subdivision explained earlier.

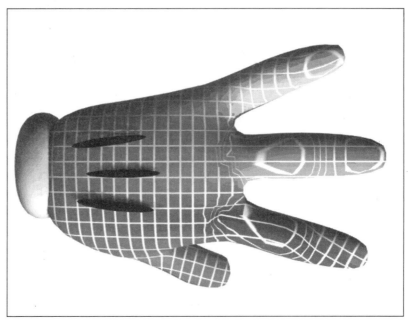

Figure 12-25: Mapping coordinates reversed by a Save Transformed object, retransformed in an MTSE chain.

With all the hassles over compatible objects and screwy mapping coordinates, why use Metamorphosis at all? Because it's one of the most effective ways of conserving both animator's and TD's time and energy. For the animator's side of the story, refer to Chapter 3.

For the TD side, consider how much time you spend on a single major character. Wouldn't you rather get as much mileage out of that work as possible, rather than having to constantly create variations on the same old theme? The biggest advantage to Metamorph and MTSE, as far as I'm concerned, is that the more you work with them, the less work it takes to do something new. You can always build on the library of work you've collected.

The next exercise gives a concrete example of what I've been saying. We'll start off with a simple object, the desk lamp that ships with LightWave 3D, and create a whole library of derivative objects that an animator can use in a variety of actions.

Exercise 12-5: Save Transformed for Metamorph Targets

This exercise shows how I modified the Metamorph targets used in Exercises 3-1 through 3-5, and demonstrates one way to model Metamorph targets using Bones deformation and the Save Transformed function. The goal of this exercise is to build 31 compatible Metamorph target objects. These objects can then be used with Replacement animation tools to animate the original object. (See Chapter 3 for details on Replacement animation tools.)

1. Clear the scene. We don't want anything interfering with saving clean transformed copies of the original object and we don't need any elaborate lighting setups to help us with this particular set of transformations.

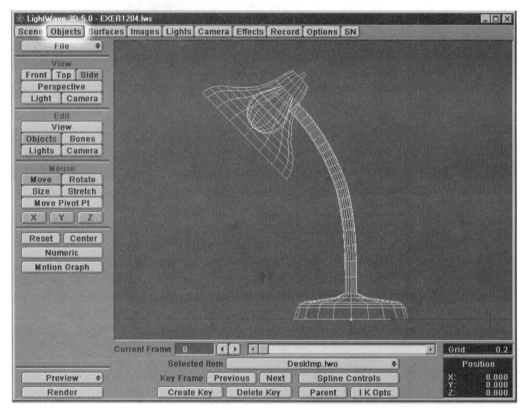

Figure 12-26: Side view of DESKLMP.LWO, before transforms.

2. Load the DESKLMP.LWO object from the Objects\Tutorials directory. This will be our original object; all the Metamorph target objects will be deformed versions of this lamp. Make sure it is positioned at the origin, 0, 0, 0. It is usually easier to manage objects that are modeled around the origin, and all the copies you are about to make will automatically inherit any displacement.

3. Adjust your views to give an adequate side view of the lamp, as in Figure 12-26.

4. Click the Objects button. The Objects Panel appears.

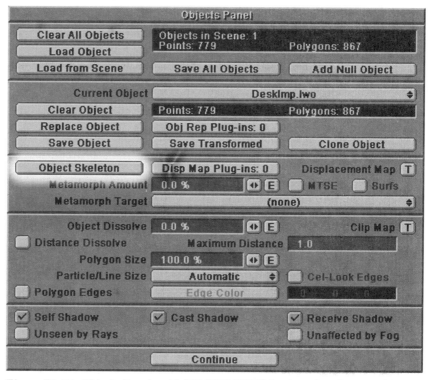

Figure 12-27: Objects Panel, with DESKLMP.LWO selected as Current Object.

5. Click the Object Skeleton button. A panel appears with the heading Skeleton for "Desklmp.lwo."

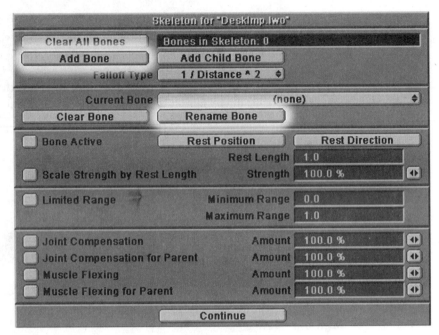

Figure 12-28: Skeleton Panel for DESKLMP.LWO.

6. The Current Bone button shows the word "none," since there are no Bones in the scene yet. Click the Add Bone button. The Current Bone button changes to read "Bone." Click the Rename Bone button. The Bone1 Name Panel appears. Type in the new name, BaseBone, and press Enter.

7. Repeat step 6 to add the first SpineBone, then press p twice to close the Skeleton and Objects Panels. You will see the two new Bones you just added, with both their axes at the origin and so closely overlapping that they look like a single Bone, as in Figure 12-29.

8. Click the Bones button. The name of the Bone you most recently created appears in the Selected Item pop-up, and the Bone is highlighted in the current view. Now is a good time to save the scene, just in case.

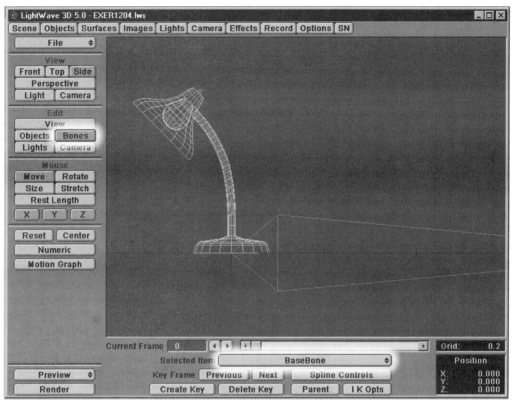

Figure 12-29: Side view of DESKLMP.LWO with Bones added.

9. Choose BaseBone from the Selected Item pop-up. Select Rest Length from the Mouse area and press n to call up the numeric data entry panel for Rest Length. Change it to 0.4, and press Enter to accept the change.

10. Select Rotate from the Mouse area and press n again to call up the numeric Rotate Panel. Change Pitch to 90, but leave the Heading and Bank settings at zero. Press Enter to close the panel and accept the changes.

11. Select Move from the Mouse area and press n again to call up the numeric Bone Position Panel. Change the Y value to -0.02, but leave the X and Z settings at zero. Press Enter to close the panel and accept the changes.

   These changes should put the BaseBone in about the position shown in Figure 12-30.

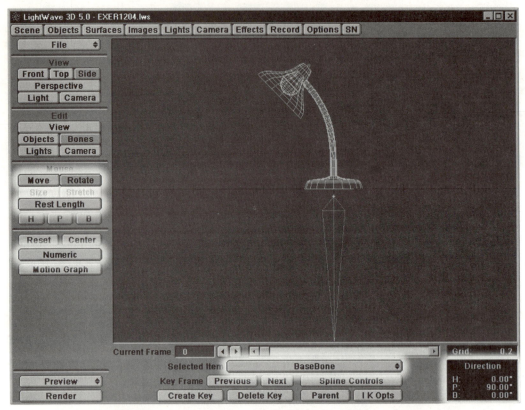

Figure 12-30: Side view of DESKLMP.LWO, with BaseBone positioned and Rest Length set.

12. Create a keyframe for BaseBone at frame 0, then press r to set the Bone's rest position. While BaseBone is still active, press p to call up the Skeleton Panel.

    For the models we are about to make, you want the lamp base to remain absolutely solid while the neck does the bending. You can lock down the vertices near a Bone by setting the Bone's Minimum value.

13. Turn on the Limited Range toggle button. Change the Minimum Range to 0.1, and the Maximum Range to 0.5. Press Enter, then press p to save the changes and close the panel.

These changes mean that any vertex in the lamp that is closer than 0.1 units to the BaseBone will not be influenced at all by any other Bone, and that any vertex between 0.1 units and 0.5 units will be affected by both BaseBone and any other Bone(s) with an overlapping area of influence.

14. Repeat steps 9 through 13 for SpineBone. Set the Rest Length to 0.044. Position the SpineBone at coordinates 0.0, 0.081, 0.0, with a Pitch of 266 degrees and Heading and Bank of zero. Leave Limited Range off. You should end up with something like Figure 12-31.

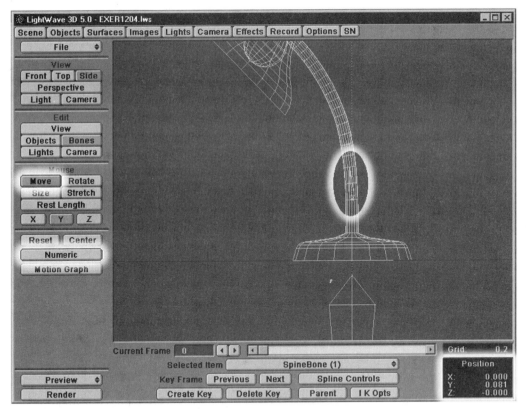

Figure 12-31: Side view of DESKLMP.LWO, with SpineBone positioned and Rest Length set.

Obviously, one SpineBone won't be enough if you want a smooth bend to the lamp's neck. Let's add a few more SpineBones.

15. With SpineBone selected, press p to call up the Bones Panel. Click the Add Child Bone button.

    This adds another Bone, but it's automatically Parented to SpineBone and with all SpineBone's settings. The new Bone is also automatically given the Parent Bone's name, with a number after it in parentheses. You should therefore see "SpineBone(2)" listed as the Current Bone in the Skeleton Panel, as in Figure 12-32.

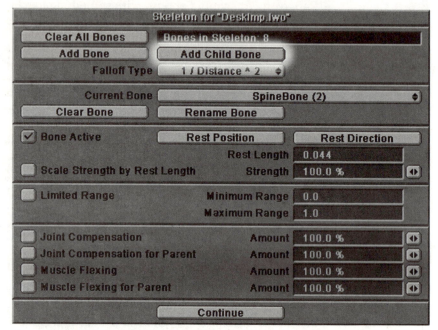

Figure 12-32: Skeleton Panel after adding a Child Bone to SpineBone.

16. Click the Add Child Bone button four more times to add a chain of Child Bones up to SpineBone(6). Make each new Child Bone inactive and close the Skeleton Panel when you are finished.

17. Change the Rest Length of the last Child, SpineBone(6), to 0.036. Change the pitch of SpineBone(2) and (6) to 5 degrees, and SpineBone(3), (4), and (5) to 10 degrees. This should keep them close to the centerline of the lamp neck, as in Figure 12-33, with the tip of SpineBone(6) near the centerline of the lamp shade.

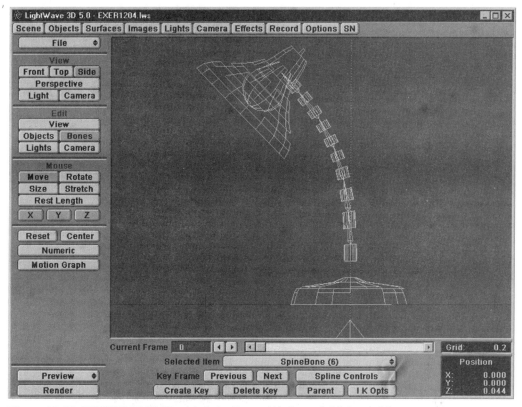

Figure 12-33: DESKLMP.LWO with SpineBones (1) through (6) in position.

18. Set a keyframe at frame 0 for everything. Activate all the Child Bones again and save the scene again.

19. Select SpineBone(6) and open the Skeleton Panel again. Add another Child Bone, but change this one's name to ShadeBone.

20. You want ShadeBone to keep the lamp shade rigid while the neck is bent by the SpineBones, so set ShadeBone's Limited Range to On, and Minimum and Maximum both to 0.09. This radius includes the entire shade, as shown in Figure 12-34. Set the Rest Length to 0.4, the same as BaseBone. Make sure ShadeBone is still inactive and close the Skeleton Panel.

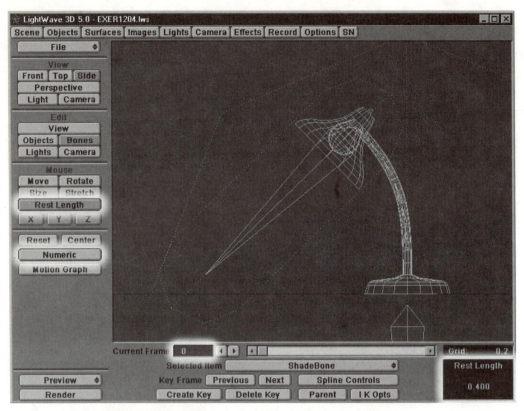

Figure 12-34: ShadeBone Limited Range includes the entire lamp shade.

21. Set ShadeBone's Pitch to -90 degrees, but keep Heading and Bank at zero. Make a keyframe for ShadeBone, then press r to activate the Bone. Make a keyframe for all items at frame 0, and save the scene again.

At this point, you should have a fairly well-articulated desk lamp. You can bend the lamp neck by progressively rotating each SpineBone a few degrees at a time. BaseBone keeps the lamp base rigid, and ShadeBone does the same for the lamp shade.

As easy as that posing sounds, there may be times you want a particular angle to this lamp and you don't want to bother adding Bones and posing it. You can avoid that hassle by posing the lamp now, and using the Save Transformed function to take "snapshots" of each pose for later use. Let's give it a try.

22. From frame 0, create a new keyframe for all objects at frame 30. Move to frame 30.

23. Bend the neck of the lamp over until it makes a smooth curve and the edge of the shade nearly touches ground level (see Figure 12-35). Be careful to change only the Pitch values for the SpineBones.

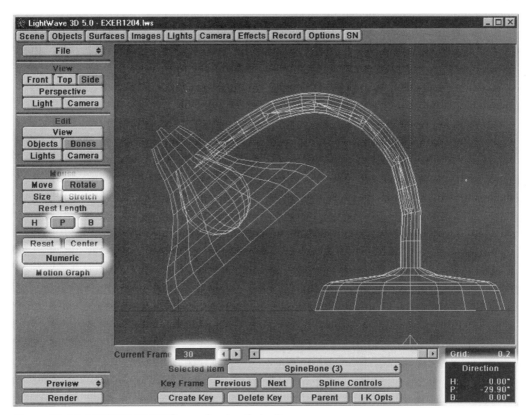

Figure 12-35: DESKLMP.LWO posed using SpineBones.

24. Create a new keyframe for all objects at frame 30. Save the scene file again.

25. Make a preview and examine it critically. If the motion of the lamp bending over is not as smooth as you want it to be, readjust the SpineBones and perhaps add some intermediate keyframes. Keep tweaking until you are happy with the preview results.

26. Create a new subdirectory in your default Objects directory to contain the new objects you are about to create.

27. Go to frame 0. Click the Objects button. The Objects Panel appears. Since there is only one object in the scene, the lamp, Desklmp.lwo appears on the Current Object button.

28. Click the Save Transformed button. A panel appears, warning you to change the filename for the new object to avoid overwriting the original. Save the new file in the directory you created in step 26, with the name REPLAC00.LWO. Press Enter to close the File dialog, press p to close the Objects Panel, and press the right-arrow key to advance to the next frame.

29. Repeat step 28 for frames 1 through 30, saving each object with the prefix REPLAC and the appropriate two-digit frame number.

You should end up with 31 compatible Metamorph target objects. If you would like to try them out, follow the directions in any or all of Exercises 3-1 through 3-5, using your new objects instead of the objects provided on the Companion CD-ROM.

As you can see, once you have a Boned object, it's relatively easy to create Metamorph targets from it by using the Save Transformed function.

Using SIMILAR

One of the difficulties with character animation using Metamorph objects is that modeling each object is time-consuming. Using object libraries is a big step forward, but you still have the problem of multiple actors in a scene. You don't want your characters to be identical, you want them to have unique, readily identifiable differences. But how can you afford the time to model even the most basic phonetic and emotional head objects for every new actor?

Together with Glenn Lewis, I've worked out one solution. Following this procedure lets you make manual changes to just one model, then a batch file and a utility program produce duplicates of all the compatible objects in your library with all your changes included.

Exercise 12-6: Creating SIMILAR Batch Files to Build Custom Object Libraries

1. Select the baseline, or "normal," object from a library of Metamorph objects.

   For this example, I'll use the Strong Man normal head from Crestline Software's HUMANOID model library. You can use any compatible objects you like; just make the filename substitutions in the following directions, where appropriate.

   If you have no other Metamorph libraries available, you might use the REPLACXX series of desk lamp objects used in Chapter 3.

2. Modify the normal object by using the Modeler and Layout tools that are legal for Metamorph objects.

   Don't delete or add any points, as you must maintain exact point counts and arrangements for the objects to Metamorph properly.

   To make my new character different, I enlarged the chin, sloped the forehead while exaggerating the eyebrow ridge, pushed the cheekbones out, and hollowed the cheeks. I also dragged the nose out and down slightly, then narrowed it. The end result was a decidedly unpleasant-looking character. That's Charley, Figure 12-36.

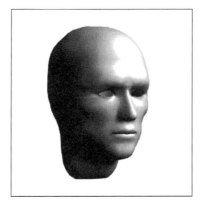

Figure 12-36: Strong Man normal head object modified to create Charley.

The key to the rest of this process is a utility program called SIMILAR.EXE, written by Glenn Lewis. SIMILAR works with a number of different file formats, including LightWave 3D. Basically, SIMILAR looks at the differences in point positions between objects A and B, and extrapolates those changes onto object C to create the new object, D. For example, the command line:

```
SIMILAR normal.lwo anger.lwo charley.lwo charangr.lwo
```

compares the normal head to the Anger morph object, then applies those changes to CHARLEY to produce Charley with a angry expression (see Figure 12-37).

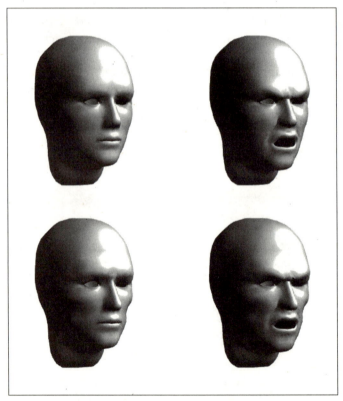

Figure 12-37: Normal compared to anger, and the differences applied to Charley to produce an angry Charley.

The FACECOPY.BAT batch file I've written, listed below, uses SIMILAR to create duplicates of all the Strong Man head objects, modified according to the changes in the head model named CHARLEY. This allows you to make whatever changes you like to CHARLEY, then automatically produce all 15 HUMANOID head objects with the same parameters.

```
REM FACECOPY.BAT
REM USES SIMILAR.EXE TO CONVERT HUMANOID HEADS TO CHARLEY PATTERN
SIMILAR.EXE NORMAL.LWO FEAR.LWO CHARLEY.LWO CHARFEAR.LWO
SIMILAR.EXE NORMAL.LWO ANGER.LWO CHARLEY.LWO CHARANGR.LWO
SIMILAR.EXE NORMAL.LWO STERN.LWO CHARLEY.LWO CHARSTRN.LWO
SIMILAR.EXE NORMAL.LWO SURPRISE.LWO CHARLEY.LWO CHARSURP.LWO
SIMILAR.EXE NORMAL.LWO SADNESS.LWO CHARLEY.LWO CHARSAD.LWO
SIMILAR.EXE NORMAL.LWO SMILE.LWO CHARLEY.LWO CHARSMIL.LWO
SIMILAR.EXE NORMAL.LWO GRIN.LWO CHARLEY.LWO CHARGRIN.LWO
SIMILAR.EXE NORMAL.LWO CRYING.LWO CHARLEY.LWO CHARCRYG.LWO
SIMILAR.EXE NORMAL.LWO 1CLOSED.LWO CHARLEY.LWO CHARCLOS.LWO
SIMILAR.EXE NORMAL.LWO 2PARTED.LWO CHARLEY.LWO CHARPART.LWO
SIMILAR.EXE NORMAL.LWO 3PRTOPEN.LWO CHARLEY.LWO CHARPRTO.LWO
SIMILAR.EXE NORMAL.LWO 4OPEN.LWO CHARLEY.LWO CHAROPEN.LWO
SIMILAR.EXE NORMAL.LWO 5WIDE.LWO CHARLEY.LWO CHARWIDE.LWO
SIMILAR.EXE NORMAL.LWO 6GAPE.LWO CHARLEY.LWO CHARGAPE.LWO
SIMILAR.EXE NORMAL.LWO 7PUCKER.LWO CHARLEY.LWO CHARPUCK.LWO
```

To create other characters, you'll need to use a text editor to edit the batch file.

3. Replace CHARLEY in the batch file with the name of your character, and CHAR, in the objects' names, with the first four letters of your character's name. You also need to replace the Strong Man normal, phoneme, and emotion object names with the appropriate object names from the library of your "normal" baseline.

   For example, to create a character named VICTORIA, first replace CHARLEY.LWO with VICTORIA.lwo, then replace CHAR with VICT throughout the batch file.

4. Copy FACECOPY.BAT, SIMILAR.EXE, DOS4GW.EXE, the object you modified in step 2, and the object library to be used as a baseline to a temporary working directory.

5. Run the batch file.

You should get a complete set of compatible Metamorph objects, all with the changes you modeled in step 2.

If you later decide to make changes to your object, simply make the changes to the "normal" model and run your modified FACECOPY.BAT again. It's fast enough that I've used it just to make minor tweaks. And every time you add a new object to your character's repertoire, you can add a line for it to the batch file.

SIMILAR can be used to make other Metamorph objects, too. For example, you can put long fingernails on hand objects, or modify them into claws for that Halloween look. You can even modify torso objects to have collars, plackets, lapels, and buttons for an easy approach to clothing your characters.

SIMILAR and related utilities are available from Glenn Lewis, 8341 Olive Hill Court, Fair Oaks, CA 95628. Some of his programs are also available for the Amiga, so please specify which disk formats you prefer. For further details, see the GLEWIS directory on the Companion CD-ROM.

Modeling From Life

There are two basic approaches to 3D digitizing: raster and manual. Laser scanners and their relatives are usually raster scanners, meaning they gather data in a tightly spaced grid pattern, scanning one horizontal line after another until they have covered the entire subject.

The *raster* method is brute force, generating a mesh of thousands of coordinates that do a good job of replicating the original object. Unfortunately, raster scanners produce points whether they are necessary or not, so you generally end up with a lot of points you don't need. This makes raster scans difficult to animate until they have been cleaned up and simplified, which takes either a lot of work or some expensive optimization software.

The existing niche for laser scanners seems to be the high end of Hollywood special effects production, where a faithful rendition of a star's face is more important than the ability to animate the finished model. If for some reason you really need that level of accuracy, there are service bureaus that will scan your model or live subject for a fee.

The *manual* approach is generally better for producing simpler objects that are easier to modify and animate. The hardware and software are also a small fraction of the price of a full-body laser scanner, and more within the reach of small studios or individuals.

The first step in manual digitizing is to make a working copy of the subject; it's going to get marked up and possibly sawn into slices. For live subjects, face or body molds are taken and positive casts made.

The digitizer operator carefully marks a grid of contour lines on the working copy. These lines should delineate the changes in slope that call for a new polygon. Areas that are—and will remain—flat don't need any polygons, so they show up as blank areas between contour lines. The lines are drawn in both vertical and horizontal directions, so the result is an irregular grid that draws together wherever there is detail, and spreads apart where there is less data to gather.

It's important that the operator at least understand what the TD or animator is going to be doing with the digitized model. It's even better if the operator is actually the TD or animator who will have to make the model work properly. If the operator doesn't understand the requirements and limits of the modeling and animation software, their mistakes are going to require extra work and maybe even a recapture of the model.

Once the operator has a clear grid of contour lines, he uses the digitizer to record the coordinates of each intersection. Depending on the software and the digitizer, this can produce a clean 3D object or another mess of coordinates that needs more cleanup.

Once the data is in the computer, the TD can go to work on cleaning it up. Small glitches or gaps in the model have to be filled in by hand; the current generation of modeling software is not something I'd trust to correctly interpret how a model should look. When the cleanup is complete and the usual pecking order (director, art director, lead animator, etc.) has blessed the object's appearance, the TD can start cutting it up and turning it into an animatable character.

A Sense of Proportion

If you are building characters from scratch, you need to study proportion and dimension from life and from caricature. "Winging it" is an excellent recipe for rebuilding models repeatedly. You should at least have a rough pencil sketch before you start modeling.

The best resources on proportion from life are not the artist's books, but the industrial designer's and engineer's. When you're planning joints and range of motion, there is no substitute for hard numbers. Henry Dreyfuss's work on ergonomics is still worth consulting, and his *Measure of Man* is generally available from your local public or university library. References on anthropometry can also help you decide on the just how long to model that arm, or how high to place the ankle Bone.

On the artistic side, two of the books in the Bibliography may be of use; Peck's *Human Anatomy for the Artist* for the realists, and for you game developers, Lee and Buscema's *How to Draw Comics*. If you are leaning toward a cartoon style, Blair's *Cartoon Animation* and the various compilations from the Warner and Disney studios have lots of examples.

And don't forget original inspiration! If all you are going to model is a 3D version of the same old caricatures, you might as well stay with ink and paint. This is a new medium; why not push the boundaries, and develop a completely original character design that belongs only to 3D CGI?

Give 'Em a Hand!

As a send-off for completing this chapter, here's one more exercise in applying Bones to an object. It's the Classic Cartoon Character Glove, with three fingers for easier animating, and the high style of three stitched lines on the back and a rolled cuff.

As you might expect, the original object was modeled with MetaNURBS. The source object is HANDLOW.LWO, and as usual you can find it in this chapter's directory on the Companion CD-ROM if you feel like fooling around with it.

Exercise 12-7: Boning a Cartoon Hand

You're pretty much on your own with this one. If you worked through the other exercises in this chapter, I think you're more than ready for it.

1. Clear the Layout workspace for a new scene. Load the HANDOPEN.LWO object from the Chapter 12 directory on the Companion CD-ROM.

2. Add, position, and set the parameters for the Bones required to pose the hand. Give it three knuckles for each finger.

   You might refer to Figure 12-18 for an idea or two about Bone placement.

One special concern is the opposable thumb's transverse bulge; this is a real pain to animate properly. I suggest you add a separate Bone with a Child handle and devote it exclusively to making the bulge swell by using Muscle Flexing, as in Exercise 12-2.

3. When you are satisfied with the animation of the Boned hand, use the Save Transformed function to start building a library of hand poses for Metamorph and MTSE animation.

   Most of Preston Blair's books have a wonderful page full of cartoon hand poses.

4. Make right hand duplicates of all the left hand models by making a copy, then scaling it by -1 on the X-axis.

Moving On

If you worked through all seven exercises in this chapter, you should have a solid understanding of the LightWave 3D tools you can use to create characters. If you are working through this book on the technical director track, this enables you to build your own characters to use later in the animation exercises.

If you add the finished hand from the preceding exercise to the arm from Exercise 12-2, you can make it wave bye-bye as we stroll along to the next chapter.

Express Yourself

Advanced Modeling for Character Faces

This chapter expands on the Modeler and Layout techniques from Chapter 12 to show you how to create character faces. You'll learn techniques for modeling and Boning heads to enable the most versatile facial animation. You'll work through exercises to produce MetaMorph model libraries for lip sync and emotional transitions. As you learn these techniques, you'll become familiar with the trade-offs in each approach, enabling you to choose the right technique for the job at hand. You'll also learn the essential criteria for realistic and caricature facial expressions.

To assist you in designing realistic and caricature faces, this chapter explains the underlying muscle and bone structure of the human face, plus dimples, wrinkles, flab, and fat. Exercises relate all this to LightWave 3D object geometry and Bones placement you can use to mimic the real structures.

Facial Modeling Options

You can model the simplest version of an animatable character face after a traditional puppet or ventriloquist's dummy. The eyes should rotate, the upper eyelids are useful for blinks, winks, and a variety of emotional expressions, and you can animate a simple hinged jaw for lip sync. That's a total of five objects in a Parented hierarchy. This approach is so simple that I'm not even going to illustrate it with an exercise. If you want to build a Pinnochio, you can refer to the later sections of this chapter on proportion and expression and plan one for yourself.

The problem with a very simple puppet head is that you can't easily animate the full range of human emotion. For real people, more subtle emotion is communicated by the softer tissues of the face than by the simple angle of the eyes or jaw. If you want to mimic emotional expression, you must try to recreate the subtlety of motion of a real human face. If you want your character to lip sync as convincingly as possible, you must be able to deform the lips to match the sibilants and fricatives of the dialog track.

It would be possible to assemble a more complex face from separate objects; some traditional puppets have many moving parts in their faces. You would have to accept the seams between objects, however, which rules out Parented objects for any animation that hopes to create a higher realism or a smoother style than puppetry.

The two remaining modeling approaches to facial animation are Bones and MetaMorph. Although you can create MetaMorph object libraries entirely in Modeler, it is such a tedious process that in the real world the production time is prohibitive. I can't recommend it, unless you are an exceptionally gifted and amazingly fast sculptor. The Bones approach, on the other hand, only requires that you model the object once, and the technique can be used straight or mixed with MetaMorph via the Save Transformed function. Accordingly, this chapter focuses on Bones and derivative modeling techniques.

Observing Nature, Again

As I mentioned in earlier chapters, observing nature is the best way to begin. It's very easy to go wrong if you try to work from memory, or from your own ideas about how a creature should function. Go to the source! When you are first considering a modeling project, even if it is pure caricature or fantasy, study everything you can lay hands on that may relate to your project. If you are modeling animals, study their physiology and visit the zoo to observe how they move. If you are modeling people, do the same—although just about any street corner will do as well as the zoo, for people watching.

There are a handful of resources I have found invaluable for modeling and animating. On my desk I keep a mirror and a model human skull, one to study the "live" play of muscles and skin, the other to study the underlying structures. Both items are cheap, available nearly everywhere, and last a long time. I also keep several books handy when designing character's heads, the most useful being Faigin's *The Artist's Complete Guide to Facial Expression* (see the Bibliography for details). The language is clear, technical only when necessary, and the illustrations seem designed especially for 3D construction. A paperback edition of Gray's *Anatomy* gets regular use, too. For caricature and more traditional "cartoon" design, I like Preston Blair's books, supplemented by various model sheets and other art from Disney, Warner Bros., and Will Vinton Studios.

All these resources boil down to a relatively small number of guidelines you should keep in mind when designing a character's head and face.

Proportion

The first guide is proportion: the size and relationship of the head's parts can make or break your character. Audiences expect a certain amount of stereotype in animated films; characters are expected to act as they look. If the eyes are a bit too close together, the nose hooked, and the forehead too low, the audience will expect a different type of behavior than that of a normally proportioned character. If you choose a realistic style, you must be especially careful to model accurate human proportions.

The baseline for the head is the *orbit*, or socket, of the eye. A line drawn horizontally through the eyes should divide the head in half. One of the most common mistakes is to put the eyes too far up the forehead, making the character look small-brained. Once the eyes are located, use the rule of thirds to divide the face: the top of the forehead (the hairline) to the eyebrow ridge is the upper third, the eyebrow ridge to the base of the nose is the middle third, and the base of the nose to the bottom of the chin is the lower third. If you get these proportions right, modeling the rest of the head goes more easily.

Bone Structure

The second guideline is to start with the bone structure. Even if you are designing a very flexible fantasy character you need to understand and borrow from normal human bone structure to create a character your audience can understand. For example, in a normal human the distances between the eye sockets, base of the nose, and upper teeth are all firmly fixed by bone. If a realistic character's eyes, upper teeth, and nose float around, the effect is very disturbing. Even if a "cartoony" character will squash-and-stretch to extremes, you should establish the same fixed relationships between facial parts before you create any distortions.

Make a baseline, then play with it any way you like, and the audience will be able to follow along. Jump straight into distorted and variable proportions without that baseline, and your audience will be so busy trying to figure out the character's face they will completely miss the story.

Muscles

The third guideline is to follow the muscles. Muscles (and their associated fat and skin attachments) provide most of the surface distortion we use to create facial expressions, so you need to understand the musculature in order to simulate it with your models. Even if you are building a dragon or other fantastic creature, you must model it with believable muscle action or the character will look like a rubber toy. This is why life drawing and anatomy are so important for artists. If you are a TD with a very focused CGI background, this may be an area where you can learn from animators with traditional art training.

The rest of this chapter examines the proportion, bone, and muscle structure of each part of the face, including specific tips on modeling them for Boned animation and opportunities for caricature and exaggeration.

Limiting the Effect of Bones

When you build a skeleton in LightWave 3D to animate an organic object like a humanoid face, there is one major headache: how to get the detailed control you need, without using zillions of Bones. The problem lies in how LightWave 3D handles Bone assignments. If you apply a Bone in the middle of a group of points, there is no effective way for you to limit the Bone's effects to an irregular selection of polygons and leave the rest alone. You can get around this by splitting the object up into separate objects, but then you lose the Bone's advantage of seamless surfaces. You can try to nail down the unwanted points with a lot of smaller Bones, but that slows down the screen redraw, interferes with still other Bones, and clutters your scene. You may also want more than one Bone to affect a particular point; for example, the cheeks should stretch when the jaw opens, but also bulge under the influence of cheek "puffers" (Bones that mimic air pressure in a closed mouth). This is a Bone setup problem that you can't easily solve using ordinary Parent/Child skeletons.

The goal of the following procedure is to enable you to set up Bones to exclusively affect a precise selection of points. Using this technique, you should be able to mimic any combination of bone and muscle structure to deform the skin of an object. The basic steps of the procedure are:

1. In Modeler, select the points to be affected by a Bone and define them as a surface.

2. Move the surface a safe distance from the other points. Save this "exploded" object.

3. Load the exploded object in Layout. In the first frame, apply a Bone to the defined surface, parented to the object's root Bone. Define the Limited Range Minimum and Maximum for the Bone to lock down every point in the surface.

4. In the second frame, implode the object by moving the Bone the reverse of the safe distance.

The approach I recommend is to define a separate surface for each part of a character's face. These surfaces should be bounded by the relatively immovable borders between the different parts. For example, looking at the face's anatomy tells you the perimeter of the nose is pretty closely attached to underlying bone, so while the nose can deform quite a bit, it can't affect surrounding tissues very much. You can therefore define the nose as a single surface, and assign a Bone to limit its influence on the rest of the face. It's much easier to select polygons for repeated operations if they are organized by surfaces, but it's not absolutely necessary. If you have a lot of surfaces already set up for some other purpose, you can get by with manually selecting the points for each "explode" operation.

When you explode the separate surfaces in Modeler, the goal is to place each surface's points far enough from all other points that a Bone can include all the selected points without affecting any other points. If you do this properly, Bones assigned to a surface will not interact with any other surface's points or Bones. Note that Bone assignments are by point, not by polygon. A polygon will stretch as far as necessary to bridge between points assigned to different Bones.

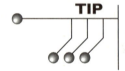

TIP Make sure you keep an intact copy of the original object when you save the exploded object. I tend to save a copy of the object after exploding each surface, so if something goes wrong I never have to backtrack further than the previous surface.

When you assign Bones to the exploded surfaces in Layout, using identical Minimum and Maximum Limited Range values effectively locks each point in place relative to the Bone. This enables you to implode the surface's points to their precise original positions simply by moving the Bone. If you need to distort or otherwise animate the surface, you can apply Child Bones that have a more flexible Limited Range. If the Child Bones are set in the object's exploded keyframe, they will also affect only their Parent Bone's points.

To return the object to its original shape you must implode all the surface's Parent Bones by the exact inverse of the explosions you applied to the surfaces in Modeler. If you exploded the nose surface 2.0 units along the Z-axis, you must implode the nose's Bone -2.0 units along the Z-axis. When you do this, you set that keyframe as the new default pose for the object. This is a modification to the usual LightWave 3D working style of setting your default scene in frame 0 and starting the action in frame 1. If you are also animating this character, don't forget to allow for this additional 1-frame offset in laying out your x-sheets. You can build even more layers of Bone interaction and control if you use additional frames to assemble and Bone combinations of surfaces. For each of these extra frames, the animator has to add another offset to their x-sheet for the scene. Make sure you document this in your character notes and model sheets.

Problems & Solutions

Unfortunately, you fragment all the surface mapping coordinates when you use the explode/Bone/implode process. If you applied a spherical map, for example, it would render as if the sphere were mapped to the exploded version, and all the surfaces would have large sections of the map missing at their borders with adjoining surfaces.

If you need to map an object you have exploded for Boning, try to figure an acceptable way to use planar mapping. If you explode all the mapped surfaces along a mapping axis, a planar map on that same axis will not distort when you implode the object. For instance, if you created a bump map for facial wrinkles (see Chapter 14), you could apply it as a planar map on the Z-axis. Knowing this, you would explode all the face surfaces along the Z-axis. The imploded face would retain the correct mapping coordinates for the wrinkle map. On the other hand, the main reason for this type of Bone animation is to make Metamorph objects, in which case mapping coordinates don't matter anyway.

You can Bone an exploded object surface by surface, you don't have to do it all at once. When an exploded object is set up in Layout you can use the Replace Object function in the Objects Panel to replace it with a similar object. The point and polygon count and distribution does not have to be identical; as long as the exploded surfaces are within the Limited Ranges of the existing Bones, the scene still works. See Figure 13-1 for an example.

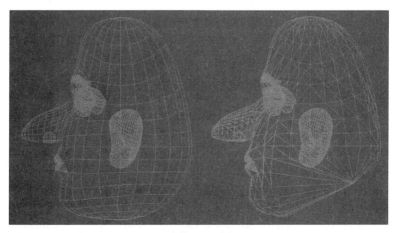

Figure 13-1: Same scene, very different objects.

This enables you to experiment with more manageable low-complexity objects before committing to the full-complexity objects for final tweaking and rendering. You can subdivide, triple, and use MetaNURBS, as long as the surface's points remain within the areas of the Bones you have already set in Layout. You can even modify and re-explode a derivative of the original object, if you keep careful track of which surface goes where.

The following exercises guide you through the explosion, Boning, and implosion of an example character face, using this incremental approach to work through one facial feature at a time.

Exercise 13-1: Setting Bones for Ear Surfaces

1. Open Modeler. Click Load. Select the object to be exploded, in this case HEAD1301.LWO, which you can find in the Chapter 13 directory of the Companion CD-ROM (see Figure 13-2).

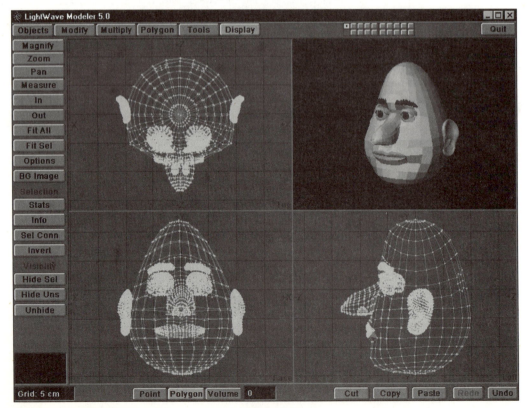

Figure 13-2: HEAD1301.LWO object loaded in Modeler.

Normally, you would next select points to define the surfaces of the object. The exact surface divisions depend on your object; the exercises later in this chapter examine some guidelines for defining surfaces. For the example object, the major facial parts have already been defined as surfaces. If you had defined new surfaces, you would now deselect all points and save the surfaced object with a new name as the baseline reference object.

2. Click Display. Switch to Polygon selection mode. Click Stats. Select the surface name Fred-Ear from the panel list. Click + to select the surface's polygons. The panel closes automatically.
   Your screen should look like Figure 13-3.

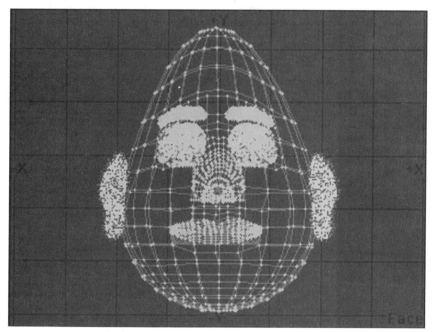

Figure 13-3: Fred-Ear surface selected.

3. Click Modify. Click Move. Click Numeric. Move the selected points, using the Numeric Panel, at least twice the part's maximum dimension away from the remaining parts, as in Figure 13-4.

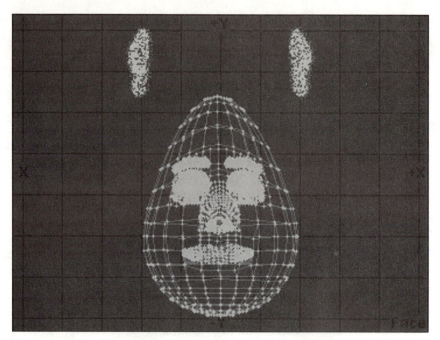

Figure 13-4: Fred-Ear surface moved.

This is enough of a safety margin for you to create a Bone that affects the entire selected surface, without including any other surfaces of the object. It's almost always best to err on the side of caution, but spreading the surfaces out over larger distances makes it more difficult to get a look at the whole object in either Layout or Modeler.

4. Write down the numbers you type in the Numeric Panel as soon as you complete each move. You will need these numbers later in the process to reassemble the object accurately. I strongly recommend that you move the surfaces by round numbers, (0.1000, 0.5000, etc.) so they are easy to remember, and type in all four digits to prevent rounding errors.

5. Click Object. Click Save as. Save the exploded object with a new name.

Make sure you keep an intact copy of the original object. I tend to save a copy of the object after exploding each surface so if something goes wrong I never have to go back further than the previous surface.

CD-ROM

6. Close Modeler. Open Layout. Open scene file CH130001.LWO, which you can find in the Chapter 13 directory of the Companion CD-ROM. This scene is set up with the original, unexploded version of the head object, just to save you the trouble of setting Camera angles and lights.

   When you are creating a new character, I recommend setting up the head in a separate scene like this until you have worked out all the Boning problems. The head is usually more complex than the rest of the body combined.

7. Open the Objects Panel, and replace the head object with the last exploded version you saved in Modeler.

8. Open the Skeleton Panel. Add a root Bone for the head with the pivot set to 0,0,0. Leave it as a null Bone for now, with Rest Length 0.0001 and Strength 0.0%. Your scene should now look like Figure 13-5.

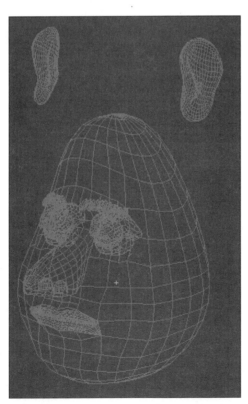

Figure 13-5: Head with root Bone set.

What you're going to do next is set a Bone for one surface, with Limited Range values that will lock down all the points in the surface. We'll refer to these types of Bones as surface Bones. The goal is to be able to move the surface Bones, and know that the surface's points follow along exactly, without any distortion. Later, you can add Child Bones to each surface Bone to enable you to animate more detailed surface distortions.

To start off, you'll set up the Bones for the left and right ears. This is about the simplest part of most characters; for many humanoid characters you won't have to Bone the ears at all, they're just immobile lumps on the side of the head. In this case, you'll set up the ears so they can wiggle front-to-back.

9. Open the Skeleton Panel again. Select the root Bone. Click Add Child Bone.

10. Rename the new Child Bone as EarsRootBone. Turn off Bone Active. Close the Skeleton Panel.

11. With the EarsRootBone selected, click Move. Turn off the X- and Z-axis buttons, and drag the EarsRootBone up along the Y-axis until it is in the middle of the ears, according to the Side view, Figure 13-6.

12. Create a key for the EarsRootBone at frame 0. Press r to set the rest length and position and activate the Bone.

13. Open the Skeleton Panel again. With EarsRootBone selected, click Add Child Bone. Rename the new Bone LeftEar. Turn off Bone Active. Set Rest Length to 0.01 and Strength to 100%. Close the Skeleton Panel.

14. Move the LeftEar Bone to the center of the left ear surface of the exploded object. Create a key frame for LeftEar at frame 0. Press r to set the rest length and position and activate the Bone.

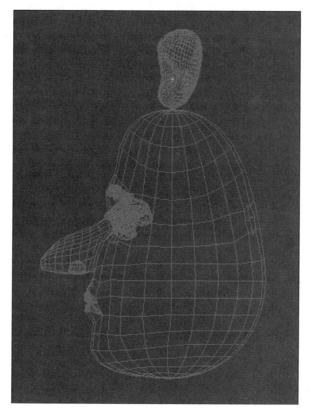

Figure 13-6: Side view of EarsRootBone position.

15. Open the Skeleton Panel again. With LeftEar selected, turn off Bone Active. Turn on Limited Range and set the Minimum and Maximum to 0.06. Turn on Bone Active and close the Skeleton Panel.

    The dotted outline of the LeftEar Bone's influence should contain all the points in the left ear surface of the head object, and no points from other surfaces (Figure 13-7). If this is not the case, repeat step 15 to correct the Limited Range settings.

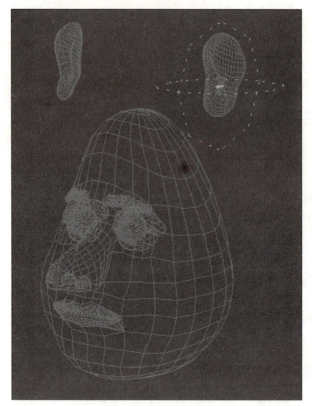

Figure 13-7: LeftEar Bone activated.

16. Repeat steps 13 through 15 for the other ear, naming the Child Bone RightEar.

17. Go to frame 1. Select EarsRootBone.

18. Refer to your notes from step 4, the explode operation in Modeler. How far did you move the ears' surface? Click Move, then click Numeric. Enter the negative value of the ears' previous move and click OK.

This should move the ears back to their precise original position. If it's off a little, try to find the cause of the error to make sure you don't repeat it for the rest of the surfaces.

19. Create a key for EarsRootBone at frame 1.

    So far, all you've apparently done is move the ears around and insulate the rest of the surfaces from the effects of the ear Bones. Now you get to the good part: setting Child Bones to move and deform the surface, without affecting the rest of the object.

    Presumably, you'd like the character to be able to wiggle his ears. If you tried to do that with a Parented hierarchy, the pivot would look very mechanical; if you tried it using an ordinary Bone set around the ear, the side of the head would deform as well. Exploding, Boning, and imploding the object solves this problem, enabling you to restrict smooth Bones deformations to a well-defined part of an object.

    The goal of the next few steps is to add a Null Bone as a pivot, near the center of the ear, and place a normal Child Bone at the rear edge of the ear. This enables you to bend the ear forward or back by changing the Heading angle of the null Bone; the Child Bone's influence is stronger near the back of the ear, while the LeftEar Bone keeps the ear securely anchored near the front.

20. Go to frame 0. Open the Skeleton Panel again. With LeftEar selected, click Add Child Bone. Rename the new Bone LeftEarHinge. Turn off Bone Active and Limited Range. Set Rest Length to 0.0001 and Strength to 0.0%. Close the Skeleton Panel.

21. Move the LeftEarHinge Bone towards the front of the left ear surface of the exploded object, as in Figure 13-8. This is the line where the deformation of a bent ear should stop, where the flesh and cartilage of the ear grow out of the head.

Figure 13-8: LeftEarHinge Bone position.

22. Create a key frame for LeftEarHinge at frame 0. Press r to set the rest length and position and activate the Bone.
    That's the hinge. Now for the "bender."

23. Open the Skeleton Panel again. With LeftEarHinge selected, click Add Child Bone. Rename the new Bone LeftEarFlap. Turn off Bone Active. Set Rest Length to 0.01 and Strength to 25%. Turn on Scale Strength by Rest Length. Close the Skeleton Panel.

24. Move the LeftEarFlap Bone to the rear edge of the left ear surface. Pitch the Bone up 90 degrees so the long axis is vertical and aligned (more or less) with the rear edge of the ear, as in Figure 13-9.

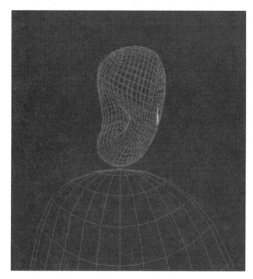

Figure 13-9: LeftEarFlap Bone in position.

25. Create a keyframe for LeftEarFlap at frame 0. Press r to set the rest length and position and activate the Bone.

26. Open the Skeleton Panel again. With LeftEarFlap selected, turn off Bone Active. Turn on Limited Range, and set the Minimum to 0.06 and Maximum to 0.06. Turn on Bone Active, and close the Skeleton Panel.

    The dotted outline of the LeftEarFlap Bone's influence should contain the entire ear surface, as in Figure 13-10.

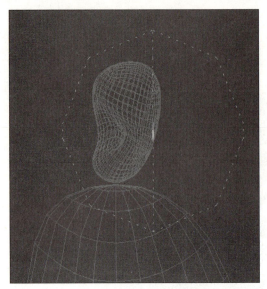

Figure 13-10: Influence of LeftEarFlap Bone.

27. To test the ear's flexibility, go to frame 1 and experiment with the Heading angle of the LeftEarHinge Bone. How far can you rotate it before the ear deformation becomes unusable? What are some good Heading values, as in Figure 13-11? Document these experiments, you will need them later when you make up the model sheet for this character's head.

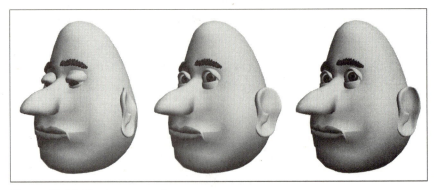

Figure 13-11: Bent ear examples.

28. Repeat steps 20 through 27 for the other ear. Save the scene.

You should end up with a head that can be animated to wiggle its ears. While of questionable usefulness, this exercise was the simplest example of a procedure you can repeat to set up every other facial feature.

Once you have set the Bones for a surface, you can make the character easier to animate by opening the Scene Panel and hiding any Bone that should not be animated. This keeps the Layout view cleaner, so the animator can find the right Bone faster and with less confusion. Hide each of the surface Bones, plus the Bones like LeftEarFlap that are active but not designed to be animated directly. The remaining Bones, like LeftEarHinge, should be color coded for contrast and remain visible.

When you've had more practice, you can build more efficient skeletons by adding the animatable Bones first, so they display near the top of drop-down lists, and the null Bones are out of sight near the bottom. For now, simply accept that you will have to do a certain amount of scrolling in the selection lists to locate the Bones you want.

Feature by Feature

The next 11 exercises are more brief, since you already know the details of the procedure. A preface to each exercise explains the musculature and range of motion of the facial feature, followed by a recommended approach to modeling and Boning, and an example figure or two.

Eyebrows

Eyebrows are controlled by two sets of muscles, the *frontalis* and the *corrugator*. The frontalis runs in two vertical broad bands from the hairline straight down to the brow ridge. The main effect of this muscle is to lift the eyebrows toward the hairline, producing wrinkles in the forehead. Each half of the frontalis can be controlled independently, raising one eyebrow at a time and wrinkling only the half of the forehead above the raised eyebrow. The corrugator is a collection of three smaller bands of muscle connecting the bridge of the nose, the lower center of the forehead, and the center of each eyebrow. These muscles pull the eyebrows together and down over the bridge of the nose, forming deep folds.

Realistic eyebrows do not have a very large range of motion. On the average, they can move up or down only about half an inch, and the outer ends of the eyebrows hardly move at all. As the eyebrows lower, they tend to compress inwards slightly. Caricature eyebrows, however, can be exaggerated to such an extent that you can actually separate them from the face and animate them as individual objects.

The eyebrows can be very important for a character's nonverbal communication, as any fan of Groucho Marx or Leonard Nimoy can attest. Eyebrows contribute to many expressions, usually in combination with the eyes and eyelids.

Exercise 13-2: Modeling Eyebrows

1. Repeat the procedure from Exercise 13-1 to define the surface, explode, Bone, and implode the eyebrows for the head object. Since the head is in a caricature style, you can choose to keep the eyebrows as part of the lower forehead, or separate them entirely and animate them apart from the forehead.

2. You can add flexibility to the eyebrows by assigning several overlapping Child Bones designed to change the curvature of the eyebrow. The Child Bones are best constructed as a hierarchy, rooted at the outer end of the eyebrow where the least motion occurs. Two or three Child Bones should give you as much animation control as you are likely to need (see Figure 13-12).

3. You can model the wrinkles produced by the frontalis and corrugator by creating closely spaced parallel rows of points, exploding alternate rows along the Z-axis, and assigning the exploded rows to a "wrinkle Bone" designed to animate along the Z-axis. Pushing the wrinkle Bone farther into the head deepens the wrinkles.

4. Test the results for effective range of motion. Wiggle the eyebrows. Attempt to pose a surprised, very angry, or quizzical expression. Do a Mr. Spock, or even a Groucho Marx impression. Document the animatable Bones for the character's model sheet.

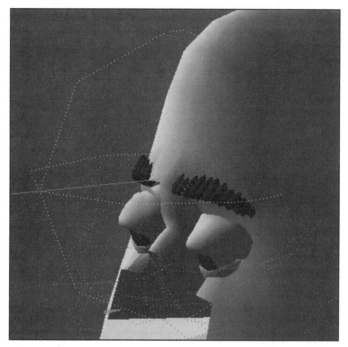

Figure 13-12: Example Eyebrow Bone layout.

Nose

The realistic human nose is nearly rigid. The *septum*, at the base of the nose just above the upper lip, does not move, nor does the entire bridge. The tip can deflect slightly when the nostrils flare or compress or the upper lip moves radically. The root (between the brows) can be wrinkled deeply by the corrugator muscles of the eyebrows. Some people can flare open or partially close their nostrils by flexing the *nasalis* muscle that runs from each wing of the nose across the crest. Since the perimeter of the nose is mostly attached to underlying bone, the nose doesn't affect surrounding tissues very much. On the contrary, the nose is usually moved incidentally by strong motions of the cheeks or upper lip.

The nose has little to do with most realistic character animation. Humans are not generally attuned to flared nostrils as a sign of anger or alertness, or constricted nostrils as a reaction to unpleasant smells. The phrase "wrinkling one's nose" is a bit misleading. The wrinkles are formed at the nose's root by the eyebrow's corrugators; the nose's midsection is compressed by the angular head of the quadratus labii superiorus muscle that runs along the nasolabial furrows that divide the nose from the cheeks. So the wrinkles are all formed by muscles around the nose, not part of it.

Caricature animation can easily employ the nose to humorous effect. Exaggerate the nose to a fleshy mass, make it bob and wobble in overlapping action, and every facial motion becomes laughable.

Exercise 13-3: Modeling a Nose

1. Repeat the procedure from Exercise 13-1 to define the surface, explode, Bone, and implode the nose for the head object. Figure 13-13 shows one possible arrangement.

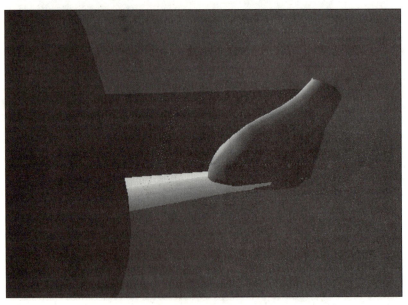

Figure 13-13: One approach to Boning the nose.

2. Add Child Bones to make the nostrils flare and enable the tip of the nose to bob and wobble.

3. Animate tests of the nose for effective range of motion. Document your results for the character model sheet.

Eyes: Realistic

Realistic eyeballs are paradoxically the easiest and among the most difficult parts to animate. On one hand, they are nearly perfect spheres, easy to model, position, and rotate; on the other hand, they are such a crucial part of nonverbal communication that your audience will be examining your character's eyes more closely than any other part of the scene. On the gripping hand, that means you can often "cheat" other parts of the scene, as long as you model and animate the eyes well.

If you're going for realism, you can't get away with modeling the eyeball as a simple sphere. You need to model the corneal bulge, and if the eye is going to be seen in extreme close shots, you will probably want to model the iris complete with a variable pupil opening and set the index of refraction for the cornea and the vitreous humor (the liquid filling the eyeball, visible through the pupil) to something near the real values. If you want to get completely obsessive about realism, consult an ophthalmologist. Then there are all the interesting possibilities for creature eyeballs, from a relatively prosaic cat's-eye slit pupil to weird glowing effects and hypnotically flowing iris maps.

For ordinary concentric pupils you have two basic choices: a set of image maps with a variety of pupil sizes, or a pupil opening that can be animated with a Bone or MetaMorph object. I personally prefer to assign a Child Bone to the points defining the circumference of the pupil, and rotate the Bone. This makes the opening close like a mechanical or camera iris, but it swirls any image map applied to the iris polygons.

If you're willing to compromise, the eyeballs modeled for the example head are adequate for a learning exercise. The pupil and iris are modeled as ordinary surfaces, and the eyeball itself is just a sphere. An hour's tweaking could turn them into really nice eyes if you're up to the challenge.

You can set up the eyes to simply rotate by using keyframes, but I think that's inefficient for the animator. I prefer setting up eyes to use full time Inverse Kinematics, as in the exercises in Chapter 4, to automatically track a Null object. This makes it easy for the animator to keep the character's eyes lined up with another object in the scene. You can also use Lock & Key or LightWave 3D's Parent to Bone plug-ins to Parent the eyes to the Head, instead of Boning them as part of the overall character. Parented object eyeballs, with or without IK tracking, are generally a better approach than Boned if you plan to use MetaMorph or MTSE for the rest of the face.

Exercise 13-4: Modeling Realistic Eyes

1. Repeat the procedure from Exercise 13-1 to define the surface, explode, Bone, and implode the eyes for the head object. Create a root Bone for both eyes, similar to the EarsRoot Bone you used in Exercise 13-1. Just as with the ears, it's handy to be able to move the eyes as a single unit.

2. Add a Child Null Bone to each eye, positioned in front of the pupil, and another Null off in the middle distance. Set up the IK options so the eyes' Null Bones track the distant Null. Turn off IK for the eyes' root Bone and set rotation constraints for the eyeballs so they can't rotate to unrealistic angles. Figure 13-14 shows the Layout screen for full time IK tracking of a target Null object.

Figure 13-14: Full Time IK approach to Boning the eyes.

3. Add Child Bones to make the pupils open and close.

4. Animate tests of the eyes for effective range of motion. Repeat the reading simulation Exercise 4-5, using the scene you just set up, to test the eyes' function. Animate the pupils as if reacting to a bright light turning on, then off. Document your results for the character model sheet.

Eyelids: Realistic

Eyelids convey a significant fraction of the eyes' expressiveness. Rotation and pupil dilation are the limits of the eyeball's repertoire, so the eyelids and brows have to do the rest of the work. As with any action involving the eyes, the tiniest changes can make a big difference in the meaning of the expression.

The eyelids are controlled by two muscles, the *levator palpebrae,* which raises the upper lid, and the *orbicularis oculi,* which encircles the eye and squeezes the lids together in squinting. The normal position of the upper lid is between the upper edge of the pupil and the upper edge of the iris. Usually, the upper lid just covers the edge of the iris. If the upper lid covers any part of the pupil, the eyes look sleepy, depressed, intoxicated, or slow. If the upper lid raises far enough to expose the sclera, or white of the eye, the eyes look surprised or alert. The lower lid has much less influence on expression. Normally, the lower lid simply follows the edge of the iris, within the lid's range of motion. If the eyeball rotates upward, the lower lid cannot follow very far and often leaves part of the sclera exposed. Unlike the upper lid, exposing the sclera above the lower lid has no particular emotional message. Even when squinting, the lower lid rarely covers more than the lower part of the iris, and sometimes the lowest edge of the pupil. Neither eyelid ever slants beyond its natural angle; this is an effect used sometimes in caricature, but in reality the illusion of a slant upwards in distress or downwards in anger is created by an extreme position of the eyebrows that deepens the shadows in the eye socket.

Modeling and Boning the eyelids can be easy or hard, depending on the style of modeling you choose for the character. Exact realism is difficult because of the wrinkling and folding of the lids; mimicking this precisely would require a plethora of Bones and take forever to animate. If you need realistic eyelids, I recommend modeling a series of MetaMorph or MTSE target objects.

A much easier approach is to treat the eyelids as simple hemi-spheres and allow them to interpenetrate the face. The seam along the penetration shows, but appropriate texture maps can partially disguise it. This makes animation a breeze, and the following exercise even shows you how to automate most of the eyelids' actions.

Exercise 13-5: Model & Bone Realistic Eyelids

1. Repeat the same procedures you followed for the eyeballs to surface, explode, Bone, and implode the upper eyelids. Assign the eyelids to track the same Null object as the eyeballs.

   The eyelids of the sample object are modeled in rest position, as if the eyeballs are looking straight ahead.

2. Set the IK limits for the eyelids to allow Pitch rotation within natural norms, and no Heading or Bank rotation at all.

   The upper lid's Pitch limits should be around +30 and -55 degrees, and the lower lids around +10 and -10. Your results may vary; each character needs IK limits that produce natural-looking angles for the lids. A sleepy character, for example, should have a rest angle that partially covers the pupil.

3. Go back to frame 0 for the upper eyelids and add another Child Bone to the eyelid Bones, keeping the same values as the Parents. Name these new Bones LeftEyelidHandle and RightEyelidHandle. Turn off Bone Active for both Parent and Child, and move the new Child Bones to the same position as their Parent Bones. Turn Bone Active back on for the Child Bones and leave it off for the Parents.

   This should give you a pair of upper eyelids that still follows the eyeball's actions in the Pitch axis, but now has an extra Bone, a handle, for animating the upper eyelid to modify the IK rotation. You can leave most of the eyelid action to full time IK, then rotate the EyelidHandle Bones in the Pitch axis to animate a wink or blink.

4. Animate tests of the eyelids for IK function in following the eyeballs. Repeat the reading simulation Exercise 4-5, using the scene you just set up to test the eyelids. Animate a blink. Animate a wink and add some eyebrow action for emphasis.

5. Document your results for the character model sheet.

Eyes: Cartoon

Cartoon eyes behave just like real eyes, only more so. The limits of various expressions are the same, but you have to model the eyeballs, lids, and brows so the animator can distort them to exaggerate and emphasize the central traits of the expression. For example, a very angry scowl for a realistic character requires drawn-down eyebrows, lowered upper eyelids, and the eyes' tracking Null positioned on the object of the anger. A caricature of the same expression requires the brows to be pushed farther down the nose, deeper wrinkles across the bridge, swelling and thrusting forward of the brows to make them appear larger and more threatening, and bulging of the eyeballs and lids toward the object of the anger. Obviously, cartoon eyes require more than a simple IK rotation setup.

The need for flexibility means the shape of a cartoon eye depends on the character and the expression. Most cartoon eyeballs are drawn as distorted ovoids, like soft-boiled eggs with the point up; but different characters may require flattened, elongated, or even triangular eyeballs. Since the shape will probably not be suitable for rotating, you don't need to model the eyeball separately from the face. You don't even need to animate the sclera, except for gross distortions like bulging and stretch-and-squash. You can create the illusion of a moving eyeball by simply animating the iris and pupil across the unmoving surface of the sclera. Therefore, you can model a cartoon eyeball as just another bulge in the face, but you need to define it as a separate surface.

You can model the iris and pupil as the same corneal bulge you'd use on a realistic eyeball, but I prefer a simple flattened sphere, imbedded just less than halfway in the sclera. This shape is more forgiving of alignment problems; if you position it a little too high or too low in the sclera, the difference is not glaringly obvious. Most cartoon characters can get by with a simple black pupil, but others look better with an iris. You rarely need realistic refraction in a cartoon pupil, so I recommend using image map sequences to animate any pupil dilation. If you are using a solid black iris, you can simply scale the iris in the X- and Y-axes.

Exercise 13-6: Model & Bone a Cartoon Eye

1. Modify a copy of the character head to give it cartoon eyes, or create a new character head from scratch. Delete the eyeball and eyelid surface points. Add a new ovoid surface for each sclera. Define the sclera as a surface.

2. Model an iris and pupil. Define them as a separate surface.

3. Explode, Bone, and implode the new eyes just as you did for the other surfaces. You will probably have to Bone the iris so it can be moved in or out as well as rotated around the sclera's center, to keep it on the eye's surface.

This isn't as easy to animate as the spherical eyeball, but you can create some great classic cartoon effects with it.

You can get more of a cartoon look for your character's eyes if you use image maps for the irises. That's what Will Vinton Studios chose to do for the recent series of M&M's commercials they animated. There are two basic approaches: create a bunch of painted image maps, select the closest match for each frame, and renumber copies of each image to create an image sequence; or animate an iris object, render the animation so only the eye shows, apply the rendered sequence to the sclera, and dissolve the iris object. I much prefer the second method, since it's easier to revise, maintain sight lines, and set up for rendering.

If there is any way you can use a regular ellipsoid (a stretched-out sphere) for a sclera, it can really make Boning and animation easier. If the eyeball surface is at all regular, you can set up a full time IK chain that can keep the iris near the surface of the eye while automatically tracking a Null, just as you did with a spherical eyeball.

Exercise 13-7: Making Cartoon Iris Image Sequences

1. Determine the center of the vertical and horizontal arcs that most closely follow the surface curves of the sclera. If the sclera were a sphere, both of these points would be in the center of the sphere. For an ellipsoid, the center of the longer vertical arc will be farther behind the surface, while the center of the shorter horizontal arc will be closer.

2. Set a Null Bone named UpDown at the vertical center, add a Child Bone named SideSide at the horizontal center, and lock all the iris's points to the SideSide Bone.

3. Set up IK Options for this chain to look at a Null object, just as you did for the spherical eyes. Set the IK limits for SideSide to keep it within the horizontal limits of the sclera, and UpDown to keep it within the vertical. Lock off the two unused axes for each Bone. The range of motion of the iris will actually describe the outer surface of a torus, not an ellipsoid, but it's close enough to match sightlines and produce usable image sequences.

4. Save a duplicate of the complete character scene as EYEMAP.LWS. In the duplicate scene, delete every surface except the iris and sclera.

5. Position the Camera directly in front of the UpDown Null, and far enough away along the Z-axis that you can use a telephoto lens setting for the Camera. This will avoid most of the distortion from a wider-angle lens, so the image map will be a little more accurate. Set the Camera resolution to precisely frame the sclera, as in Figure 13-15.

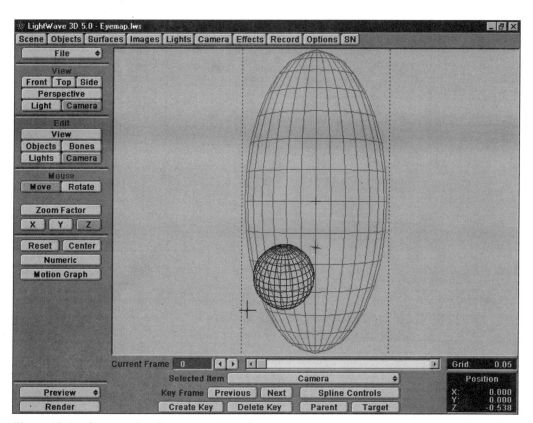

Figure 13-15: Camera view in EYEMAP.LWS.

6. Delete or 100 percent dissolve the sclera, leaving only the iris visible to the Camera. Set the Background color to pure white and set the lighting to produce an acceptable hot spot on the iris. Save the scene.

   At this point, the original scene can be animated, moving the target Null to match the iris movement to the action. When the animation has been approved, you can proceed to the next step.

7. Save the motion graphs for the iris's IK chain from the finished scene. Load the EYEMAP.LWS and apply the saved motion graphs to the appropriate objects. The iris should move exactly as it did in the animated scene. Render EYEMAP.LWS as an image sequence (see Figure 13-16).

Figure 13-16: Iris and sclera, and finished image map.

8. When rendering is complete, reopen the original animated scene, delete or dissolve the iris, and apply the image sequence to the sclera surface. Render the scene.

   The finished animation should show the iris applied precisely to the sclera. Since the image is mapped only to the sclera surface, the iris disappears if it crosses the edge of the eye, as if passing under an eyelid.

Eyelids: Cartoon

If the sclera shape of a cartoon eye is irregular or distorted, MTSE sequences of hand-modeled targets objects is the only reliable way to conform the eyelids to the eyeballs. Boning gets too complex too quickly when you start trying to compensate for irregular outlines.

Start modeling the eyelids with the fully closed version. It's easier to compress the longer complete eyelid to cover only a third of the eye, than to stretch a one-third eyelid over an irregular eyeball shape. You can either use LightWave 3D's Parent to Bone plug-in, or get Lock & Key (for more flexibility) to Parent the eyelid MTSE sequence to the character's head Bones. Fortunately, most eyelid movement is nearly a straight vertical line, and rapid enough that in-between errors are very small. Relatively few target objects are required, even if you build a model library that includes all the emotional reactions. If you keep the face symmetric, you should be able to model just one side's eyelids, then scale the entire library by -1 to create a matching library for the other side.

One of the problems with cartoon-style eyes and eyelids is the difficulty of keeping an animated pupil underneath a relatively thin modeled eyelid. Image mapping the iris to the sclera is a handy way to solve this problem.

Exercise 13-8: Model & Bone Cartoon Eyelids

1. Model a simple set of eyelids to match the eyes you created in Exercise 13-6. The minimum library includes objects for the following eyelid positions: fully closed, just above halfway open, normal rest position, and wide open.

2. Load the rest position eyelids into the cartoon eye scene and use the Parent to Bone plug-in to assign them to the same Bone that controls the sclera.

3. Set up the rest of the eyelid objects in an MTSE sequence, based on the rest position object.

4. Test the eyelids. Animate blinks and winks. Write up the scene for the character's model sheet.

Jaw

Most of the expression in a person's face is due to muscles and other soft tissues. Very little unique expression is contributed by the position of the jaw, but it acts as a modifier for many emotions and is important for lip sync. A human jaw is basically a hinge on the local X-axis, with a small amount of play allowing X-axis and Z-axis movement. The jaw does not pivot on either Y- or Z-axes, unless it has been broken or dislocated. The pivot of the jaw is located just under the rear end of the zygomatic arch, the ridge of bone that runs from the cheekbone back toward the ear. If you draw a horizontal line from underneath the eye socket to the opening of the ear, the pivot will be on that line and just forward of the ear.

The jaw carries the lower mouth, lower teeth, and the tongue along when it moves or rotates, and stretches the cheeks between their upper attachments and the jaw line. You can get a better feel for this if you run a finger inside your mouth, along the outside surface of your lower gums, pushing outward on the cheek to note where the flesh is fixed to the jaw and where it stretches to meet the rest of the face. You may be surprised at just how much of your face isn't really attached to anything; from just below the orbits to the jawline, it's all hanging loose. This is one of the times a model skull comes in handy, to correlate what your fingers are telling you with what the bone structure looks like.

The upper palate and teeth are locked to the rest of the skull; you should never try to animate them, unless you're trying to upset your audience with a really unnatural character. The upper front teeth are handy as reference points for facial maps, as they are visible in wireframe, do not move, and are near the center of the face.

When you model the lower face, remember that the lower jaw, teeth, lower edge of cheeks, and the base of the tongue are all attached and should share the same Parent Bone, with the X-axis of rotation at the hinge of the jaw. The tongue itself is extremely fluid and versatile, a mass of muscle with no limiting bone structure. It may be best to limit its use to phonemes that prominently display the tongue, or use one of the replacement techniques to allow detailed modeling of different tongue objects.

Exercise 13-9: Model & Bone the Jaw

1. Follow the usual procedure to surface, explode, Bone, and implode the jaw for the character's head. If you like, you can model and append a tongue and teeth.

2. Bone the jaw so you can animate it to open and close. Make sure the Parent Bone for the jaw is at 0 degrees Pitch when the jaw is closed; this makes it much easier to close the mouth during animation.

3. Test the Boned surfaces for effective range of motion (see Figure 13-17); open and shut the jaw, wiggle the tongue, and so forth. Write up the finished jaw for the character's model sheet.

Figure 13-17: Jaw Boned and slightly Pitched before setting Mouth Bones.

Mouth

The mouth is one of the most complex areas of a character's face, and contributes almost as much expression as the eyes. In nature, the mouth is a ring of muscle, the orbicularis oris, which forms the lips; there are at least five other major groups of muscles that pull, push, or otherwise affect some part of the mouth. The mouth can be complex enough to justify its own animation hierarchy, depending on how realistic you want your character's face to be.

The mouth is bounded by the rigid septum of the nose above, and the equally rigid attachments to the chin and jawline below. Between these extremes, the musculature of the mouth is almost completely free. This shows us where to begin to model and Bone the mouth: Parent the upper mouth to the root of the head and the lower mouth to the jaw. This takes care of the grosser movements required for lip sync and extreme emotions. Leaving the larger motions to a Parent Bone also leaves you more flexibility in setting Child Bones to animate the subsidiary surfaces.

The next level of the animation hierarchy is the lips. Generally, you can get away with leaving the upper surface of the upper lip and the lower surface of the lower lip to fend for themselves; the tension between the Bones controlling the lips and the Bones nailing down the jawline and upper face stretches the intervening polygons enough for most expressions. The lips proper need a fair number of Bones to provide an acceptable degree of control, but laying them out is intuitive enough that it's not very difficult.

A labor-saving technique for lips is to alternate short chains of Bones with IK goals the Bones are targeted to.

Before you begin adding Bones to the lips, you should consider ways to reduce the animator's workload without sacrificing flexibility. A labor-saving technique that is good for the lips is to alternate short chains of Bones with IK goals the Bones are targeted to. This means you only have to animate the root Bones and the IK goals, and the Child Bones help smooth out the lips' curves automatically. This can reduce the number of animation controls for a mouth by a factor of two at least, and perhaps a factor of four. One of the worst things you can do in creating a character's face is to simply set an independent Bone for each cross-section of the lips, forcing the animator to endlessly noodle for even the simplest lip sync. Keep it simple!

Keep in mind that the corners of the mouth have to move somewhere between the lower jaw's position and the rest of the face, but not exactly halfway. The lower lip usually stretches more with the jaw opening, and the upper lip stays relatively close to the upper face. The lips also should be able to pucker outwards or suck in, especially for pronouncing Ps, Vs, and Fs.

Exercise 13-10: Model & Bone the Mouth

1. Follow the procedure again to surface, explode, Bone, and implode the lips and mouth area. Make the upper mouth a Child of the head's root Bone and the lower mouth a Child of the jaw Bone.

2. Add enough Bones to the lips that you can animate it to lip sync and express basic emotions. Try to minimize the number of Bones or Nulls an animator will have to use.

3. Test the mouth for effective range of motion. Try a pucker, open wide, smile, fricative, and sibilant.

Cheeks

The cheeks are an interesting challenge after the complexities of the mouth; they can be deceptively simple. The main purpose of the cheeks is to bridge the distance between jaw and eye socket. For a low-resolution character, cheeks can even be single polygons stretched between the jawline, nose, mouth, and lower eyelids. Cheeks bulge up and out near the top when the corners of the lips are pulled up or the eyes squint. They stretch when the jaw is opened, and bulge from air pressure just before plosive phonemes or when the character is making a face.

The dual role of the cheeks requires a special solution. The stretching to connect the jaw is pretty easily handled, simply by being careful with positioning of points in the cheek surfaces. Air pressure bulging, on the other hand, is a bit of a challenge. I recommend tackling it with an additional Bone or set of Bones designed specifically to puff out the cheeks.

The CheekPufferBone should affect the lips, the upper lip to the base of the nose, the lower lip to the chin, the cheeks up to the lower eyelids and down to the jawline, and up to the edges of the nose on both sides. This is the outline of attachment for the loose skin of the cheeks. The CheekPufferBone should not affect the nose, the eyeballs, the jawline, the chin, the eyelids, the eyebrows, or any part of the top of the head above the eyes or back of the head behind the temples. These are either firmly attached to underlying bone, or beyond the cheeks' range of influence.

You can Bone the CheekPuffers by adding another frame to the implosion process, between fully exploded and fully imploded. Bring together in this frame only the surfaces affected by the CheekPufferBone, and keep them separated from the unaffected surfaces. In this way, you can combine surfaces for Boning in several different permutations.

Exercise 13-11: Bone Egghead's Cheeks

1. In the Scene Panel, shift all keys from frame 1 to frame 2. This leaves frame 1 available for the intermediate imploding you need to Bone the CheekPuffers.

2. Move the surface Bones for all those to be affected by the CheekPuffers into the planned Bones' effective range. Set a keyframe for each surface Bone at frame 1.

3. Add the CheekPuffer Bone(s). Try to get the effect with a single Bone if possible; most characters require at least two, one on each side, and may need more to get adequate expansion within other Bones' range of effect. Experiment with strength and range settings.

4. When you are satisfied with the performance of the CheekPuffer Bones, go to frame 2 and move the CheekPuffer into final position along with the other surface Bones.

5. Test and document the CheekPuffers for the character model sheet.

Miscellanea

Beyond the standard muscle groups and their effects are a whole range of special purpose Bones that can be very useful in modeling and animating characters. Very small Bones with high strength and small Limited Ranges can make dimples or muscle attachments; whole-head Bones can be used to create wild takes and squash-and-stretch. You can even set Muscle Swell for collections of small Bones, to make objects ripple and bulge.

Use Your Head

The Boned head you just created can be used directly in animations, but is at least as useful as a tool to create Metamorph and MTSE object libraries for Replacement animation techniques.

Exercise 13-12: Build a Basic Library

1. Animate the character head you just Boned to create poses for the major phonemes and emotions.

2. Use the Save Transformed function to create objects of each of the poses.

3. Save the new objects in a separate directory. Document the library and set up an MTSE sequence in a scene to enable easy loading of the complete library. As you add poses, update the MTSE sequence to include the new additions.

Moving On

This chapter and the preceding one have equipped you with the techniques to model complete characters. The next chapter shows you how to dress those characters up, giving them appropriate textures and colors and even using maps to substitute for detailed modeling.

Makeup & Wardrobe

Applying Maps & Shaders to Characters

This chapter is the equivalent of the wardrobe and makeup departments of a motion picture studio. Once you have modeled and set up the basic character, your next step is the coloring, texturing, and embellishments that add the realism—or that extra touch of fantasy—for the finishing touch. This chapter also shows you some general principles for modeling, Boning, and object library creation for animating fabrics.

Surface appearances are critical for any style of CGI character animation. A great job of texturing may not redeem a lousy piece of animation, but a lousy job of texturing can distract the audience from an otherwise excellent animation. The appearance of the character should agree with its actions; if a character moves as if made of rubber, but you texture it to look like chrome, you will confuse the audience. Your texturing should help tell the story without intruding. Ideally, no one should specifically notice the maps and shaders you apply; the audience should simply accept them as a natural part of the character.

What Are Your Options?

The basic map types for LightWave 3D are color, bump, diffusion, reflection, specularity, luminous, transparency, clip, and displacement. Theoretically, you could create a character that uses at least one map of each type, but most of the time you'll probably only use a few map types.

Color maps are the most obvious choice, but you can create more subtle effects with the others. A good TD can make an object look like almost any material, without using any color map at all. Conversely, even a photographic-quality color map is going to look wrong if it isn't complemented by other map types. For that reason, I recommend using color maps only as references early on and not actually applying them until last. Instead, I recommend using a neutral gray. Color is so overwhelming that it can distract you from getting the other settings just right, but if the character looks good with the other maps in place, it will look great with color added.

Characters need complex surfaces for facial features, skin, and clothing. If you are working in a style that lets you get away with solid colors and uniformly smooth surfaces, you can ignore this; but the closer you work to realism, especially matching to live action, the more complex surfaces you have to create for your characters. Maps for facial features have to reproduce the shape of the modeled features they replace; skin must look like it has a subtle roughness, that it grew, aged, and wrinkled from use; clothing has to look like it's really made of thousands of separate fibers with a definite weave, drape, and nap. Sheet materials like polished leather and vinyl must have the right "shine."

Make sure surfaces you apply suit the geometry of the object.

Make sure the surfaces you apply suit the geometry of the object. This can be especially challenging for objects that are exploded and Boned, as in Chapter 13. The mapping coordinates are based on the exploded object, so any map that bridges from one part to another will show severe distortion along the exploded seam. You can work around this by applying planar maps only along the same axis you used for the explode operation.

For example, most of the head object in Chapter 13 was exploded along the local Z-axis. If you look at the object in the Face view, almost everything is still aligned. So, if you apply a map along the Z-axis, you won't get any distortion at the seams. One problem with this work-around is that you can't use spherical or cylindrical mapping, since there is no way to avoid the exploded seams. If you apply a planar map to a round object like a head, you still get map smearing along the sides.

If you split the object into surfaces for the explode operations, you should probably redefine the surfaces again after all the explode and Bone operations are complete and you no longer need the surfaces as modeling selection tools. It's much easier to apply textures to surfaces defined by common surface appearance rather than Bone assignment. Having a single surface named Skin makes it easy to assign a skin texture, for example, rather than having to repeat identical settings for a number of surfaces like Head, Nose, Ears, and Eyelids.

If you are designing a character for replacement animation, remember that the surfaces don't morph with the objects.

If you are designing a character for Metamorph or MTSE replacement animation, you'll save time if you remember that the surfaces don't morph along with the objects. LightWave 3D uses the original object's UV mapping coordinates to stretch or compress the map to match the morph targets. In effect, LightWave 3D applies the surface settings of the original object in a Metamorph chain to each following object. This can save you a lot of production-line work; instead of having to painstakingly reapply all the surfaces to a derivative object created by a Save Transformed operation, you can leave the new object "as is," as long as you never try to use it without morphing it from the original textured object. You can also use Metamorph to evaluate textures for animation. Set up an MTSE chain of as much of the object library as you can manage, at one object per frame. Each time you revise the textures, rerender the scene, angling the camera to view the part you're working on. You'll have a much better idea of how the textures look when deformed by the character's animation. This is especially useful when the character's face can deform a great deal; you may find you have to use higher resolution maps to keep the stretched areas from showing individual pixels. The general rule of thumb regarding map resolution is that one pixel in the map should be no larger than one pixel in the final rendering.

Mapping Faces

Very simple character Head objects can use animated maps instead of modeled features to provide facial details. This approach works best for cartoon-style caricatures and features that do not protrude very much in profile. You can generally get away with mapping eyes and mouths, but you are better off modeling noses. If you are a good 2D artist, you can probably paint a set of lip sync mouth maps faster than you can model a single mouth object. You may want to consider doing tests for a new character with drawn maps for experimental features, and model them when your ideas have firmed up a bit.

The simplest approach to facial feature mapping is to paint just the color image maps to be applied to the character's lower face. You can use any paint software that can save an image compatible with LightWave 3D. There are advantages to using a program like Adobe's Photoshop, which enables you to use foreground and background layers to paint over rendered images. Whatever paint software you use, keep backup copies of any drawing templates you create. Just as with objects, there will always be additional demands on a character's dramatic and spoken range as the project progresses. If you can pull up the original mouth templates, it will be much easier for you to create more maps or to revise the existing libraries.

When you paint mouths for lip sync you should consider keeping them compatible with the Magpie lip sync software explained in Appendix H. Even if you use higher resolution maps for the finished animation, creating a duplicate set of thumbnail images for Magpie does not take very long and can be a great time saver for the person doing the lip sync exposure sheets.

Exercise 14-1: Paint a Mouth

1. Load scene file EXER1401.LWS from the Chapter 14 directory of the Companion CD-ROM.

2. Render frame 0 at high resolution in wireframe.
   This image is the starting point to create a map template you can load into your paint software.

3. Load the rendered map template into Photoshop or another image editor that can use multiple layers. Crop the image to include only the area below the nose and above the chin. Try to keep the proportions of the cropped image close to square; this makes it easier for the animator to work with Magpie for lip sync. Save the cropped image, as in Figure 14-1.

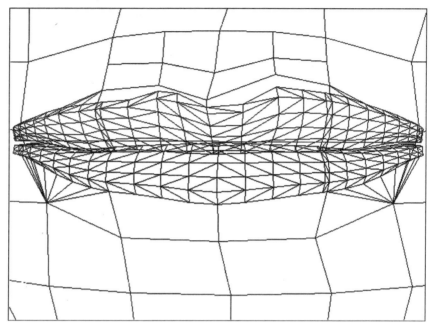

Figure 14-1: Map template for head object.

4. Use the cropped map template as one layer and paint your maps in another layer. You can use the lines of the original modeled mouth as guides, or you can do something completely original.

5. Paint an image of the mouth at rest—a nice default image. Save the new layer as a separate image. Repeat to create image maps of the mouth for the basic emotional and lip sync mouth shapes: Smile, Grin, Frown, Fear, Disgust, Stern, Crying, Sad, Disdain, and AI, CDGK, Closed, D, E, FV, LTH, MBP, O, U, and WQ.

   You can refer to the default mouths supplied with Magpie for examples of the lip sync shapes. Figure 11-2 shows a complete model sheet. You might also look in either Levitan's or Blair's books from the Bibliography. Both contain good mouth model sheets.

6. If you like, make 128x128 resolution BMP format thumbnails for each lip sync image. These thumbnails are compatible with Magpie.

7. Paste together a model sheet of all the thumbnails, and write the file names of the full-size maps under each image, as in Figure 11-2. This is another item for the character model sheets you deliver to the animator when the character is complete.

   You can repeat Exercise 11-1 if you'd like to test your lip sync maps.

Exercise 14-2: Bump It

The goal of this exercise is to create bump maps that match the color maps you painted in the preceding exercise. A properly executed bump map gives a sense of depth to the object and smooths out some of the disparity between the drawn maps and the modeled object.

1. Load the first color map into one layer of your paint software. You can either save and load a duplicate of the color map, or start off with a clean slate in another layer.

2. Paint over the mouth opening (if any) with solid black. Cover the teeth or tongue with very dark gray.

3. Draw pure white lines down the middle of the lips, tracing the high points.

4. Trace the perimeter of each lip in medium gray, defining where the slope of the lips drops back toward the level of the face.

   If you feel like cheating a bit, look ahead to Figure 14-4. This image is a depth-cued rendering of the modeled lips. You're trying to paint the same sort of gradient for the lip shape you defined in your color map.

5. Create gradient fills between the white "high" lines and the medium gray perimeter lines.

6. Paint a white line around the perimeter of the map. Create a gradient fill between the outermost perimeter line and the borders of the map.

   This is to smooth the mapped area back to the normal height of the unmapped area. The smoother your gradients, the better your bump maps look. If the jump between adjacent gray levels is too large, the bump map creates a stepped appearance.

7. Save the new layer as a separate image. You don't have to create Magpie-compatible thumbnails for the bump maps.

8. Repeat for the remaining color maps.

CD-ROM

You can test your bump map by applying it and the matching color map to the head object in scene file EXER1402.LWS, which you can find in the Chapter 14 directory of the Companion CD-ROM. This head has no modeled lips, just a flat area suitable for mapping.

Exercise 14-3: Clip & Save

The ultimate mapping for a mouth is a matched set of color, bump, and clip maps. Color and bump maps provide the surface appearance, and the clip map cuts away the mouth opening to create an unmistakably 3D effect. Of course, if you apply a clip map, you also have to model and animate a set of teeth and a tongue.

Clipping occurs precisely where the luma (brightness) value for the map drops below 50 percent. Since the edge of a clip map can't be dithered, if you use a low-resolution clip map, any curved or diagonal edge will show jaggies. If the bump map you are matching has a dithered edge, you can make the clipped edge smoother by duplicating the bump map, doubling or quadrupling its resolution, and converting it to a black-and-white bitmap. This image saves space, even though it's several times the size, makes the clipped edge jaggies much smaller, and still precisely matches the bump and color maps it is derived from.

1. Open a copy of one of the bump maps you created. Quadruple its resolution. Save it under a new name.

2. Change the mouth opening to pure black. Change the remaining areas to pure white. Save the modified image as a clip map.

    In Adobe Photoshop, one way to do this is to lighten the entire image about 60 percent, then use the magic wand to select the mouth opening, varying the range of the wand to get exactly the selection you want. With black as the foreground color, use Fill. The mouth opening should be solid black; use the Brightness and Contrast settings to keep the mouth opening dark and to lighten the rest of the image below 50 percent gray. Change Mode to Bitmap, using 50 percent threshold, to turn the image into a black-and-white clip map.

    When you apply the clip map, be careful to set its Center in the Z-axis to match the surface of the mouth area, and set Texture Falloff so the clipping doesn't go clear through the object. If the teeth or tongue are part of the same object, you will have to be especially precise with the Falloff or you'll clip them, too.

Hold It

If you choose to animate any part of a character using image sequences, you must pay careful attention to transitions. Since there is no automatic interpolation between images as there is for Metamorph objects, maps are inherently more jerky and difficult to smooth. Smooth interpolation is especially important for emotional transitions, which can take several seconds. Held vowels are also prime candidates as there is usually a slow transition from the first extreme pose to the more relaxed hold. Either of these situations will be unacceptably jerky with only the basic extreme pose maps. If you need a smoother transition, your only option is to create interpolated image maps. It's more work, but the difference in your lip sync and other transitions will be well worth it.

Skin 'Em

Unless you're animating the Invisible Man, you're going to have to texture your character's skin. A variety of skin maps is the core of a character TD's image collection. You can start off with high-resolution images of leather, which seem to be popular in clip-art and background collections. When converted to grayscale and applied at smaller sizes, well-grained leather does very nicely as human skin. For more bizarre characters, keep an eye out for images of snakeskin and reptile hides, and for the truly disgusting characters that populate some role-playing games, you might skim through a dermatology textbook or two for the worst-case photos. Then there are the procedural textures like Orange Peel, which work especially well at very small values.

In addition to the general skin maps, you may want to add bump maps to specific locations like the hands and eyes. Knuckles, palms, and eye corners tend to wrinkle deeply when flexed; if the character's style leans toward realism, you need to simulate this, too. Unfortunately, LightWave 3D doesn't allow you to animate a map's settings, so your only option is to create an image sequence.

Exercise 14-4: Wrinkle Map Sequences

1. Paint a knuckle wrinkle bump map. Look at your own knuckle for a model. Make the background white, and the folds grade down to black in the middle. Design it for planar mapping, applied from the top of the hand.

2. Create a range of knuckle wrinkle bump maps with decreasing contrast, ending with a map that is almost all white. In Adobe Photoshop you can use the Blur filter and the Brightness setting to gradually spread out and lighten the wrinkles.

3. To test the bump maps, create an image sequence from numbered copies of the maps, and apply it to the glove from Chapter 12; match the lightest images to the greatest bending angles.

Obviously, setting up animated bump maps is nearly as tedious and demanding as lip sync. Animating wrinkles should be one of the finishing touches, after all the action has been finalized. The animator may find it useful to print a copy of the motion graph for the mapped joint, and correlate specific angles with particular bump maps, creating a sort of exposure sheet for the knuckle.

Displacement?

You may be wondering why I haven't mentioned displacement maps. I don't recommend using them, except in certain special situations where their advantages outweigh their drawbacks. It's relatively easy to use a displacement map on a finely divided primitive, then optimize the results to create a complex object. Unfortunately, animation using displacement maps requires you to keep that initial complexity—which means one object point per map pixel, or you start getting 3D jaggies. Combining an unnecessarily complex object with the hassles of image sequence management seems to me to be the worst of both worlds.

Realism

When you are called on to match live action, especially inserting a CGI character into live footage, you have to use all the realism tricks. Materials have to be an exact match, their appearance under the matched lighting has to be identical, and in general you have to nearly duplicate reality.

If at all possible you should photograph and digitize materials on-site at the time of the live-action shoot. This gives you the opportunity to get extreme close-ups of textures and materials that may not show up clearly in the match footage. If a character is going to extrude itself from the tile floor it's a good idea to have an exact full-color scan of that tile floor to use as a map. If you can't get shots onsite at the time, talk to the set and prop crews afterwards to see if you can get shots of the materials later.

You should also shoot general coverage of the scene for use in reflection maps. Even a clean plate shot for the compositing effects may not be what you need for reflection mapping, but if you've got some nice clear 35mm prints you can usually piece together a decent environment map. Make sure you make the map large enough; if a reflective object has some broad convex curves, a tiny fraction of the reflection map can be stretched across quite a bit of the object.

If you have to work exclusively from the match footage, use image-processing software with an eyedropper tool to sample the footage for material colors. You also need to sample hot spots or a white card to pick up the original light colors since they affect the materials as well.

The usual giveaway for CGI elements composited into live action is not enough dirt. In the real world, anything outside a sterile clean room is going to collect crud. Corrosion, contaminants, precipitated smog, you name it—dirt is everywhere. Spread some of it on your characters if you have to get realistic. Add some rust, some dust, and some smudges and smears to your map collection. You can add a fractal noise texture in the specularity and diffuse channels for a quick and dirty (excuse the pun) weathered look. And keep your eyes open in the real world to observe and remember how materials change as they age and are abused. Take a look at an old, scuffed shoe, for instance; how would you texture a pristine CGI object of the same shoe? What color, bump, diffusion, and specularity maps would you use?

Clothing

Fabric is second only to skin as an important part of the character TD's mapping palette. With the obvious variety of fabrics available, you might think you'll have to build a huge library of fabric maps. Not so! I'm never one to discourage map collecting, but you can fake a surprising number of fabrics with a handful of basic elements.

Fabrics are either woven or sheet. If it's a sheet material like leather or vinyl, the texture is easy enough to figure out. If it's a woven material then simulating the texture gets a little more complex.

Here are some guidelines for creating clothing:

1. Identify the weave. Fabrics are manufactured in a wide variety of weaves, but half a dozen good bump maps will enable you to fake most of the materials you'll run across. I like digitizing shots of fairly coarse-woven cloth like canvas and burlap, then applying them at a very small size to simulate finer materials.

2. Identify the finish. Fabrics can be rough and slubby, or smooth and satiny. The finish will determine what type of specularity and diffusion maps you apply. These can generally be modified versions of the bump map.

3. Identify the color. This is where you may have to collect a lot of swatches, especially for patterned materials. On the positive side, you can create original tileable patterns and overlay them on the standard weave and finish maps to create your own fabrics.

Modeling the clothing itself is a more painstaking job. There are, as of this writing, no easy solutions to the simulation of cloth. It's on the "to do" list of studios all the way up to Pixar; it's a tough set of problems. The only currently available solution for character animation in LightWave 3D is to model, Bone, and animate the character's clothing as just another part of the character. Guess why so many CGI characters seem to be wearing tights?

If the point is to mimic the real behavior of fabrics, you should (big surprise) start off with observation. Pull some different materials out of your closet and practice draping them across your hand and arm. Note how the drape of the cloth depends on the thickness, the weave, the stiffness of the material, and on the shape of the object under it. Observe how the fabric responds to motion; wave a piece back and forth, tap your hand against it from behind, and set up a small fan, if you can, to observe how it billows in a breeze.

Those tights are starting to look like a better idea, aren't they?

Creating clothing for a character is usually a matter of building the character, then extrapolating their clothing from their general outlines. It's easier to take a cross section of a figure and scale it up slightly than to try reconstructing the same shape from scratch; you have a better idea of where and how the underlying figure would motivate or restrict the movement of the fabric. For example, let's look at how to construct a kilt for the Puppet character from Chapter 6.

Exercise 14-5: Modeling & Mapping a Kilt

The first step is to define the line where the fabric stops resting against the body and starts draping free.

1. Load the Hips object into Modeler. Rotate the object on the Y-axis, a few degrees at a time, and select the outermost points (one from each side) in each rotation's profile. When you've rotated the object 180 degrees, you should have a continuous line of selected points.

2. Duplicate the selected points. Extrude the duplicated points down to the hemline of the kilt. Turn on OpenGL preview to see if any part of the puppet penetrates the kilt.

3. Subdivide the kilt until you believe it has enough flexibility to drape properly. Delete the unnecessary parts from Modeler. Define the kilt as a single surface named Tartan. Save the object as KILT01.LWO.

    Modeling the kilt from the Hips object should keep the Pivot in the same place. When you load the kilt into Layout, you should be able to parent it directly to the Hips object and know that it will be perfectly aligned.

4. Load the Puppet walking scene you completed in Exercise 6-1 or 6-2. If you are working through this book on the TD path, and have therefore not worked through Chapter 6 yet, open scene file EXER1405.LWS from the Chapter 14 directory of the Companion CD-ROM. Open the Objects Panel and load the kilt object. Close the Objects Panel.

5. Open the Surfaces Panel. Select the Tartan surface. Apply a color map with a suitable pattern, as a tiled cylindrical map. The stock Windows tartan pattern will do nicely. If you like, add a bump map with the appropriate weave.

6. Add Bones to the kilt, running in chains down each lengthwise seam. Set a series of Null objects like dangling charms, one at the end of each Bone chain. Set up each Bone chain for full time IK, with the final Bone at the hemline set to target the nearest Null object (see Figure 14-2).

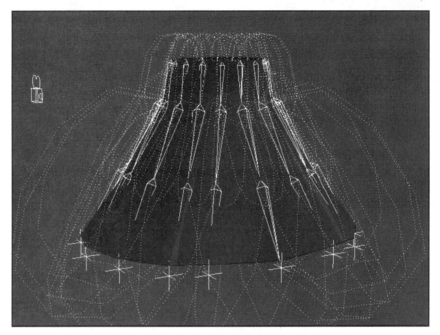

Figure 14-2: Boned kilt.

This makes it easier for you to animate most of the kilt's behavior by moving the IK goal objects.

7. Animate the kilt for one walk cycle. Make sure the kilt never passes through any part of the Puppet, and vice versa. Animate the kilt's individual Bone chains with overlapping action to convey an impression of heavy cloth. Animate the follow-through each time the Puppet decelerates, and the overlapping action delay each time the Puppet accelerates.

8. When you're satisfied with the kilt's posing, render the animation. Play it back. Does the cloth look real enough?

9. Document the kilt for the Puppet's character model sheet.

Mapping When You Can't Model

There's another way to get detailed, well-graded bump maps for
characters: model them first! You can use the Fog feature in
LightWave 3D's Effects Panel to create grayscale bump maps directly
from 3D objects. If you animate the objects, you can even render
bump image sequences. This can be very useful in situations where
texture maps are acceptable, but complex Boned objects aren't.

Exercise 14-6: Rendering a Bump Map

1. Open a scene with an animated character. A lip sync exercise is a
   good choice. Save a copy of the scene as BUMPMAP1.LWS.

2. Set the Camera to look straight on at the character's lips, and
   change the Camera Panel resolution to crop out everything but
   the lips and their associated surfaces. Your Camera view should
   look something like Figure 14-3.

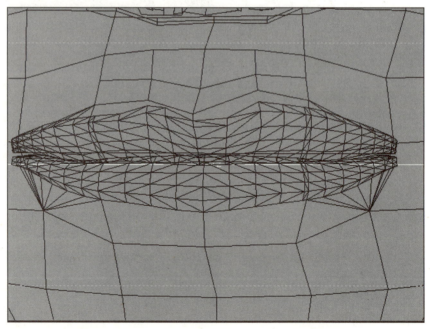

Figure 14-3: Camera view of modeled lips.

3. If you want matching color maps for the bump maps, you should render them now.

4. In the Surfaces Panel, change the visible surfaces to a matte white, with no specularity or reflection, and 100 percent diffusion.

5. In the Lights Panel, turn off all the lights. Set Ambient Light to 100 percent.

6. In the Effects Panel, set Background Color and Fog Color to black. Select Linear for Fog Type. Set the Maximum Fog Amount to 100 percent. Set the Minimum Fog Amount to 0 percent. Set Minimum Fog Distance to the distance between the Camera and the nearest visible point of the object. Set Maximum Fog Distance to the distance between the Camera and the farthest visible point of the object.

These settings create a black fog that darkens the parts of the object farther from the Camera. If you turn on the Show Fog button in the Options Panel, Layout will draw a black circle representing the Maximum Fog Distance. This can be a big help when you're trying to get the fog to cover just the right area. The resulting images show white at the "highest" parts of the object, and black at the lowest. You should end up with rendered images like Figure 14-4. You can also render inverted bump maps by changing the object's surfaces to black, and the background and fog to white.

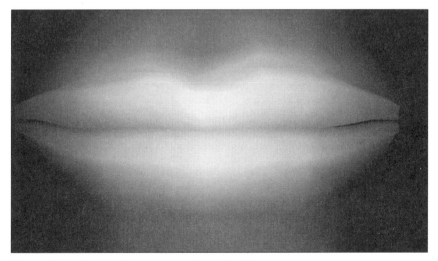

Figure 14-4: Rendered bump map of modeled lips.

Moving On

This chapter showed you a few new tricks for texturing character objects. The next chapter is about making life easier for the animators, and incidentally for yourself, by setting up default character scenes properly.

Setting Up Default Character Scenes

Whether you are making an entire animated film yourself, or just doing setup work for a team of animators, you should try to make the animator's job as easy as possible. One of the ways you can save the animator a lot of time and effort is to set up default scenes for each character. This chapter shows you how to set up a basic default scene for a complete character.

It's All Your Default

A default scene contains a character with all its associated textures, Bones, hierarchies, motion plug-ins, and lights set up and ready to animate. A good rule of thumb for including items in a default scene is: would the animators have to set this up before they could start animating the character? If the answer is yes, include it. If no, you can let it slide unless the animator specifically asks for it.

Depending on the preferences of the animators, you may also have to pose the character in a default posture. There are several advantages to assembling a character spread-eagled on the ground; if you build the character this way, the animator shouldn't have to stand the character up and move the arms to a more normal pose every time; you should do that in the default scene.

Animators can work faster and more efficiently if they can get a clear picture of the part of the character they are posing without having to tweak a view every time. This is difficult with the standard views, but since LightWave 3D allows you to use each light as a view, there is a workaround. Simply add a set of inactive lights, assigned to the various Bones or objects that require close-up views, so the animator can change views by changing lights. You can add as many lights as you need, and once they are set you never have to tweak them. Also, any time you use Load From Scene to import the character, you can import all the View Lights at the same time.

Setting up these View Lights for a Parented object hierarchy is no problem, you just Parent the View Lights to the appropriate objects. Boned objects are a little more difficult; the easiest way to set up View Lights for a Boned hierarchy is to use Dynamic Realities' Lock & Key motion plug-in. LightWave 3D's ParentBone motion plug-in can do most of the same job, but the setup is unacceptably tedious and counterproductive.

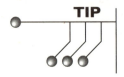

TIP

Have at least one View Light covering each area the animator needs to see in detail. Generally, anywhere there are a lot of active Bones, or an especially tricky piece of a hierarchy, you'll want to set a View Light. A typical character might need face front, right face, left face, left hand, right hand, left foot, right foot, and perhaps full body front and full body side View Lights.

Keep in mind that lights are always displayed in selection lists in the order they are added to the scene. You should use Load From Scene to add the character before any other lights are added, so the View lights are at the top of the selection menu and are the easiest to find. If you work with OpenGL, you should leave one active Distant Light (the default scene light will do) at the top of the list. OpenGL can only use the top eight lights in the scene's list, so you could easily end up with all eight eligible slots filled by inactive View Lights. Once you start setting active lights for the character (see Chapter 17), you should put the first key light at the top of the list. All these considerations mean you should carefully plan your View Lights before you start building the scene.

Lock & Key Combos move the keyed item precisely to the lock item's coordinates. For most View Lights, you want to offset the light from the lock item. For example, a key Light locked to the root Bone of the character's head, with no offset, would be located at the pivot of the HeadBone; this view from inside the character's head wouldn't be terribly helpful in posing the face.

The simplest way to do this is to set combos to key a Null object to each lock item, then Parent the View Lights to the appropriate Null objects. For example, the head and face would only need one Null, locked to the Head Bone. The three View Lights, face front, left, and right, would all be Parented to the Null, and positioned and rotated to give the intended view.

Exercise 15-1: Create a Default Scene for Fred

1. Load scene file EXER1501.LWS from the Companion CD-ROM.
   This file contains an early version of the main character in the example script. All the Bones have been set, and there is only one light in the scene, which is the default used for OpenGL viewing. If you have trouble with screen redraw times, you can replace the object with the low-polygon version, also in the Chapter 15 directory.

2. Add six Null objects and name them for the Face, Right and Left Hands, Right and Left Feet, and Body.

3. Use the Lock & Key plug-in (if you have access to it) to set combos for each Null object as a key to the appropriate Bone's lock.
   The Bone names in the character are pretty descriptive; I prefer setting the combos to the Toes and Fingers, to better center the extremities in the lights' views.

4. Add nine lights to the scene. Set them all for black, 0 percent Light Intensity, Lens Flares and Shadow Maps disabled, No Diffuse and No Specular, and Shadow Type off. Give them appropriate names.

5. Parent each light to the appropriate Null. Move and rotate them to give views like the nine shown in Figure 15-1, and set a keyframe at frame 0 for each of them.

You should end up with a scene that looks like the central image of Figure 15-1, with lights pointing at the face, hands, feet, and body.

Figure 15-1: Nine View Lights images covering a character.

If other complex lighting setups are required, it is a good idea to create a Null object at the origin, set up all lights as Parented to the Null, then save the Null and lights in a scene of their own. The animator can then create a new scene, load the character (and View Lights) from the character's default scene, then load the lighting setup from the lights' default scene. This makes very quick work for variations on a reusable set or character.

Write It Up

Once you've set up the default scene, you should document the whole thing, including the view and name of each light. You might just make a sort of contact sheet like Figure 15-1, and hand-write your notes around the images. Include this with the model sheet and other documentation for the character.

Exercise 15-2: Document the Default Scene for Fred

1. Write up the lights, positions, and views for the default scene you just set up.

Moving On

You should now be able to set up a default character scene that is faster and easier for an animator to use. A lot of these tips apply as well to sets, which we cover in the next chapter.

Backgrounds & Sets

Sets and backgrounds help you tell the story by placing your characters in an environment that helps define them. If the characters were acting on a bare stage, all their definition and development would have to come from their actions and appearance. A man sitting in a plain chair on a bare floor might be anyone; a man sitting on a throne in surroundings of rich ornamentation is most likely a king. A great actor can sit on a plain chair and make you believe he's a king, but animating that level of performance is a very tough job. Sets and backgrounds can carry some of the dramatic load, making the animator's job a little easier.

Backgrounds

Using images as backgrounds can simplify the animator's and TD's jobs, while adding realism and a level of detail that would be difficult or impossible to duplicate with objects or procedural textures. The most common use of backgrounds is for skies, landscapes, and live action footage to be matched. In LightWave 3D, you can apply images to the background or foreground layers in the Effects Panel, or you can create mapped objects called *backplanes*. Backplanes are often more useful since you can animate them separately, unlike the background and foreground, which are locked to the Camera view.

Exercise 16-1: Setting Up Photographic Backplane Objects

1. Load scene file EXER1601.LWS from the Chapter 16 directory of the Companion CD-ROM. This scene contains the street and building used in Chapter 9.

2. Open the Objects Panel and add SKYPLANE.LWO to the scene. Position the new object near the end of the sidewalk, about -75 on the X-axis, and a little below the level of the road, about -1 on the Y-axis. Rotate SkyPlane's heading 90 degrees so it crosses the sidewalk.

   If you position the Camera to look down the sidewalk from in front of the building's doorway, the SkyPlane should now cover the Camera's entire field of view.

3. Open the Images Panel and load CLOUDS4.IFF into the scene. Open the Surfaces Panel and select the Sky surface. Set Surface Color Luminosity to 100 percent. Open the Color Texture Panel and apply the Clouds4 image as a planar map on the Z-axis, using Automatic Texture Sizing to match the image to the object's dimensions. Close all the panels, then open the Objects Panel and save the SkyPlane object with the new surface settings.

4. Position the Camera to the right of the building's doorway and looking down the sidewalk toward the SkyPlane. Make sure none of the SkyPlane object's edges are showing.

5. Save the scene. Render an image. You should get something like Figure 16-1.

Figure 16-1: Photographic backplane in scene.

A fixed backplane looks very pretty for still images, but what about animation? As soon as the Camera moves, the visible change in the backplane is a dead giveaway. You don't expect the view of the sky to change dramatically just because you move a few steps. You can fix this by Parenting the Camera to the backplane object, then using the backplane to control the position of the Camera in one axis. As long as the distance between the backplane and the Camera is the same, the Camera can move all you want in the other two axes, and you can rotate it freely in all three.

Exercise 16-2: Matching Backplane to Camera Motion

1. Reload the scene you created in the preceding exercise.

2. Parent the Camera to the Skyplane object. Move the Camera to a good viewing position, as you did in step 4 of the preceding exercise. You need to offset the Camera along the SkyPlane's Z-axis, probably about -7 units. Make a keyframe for the Camera at frame 0.

3. Animate the SkyPlane along the global X-axis, making sure it doesn't move into the area of stronger light near the streetlight or off the end of the sidewalk, either one of which could spoil the illusion.

4. Make the Camera do a fly-by of the building front. Animate the Camera along the X- and Y-axes and rotate around all three axes, being careful not to expose any edges of SkyPlane. Do not move the Camera along the Z-axis or you'll change the offset from the SkyPlane and spoil the illusion. Set the necessary keyframes for the Camera.

5. Save the scene under a new name. Render the animation. You should end up with something like EXER1602.AVI (see Figure 16-2), which you can find in the Chapter 16 directory of the Companion CD-ROM.

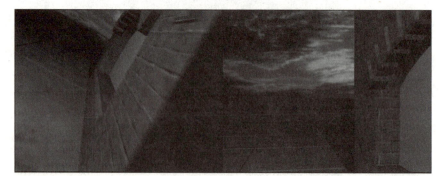

Figure 16-2: Two frames from EXER1602.AVI.

Note how the backplane keeps its appearance in relation to the horizon line, creating the illusion that the sunset is actually part of the scene.

You can simulate the view from a vehicle by varying the procedure you just learned. Add a backplane object to a scene and Parent a vehicle object to the backplane, just as you did for the Camera. Parent the Camera to the vehicle, and place the Parented Camera at the driver's point of view, with the vehicle's controls and windscreen bordering the frame. If you use an image sequence on the backplane to mimic the view from a moving vehicle, remember to match the scene's lighting to the lighting in the backplane.

Move Matching

It's fairly easy to composite CGI characters into live action footage that has been shot with a locked-down camera. You can pick a set of reference points in the first image, set up your objects and Camera to match those points, and animate the entire shot without worrying about matching anything else. The problem is that live action directors hate to lock down their cameras. A lot of the dramatic range available to the director depends on moving the camera.

To give the director the freedom to move the camera, a technique called *move matching* was developed. Move matching requires you to animate the LightWave 3D Camera to match the live action camera position and attitude in every frame of live action footage. Depending on how the camera is moved, you may end up setting key frames for all six rotate and move axes for every frame. That's the worst case; if the camera is mounted on a fairly solid dolly or a damped mount, the motions on at least a few axes will be more regular, gentle, and easily matched with the motion graph tools.

Documenting the Set

Move matching is much easier if you can get on the set before the shoot and gather some basic information. If you have to do it all from the match footage, animating the Camera's match moves is a pain in the neck.

Your number one priority is camera information. If you can get motion path information digitally from a special instrumented camera, most of your work is done. If it's an uninstrumented camera, measure everything. Ask the cinematographer about the lenses and settings they will be using. Talk to the crew about anything affecting the camera motion, from the layout of the dolly tracks to the offset between the film plane and the camera mount swivel. It's amazing what kind of information can save your sanity during a difficult match move.

At the same time, you need to be polite and professional with the entire crew. They've got a job to do, and usually not enough time in which to do it. Most of them are probably making more money than you, and if the rationale is that delaying a shot 15 minutes saves you 10 days, the production manager may well decide that your 10 days is cheaper than the crew's 15 minutes.

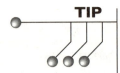

TIP Be prepared to work around the edges. Collect your measurements when you can, and otherwise keep out of people's way. Measure everything three times with an accurate steel tape. You'll be building models of most of it, at least enough for reference points.

It also makes your job easier if you can place four or more bluescreen balls in the scene as reference points. These are ping-pong, golf, or other small balls painted in chroma key colors. You need to place them inconspicuously so at least three of them are visible to the camera at all times, so that you can derive the matching LightWave 3D Camera position by triangulation in each frame. You should also place them where the background will be easy to cut-and-paste or chroma key over them. Repeated patterns like brick, wallpaper, or wood are good choices. Sticking your markers on complex or reflective surfaces is a big no-no. If you can't place your own markers, make sure you have accurate measurements to corners, seams, patterns, or any other kind of detail that will be visible in the match footage.

The complement to move matching is match lighting. Refer to Chapter 17 for some important on-location tips for gathering lighting information.

Back in Your Studio

Once you have your match footage digitized, load it in Layout as an image sequence and use the Effects Panel to select it as the background. Set your Camera Panel resolution and aspect ratio to match the lens and frame used. If you have a set of accurate measurements for your reference points, place color-coded Nulls at each of the points, as precisely as possible. Position another Null at the location of the live action camera for the first frame of the match footage. You don't want to position the Camera directly; it's much easier to match camera moves if you separate the XYZ motion from the HPB rotation. Move the CameraNull to match position, Parent the Camera to the CameraNull, and rotate the Camera to match rotation.

If all your measurements were accurate, the first setup of the Nulls should put the marker Nulls pretty close to the reference points in the first frame. If not, try to track down the problem before you go any further; odds are the same problem will affect every frame, so you should try to fix it now.

Tweak the Camera and CameraNull until the nulls precisely match the background reference points in the first frame. Set a keyframe for each one. Compare the actual settings against the measurements you took, and make a note of the differences. You may have to apply those corrections to every frame. Go to the last frame of the match footage, set the position and rotation by your notes, and tweak them again until you get another perfect match.

Keep repeating this process, splitting the difference between key frames until you get smoothly matched movement for the entire scene. You may find that one or more axes can be defined by a small number of keyframes, especially if that axis was locked down or controlled by an accurate mechanical device. If an axis was controlled by a human hand, you're going to get slaloms and jitter in the motion graph, and will probably end up making every frame a key.

The One-Object Set

You can make Layout setups a lot easier for both TDs and animators if you combine all the immovable objects in a scene into a single object. Furniture, walls, and architectural details rarely need to be animated. You can also delete unnecessary polygons once you know they won't be seen in a shot, and conserve memory and save redraw and rendering time. You can add simple looping actions to a set as Child objects. You can set fan rotation, clock hands, even dripping water to Repeat in the Motion Graph Panel.

If you think ahead about set construction, you can build reusable objects that you can customize with a minimum of effort. Suppose you assigned a Bone to lock down all the points defining a window opening; you could drag the Bone to move the window, use Save Transformed, and have a new room layout. With a judicious placement of Bones and definition of surfaces, you can make a "chameleon room" that you can transform into the basis of almost any interior set.

When you're ready to furnish a set, don't neglect 3D clip art. If the animation's style is very quirky and unique, you'll probably have to model everything from scratch; but if the sets are at all "normal," you can probably find some clip art that will save you modeling time. CD-ROM collections are available, including inexpensive compilations from Internet FTP sites. Those sites are also good hunting grounds, if you have the time to browse.

Exercise 16-3: Building a Simplified Set

1. Assemble a generic office set as a single object in Modeler, with floor, ceiling, walls, door, window, desk, chairs, credenza, shelves, and lamp, using prebuilt objects. Cull objects from the Internet, NewTek's LightWave 3D CD-ROM, and any other sources you find useful.

2. Define surfaces so you can select the individual parts, as necessary.

3. Build Child objects for a clock, ceiling fan, or other object that will make cyclical motions. Set up a looping motion graph, and set it to Repeat.

Moving On

This chapter has shown you some techniques to make your character's environments more effective for storytelling, and to save you time and effort. The next chapter shows you how to illuminate them to best effect.

Lighting Design

Lighting design is a whole profession in itself, and much has been written elsewhere on creating good lighting designs with LightWave 3D. This chapter therefore concentrates on lighting tips specifically for character animation. Appropriate lighting can help tell your story; poorly designed or inappropriate lighting can obscure or ruin it.

You can save time and effort if you set up lighting last, after all camera and character animation has been finalized and approved. You will modify the lighting to support the animation, so if there are revisions to the action you will have to revise the lighting as well. There's no sense doing a job over if you don't have to.

A useful way to light the shot before turning it over to the animators is to turn off all the other lights and crank up Ambient to between 25 and 50 percent. This makes the whole scene clear enough for the animators to see what they're doing and keeps rendering times for tests to a minimum. After the animation is final, you can set up a more aesthetically pleasing and dramatically useful lighting design.

Basic Three-Point

The standard three-point lighting setup of *key* light, *fill* light, and *rim* (or back) light works just fine as a starting point for character lighting.

◈ Key light illuminates the strongest part of the character's face or action and casts the strongest shadows.

◈ Fill light softens the shadows to bring out the remaining areas.

◈ Rim light outlines the character's profile.

The usual photographer's three-point setup is a key light high and to one side of the camera, a fill light low and to the other side, both pointing toward the subject, and a rim light high in back of the subject and on the same side as the fill, pointing toward the camera.

Exercise 17-1: Three-point Lighting for Fred

1. Load scene file EXER1701.LWS. This scene contains the basic object of a character, but no Bones or animation; this is just for lighting tests.

2. In the Lights Panel, turn off Ambient. Set up a 100 percent white key spot. Add a 50 percent blue fill spot set to No Specular. Add a 200 percent white rim spot set to No Diffuse. Arrange the lights in a standard studio photographer's three-point, with all three spots targeted on the object.

3. Render an image. You should end up with something like Figure 17-1.

Setting the Mood, Telling the Story

The three-point setup is adequate for illuminating the character, but it doesn't do much for telling the story. Lighting can set the mood of a shot, highlight an action, even foreshadow a character's behavior.

You can help establish the mood of a shot by carefully selecting and balancing the lighting colors.

Light for the story, light for the character, but never light to show off. Your audience will rarely care that you can light every form of lens flare known to cinematography, or that you can simulate light refracting through a lava lamp; the audience wants you to tell them a story. No one should notice your lighting, it should be completely taken for granted. If the lighting stands out enough to be noticed by a nonprofessional audience, you've been soloing when you should have been harmonizing.

Figure 17-1: Fred illuminated with a standard three-point setup.

You can help establish the mood of a shot by carefully selecting and balancing the lighting colors. Generally, warm lights (daylight and firelight, warm whites to reds) as keys make for a positive mood, accented by cooler fill and rim lights. Cooler lights (night and moonlight, cool whites to blues) as keys, especially in an overall darker shot, can create a sense of foreboding unless they are strongly balanced by warmer fill and rim lights.

You also need to consider the effect of colored lights on the character's textures. Complementary colors in light and surfaces can go black or otherwise produce unintended effects.

Shadow is at least as effective as light in setting a shot's mood. What you do not light is often more important than what you do light. Your audience's eyes are drawn to the bright areas of the frame; keep the character in the light while shading the rest of the scene, and the audience will keep their eyes on your character. Go easy on the shadows, not only to minimize rendering time but for simplicity in the shot composition. I usually prefer to leave all but one light's Shadow Type set to Off. Only one light in a scene is the best one to create a shadow that helps tell the story or define the character; find that light and set its Shadow Type to Shadow Map. Also, if you use only one light's shadow mapping, that shadow is colored by the other lights, producing an elegantly realistic effect.

I'm Ready for My Close-Up, Mr. DeMille

If you can, start off with lighting the character. In a minimalist stage production, it's just the actor and the lights, right? It's the same principle here; you can create a good story with just the character shot against a plain background, but the lighting still has to show that character to the audience. A completely dark stage doesn't have a lot of dramatic range. There will be times you have to start with the lighting of the set, but try to put the character first whenever you can.

You shouldn't plan to set up a character's lighting just once for an entire sequence. To get the right effect, cinematographers and gaffers usually relight the subject for each change in camera angle and shot composition. This is especially important when lighting a character's face; a perfectly good lighting setup for one camera angle may give a completely wrong effect from another angle. You also want to set up lighting for any other character action. Bringing up a supplemental key on a hand, just before the hand gestures, can be as strong a precursor for the audience as the traditional staging motion.

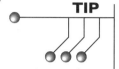

TIP

Good people are lit from heaven, bad people are lit from hell. Key lighting a character's face from a low angle is a common technique in horror and mystery films when a sinister effect is desired. Keep the key light high for more sympathetic characters, and nearly overhead for that angelic, haloed effect.

The eyes are the windows to the soul. If the audience can't see your character's eyes, the animator has a harder time communicating emotional transitions and the character's mental processes. The character's eyes should show a bright specular spot unless they are unhappy or otherwise emotionally down.

Lights used in cinematography specifically to bring out that spot are called *eyelights*. You can set up good eyelights by parenting a pair of tightly focused spots set for No Diffuse to the eyeball goal object, and targeting them at the eyeballs. The spots should be tight enough to only illuminate the eyeballs themselves, and must have an Envelope for intensity so you can dim them when necessary, as during a blink or when the character transitions to a "down" emotional expression. Literally, the light should go out of their eyes.

It doesn't take much light to get that sparkle in the character's eyes. Start off with a very low intensity and work your way up to the lowest value that gives you an acceptable specular highlight.

Miscellaneous Tips

- When you're ready to start lighting the finished animation, turn down the ambient light to 5 percent or less. Ambient light may be good for sunny outdoor scenes, but too much washes out a shot and leaves it looking flat. You can create a more natural look by using soft lights for area lighting. For a nice soft fill light, use a Distant type light set for No Specular.

- Don't use lens flares in character animation. Most cinematographers are very careful to prevent lens flare, so why should you deliberately add it? It's also been overdone so much that lens flares on a demo reel are usually interpreted as an amateur's touch.

Making Reference Objects

When you need to match live-action footage, you should try to take measurements and a clean plate at the time of the original shoot. If you can place a reference object in the scene, it makes matching shadows and light colors much easier.

For reference objects, I recommend two items: a sundial-type arrangement with a grid pattern around the gnomon, so you can reproduce the sun angle and any other shadows from the scene's lighting; and a full- or half-sphere at least a foot in diameter, painted matte white, to pick up the colors of any lights plus the ambient levels.

I found a Plexiglas half-sphere at a hobby shop and constructed the sundial to fold up and fit inside it, so carrying both items around wasn't awkward. Just set up the sundial so it's level and the camera has a clear view of its grid, and point the white sphere's convex side directly at the camera lens.

◈ If you have a lighting setup you really like, set up a scene with just those lights, Parented to a null object at the origin. You can later use the Load from Scene command in the Objects Panel to load the null and its Parented lights into your current project. Also, it helps to name your lights in case you want to tweak them later. WarmKeyLight is a lot easier to understand than Light003.

◈ Experiment with lighting every chance you get. Lighting often takes as much time as staging the scene. A lot of that time goes to the numerous test renders needed to get things lit exactly right.

Moving On

With this chapter's tips firmly in mind, you should be able to light any character's action to good effect. The next chapter, "Rendering," shows you how to get the best images possible, considering your computer, budget, and schedule.

18

Rendering

This chapter points out some of the tips and tricks you can use to minimize rendering time. This is especially important in a production environment, but even hobbyists like to see their animations as quickly as possible. Sometimes you have to choose between rendering time and image quality, but many of the following techniques can be used without reducing quality. If you can reliably get good images out of the system faster than anyone else, you'll never be unemployed for long.

Your Computer

You can never have too much RAM, hard disk space, or processing speed.

The first thing you should do to shorten rendering time is get a bigger, faster machine. Just kidding! Although you can never have too much RAM, hard disk space, or processing speed, most of us have to work in the real world. Fantasies about the ideal rendering monster system won't help your TD work. On the other hand, if you can produce really outstanding work on a rinky-dink machine, your problem-solving skills and can-do mindset will be valuable assets even when you're wrangling a 20 teraFLOP network.

LightWave 3D follows the same steps every time it renders an image. It loads the objects, maps, and other files required for the current frame into RAM, calculates the image, and saves the image to storage. You can add optional steps (post-processing plug-ins, image file compression, etc.) to this process, but most of them slow it down. Each step in the rendering process is a potential bottleneck; learn the bottlenecks of your particular system's RAM, storage drives, and CPU, and how to work around them.

If you have plenty of hard disk space, but little RAM, you can split up scenes into more manageable layers, render each layer as an image sequence, and composite the layers together. This enables you to render complex scenes that would otherwise overload your machine. If you don't have enough RAM and you try to render the scene anyway, LightWave 3D treats part of your hard disk as if it were RAM (a swap file) and moves bits of the scene to and from your hard disk as necessary. This is sometimes referred to as *thrashing*. As you may imagine, this really slows down the rendering process and doesn't do your hard disk any good, either.

If you have plenty of RAM, but loading files from the hard disk seems to take up a lot of time, you might try allocating a RAM disk. (The exact procedure depends on which hardware platform you are running.) If you load some or all of the scene's files to the RAM disk, LightWave 3D can load them for rendering much faster.

If you are thinking about upgrading or purchasing a machine, pay as much attention to the bus speed as to the CPU speed. The bus speed determines how fast LightWave 3D can push data around your system, from hard disk to RAM to CPU and back again. If the bus speed is significantly lower than the CPU speed, you may not be getting all the performance you should. The CPU may render images fast enough, then sit there wasting cycles waiting for the next batch of data from the bus.

Files

LightWave 3D can render much faster if the object and image files you add to a scene are designed to load and render efficiently. Following are a few simple guidelines that can speed up your rendering.

For images, keep it simple. If an image is going to occupy a quarter of the screen at the Camera's closest distance, and your output resolution is 640x480, any resolution higher than 160x120 will be wasted.

Design your image, bump, and other maps to suit the resolution at which you will actually render them. The same goes for color depth; it's just wasting RAM and disk space to use a 24-bit color image for a bump map when only 8 bits' worth of luminance information is used. Make a habit of asking yourself, "How much detail is the audience able to see?" Whenever possible, use image maps instead of procedural textures, since maps render much faster. One approach is to apply a procedural texture to an object, render an image of it, and apply the rendered image as a map to the original object.

For objects, again, keep it simple. If an object is going to appear small or in the background of a shot, replace it with a simplified version. Save the full zillion-polygon versions for extreme close shots where all the detail will show. If you will be using a character in a number of different shots, you may be able to save a lot of rendering time by creating different versions of the object for different Camera distances. Even if an object is seen only in close shots, if it is very complex you may find it worthwhile to model alternate versions with back surface polygons deleted. If a shot only shows the character's face, loading the polygons that form the back of his head is a waste of time.

Objects Panel

After you've finished laying out a scene and have done your test renderings, take a good look at where the shadows fall. Note which objects have to cast shadows, receive shadows, or shadow themselves. For each object, open the Objects Panel and turn off the Shadow options that aren't needed.

Lights Panel

Just as for objects, turn off Shadow options for lights that don't need them. Use only the minimum lights necessary to the scene. More lights always cause a longer render, but do not always produce better-looking results. If you must set up a complex lighting scheme, try separately lighting layers of a scene to save rendering time, since a rendered layer applied as a background image needs no lights.

Use shadow maps rather than traced shadows whenever possible. They render faster, and generally look better because of their soft edges. You can fake shadows, too; if you are really pressed for rendering time, you can model shadow objects. For example, if a table has a shadow below it, make a dark transparent polygon shadow and place it beneath the table.

Camera Panel

One of the options that beginners tend to waste a lot of time on is raytracing. Other than the gee-whiz factor of creating complex scenes, do you really need photorealistic glass, chrome, or other raytraced surfaces? You should keep in mind that potential employers have seen a lot more CGI than you have, and are thoroughly sick of raytraced reflection studies. They will be more interested in a good application of shadow, reflection, and projection maps to achieve a realistic effect with more finesse. If you have a lot of obviously raytraced stuff on your demo reel, it won't say much about your ability as a TD to fake a "look" without resorting to brute-force rendering. It's better to dazzle them with your skills, not your tools.

You should always try to keep enough RAM free to render the scene in one segment. Split the rendering into foreground and background layers if necessary; you'll still save time overall. Select an appropriate antialiasing level; overdoing it for a particular resolution just wastes time. Motion blur can be increased to cover a number of problems, but can also increase rendering times. If you plan to use a lot of motion blur, you may want to split the scene into layers again. You can generally render a background layer without motion blur, but the foreground characters should have as much motion blur as they can handle.

If you are rendering an animation to put on a demo reel or otherwise impress someone, you might try rendering it in widescreen. You will actually be rendering a smaller size image, but it looks like a letterboxed film so people tend to think of it as higher quality work.

Record Panel

If you are compositing any layers of animation and have plenty of hard disk space, you can save a little processing time by leaving Save Animation off and saving the rendering as a numbered sequence of TGA or IFF image files. LightWave 3D won't have to run compression for an AVI after rendering, and the rendered images will look a lot nicer than the compressed AVI frames. Choose an image format that your compositing software can load in numbered sequence, or just reload them as an image sequence backdrop in Layout.

Options Panel

The only setting in this panel that saves rendering time is the Show Rendering in Progress check box. Make sure it is turned off. It takes LightWave 3D a significant amount of time to refresh the screen display while it is rendering. If you are experimenting and need to observe the rendered images as they are completed, you have a legitimate use for this option. Otherwise, it's just distracting and a bottleneck.

Further Study

If you are interested in the technical theory behind LightWave 3D's rendering, you can find out more by reading some of the computer graphics textbooks cited in the Bibliography. The ACM SIGGRAPH publications mentioned in the Part II preface are also good resources, once you have a basic grounding in CGI theory.

Moving On

In this chapter we've covered a number of simple tricks to render your LightWave 3D scenes faster. This wraps up Part II, "The Technical Director." Part III introduces you to the work of the other members of the production team, and techniques for producing your own short film or demo reel.

All Together Now! Assembling a Demo Reel

If you've worked through all the exercises in the first two parts of this book, you should have a solid understanding of the principles of character animation using LightWave 3D. At least a few of the exercises should have produced decent-looking actions.

However, just being able to complete these step-by-step exercises will not get you a job. You need to go beyond this, to put together a presentation that tells potential employers that you can breathe life into any collection of polygons. This presentation will be your demo reel.

You should be keeping all your material, including textbook exercises, on an archive reel. You can take this to an interview, where you may have the opportunity to discuss your learning experiences and techniques. All those bits and pieces of work in progress help convince a potential employer that you actually did the work on your demo reel.

For your demo reel, select at least three minutes of your best work from your archive reel. You can get by with less than three minutes if your work is very good, but have a reasonable explanation ready if you're under two minutes. Don't go over five minutes. Reviewers decide in the first few minutes whether they want to talk to you; anything over five minutes is probably not looked at.

If you have a lot of material you want to show, resist the urge to do an MTV-style montage of fast cuts. Some reviewers don't mind this, but it annoys others and you don't want to risk that. If at all possible, arrange your pieces in some logical order to minimize the jarring effect of cuts.

Put your name and contact information at the beginning and end of your reel, and don't put a date on it. Don't explain what software you used in your animations, either. Some houses will automatically turn you down if you don't use their favorite software. On the other hand, if you apply to a house that relies on the same software you used to produce your reel, it is pretty easy to put an explanatory printed insert in the cassette case. Your philosophy should be to let your work speak for itself, and don't give the reviewer any irrelevant information they could use to weed you out. One exception to this is credit for others' work: make sure everybody who contributed to the work on your reel is credited on the insert. It's a lot better to volunteer this information up front than to be answering awkward questions at an interview.

Depending on how good your material is, and on how paranoid you are, you may want to rig your demo reel so nothing can be lifted from it by unscrupulous persons. One simple technique is to run an animated streamer through the middle of each scene, traveling behind your main characters but in front of the sets and background. The streamer can say something like "Doug Kelly's Demo Reel—Not For Commercial Use." If you use color cycling in the streamer, or vary it's transparency values, it is very difficult to remove. If you choose to do this, make sure the "protection" you employ doesn't protect you from becoming employed! Keep it as subtle and unobtrusive as you can.

Animation houses are going to be looking for some very specific elements in your reel. They want to see that you can do the work you are applying for, not just that you have the potential to be able to do it someday. If your demo reel doesn't show what they are looking for, you can expect a polite letter to the effect that "we have no requirement for your services at this time."

So, what do you need to show? That all depends on what job you are applying for. If you want to be a character animator, then show character animation in your demo reel. Animators who review your reel look for a clear understanding of squash-and-stretch, anticipation, secondary motion, timing, and the other animation concepts you worked through in Part 1. Beyond that, they look at the whole effect of your work. Do your characters seem motivated? Do they act convincingly? Do they appear to be thinking? Can the viewer understand what the character is expressing?

You are only as good as the worst piece on your reel.

What you leave off your demo reel is at least as important as what you put on. You are only as good as the worst piece on your reel. If you want to be employed as a character animator, leave the flying logos, bouncing checkered balls, zooming spacecraft, architectural walkthroughs, and game rides on your archive reel. And even if it looks like good character animation, leave off the dinosaurs. Everybody has seen dinosaur animations by now, and they are definitely "old hat." The same goes for monster animations; most game monsters show very little in the way of acting (I see you! I kill you!), and unless they show very good posing and timing, you're better off without them.

If you are looking for work as a technical director, your reel should focus on modeling, lighting, and texturing. Unlike animators, you want to put examples of work in progress on your demo reel. Include shots of your best models rendered in wireframe and close-ups of the especially tricky parts. You may want to include prints of some of your best images, as you can get better quality than videotape and the reviewer can examine them at leisure.

Your lighting samples should show a solid understanding of the principles in Chapter 17. Subtlety is usually better than an overwhelming light show. The exercises on lighting the same set for different moods are a good place to start.

Any effects shots should go well beyond any tutorial you may have read. As a TD, you will be expected to solve new problems, not just use the solutions of others. Show that you understand your tools well enough to push their limits.

It may be to your advantage to work with a complementary partner to produce a joint demo reel. If your talents are in the area of technical director, working with an animator can build a reel that is more coherent, entertaining, and demonstrates that you work well as part of a team. On the other hand, as an animator you will find that working with a good technical director gives your reel an extra polish that puts it above the competition.

How Many Hats Can You Wear?

One of the really liberating things about the revolution in desktop animation software is that you really can do it all yourself. There are software tools that can assist you in doing screenwriting, storyboard and layout art, modeling, texturing, audio digitizing, track breakdown, animation, rendering, record keeping, financial and scheduling project management, music composition and recording, audio and video mixing and editing, title design, and film or video recording.

The question is do you want to handle it all?

If you really have a driving, unique artistic vision that you feel only you can realize, then more power to you (just don't try to be your own agent and attorney, as well!). If you prefer to concentrate on one specialty and do it well, then more power to you also. Whatever your approach, these last two chapters show you how to put all the necessary pieces together in a coherent, story-telling demo reel that will give you a good chance at landing a job interview.

Along the way, you learn a little more about the other professions and trades associated with animated film production. I hope this information will help you become a more effective animator or TD, whether you pursue a solitary career or join one of the growing number of animation production houses.

Plan Your Work, Work Your Plan

From Script to Exposure Sheet

Character animation, like many other complex endeavors, benefits from thorough planning. This chapter shows you some proven planning techniques that will help you in producing your own animation, especially a demo reel.

For any complicated project involving different talents or groups of people, a successful plan evolves and grows. It never springs full-grown from the mind of even the most Zeus-like director. The plan starts with a basic idea, that idea is fleshed out and detailed, and those details are in turn filled out to the next level of detail. At each level, changes and revisions can be made with a minimum of disturbance to the rest of the plan. If a level were skipped over or not developed completely, revisions to later levels would echo catastrophically back through every part of the project.

In animation, the initial idea is usually a story to be told, and the final level of detail is the individual frame. Getting from one to the other is a series of logical steps: story, script, storyboard, bar sheets, exposure sheets, animation. This chapter is about the first five steps; the first 10 chapters of this book are about the sixth.

Each step produces its own characteristic set of documents, a record of the work completed that also forms the skeleton for the next level to flesh out. Take each step one at a time, with a little thought and practice, and you will be able to master them all.

The Importance of a Story

A good story, even if it is very small, is crucial to a successful animation. Even a five-second television station ID has a story to tell. If you want clients, employers, or any other audience to pay attention to your animation, make sure you are telling an interesting story. This is especially important for your demo reel. A series of brief, unrelated clips is simply not going to hold the reviewer's attention as well as a good, coherent story built around an engaging character.

Every good story must have a premise, which must suggest character, conflict, and a conclusion. The premise should be simple, as in "haste makes waste," "love conquers all," and the premise selected for the example script, "easy come, easy go." A complex premise generally leads to a muddled and confusing story, and should therefore be avoided.

The essential element of a story for character animation is, appropriately enough, character. Other dramatic forms may emphasize different elements of the storytelling traditions, but this book—and your work—are about character animation.

Character is defined by action. When we first see a character, we have no idea what they may do next. An undefined character can perform any action, or speak any line of dialogue, without having the least effect on your audience. It is your job as an animator to make that character tell the audience about themselves, to define who they are, so that the actions you animate and the lines your character lip-syncs have an effect on the audience, and so advance your story. This can be a daunting task. For some television commercials, you may have as little as two seconds, a mere 60 frames, to define a character. In longer formats you may have the luxury of developing your character in terms of physiology, sociology, and psychology (for example, Quasimodo in Disney's remake of *The Hunchback of Notre Dame*). In the shorter formats, you usually must resort to caricature and stereotype to establish your character as quickly as possible.

Conflict builds character. This sounds like what they tell you as they cart you off the field, doesn't it? Nevertheless, it's true. Conflict is the friction between the character and it's environment (including other characters) that forces the character to change and grow. This change and growth must be in a direction consistent with what we have already seen of the character. A miser shouldn't suddenly empty his wallet into the nearest charity box unless we first tell the whole series of conflicts leading up to his redemption, as in Dickens's *A Christmas Carol.*

Conflict also serves to draw the characters more clearly. Even if the change through conflict is very small, with each conflict your audience sees the character a little more clearly.

So how do you devise a conflict? No need, the characters create their own plots. If the character is initially a miser, then obviously the strongest conflict would be if the miser's savings were threatened. Depict your character strongly and conflicts will present themselves.

Another concept I'd like to introduce here is transition. While the term means something different in screenwriting and editing, in the dramatic sense the word refers to the dominant emotional state of a character. A transition occurs when a character, expressing one emotion, progresses through a conflict and changes to expressing a different emotion. Leaving out the transition, or shortening it so the audience does not see it clearly, makes a jump in the character's development that can ruin the story. This is especially important for character animation, as emotions must be displayed more obviously than in live action and require a good deal of planning from the animator.

The end of the story should follow naturally from the growth of the original character through conflict. Don't try to get fancy, outfoxing your audience with surprise endings and bizarre last-act plot twists. They won't thank you for it. Just finish the story with the last transition, in a manner that completes the premise, and leave it at that.

Exercise 19-1: Develop a Story Line

Select a simple premise and develop a brief story line from it.

Is your premise 10 words or less? Is the premise one you, personally, can believe in? (Remember, you're going to be spending a lot of quality time with the little monster.)

Can your character fulfill the premise? Is your conflict one that will expose the character more fully, or force the character to grow? Does the story provide for interesting transitions that will hold your audience's attention? Does the end of the story follow naturally from the character's growth or exposition, and does it fulfill the premise?

If all your answers are "Yes," why aren't you a screenwriter? Just kidding! Let's take your story to the next level.

Drafting the Script

So now you have an interesting story to tell. The sheer expense of character animation, whether measured in money or man-hours, demands that the story be told as succinctly and effectively as possible.

If you want to tell your story effectively, you need to have a plan, a blueprint that lays out all the parts in their proper place. The script is your blueprint. A properly formatted script tells each member of the production team what has to happen to tell the story. From this information, each specialist can plan the work they will contribute to the project.

If you can't write up your story as a script, you don't have a clear idea of what you are trying to say. The act of putting words on paper has a great clarifying effect on even the most obscure daydreams. It is also a useful test of the writer's creative vision: if the vision can't survive being translated into a script, it certainly isn't robust enough to survive the rigors of animation production.

"Reshooting" to correct problems that should have been caught in the script is a good way to blow your budget, your schedule, and your career as a director. A well-formatted script can go a long way toward preventing that kind of disaster. Each conflict and transition is written there in black and white, and if more than one member of the production team can't "see" a particular shot, that's an excellent indication that a rewrite is needed. Paper's cheap, but time and film aren't.

The script is intended as a working tool, not a literary form. Get used to writing in the standard format expected by Hollywood and Madison Avenue. Even as an independent or hobbyist, you may find it useful to consult a working professional about some production matter; if you show them an unkempt collection of odd formatting that you call a script, they are not as likely to take you seriously. Writing in the standard format costs you nothing in creativity, helps you stay organized, and makes your eventual transition to professional work that much easier.

The correct format for a shooting script is an easy thing to master. Get a copy of Blacker's *The Elements of Screenwriting*. This slender but dense volume covers the simple mechanics of punctuation and formatting in less than 10 pages. You may also want to use the Script

Maker template for Microsoft Word. This shareware template distributed by Impact Pictures can be found in the Chapter 19 directory of the Companion CD-ROM. This template was used to create the sample script in Appendix D.

One modification I would make to Blacker's advice, specifically for animation scripts: go ahead and direct the camera. Especially if you are playing Omnipotent Person Wearing All Hats, you probably have some idea of the camera angles and lenses you want for each shot. If not, trust me, you'll get those ideas while you're typing the script. Put them in; it's easier to line them out later than to pencil them in.

Take a look at the script reprinted in Appendix D. Note that each character, sound effect, and animated prop or "live" set is typed in all caps. This is an extension of the standard script format. The characters are capped so the animator for each character can see their shots, the sounds are capped so the sound crew can plan their work, and the sets and props are capped so the TD and animator can plan for the additional modeling and animation. If you are given a more traditional script to animate from, you may want to amplify it along these lines.

Each shot is described by camera lens, angle, and the subjects contained in the shot. This is overdirecting for live-action, but it really helps for animation.

Each emotional transition is clearly written out. You wouldn't want to be this heavy-handed with directing live actors, but for animation it's a necessity. After months of looking at dozens of shots, often out of order, you will have no idea what emotion was supposed to be portrayed unless it's written down somewhere. It might as well start with the script. Also, if there is to be any dialog, the written transition instructions help the voice talent replace the normal interaction between the actors. In many animation productions, a voice talent records each half of the dialog in separate sessions. This can be a challenge, and the transition notes can help.

Exercise 19-2: Draft a Script

Expand the brief story line from Exercise 19-1 into a properly formatted animation shooting script. When you are writing your shot descriptions, remember the principles of composition and camera motion discussed in Chapter 9.

If you don't want to script your own story, select and videotape a 30- or 60-second television commercial, then translate it to a script. The purpose of this exercise is to make you familiar with screenwriting conventions. Whether you write your own or work exclusively with other writers' scripts, you need to be able to read these blueprints accurately.

Have your script read by at least three other people. Be polite when they suggest plot changes, "improvements," or make other comments. Look for answers to these three questions:

1. Could you visualize each shot?

2. Did the characters act consistently?

3. Did you have an emotional reaction to any part of the story?

If you get a lot of "No" answers, you probably need to rewrite. If that seems too much for you, set your script aside and try to rewrite it later. You can complete the exercises in the rest of this chapter by using the example script provided; you don't have to create everything from scratch. This book is about animation, after all, not screenwriting.

Creating Storyboards

A storyboard is a collection of individual story sketches, each illustrating a particular shot from the script as it would appear to the camera. The storyboard itself can be a large piece of board or section of wall with the sketches pinned to it, a portfolio with a few sketches on each page, or even a loose-leaf binder intended to show only one story sketch at a time.

Storyboards were developed in the Disney studio in the late 1920s as a way of visualizing the shot flow of the entire story at once. By the mid-30s, most Hollywood studios were using them as a means of preplanning and managing film production.

The storyboard is one of the most valuable tools an animation director can use. A well-done storyboard bridges the gap between the script and the actual animation, providing the next level of detail in visualization. As with the script, if you have trouble creating the storyboard, you may want to revise or clarify your ideas.

Storyboards are also necessary for dealing with most employers and partners. If you are working in feature films, television, or advertising, the producers and other team members need to see the storyboards. In advertising, even the client sees the storyboards; ad agencies are notorious for over-approving everything. For an animated ad, expect to produce detailed, finished artwork for storyboards, and to have it all second-guessed and revised repeatedly. While it's true that most CGI animation can be laid out and rendered faster than an artist can produce the finished storyboards, speed is not the issue. Client approval and protecting the agency, are the issues.

If a particular employer requires more storyboarding than you want to do, plan to hire a storyboard artist to do the extra work and increase your fee accordingly. If there will be several cycles of storyboarding and approval before you can get down to animating, make sure your contract spells out your compensation for the delays and extra work. Pay particular attention to the clause that states you get paid for out-of-pocket expenses and work completed, even if the client changes their mind or cancels the project.

If you are working on an independent project like a demo reel, you have a lot more leeway in the production values of your storyboards. Stick figures and rough sketches are adequate if you are doing a solo project, but putting in more information will make your work easier later on. After months of posing and tweaking, it's sometimes difficult to remember exactly what you had in mind for a particular shot. A detailed story sketch is one of the best memory-joggers you can have.

You can also abbreviate storyboards by using a single sketch for several shots (or a traveling shot) of the same backgrounds and characters. Place numbered frame outlines in the sketch, especially if the shots use complex cuts or travel.

I'd still recommend using complete storyboards, both to help clarify your vision of the story and as evidence that all the work is actually yours. Some animation houses will ask you to prove that you created the work on your demo reel. The script drafts, story sketches, and other production notes should be saved and carried to interviews.

Script to Storyboard

So exactly how do you expand a script into a storyboard? There are almost as many approaches as there are professional storyboard artists. You can choose the size, media, and style to suit yourself, and several books listed in the Bibliography can give you ideas.

My personal approach is, I think, simple and effective. Having the finished script in a Word document, I save a copy of the script and then make some page layout changes to the duplicate:

1. Change the page orientation to landscape.

2. Change the page number in the header to read SHOT #.

3. Immediately after the shot number, insert a carriage return followed by a frame measuring 8 x 6 inches, centered in the header, flush against the top margin, and spaced 0.2 inches from the following text.

4. Change the cover page to read DRAFT STORYBOARD rather than FIRST (or whatever) DRAFT.

Take a look at the storyboard reproduced in Appendix B for an example of this formatting.

This starts off every page (except the cover) with a blank 8 x 6 frame, which is the "standard" aspect ratio for film work. If you are going to work in another aspect ratio, change the dimensions of the frame to match. Working with landscape format 8 1/2- x 11-inch paper also enables you to put the storyboard in a standard three-ring binder. A number of directors prefer working this way, as you can flip through the pages rapidly to get an idea of the timing for shot flow.

The shots are numbered automatically. If you need to insert a new shot later, it will probably be easier to hand-letter on a blank page than to fool around with reformatting the entire document. This was the procedure for the montage (Shot #49) of Fred's excesses in the restaurant in Appendix E. The composite shot was numbered from the original script breakout. The individual shots used to compose the montage (which was edited together in post-production) were designed later, their descriptions handwritten on blank sheets, and the finished sketches numbered 49A, 49B, and so on.

To create the blank pages in Word, add a section break and a page break after the last FADE OUT, turn off the Same as Previous toggle, and change the new section's header to replace the page number with a few underscores. You may want to type the label SHOT DESCRIPTION: under the frame. Print a single copy of this last page and photocopy it or print off a lot of copies to keep in the binder for making changes.

The next step is to go through the script line by line and insert a page break after each shot. I carry this a little further for character animation storyboards by breaking after each action or moving hold.

Let's look at an example from an earlier draft of the "Easy Come, Easy Go" script. The shot where Fred leaves the barber shop was much longer in the earlier draft and involved a visible barber character. This sequence was cut because, even though it was an opportunity to animate some interesting actions, it didn't advance the premise of the story. This shot broke down to five sketches even though cinematically it's a single shot (see Figure 19-1). From a character animator's viewpoint, the actions to be animated are very different and can be handled as a series of separate shots connected by overlapping action:

1. The door opens and Fred exits the barbershop with a particular gait. The main action ends when Fred halts, just before beginning the turn. All the overlapping actions that are part of Fred continue into the next main action.

2. Fred turns and bows to the barber. This should be a single action, flowing and graceful (if a trifle over-acted). The action ends when Fred straightens into a moving hold, which overlaps the next action.

3. The barber's hands wave. The action ends when the door closes. The overlapping action here would be Fred's reaction, beginning just before the door is completely closed.

4. Fred turns again and scans storefronts. This turn is slightly different from the second action in both timing and emphasis, as he now has another purpose in mind. The action ends when he identifies his goal and sets himself to begin walking. Again, the overlapping actions are all associated with Fred.

5. The last action is Fred walking out of the frame. There is no overlapping action because the set is empty of characters.

As you can see, this breakout increases the number of story sketches. I prefer this approach because it helps bridge the transition from storyboard to bar sheet, giving you more breaking points than a simpler shot breakout. This makes it a little easier to time each action, and you can pencil your timing estimates right on the story sketch margin. This is a big help when you first meet with the music director or composer.

If I'm doing the entire production myself, I prefer working in pencil. I'm not a graphic artist by any stretch of the definition, so most of my storyboards are simple perspective layouts of the sets populated by somewhat-proportional stick figures. For the example production, I planned to work with a production team and therefore arranged for a professional artist to do the storyboards.

At some point during the script revision process, you need to do the preliminary character design, as detailed in Chapter 12. The storyboard artist will need a copy of the character model sheets, plus whatever concept sketches are available for sets and props.

Figure 19-1: Preliminary character designs for Fred. Copyright 1996 Mike Comet.

If the project is a continuation of a series using existing sets, it's helpful to provide the artist with some appropriate rendered backgrounds from previous projects. There's no need to expend creative effort on a stock interior that has appeared in 12 episodes already—at least not if you want to stay on good terms with your storyboard artist.

You should also have sketched plans and elevations (the top and side views, respectively) of the original set elements called for in the script. If you mention a storefront, make sure the storyboard artist has some idea of what kind of storefront you mean. A trendy big-city designer boutique should have a very different look than a small-town barber shop.

At this point you will find it useful to make some schematic sketches of the objects and their eventual positioning in LightWave 3D's Layout. A simple plan sketched on scaled grid paper, as in Figure 19-2, greatly reduces the time you spend setting up the master scene.

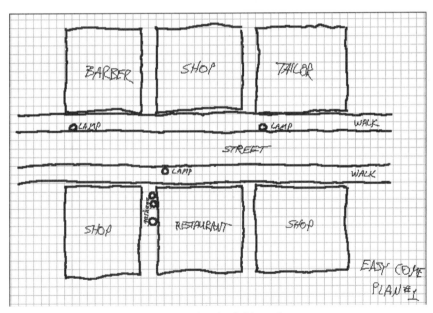

Figure 19-2: A simple preliminary sketch of object placement.

It's important that you discuss with the artist any limitations you want to keep in mind. For example, since everything described in the sample script was to be constructed from scratch, I wanted to limit extraneous backgrounds. One way to do this is to limit camera angles.

If the camera is always looking below the horizon line and buildings are in the near foreground, you'll never have to create a sky. Similarly, if the camera is on a slight down angle in a medium shot of a building, nothing above the first floor needs to be modeled. A matter of a few degrees in panning the camera can mean the difference between modeling an entire street scene and being able to get away with a few false-front shops and a dozen feet of road and sidewalk.

It may help if you think of the camera view as a pyramid, with the point at the focal plane of the camera and the base way out at infinity. The frame of the shot is a slice through the pyramid. Anything within the volume of that pyramid is something you are going to have to model, buy, or fake. It's in your interest to keep that pyramid as empty as possible while still telling an interesting story.

You can't always get away with dodges like these, but for a character animation demo reel you should concentrate on the animation and avoid having to recreate the whole world.

Exercise 19-3: Make a Storyboard

Break out your script from Exercise 19-2 into a properly formatted storyboard. Stick figures are acceptable, but try to keep them in proportion. If the characters are interacting with part of the set (looking out a window, opening a door), draw that part of the set.

If you don't want to storyboard your own script, either use the example script provided in Appendix A or select at least four pages from a motion picture or television script. Break it out as if you will be animating it, even if the script is for a live-action show.

If you use the example script, make your version of Fred markedly different. How would you compose the shots if Fred were tall and thin? Short and fat? Make all the action work from the opposite side of the street. Do not simply copy the storyboard from Appendix E.

This exercise is intended to get you thinking visually, converting the shot descriptions in the script into images that are closer to what you want in the final film.

Use a blank sheet of paper to cover the shot description under each sketch. At random, pick a sketch and see if you can tell what the action is and what the character is expressing. Repeat this for several of the shots.

Flip through the storyboard in order, looking only at the sketches. Are you starting to get a sense of the rhythm, the timing for the shot flow? Are there gaps or jumps in the shot flow?

If you can, show your storyboard to someone who can think visually. Ask them to tell you the story represented by the boards in their own words.

If the responses to all three of these critiques are close to what you intended, your storyboard is working. If not, remember that storyboarding, like writing or animating, is a skill that improves with practice. Keep at it!

Putting the Storyboard to Work

So you've got a storyboard. Now what? Put it to work, of course, to save you time and effort!

The number one value of a storyboard is saving effort for the production team. For example, if there are no shots in the storyboard where the camera is closer than a hundred feet to a particular object, you don't have to build any details into that object that aren't visible at a hundred feet. If every camera angle cuts off at first floor height, there's no use in modeling and texturing the upper floors and roofs.

Take another look at the sample storyboard, this time from the point of view of the technical director. Fred is the only character who needs to have a head, feet, or a body. The bouncer and waitress are represented by disembodied hands and arms that appear from off-screen. This is an enormous saving in modeling and animation. There is a slight cost in terms of expressive range, as you can only communicate so much with hand gestures (we have to assume most of the audience doesn't read American Sign Language).

The sets are almost all false-front shops, with simple (and reusable) sections of sidewalk, street, and alley connecting them. The single interior is also deliberately vague and simple, kept shadowy by lighting so minor details need not be modeled.

Take a look at your own storyboards. Look at each sketch. Is there any object in this sketch that doesn't appear somewhere else? Is there a different way to compose the shot so that object doesn't have to be modeled? Will cropping it out have a negative effect on telling the story? Could a simpler or stock object be substituted? There's no reason to custom-build a 1931 Duesenberg if it's only in one shot for a few seconds and the character could just as easily be stepping out of a stock-model taxi.

Decisions like these make storyboards an absolute requirement for any sizable animation. Budgets can be broken and deadlines blown by a few overly complex shots. If they are necessary to tell the story effectively, the finance people might accept the overrun; if the shots are superfluous, you are likely to hear references to *Heaven's Gate* or *Waterworld* as they tell you to clean out your desk.

Bar Sheets: Planning for Sound

Silent animations are boring. Even a little generic background music will liven them up, and synchronized sound effects will do wonders. If you are producing a demo reel, you can increase your chances of an interview if you pay a little attention to your soundtrack. The reviewer is more likely to watch your reel, and less likely to cut it off short, if the audio track adds to the flow and continuity of your animations.

You have a variety of options for adding sound to your animation: borrow, buy, or make it yourself. You can always opt for a silent piece—a bad idea in general but sometimes necessary if your resources are limited.

General background music and sound effects are the next step up. At minimum, try to dub a song that has similar mood and length to your animation. If your animation has been laid out to a steady beat you may even be able to find prerecorded music that matches your animation's accents.

If you intend to send your demo reel only to potential employers, you may be able to get away with using commercial recordings; this is a gray area of the fair use doctrine regarding copyright. You definitely cannot use a copyrighted work to make money or in public performance, and any use on a demo reel must be strictly for "educational or research purposes." That is, a student piece, even if you are self-taught. If you are already in the graphics business and the reel is distributed to advertise your services, you can't use the fair use defense. Also, if there is any chance that your reel will be shown in public, you need to comply with all the copyright restrictions or prepare to be sued. To play it safe, if you can afford to, you should buy an appropriate piece from a music or sound effects library.

Custom music and sound effects, synchronized to the action, are the most expensive but highest quality sounds for animation. If you don't have the budget to hire professionals you can try to do it yourself, or you can find a friendly musician or composer who is willing to work with you. The same is true of sound effects and vocal tracks; locate people willing to help, or do it yourself if you can. Foley work (recording sound effects) can still be done effectively by nonprofessionals. You don't need a license to play the coconut halves, and most theatre arts schools have books on low-end sound effect recording techniques.

What Is a Bar Sheet?

Animation and sound are a chicken-and-egg problem. Which should be done first? The answer is an unsatisfying "that depends."

The most common tool in coordinating sound and animation is the bar sheet (Figure 19-3). This is similar to the blank sheets a composer would use, except the three middle staff lines are missing. The measures are marked, and the number of beats to each measure is penciled in.

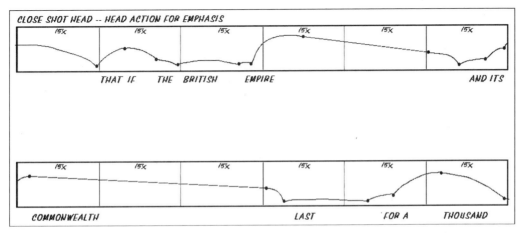

Figure 19-3: A bar sheet.

The director uses the bar sheets to plan the flow of the whole animation, condensing a hundred or more story sketches down to a few pages of cryptically penciled notations. This is where the mood and tempo of the finished film are determined. Prior to this, there has been a great deal of flexibility in how shots are paced and connected and what the mood of each segment can be. Once the director establishes the rhythm and timing of every shot via the bar sheet, the flow of the film is much more definite.

The bar sheets are especially useful because the director, composer, and other members of the production team can easily see if a particular action, sound, or musical passage fits properly in the time allotted. This helps in negotiating the inevitable tradeoffs and compromises necessary to make the sound and animation work together. All these changes are also recorded on the bar sheets. Other people may contribute during the bar sheets' revision, but the final responsibility is the director's.

The bar sheets track most of the information needed to coordinate the entire animation production team. The director, animator, and most of the rest of the crew will live and breathe by these sheets before the project is completed. Keeping track of the sheets is an important job, whether you are being paid to do it as an assistant director or are doing it all yourself on a private project.

There are four basic approaches in coordinating sound and animation, plus combinations of two or more of the basics. All of them depend on accurate bar sheets:

- Music first. Compose and record the music first, using a strictly regular beat. The director lays out the musical beat in the bar sheets, so the animators can match the action to it without hearing the score. This approach can force animation into the realm of choreography. It is challenging for the animator to squeeze a long action into a fast passage, or stretch it to fill up a slow one. This approach is best used when there is a strong reason to adhere to a prerecorded piece of music.

- Music first, but this time with a variable tempo. The music track is analyzed as if it were dialog, and the beats noted on the bar sheets.

- The director and composer negotiate between the director's timing of planned actions and the composer's scoring of individual phrases or passages.

- Scoring to the action. The action is laid out in the bar sheets with each accent marked in a dummy score. Then the composer writes a free tempo score to match the action's emphasis with the music's beat.

Timing for Bar Sheets

For any approach that includes voice or sound effects, you are going to need timing information to help build your bar sheets. If you have recorded dialog, you should have several takes of each line from the script. Extracting timing information from these takes is called *sentence measurement*. In addition to extracting the amount of time each line of dialog takes, you also need to note the interval between the line being measured and both the preceding line and the following line.

One way to do sentence measurement is to digitize each usable take from the recording session, then open up the digitized files in a sound editor. It's fairly simple, then, to note the time of each sentence.

Exactly how the information is organized depends on your working style, but I prefer typing it all into a spreadsheet with session, take, time, intervals, clip file name, and comments organized in separate columns. This is probably overkill on small projects, but it can save you a lot of hassle on big ones by enabling you to sort and search for just the right clip.

It's a good idea to do the same for any sound effects you plan to use. If you will be matching action to the sounds, it's essential.

If you are following the last method listed above, or are animating a sequence with no sound effects, musical, or vocal timing guidelines, you will have to wing it. That is, estimate each action's timing to the best of your ability.

Veteran animators became masters at this, partly through necessity. Management pressures at some studios dictated the precise length of animated shorts, and directors quickly learned to time an animation exactly to the frame. Similar pressures still exist today in advertising and television, but there is a lot more slack in independent and feature-length productions.

You can develop your ability to time actions accurately by working through the exercises in Chapter 5.

In learning to time action, use any technique that helps. I recommend acting the actions out and using a stopwatch to time them. Repeat each action until you are satisfied with your "performance," then take three more timings and average them to get your working time.

Other useful tools for acting out timing include a videotape recorder (VTR) and camera with an SMPTE timecode display, a laserdisk player and a collection of disks with appropriate action sequences, or a metronome (for you traditionalists). There are special stopwatches that are marked in frames; if you will be doing this a lot, consider acquiring one.

Exercise 19-4: Timing the Sketches

1. Beg, borrow, or otherwise acquire access to a stopwatch or a VTR with timecode display.

2. Act out each shot in the example storyboards. Repeat each action at least three times. Record the time for each action.

3. Average the performances to give a working time for each action.

4. Convert the working time to frames.

5. Note the working time in the margin of each story sketch.

6. Repeat this exercise with your own storyboards.

The Story Reel

So how do you know if your timings are any good? One way to check them is to make a *story reel*, a motion picture assembled using the story sketches. Each sketch is held on screen for the exact length of time the action depicted is supposed to take. No illusion of motion is created, but the overall timing and shot flow of the animation becomes obvious. Fortunately, modern technology has made assembling a story reel almost trivial.

The first requirement is to convert the story sketches to electronic image files. You can do this with a scanner, a video camera, and digitizer, or my favorite low-tech approach: a fax machine!

If you are strapped for cash and don't have access to a scanner, a cheap used fax machine can be just what the doctor ordered. There are a lot of old fax machines out there designed to print on the slick, expensive thermal paper that everybody hates. These machines are usually retired as quickly as possible, and you may even be able to pick one up for free.

The other side of this technique is the fact that most machines capable of running LightWave 3D include a fax modem as standard equipment.

What a lot of people don't seem to realize is that you can hook a fax machine directly into your fax modem without tying up your phone line. Just drop your sketches in the hopper, tell your fax software to pick up, and press the fax machine's Send button. Presto, you've got scanned sketches in your computer!

The disadvantages to this technique are that the resolution on fax machines is only about 200 dpi and you still have to translate or export the page images from your fax software to an image format that LightWave 3D can work with.

Exercise 19-5: Check Your Rough Timing With a Silent Story Reel

You will find low-resolution story sketches in the Chapter 19 directory of the Companion CD-ROM to use for this exercise.

1. Make a duplicate of all the story sketch files. Put the duplicates in their own directory on your hard drive.

2. Using the timing notations from Exercise 19-4, calculate the beginning frame number for each story sketch.

   For example, if the first and second sketches are each to be held for 60 frames, and the third is held for 120 frames, the fourth would start at 60+60+120, or frame 240. The easiest way to do this is by using a printing calculator that prints the running total as you add in each sketch's timing.

3. Rename each duplicate story sketch to match the appropriate beginning frame number, for example: SKET0090.TGA.

   You should end up with a numbered sequence of images.

4. In LightWave 3D Layout, open a new scene and click the Images button. In the Images Panel, click Load Sequence. Select the first image in the sequence you just created, and click Continue.

5. Click the Scene button to call up the Scene Panel. Set the number of frames equal to (or slightly greater than) the total of the story sketch times. Click Continue.

6. Click the Effects button to call up the Effects Panel. In the Compositing layer of the Effects Panel, set the Background Image to the image sequence you loaded in step 4. Click Continue.

7. Click the Record button to open the Record Panel. Choose a directory, filename, and format for the animation you are about to render, and click on Continue.

8. Click the Camera button. In the Camera Panel, set rendering to Wireframe, antialiasing off, and whatever resolution your machine can play back at 30 frames per second. Click Continue. (You don't need antialiasing or anything other than Wireframe, because the only purpose of this scene is to duplicate the background images into an animation.)

9. Render the animation.

   Make sure you've got plenty of disk space available; even though there are mostly very small *deltas*, changes in pixel values between successive frames, AVI and FLC compression algorithms are not very efficient with this sort of file.

This approach is adequate only for a really quick timing check, as it has no provision for music or other sound tracks. However, it's handy, quick, and doesn't require any software besides LightWave 3D.

Exercise 19-6: Writing Up Your Bar Sheets

The purpose of this exercise is to create bar sheets from your demo reel storyboards.

1. First, get some blank bar sheets, or draw up your own. Set the space between bar lines equal to 30 frames.

    This is arbitrary, but I like it since it gets an adequate amount of animation onto a single sheet, while leaving room for a moderate amount of scribbled notes.

2. Mark the important accents, especially the beats the composer needs to match. Steps, strong actions, starts or peaks of sounds, and dialog accents should all be noted.

    Refer to Figure 19-3 for an example of a filled-in bar sheet.

3. From each accent, arrange the boundaries of the sound effects and dialog, using the sentence measurements you performed earlier.

    This should immediately show up any glaring inconsistencies, like a seven-second speech that is supposed to match an action timed for five seconds, or an originally brief interval between sentences that now stretches interminably.

4. Interpolate minor actions and accents in between the major ones.

    As you will do later with the actual animation, work from the most important element down to the least significant. The important actions have to be timed to certain frames or musical hits; the less important actions can slide around the bar sheets more without adversely affecting the story.

Depending on the approach you take to coordinating sound and music, you may want your composer or other musical talent to have a hand in developing the bar sheets. When the bar sheets are complete, you are ready to put together your next production tool—the story reel.

Checking Your Plan: the Story Reel

For a better idea of how your film is progressing and to assist in making various production decisions, you need to make a more complete story reel. This requires an almost complete set of sound tracks, including voices, music, and sound effects. You will also need the completed bar sheets and digitized story sketches.

Exercise 19-7: Assemble a Story Reel

The following exercise is written for Adobe Premiere 4.2. Other compositing and editing software may be usable if it has similar functions.

1. Start Adobe Premiere. Choose the Presentation-160x120 Preset for the new project. Set the timebase to whatever you will be using for the final output, most likely 30 fps NTSC video.

   The Project, Info, Preview, Construction, and Transitions windows appear. You can immediately close the Transitions window, as you won't be using any transitions for this exercise and there's no sense in cluttering your workspace.

2. Choose the File | Import | File option, or press Ctrl+I. The Import dialog appears.

3. Drag-select the story sketch files from the Chapter 19 directory of the Companion CD-ROM. Click Open to import the images.

   The story sketch files appear in the Project window as thumbnails, or smaller versions of images that are more suitable for on-screen viewing.

4. Repeat the preceding step for the sound effects, voice tracks, and music tracks, as appropriate. The sound files also appear in the Project window, but as audio waveform thumbnails.

   So far so good. Now you need to set the duration of each story sketch. Premiere has a default setting of one second for still images, which is probably too short for any of the shots from the sample storyboards.

5. Double-click on the first story sketch in the Project window. The Clip window opens. Click the Duration button at the lower left. The Duration dialog appears.

6. Enter a duration for the first sketch, expressed in SMPTE timecode (HH:MM:SS:FF). This should be equal to the number of frames penciled in the sketch margin from Exercise 19-4.

7. Click OK. Close the Clip window. Double-click on the next sketch in the Project window.

8. Repeat the process until you have set the duration for each sketch. Save the project with an appropriate name.

9. Drag the first story sketch from the Project window to the top row of the Construction window. Drag the sketch to the left until it is flush with the first frame of the time ruler.

10. Drag the next story sketch from the Project window to the top row of the Construction window. Drag the sketch to the left until it is flush with the right edge of the preceding frame.

    The duration you set for each sketch automatically sets the timing for the whole story reel.

11. Repeat until all the sketches are loaded in the Construction window. Save the project again.

    At this point you have the same results as when you used LightWave 3D in Exercise 19-5. The next step adds synchronized sound, which LightWave 3D can't handle—yet.

12. Drag the first sound clip from the Project window to the top track of the Audio part of the Construction window. Drag it left or right until it matches the timing laid out in the bar sheets.

13. Repeat step 12 for the rest of the sound clips. If the timing marked in the bar sheets indicates two or more sounds will overlap, position the sound clips in the lower tracks.

    Premiere can handle up to 99 audio tracks at once, so you shouldn't have any problems with overloading.

14. When everything is set up according to the bar sheets, save the project again. Choose Make | Make Movie. The Make Movie dialog appears. Choose the directory and filename for the movie, then click the Output Options button.

15. Set the options to create a movie that can play back at full frame rate on your system. Click OK, then repeat with the Compression options. Click OK again.

    This may limit you to a 160x120 preview, or you may be using a monster machine that can handle full-screen 30 fps playback with stereo sound and lossless compression. Use whatever works; this is just for a working preview!

16. Click OK in the Make Movie dialog to begin compiling the story reel. When it's complete, open and play it.

Are all the sounds synchronized correctly? Does the story reel "read" well? Does it give you a better idea of the effect of timing on how the story reads? Is there anything you want to change?

You can adjust the timing of sounds by dragging them left and right in the audio tracks. Adjusting the timing of the individual sketches is a little trickier:

1. In Adobe Premiere, double-click on the thumbnail you want to re-time in the Construction window. The Clip window appears.

2. Enter a revised duration for the sketch, expressed in SMPTE timecode (HH:MM:SS:FF) and click OK.

3. Select and drag the thumbnails to either side of the retimed clip, if necessary, until they are all flush again.

Retiming the story sketches is a lot easier than reanimating finished sequences, isn't it? That's why story reels are an integral part of the workflow for most animators. It's standard procedure, because it pays off.

When you start producing finished renderings, you can selectively substitute them for the corresponding story sketches and recompile the movie. This way, the movie fills out as you make progress, and at any time you can view the whole thing. It's a wonderful feeling to watch your creative efforts grow this way.

Exercise 19-8: Make Your Own Story Reel

Repeat Exercise 19-7 but use your own story sketches, bar sheets, and sound files.

Synchronizing Sound

You can add synchronized sound effects to an animation by noting where a sound should start and pasting the appropriate sound file into a sound track at that frame.

Exercise 19-9: Synchronizing a Sound Effect to an Animation Using Adobe Premiere

This exercise syncs a simple "boing" sound (BOING.WAV) to an animation of a vibrating desk lamp, BOING.AVI. Both files can be found in the Chapter 19 directory of the Companion CD-ROM.

1. Start Adobe Premiere. Choose the Preset and Timebase for the new project.

2. Choose File | Import | File, or press Ctrl+I. The Import dialog appears.

3. Select the BOING.AVI file. Click OK. The AVI file appears in the Project window as a thumbnail.

4. Choose File | Import | File again. Select the BOING.WAV sound clip. Click OK. The sound file appears in the Project window. Note the spike at the beginning of the waveform.

5. Drag BOING.AVI from the Project window to the top row of the Construction window. Drag the thumbnail to the left until it is flush with the first frame of the time ruler.

6. Drag the BOING.WAV sound clip from the Project window to the top track of the Audio part of the Construction window.

7. Watch the Preview window as you drag the pointer to find the exact frame where the desk lamp is first hit. This is where the sound of the impact should also occur.

8. Slide the WAV file along the Audio track until the boing spike lines up with the frame where the desk lamp is hit.

9. Compile the animation. When it's complete, play it back.

Sometimes it's a good idea to add a two- or three-frame delay from a visual cue to the matching sound; for some reason, this "reads" better with most audiences. This is known as "slipping" the track.

You can also synchronize a longer sound effect within an animation. Simply note where a significant point (preferably a peak in the waveform) in the sound should appear in the animation, and slide the sound file in Premiere's audio track until the chosen point lines up with the correct frame number. For example, a long slide-whistle sound ending in a splat, and immediately followed by clanking and crashing, could quickly be synchronized by the initial spike in the waveform at the beginning of the splat.

If it's necessary to precisely position a sound, use the time unit selector at the bottom of the Construction window to zoom in on the frames in question. This makes it much easier to match the sound to a single frame.

Exposure Sheets for Lip Sync

Lip sync is essentially the same as synchronizing the bouncing ball to the music's beat. But instead of just a ball's position and maybe a little squash-and-stretch, you have to match the appropriate mouth and face shape to the phoneme being pronounced.

This is a lot more complicated, with many more opportunities for error. If you want to make as few mistakes as possible, you should plan your lip sync work using an exposure sheet. This is a table that is laid out with a line for each frame and a column for each kind of information needed to plan and track the production of the animation.

The x-sheet tracks the frame-by-frame information needed by the animator. For the animator, and to a lesser degree the technical director, exposure sheets are crucial. These sheets are an order of magnitude more detailed than the bar sheets, and are therefore not as useful to most other members of the production team. There's just too much information! Most of the team will be working in units of a complete shot, or of tens of seconds at least. An exposure sheet gets pretty crowded if it contains as much as three seconds' worth of information.

Different production houses use different forms for exposure sheets. I have made up a document that I like to use for character animation with LightWave 3D, and included it on the Companion CD-ROM in Microsoft Word and Adobe Acrobat formats. Several filled-in examples are shown in Appendix F.

CD-ROM

To fill in your own exposure sheets you can photocopy the blank form from Appendix F, or laser print multiple copies from the Word or Acrobat files, and pencil in all your notes and changes. This is helpful when you need to make revisions later on, as you can easily erase the pencil marks while leaving the printed form intact.

The sheets should be labeled with enough information to keep them in order, and to know who is responsible for any changes to their contents. At a minimum, the project name, the animator's name, and the scene number should be written in. Since most scenes will run longer than three seconds, the sheet number is also a requirement. It is advisable to write in the sheet numbers as "1 of 4," "2 of 4," and so on, so you know how many sheets should be attached.

The sample exposure sheet is long enough to hold 90 frames, or three seconds of NTSC video, on each page. The first column of the sheet contains a waveform of the audio track. A little later we'll go through the steps needed to capture these waveform images.

The second column is titled PH for phoneme. Here the breakdown editor writes in the phonetic spelling of the sound being pronounced, and marks duration and transitions as well. This process is called *track analysis*, and it takes a good deal of practice.

The next column, DIALOG, is for the dialog and sound effects from the script. These words are written with their usual spellings, and begin on the frame when the word or sound begins.

The fourth column is labeled ACTION. This is where the director or their assistant writes in a description of the action that must take place during the indicated frames. A door slamming, for instance, requires the complete closure of the door to be written at the frame where the sound of the slam begins.

The column labeled SMPTE is for the convenience of those who are synchronizing their work to film or video footage. Some foley (sound effects) artists or composers also work with SMPTE timecodes.

The next column, FRAME, is intended for the frame count of this specific scene or shot. Note that the numbering begins with frame one, and only the last digit is preprinted in the form. You can pencil in your own leading digits; typically, only the tens line is actually filled in.

As with all LightWave 3D animation, it is safest if you establish all your baseline keyframes in frame zero, but do not render the frame. This prevents a number of problems. The exposure sheet begins with frame 1 so the beginning of the audio track can simply be matched to the first frame of the rendered animation for perfect sync.

The BACKGROUND column provides a place for you to note any image sequences or stills that are to be used as backdrops. This is especially useful for compositing with other animations, digitized video sequences, or "matched" stills.

The last column, CAMERA, is a place to put your notes about special camera, post-processing plug-in, or compositing effects. In traditional animation, this information was used by the camera operator. Changes in lens size and other parameters for camera zooms, tracking, and pans should be listed here.

Exercise 19-10: Track Analysis

This exercise shows you the basics of track analysis, the craft of breaking out sounds for the animator's exposure sheets.

To begin filling in the exposure sheet we'll need a clean image of the waveform. It's easy to do this in the Windows environment. Just open the sound file in an editing program that displays the waveform, take a screenshot, and cut-and-paste the image of the waveform into an exposure sheet.

Most Windows sound editors can display a waveform. It is to your advantage if the editor you use can display a timecode or frame count alongside the waveform. My preference is for a shareware package called GoldWave, written by Chris Craig. It has a lot of useful tools for sound editing, the waveform ruler is clear and legible, and the screen colors can be customized for the best printing contrast. The only downside is that the ruler is marked in decimal units of time rather than frames. See Appendix C for downloading and contact information for GoldWave.

This exercise requires that you keep Word, Photoshop, or other graphics software, and your sound editor open at the same time. You may need more memory. If you can't keep all the programs open at once, you will have to open and close them in turn for each three-second waveform image; a tedious business, at best.

For this exercise, we'll be using a digitized sample from a speech by Sir Winston Churchill, THISHOUR.WAV, which can be found on the Companion CD-ROM.

1. Copy the sample waveform image file WAVEFORM.BMP from the Companion CD-ROM to your C:\TEMP directory. The exposure sheet document has a built-in link to that file and path. If you do not have a C: drive, you may have to edit the exposure sheet to change the link path.

2. Open THISHOUR.WAV in the sound editor.

3. Adjust the waveform display for full screen width resolution of a three-second selection, as in Figure 19-4.

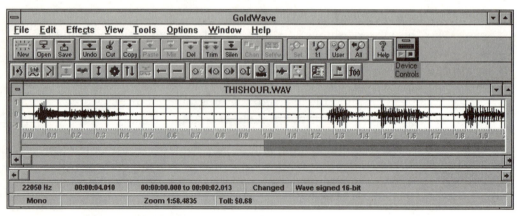

Figure 19-4: GoldWave sound editor showing THISHOUR.WAV.

4. Run Photoshop. (If you use different graphics software, make sure it can paste from the system clipboard.)

5. Open X_SHEET.DOC in Microsoft Word. Note whether the document found the WAVEFORM.BMP image file in the C:\TEMP directory. If not, you will have to change the link to the exposure sheet document before proceeding with the rest of the exercise. To do this, select Edit|Links to call up the Links dialog. Click the Change Source button, and choose the directory and filename you want to link to. Press Enter or click OK to return to the exposure sheet; the image you specified appears in the waveform column. You may have to resize it. If you have further difficulties, refer to Appendix G.

6. If everything seems to be in order, press Alt+Esc to switch back to the sound editor.

7. Press the Print Screen button to take a screenshot of the sound editor display.

8. Press Alt+Esc again to switch back to Photoshop.

9. Press Ctrl+N to open a new document. Accept the default values Photoshop suggests; they match the image currently held in the system clipboard.

10. Press Ctrl+V to paste the clipboard contents into the new blank document. Click once in the middle of the document to deselect the pasted area.

11. Zoom in if necessary to see details. Drag-select the two-second waveform section you want to paste into the exposure sheet. Make sure you precisely outline the start and stop points. Include the frame numbers if they are displayed, they will be useful later on.

     Steps 12 through 15 can be saved as a macro. This saves a great deal of time when you have minutes of audio track digitized and waiting for analysis. It cuts the cut-copy-paste-print cycle down to less than a minute per sheet, once you really get rolling.

     If you'd like to try it, I've included my own Photoshop macro on the Companion CD-ROM, file WAVEFORM.REC.

12. Choose Edit | Crop. This gets rid of everything outside your selection area and resizes the document.

13. Choose Image | Rotate | 90 degrees Clockwise. This changes the waveform image from horizontal to vertical, which is much easier to use in exposure sheets.

14. Choose Mode | Grayscale. This gets rid of stray pixels of odd colors, which can sometimes cause problems with a black-and-white laser printer.

15. Choose File | Save As, and type in the filename and path: C:\TEMP\WAVEFORM.BMP. The system asks if you want to replace the older file with the new one of the same name; click Yes.

16. Press Alt+Esc again to switch back to Word. The X_SHEET document has a locked link to the original WAVEFORM.BMP image, so it automatically updates to the one you just saved.

     I set up this exposure sheet for exactly three seconds of video, or 90 frames. Make sure each of your drag selects clips out precisely three seconds worth of audio waveform, or the sound and the frames won't match up. Note that it will sometimes be necessary to append a small amount of silence to the end of each audio sample to bring it up to the next three-second mark. It's easier to deal with exact measures than to readjust the size of the pasted-in waveform for each sheet.

17. Click the Print icon button to print the exposure sheet. Number it immediately; you'll be printing several and you don't want to get them mixed up.

18. Return to the sound editor, and adjust the waveform display for full screen width resolution of the next three-second selection.

19. Repeat steps 7 through 18 until you have all the sound files laid out in a series of exposure sheets. You might want to make photocopies of these sheets just in case you ruin one.

    You now have the raw materials for the track analysis. The only other tools you may need are more patience, quiet surroundings, sharp pencils, and a good dictionary.

    Track analysis is not really difficult, just painstaking. There are a relatively small number of phonemes, or unique sounds, that are used by all spoken human languages. If you are only working in one language, your task is even simpler.

    You can find a pronunciation guide in the front of any good dictionary. This guide will list all the phonemes for the dictionary's language, and explain the letters and diacritical marks used in phonetic spelling. I highly recommend keeping a good dictionary like this handy while analyzing vocal tracks; it can save you a lot of time while you are developing your track-reading skills. Until you can rely on those skills, I recommend that you cheat.

20. Make up a copy of the script for the vocal track, double- or even triple-spaced so you can write legibly under or over each word.

21. Look up each word in the dictionary. Copy the phonetic spelling of each word under the normal spelling in the script. Now you know exactly what phonetic symbols you need to write in the PH column of the exposure sheet; all that's left is figuring out exactly where to put them!

    What you should do next is look—and listen—for characteristic shapes in the waveform that correspond to phonemes. Human speech is made up mostly of clicks, buzzes, and hisses. For example, a sharp spike—a click—can represent a plosive sound such as P or B. The word "baby" would therefore have two spikes, and you would mark the frames next to those spikes with the letter B. Buzzing phonemes like M or N show up as relatively even zigzags with very similar individual waveforms, sustained over a number of frames. Hissing Ss or Cs look a lot like static, just a little louder.

    Rather than go into a rambling theoretical discussion of all the different phonemes and how they are produced, I'm going to encourage you to experiment and develop your own rules. This all goes back to the principles discussed in Chapters 7 and 8; you can take someone else's word for it, or you can observe and draw your own conclusions. Observing speech is a wonderful way to lose your preconceptions about how people communicate.

22. Using the sound editor and the sample WAV file, highlight and play back a word at a time. When you have located the actual beginning of a word (which can be difficult when they are slurred together), write the complete word, spelled normally, on the exposure sheet frame where the word starts. Do not simply copy from the filled-in exposure sheets in Appendix F. You can check your work with it later, but don't look at it now.

23. Find the plosives and clicks. Look for peaks or other sharp changes within the word. Select and play them back until you can identify their start at a particular frame. Mark the frame.

24. Find the buzzes and hisses. These appear as relatively even areas, drawn out over several frames. Mark the beginning with the appropriate phonetic symbol, and draw a short line through the succeeding frames to the end of the phoneme.

25. Find and write in the phonetic symbols for the remaining sounds, which will probably be mostly vowels. They tend to fill in everywhere but the clicks, buzzes, and hisses. They are also the most visible mouth shapes to animate, as they are held longer and generally require more facial distortion.

Congratulations! You've completed your first track analysis!

Compare your exposure sheet for FINESTHR.WAV to the exposure sheet in Appendix F. Did you differ by more than a frame or two for the beginning of any word? Did you use any different phonetic symbols?

Don't worry about minor differences, this is largely a matter of opinion. People use a variety of dialects and personal speech idiosyncrasies that make insistence on absolute answers in track analysis a moot point. However, if your reading of the track was significantly different, you might want to recheck your work.

Exercise 19-11: Analyzing Your Own Voice

Repeat the previous exercise, but analyze a sample of your own voice giving a brief dramatic reading. Compare your pronunciation to the phonetic guidelines in the dictionary; what phonetic symbols might you change in the exposure sheet to represent your own speech patterns?

Exercise 19-12: Using Your Exposure Sheets

1. Repeat Exercise 11-1 where you mapped a face object with a lip sync image sequence, substituting each of the exposure sheets you just completed.

2. Dub each WAV file onto the appropriate finished AVI animation.

How close did you get? Was the lip sync convincing? Try slipping the audio track two or three frames in dubbing it, to see if the lip sync looks better delayed than with a precise match. Many studios slip the track as a general policy.

If you had trouble, go back over the track analysis exercises and see if you can spot what's going wrong. If it's just a matter of a few frames here and there seeming "off," don't worry about it. Your track analysis will improve with practice, as with so many other aspects of animation.

Now that you've got the basics of track analysis, you're ready to make up the exposure sheets for your demo reel. If your story depends on synchronized speech, sound effects, or existing music, digitize the sound track and analyze it. Write it all up on the exposure sheets.

Moving On

If you've worked through the exercises in this chapter and all your exposure sheets are finished, you're ready to animate the shots using the procedures detailed in Part One. When you have all the shots rendered, move on to Chapter 20 to put it all together.

Finishing Touches

Compositing, Title Design & Final Output

This final chapter shows you how to finish off your demo reel. You'll learn the basics of compositing and editing your animations, creating main titles and end credits, and transferring the finished work to videotape.

Video Compositing

Compositing is the process of adding parts of one image to another. In photography, this refers to procedures on a single image; in video and film work, it usually means performing similar compositing operations on a sequence of images.

Compositing was originally done using optical printers and several layers of film, one layer for each piece of original footage, matte, or special effect. Each layer would add film grain to the composited footage, so there were limits to how many layers you could composite without losing image quality. Digital compositing does not add film grain, so you can composite as many layers as you want without sacrificing image quality. This is a mixed blessing: if you are matching live action digitized from film, you may need to overlay a film grain effect on your CGI images. Otherwise, they may look too "clean" and stand out from the live action footage they are supposed to match.

Film and video work uses compositing for several functions. You can composite parts of a duplicate background, or clean plate, to cover unwanted parts of the image and salvage footage that might otherwise have to be reshot. This is often used to conceal safety lines and other equipment in live action. You can also composite shot transitions such as dissolves, wipes, and special effects. If you have to split LightWave 3D scenes into layers to speed up rendering or stay within your computer's capacity, you can reassemble the scene with compositing. The most important use of compositing in this book, however, is adding an animated character to background or live action footage.

Exercise 20-1: Match Dissolve

The most basic compositing effect is the *dissolve*, a gradual transition from one shot to the next. You can vary a dissolve from a long, slow transition for dramatic effect, to a very short dissolve that is almost a cut. A *match dissolve* is a transition where the beginning and end scenes are roughly the same, but a visible difference helps tell the story. This is a popular cinematic technique, but has been used so much it has become cliché. This exercise shows you how to set up a match dissolve.

1. Open Layout. Open the Images Panel (Figure 20-1) and load the image sequence 20_A0000.IFF from the Chapter 20 directory of the companion CD-ROM.

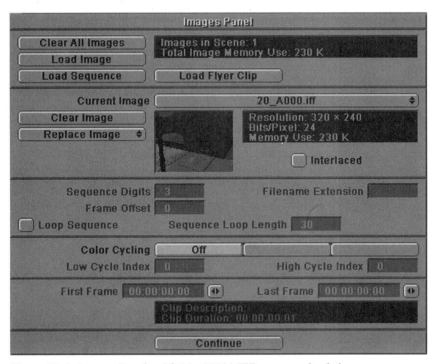

Figure 20-1: Images Panel, with 20_A0000.IFF sequence loaded.

If you would like to create your own image sequence, set up the street scene from Chapter 9 with a daylight lighting pattern and animate the Camera to dolly backwards down the sidewalk while looking toward the storefront. Render at least 200 frames to give yourself room for a smooth dissolve.

2. Load the image sequence 20_B0000.IFF. Set the Frame Offset to -100. The dissolve starts at frame 100, so you don't need to show any of the second sequence until that frame. Close the Image Panel.

If you would like to make your own version of the second image sequence, repeat the previous setup but substitute night lighting and animate the Camera moving in the opposite direction, as if retracing its path.

3. Open the Effects Panel and select the Compositing tab. Choose 20_A0000.IFF as the background image and 20_B0000.IFF as the foreground image, as in Figure 20-2.

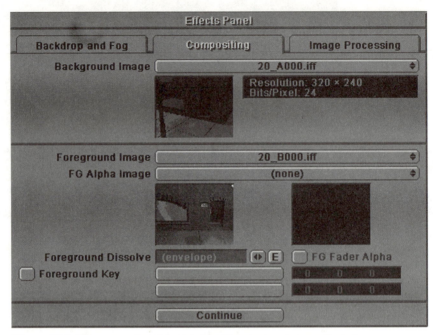

Figure 20-2: Foreground and background image sequences selected.

4. Click the E-for-Envelope button next to Foreground Dissolve to open the Dissolve Envelope panel. Create an envelope like Figure 20-3, where the second image sequence starts off 100 percent dissolved (invisible), and transitions smoothly to 0 percent (covering the background image sequence) during frames 100 to 128.

5. Set the Record and Camera Panels to render the animation in the same aspect ratio as the image sequences, and render the complete animation to the end of the second image sequence. If you used the example image sequences, this should be frame 228.

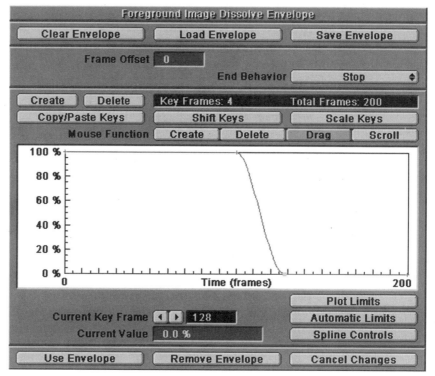

Figure 20-3: Foreground Image Dissolve Envelope.

The match dissolve from day to night lighting tells the audience that time has passed. As I said before, this is a cliché, but it still works. You can create most of the transition effects used in film and television by combining the Background, Foreground, Foreground Dissolve, and Foreground Fader Alpha functions in the Effects Panel.

If you'd like a more dramatic match dissolve exercise, you can load the walking puppet from Chapter 6 into the storefront scene. Set up the Camera in a tracking shot that allows the puppet to walk gradually out of the frame. For the second scene, set up the puppet to walk back into the shot, as if returning from a long walk, with the night-time lighting setup showing that time has passed.

Exercise 20-2: Key Compositing

This exercise shows you how to use LightWave 3D to create a *chroma key*, a technique of seamlessly combining a part of one image with another by selectively excluding specified colors. This is commonly referred to as *blue screen*, from the color most often used as a key.

1. Open Layout. Open the Images Panel and load the image sequence 20_A0000.IFF again from the Chapter 20 directory of the companion CD-ROM.

2. Load the image sequence 20_C0000.IFF. Close the Image Panel.
   If you would like to make your own version of these two image sequences, you can modify the street scene from Chapter 9.
   Set up the scene with a daylight lighting pattern and animate the camera to dolly backwards down the sidewalk while looking toward the storefront. Render the first sequence from this scene. Add the walking puppet from Chapter 6 to the scene and animate it to walk down the sidewalk. Delete all objects except the puppet, and set the background to a solid luminous color that does not appear in the puppet itself or the lighting of the scene. Make a note of this color, you will use it in the Effects Panel.

3. Open the Effects Panel and select the Compositing tab. Choose 20_A0000.IFF as the background image, and 20_C0000.IFF as the foreground image.

4. Click Foreground Key. Click Low Clip Color. Set the Low Clip Color equal to the color of the foreground image sequence's background area. For the 20_C0000.IFF sequence, this is 0, 0, 255, a pure blue. If you are working with your own image sequences, you may have to use a different color. Click OK to accept the color and close the panel. Repeat for the High Clip Color, using the same values.
   If you ever composite live-action blue screen footage into an animation, you'll have to deal with a range of shades instead of the precise values of a rendered background. The Clip Color Panels enable you to adjust for variations in lighting and blue screen colors to produce a clean key. The color you select for a key should not appear in any of the lights, objects, or textures in the keyed image. Blue is commonly used, but any color works.

5. Set the Record and Camera Panels to render the animation in the same aspect ratio as the image sequences, and render the complete animation.

You should end up with something like Figure 20-4.

Figure 20-4: An image composited using chroma key.

Exercise 20-3: Alpha Channel Compositing

If you need to composite a CGI character into a complex live-action background, the matched lighting (see Chapter 17) or reflection maps may not leave you a clear choice of color for a chroma key. For these situations, LightWave 3D enables you to render an alpha channel mask, a separate sequence of images that exactly silhouettes the scene's objects in grayscale. Alpha channel compositing uses this grayscale as a filter to combine the foreground image with the rest of the scene.

1. Repeat exercise 20-2 through step 3. If you want to use your own image sequence, you'll have to rerender the puppet walking with the Save Alpha Images option turned on.

2. Open the Image Panel. Load the image sequence 20_D0000.IFF. This is an alpha channel rendered to match image sequence 20_C0000.IFF. Close the panel.

3. Open the Effects Panel. Select 20_D0000.IFF as the FG Alpha Image. Click on FG Fader Alpha. Close the Effects Panel.

This sets up the matching alpha channel images for the foreground image sequence.

4. Set the Record and Camera Panels to render the animation in the same aspect ratio as the image sequences. Render the complete animation.

Title Design

Even a great animation won't look as good without titles. And even a bad animation looks a little more professional with good titles. Titles are easy to animate, but they should conform to principles of typographic design since the audience has to read them. Keep them on screen long enough to read, at least one second for every five words.

Titles must be limited to the text-safe areas for video work, as most televisions cut off the outer edge of the picture. LightWave 3D makes this very easy; just click on Show Safe Areas in the Layout View tab of the Options Panel. The Camera view shows two concentric rectangles with rounded corners. The outer one is the action-safe area; the inner one is the text-safe area, where your titles are least likely to be cut off. Even if you are working in film it's smart to title with eventual TV broadcast in mind. Keep your titles in the safe area, or the work will have to be retitled for broadcast—and you won't necessarily have control of the new titles!

Many fonts are unsuitable for modeling and animation. A typeface that has many fine strokes, is complexly interwoven, or leans in odd directions is difficult to read. See Figure 20-5 for examples. Your audience presumably is interested in your animation, not the number of oddball fonts you keep on your computer. Choose title fonts carefully!

Figure 20-5: Good and bad font choices for titles and credits.

Exercise 20-4: Main Titles

This exercise gives you a few guidelines for creating your main title sequence, but since titles can vary so much, the creative details are left up to you.

1. Build text objects for your main titles.

    If you haven't created text objects before, you should work through the first part of Modeler Tutorial #5 in the *LightWave 3D User Guide*. Remember your typography, and don't make the text hard to read.

2. Animate the text objects for your main title sequence. If you want a real challenge, why not animate a character putting the title together, or otherwise interacting with the letters?

As you lay out the animation, be creative; but don't move the camera around, don't use chrome textures on the text objects, and don't use lens flares or any other techniques that scream "Beginner!" This is not some cheap cable TV flying logo. This is supposed to be the introduction to your best work. Trust me, a cheesy title practically guarantees your demo reel will be ejected immediately. This is the consensus of a number of professional animators who have to review demo reels on a regular basis.

Are all your titles legible at the resolution your audience will be viewing them? Do they detract from the value of your animation, or add to it? When in doubt, keep it simple; your character animation should be able to speak for itself.

Exercise 20-5: End Credits

This exercise shows you how to lay out your technical end credits. There are two common ways to handle end credits, the scroll and the dissolve. I prefer the dissolve, just because the text holds still and is therefore easier to read. LightWave 3D's Foreground Dissolve and Image Sequence functions make dissolving credits very easy to create and modify.

1. Use the graphics software of your preference to create a series of black-and-white images, one for each credit. Make them the same size as the final resolution of your demo reel, and use antialiased text if you can. Make a solid black image to use at the beginning and end of the credits.

   I used Adobe Photoshop to create the credits images for "Easy Come, Easy Go," located in the Chapter 20 directory of the Companion CD-ROM. If you use any of the provided sample materials to create your own demo reel, please include the appropriate credit images (or your own versions with the same phrasing) in your demo reel's end credits.

2. Figure out the beginning frame for each credit. Remember to leave at least 30 frames, one second, for each five words. You can use more, but try not to let your credits drag out longer than your animation.

3. Rename each credit image with its starting frame number, TITL0000.IFF, TITL0050.IFF, and so on.

4. Open Layout. Open the Images Panel and load the image sequence TITL0000.IFF.

5. Open the Effects Panel and select the Compositing tab. Choose TITL0000.IFF as the foreground image.

6. Click the E-for-Envelope button next to Foreground Dissolve to open the Dissolve Envelope Panel. Create an envelope like Figure 20-6, where the foreground image sequence is normally at 0 percent, but transitions to 100 percent just before and after the credit images change. You can do this most efficiently by copying and pasting the first set of transition keyframes to each of the other transitions.

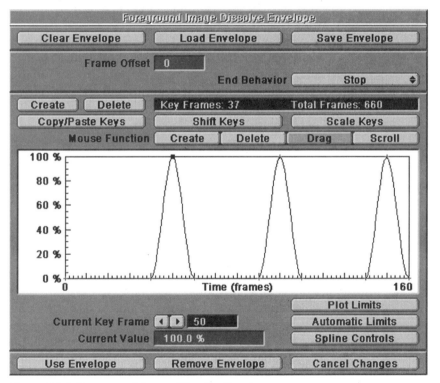

Figure 20-6: Foreground Image Dissolve Envelope.

7. Set the Record and Camera Panels to render the credits in the same aspect ratio as the original images. Render the complete animation.

This is a low-memory method of creating titles or credits, since only one image map has to be loaded in RAM at a time.

Final Output

You have several options for recording and showing your finished demo reel. The most commonly accepted format in the United States is VHS videotape. The larger studios usually have a selection of machines capable of playing back just about any format, but if you're looking for work you don't want to put your potential employer to any extra bother. If you have access to higher quality equipment, make your master reel on the best format you can handle, but make VHS dubs to mail out with your résumé.

Transferring animation to video is relatively inexpensive, but cutting corners with cheap compression boards can really hurt the final appearance. The most cost-effective solution at present is to use a special hard drive recording device that also works with your choice of editing and post-processing software, then dump the finished piece to broadcast-quality videotape. I've had good experience with DPS's Personal Animation Recorder (PAR) and the more recent Perception Video Recorder, but there are a number of competing products you may want to investigate as well. You're still looking at several thousand dollars, so you may be better off finding a service bureau or fellow animator who has equipment you can borrow or lease.

If your system's output resolution justifies it, rent a professional quality recording deck for a day to make your master tape. You can usually get a BetacamSP deck for under $200 a day in most major cities. Do all your prep work before you pick up the deck; you don't want to have to pay for another day because you couldn't find a cable or a blank tape. Buy short videotapes in bulk for your demo reels.

> You have to look at demo reels as résumés. Make lots, send out lots.

This is important; you have to look at demo reels as résumés. Make lots, send out lots. You're going after some pretty high-paying jobs, either as a TD or animator. Would you worry about the price of each sheet of paper if you were getting your résumé duplicated? What fraction of your first year's income are you willing to spend on a résumé that gets you a job? You'll be sending out quite a few demo reels before you get that first job, so resign yourself to spending the money or working a barter. Nothing ventured, nothing gained. Ten-minute videotapes are relatively inexpensive by the case, and the short length keeps reviewers from taping TV shows over them.

If you are an independent filmmaker, you may want to stick with video formats until you can find backing for film transfer. If you carefully archive all your animation scenes, objects, and related files, you can always go back and rerender to higher resolution for film. Film output is expensive, but it definitely gives the best looking results. Unless you can afford your own film recorder with a pin-register camera back, you will be sending your rendered images to a service bureau to be transferred to film. I recommend against trying to save money by transferring to 16mm. Go with 35mm; the price difference in film is relatively small compared to the transfer charges for the recorder. Also, if you are trying to get into film festivals or to sell your animation, 35mm prints have a wider potential audience.

If you can't afford film or professional video, you may be able to record a low-budget demo reel using direct computer playback. This is currently very limited by tradeoffs in resolution, speed, color depth, or all three, but is cheap. You use a relatively inexpensive device called a scan converter to convert your computer's video signals to something acceptable to your consumer-grade VCR.

Generally, the cheaper the converter, the lousier the videotaped images. The bottom end is around $250 as of this writing, and the upper end converters cost more than a DPS PAR. Don't despair if this is all you can afford; several studios have assured me that they look for the quality of the animation, not the professional polish on the tape production. Make sure the playback is at the same rate as you animated it, the images are relatively clear, and the tape tracking doesn't wander all over the place, and you should be all right.

Conclusion

If you've worked through the entire book, you should now have a solid understanding of character animation and a pretty good demo reel. Congratulations!

If you choose to pursue a career in CGI character animation, I hope you will continue to practice and learn. If you have any questions about this book, suggestions for future editions, or just want to chat about character animation, please drop me an e-mail at kcc@apk.net.

Appendices

About the Companion CD-ROM

The CD-ROM included with your copy of *LightWave 3D 5 Character Animation f/x* contains a software program and example files from the book.

To View the CD-ROM:

WINDOWS:
Double-click on the CD-ROM drive icon file from your Window Explorer or File Manager.

You'll see a root structure for the contents of the CD-ROM.

MACINTOSH:
Double-click on the CD-ROM icon on your desktop.

Software on the CD-ROM

MAGPIE (Shareware Version)   MAGPIE is a tool that helps in the analysis of a recorded dialog track for accurate lip sync animations. MAGPIE can be accessed by opening Appendix H on the CD-ROM.

Files on the CD-ROM

The CD-ROM contains files provided by the author to supplement the text of the book. The file directory is set up to mirror the structure of the book with a folder of examples for each chapter. There are also Appendices A through H which contain a variety of files related to the book's text. Other examples mentioned in the text of the book are located in the named folders at the bottom of the directory structure.

Technical Support

Technical support is available for installation-related problems only. The technical support office is open from 8:00 A.M. to 6:00 P.M. Monday through Friday and can be reached via the following methods:

Phone: (919) 544-9404 extension 81

Faxback Answer System: (919) 544-9404 extension 85

E-mail: help@vmedia.com

FAX: (919) 544-9472

World Wide Web: http://www.vmedia.com/support

America Online: keyword Ventana

Limits of Liability & Disclaimer of Warranty

The authors and publisher of this book have used their best efforts in preparing the CD-ROM and the programs contained in it. These efforts include the development, research, and testing of the theories and programs to determine their effectiveness. The authors and publisher make no warranty of any kind expressed or implied, with regard to these programs or the documentation contained in this book.

The authors and publisher shall not be liable in the event of incidental or consequential damages in connection with, or arising out of, the furnishing, performance, or use of the programs, associated instructions, and/or claims of productivity gains.

Character design drawings in Chapter 12 and Chapter 19, rendered images of creature in Chapter 9, and several rendered images of creature and cyborg for color insert are copyrighted 1996, Mike Comet, from the game Vicious Circle, used with permission by Digital Storm.

Musical composition, "Easy Come, Easy Go," copyrighted 1996, Patrick Kelly.

Online Updates

As we all know, the Internet is constantly changing. As hard as we've tried to make our information current, the truth is that new sites will come online as soon as this book goes to press (and continually thereafter). Ventana provides an excellent way to tackle this problem and to keep the information in the book up-to-date: the *LightWave 3D 5 Character Animation f/x Online Updates*. You can access this valuable resource via Ventana's World Wide Web site at http://www.vmedia.com. Once there, you'll find updated files from this book as software development continues. When NewTek or third-party developers announce new features or plug-ins for LightWave 3D, you can count on Ventana Online to show you how to use them. Ventana Online also provides links to various LightWave 3D resources on the Internet, including discussion groups, newsgroups, databases, and more. Plus—enjoy access to free services on Ventana Online.

Resources

This appendix is intended to provide information you can use to start or further your career in character animation. This information is as accurate as I could make it, but this industry is moving fast and information changes all the time. I encourage you to check Ventana's online updates (see Appendix B) before making any irrevocable actions—like mailing your last copy of your demo reel to an out-of-date address!

Just the FAQs, Ma'am

A FAQ, or Frequently Asked Questions list, is a document containing questions and answers that are often asked of a discussion group or help desk. Just about every major newsgroup, mailing list, or World Wide Web site has a FAQ. Smart vendors compile their own FAQs for technical support and make them freely available via the Internet.

Reading FAQs has got to be the easiest, cheapest way in the world to fake being an expert. Contrariwise, jumping into a newsgroup or mailing list and asking the Number One Question from that group's FAQ instantly labels you as a dweeb too dumb to pour sand out of a boot.

Remember what I said in Chapter 3: learn from others' mistakes—it's much cheaper, and certainly less painful!

LightWave 3D FAQ

The first FAQ you should read is, logically enough, the one for LightWave 3D. This pertains to the Usenet newsgroup comp.graphics.apps.lightwave and to the LightWave 3D listserv operated through garcia.com.

This FAQ is compiled and maintained by that selfless, generous paragon of virtue and incredibly talented Technical Director and Animator Extraordinaire, Mike Comet. (There, I mentioned you, Mike; can I have my dog back now?)

The full text of the LightWave 3D FAQ is located in the Resources directory on the Companion CD-ROM. For the most recent version, follow the link from the NewTek home page at http://www.newtek.com/ or go straight to the source, Mike Comet's home page at http://www.apk.net/comet/.

While you're there, check out Mike's artwork and animations.

comp.graphics.animation FAQ

Next on your reading list is the FAQ for the Usenet newsgroup comp.graphics.animation. This is probably the largest and broadest of the groups and lists dealing with computer animation. As such, it covers many areas that will probably be of little interest to you. The advantage is that many people from diverse backgrounds and approaches read and contribute to this group. A seemingly insoluble problem posted here is usually solved quickly.

Due to the volume of traffic on this group, it is especially important that you read the FAQ thoroughly before you post. Again, you don't want to look like a dweeb for asking a question that's answered in the FAQ.

The FAQ is maintained by F. X. DeJesus, and the most recent version can be found at http://www.ridgecrest.ca.us/fx/cga-faq.html or via FTP at ftp://avalon.viewpoint.com/pub/FAQs/cga-faq/.

comp.graphics.misc FAQ

If you have any remaining questions about standards, algorithms, interest groups, or references, try this FAQ. It's a grab-bag of useful stuff that just doesn't seem to have an obvious home elsewhere.

This FAQ is maintained by John T. Grieggs, and the most recent version can be found at http://www.primenet.com/~grieggs/cg_faq.html.

Internet Filmmaker's FAQ

If you are interested in producing your own film, or simply want to understand the process better, this is an excellent place to start. The focus is on live action, but many of the issues are the same and there are a lot more people contributing than for animation or CGI.

This FAQ relates to the Usenet newsgroups: rec.arts.movies.production; alt.movies.independent; misc.writing.screenplays; and aus.films. Most of these are worth reading, especially if you find the FAQ useful or interesting.

You Name It FAQ

Browse the Usenet FTP archives at MIT for FAQs on just about every subject imaginable: rtfm.mit.edu/pub/usenet/rec.answers.

The Gang's All Here

Here are a couple of organizations you should consider joining if you are pursuing a career in animation.

ASIFA

ASIFA, Association Internationale du Film d'Animation, is "devoted to the encouragement and dissemination of film animation as an art and communication form." It has over 1,100 members in 55 countries. The United States has the most members, 280, and Canada is a close second with 250.

ASIFA produces a newsletter, annual calendar, and animation school list. It also maintains an employment database and a film archive. The ASIFA Workshop Group runs animation workshops for children in over 30 countries.

ASIFA membership is open to all individuals interested in animation. For more information, contact ASIFA-Central at http://laotzu. art.niu.edu/asifa.html or ASIFA-Hollywood at http://www.awn.com/ asifa_hollywood/.

Local 839

The following is a quote from the Local 839 Web site:

> What is Local 839? Simply put, we are a union of artists, writers and technicians making animated films. We've been around since 1952 helping animation employees get decent wages, better working conditions . . . and a little respect.
>
> Animators are among our members. Writers of TV cartoons hold MPSC union cards. Digital painters, computer animators and modelers are part of the MPSC. We negotiate contracts, create resumes, provide legal and negotiating advice to artists and technicians working for the largest and most profitable animation companies in the world.

For more details, contact:

MPSC Local 839 IATSE
4729 Lankershim Boulevard
North Hollywood, CA 91602-1864
Phone: (818) 766-7151
Fax: (818) 506-4805
E-mail: mpsc839@netcom.com
http://www.primenet.com/~mpsc839/
or (coming soon)
http://www.mpsc839.org/

Don't Call Us, We'll Call You

Following is a list of major animation and special effects houses that have advertised recently for TDs or animators. As always, contact information is subject to change without notice. Sending a reel is the best approach, but this has some drawbacks since the most popular studios receive hundreds of reels.

At some studios a nonanimator, often a secretary, filters out the absolute trash before any of the creative or supervisory staff gets to see it. This can occasionally result in a reel being trashed for reasons having nothing to do with the talent of the animator; the "filters" simply don't know what they are doing.

If you are sending a demo reel, it is a good idea to get the e-mail address, fax, or phone number of a senior animator or director at the studio, and send them a polite message that you would like to send in your reel. If they agree, tell them exactly when you are sending it, and if they give you permission, add their name to the Attention line. This way, the reel is more likely to be put aside for someone who knows what they are looking at, and the person you contacted may even ask to see the reel before the "filter" gets to it.

Remember that your contact person is doing you a favor. Be polite. Don't call them at home. Don't nag. Send a follow-up thank-you note. And never broadcast whatever personal contact information they give you!

Potential Employers

※ Blue Sky Productions does CGI animation for TV and feature film, including *Joe's Apartment*.

Blue Sky Productions, Inc.
Fax: (914) 923-9058
Phone: (914) 941-5260
http://www.blueskyprod.com/

◈ Digital Domain, James Cameron's effects production house, is easily one of the most popular "dream jobs" in the industry. The corporate culture is . . . interesting. They did effects for *True Lies*, and are currently at work on an all-CGI film.

Digital Domain
300 Rose Avenue
Venice, CA 90291
Phone: 310-314-2934
E-mail: digital_hiring@d2.com
http://www.d2.com/

◈ Dream Quest Images, a division of the Walt Disney Company, does feature film digital visual effects.

Dream Quest Images
Attn.: Geoff Brooks-Talent Recruiting
2635 Park Center Drive
Simi Valley, CA 93065
E-mail: talent@dqimages.com

◈ DreamWorks Animation is part of DreamWorks SKG, the start-up studio headed by Steven Spielberg, Jeffrey Katzenberg, and David Geffen.

DreamWorks Animation
Attn.: Michele Henderson
P.O. Box 7304 #132
North Hollywood, CA 91603
E-mail: animhr@dreamworks.com

◈ Industrial Light + Magic, or ILM, is a division of Lucas Digital, Ltd., and does effects work for Lucasfilm and other studios as well. Most recently, they animated Draco for *Dragonheart* and tornadoes for *Twister*, but their line of award-winning effects goes back to the original *Star Wars*.

Lucas Digital
HR Dept.
P.O. Box 2459
San Rafael, CA 94912
Phone: (415) 662-1800

❀ MetroLight looks for TDs and animators who are comfortable in a UNIX, high-end environment. If you have exclusively LightWave 3D experience, you will need programming skills or something extra to convince them.

MetroLight Studios Inc.
Attn.: Resumes
5724 W. 3rd St., #400
Los Angeles, CA 90036
E-mail: resumes@metrolight.com
http://www.metrolight.com/

❀ Origin Systems is a major game developer, with too many credits to list. They use LightWave 3D, among other software.

ORIGIN Systems, Inc.
Attn.: Human Resources
5918 W. Courtyard Dr.
Austin, TX 78730
E-mail: nvargas@origin.ea.com

❀ Pacific Data Images does feature film digital visual effects using proprietary software. PDI's been around a long time; recent work includes the 3D Homer and Bart in last season's *The Simpsons* Halloween special, and the aliens in *The Arrival. Ants* is currently in production.

Pacific Data Images
Attn.: CG Animation Search
3101 Park Boulevard
Palo Alto, CA 94306
Fax: (415) 846-8101
Phone: (415) 846-8100
http://www.pdi.com/

❀ Pixar Animation Studios produced *Toy Story, Tin Toy, Luxo Jr.,* and the Listerine and Gummi Savers TV ads. As if you didn't know.

Rachel Hannah
Pixar Animation Studios
1001 West Cutting Blvd.
Richmond, CA 94804
Fax: (510) 236-0388

◈ Square L.A. produced best-selling role-playing games Final Fantasy and Chrono Trigger.

Square L.A.
4640 Admiralty Way
Suite 1200
Marina del Rey, CA 90292-6621
Phone: 1-888-470-8273

◈ Sony Pictures Imageworks does digital visual effects. One major project in the works is *Dinotopia*. They accept reels, résumés, and portfolios.

RT/HRANI
c/o Sony Pictures Imageworks
Room #1221
9050 West Washington Blvd.
Culver City, CA 90232
Fax: (310) 840-8888
Phone: (310) 840-8000
E-mail: resumes@spimageworks.com
http://www.spiw.com/

◈ Tiburon Entertainment develops games for Electronic Arts, including Soviet Strike and Madden NFL '97. They're expanding.

Tiburon Entertainment
HR Department
P.O. Box 940427
Maitland, FL 32794-0427
Fax: 407-862-4077
http://www.tibent.com/

◈ Walt Disney Feature Animation is going digital in a big way; currently they are gearing up for production of *Dinosaur*.

Walt Disney Feature Animation
Attn.: Human Resources HR 7.6
500 S. Burbank Street
Burbank , CA 91521-8072
Fax: 818-544-5400
E-mail: resumes@fa.disney.com

❧ Warner Digital, a division of Warner Bros., says it wants to be a full-service digital visual effects company. Send a fax before you send a demo reel; their contact info was incomplete.

Warner Digital Studios Recruiting
1935 Buena Vista Street
Burbank, CA 91504
Fax: (818) 977-0530
http:/www.warnerdigital.com/

❧ Windlight Studios did the animated Gymnast Barbie ads. They specialize in long-format computer character animation.

Windlight Studios
Attn.: Human Resources
702 North First Street
Minneapolis, MN 55401
E-mail: hr@windlight.com

A Few Needles From the Haystack

The dire warnings you may have heard about the information explosion are no joke. It's just as true for CGI animation as for any other subject. There's a lot of data out there, and it makes one big haystack to sort through for the right needle to sew up your animation.

These are the journals I use myself—long on information, short on fluff, and generally reliable to get the story straight:

❧ *3D Artist* is the best collection of tutorials and hands-on information for artists using desktop 3D software. The focus is on what works, the tutorials are generally written by artists actually working in 3D for a living, and the product reviews are honest. There is usually at least one article specifically on LightWave 3D, and tutorials for any software are often written to be applicable elsewhere.

Columbine Inc.
P.O. Box 4787
Santa Fe, NM 87502
ISSN: 1058-9503
http://www.3dartist.com/

❧ *ACM Transactions on Graphics* is a quarterly research journal dealing with the algorithms and other theoretical arcana behind graphics programming. Techniques first published here sometimes take years to show up in commercial desktop software. Smart TDs read this journal and work out their own implementations to stay ahead of the commercial pack.

ISSN: 0730-0301
http://www.acm.org/pubs/tog/

❧ *Computer Graphics* is a sister publication to *Transactions*. The contents are more about implementations and tutorials, and the annual *SIGGRAPH Conference Proceedings* are always a worthwhile collection of eye candy and solid information.

Association for Computing Machinery
11 West 42nd Street
New York, NY 10036
http://www.siggraph.org/

❧ *Animation Magazine* is a trade journal covering traditional and CGI animation. Industry news, help wanted, bios, retrospectives, and business-related articles are a big help to novices and old pros alike. This one's definitely worth a subscription.

Animation Magazine
30101 Agoura Court, Suite 110
Agoura Hills, CA 91301
E-mail: Animag@AOL.com
http://www.imall.com/stores/animag/inc/index.html

❧ *Cinefex* is the trade journal of the feature film special effects community. Slick and heavily illustrated, this quarterly publishes long, in-depth, nuts-and-bolts articles on f/x techniques. Stopmo, miniatures, CGI, you name it, if it ends up on the big screen Cinefex shows how it was done. Even the issues that don't include CGI articles have lots of useful information for character animation, and the advertiser's index reads like a who's who of houses you'd like to work for.

Cinefex
P.O. Box 20027
Riverside, CA 92516

❧ *Computer Graphics World* covers pretty much what the title says. You'll find articles here about hardware, software, and other technical issues, and the industry news leans more toward hardware and software vendors than animation houses. The down side is that space constraints force tutorials to be less detailed than one would prefer.

CGW
10 Tara Blvd., 5th Floor
Nashua, NH 03062-2801
http://www.cgw.com/

❧ *fps* is an eclectic mix of tutorials, industry news, and fanzine for animation. Most of the material pertains to traditional methods, but CGI and computer-assisted techniques are covered on occasion.

fps
P.O. Box 355
Station H
Montreal, Quebec, Canada H3G 2L1
ISSN: 1203-396X
E-mail: pawn@cam.org
http://www.cam.org/~pawn/fps.html

❧ *Game Developer* is a slim magazine that is short on animation-specific articles, but long on contact info and industry buzz for the game community. If you're looking for a way to break into the character animation business, game developers are often less picky about your demo reel than feature animation houses. If you're not already a gamer, read the back issues so you understand the problems and can talk about them intelligently at your job interview.

Miller Freeman Inc.
600 Harrison Street
San Francisco, CA 94107
ISSN: 1073-922X
http://www.gdmag.com/

❧ *LIGHTWAVEPRO* is the only magazine that focuses exclusively on LightWave 3D and supporting software. Fortunately, they do a nice job of it, and have a solid, useful balance between step-by-step tutorials, news, and general articles. If you invested in LightWave 3D but don't have a subscription to this magazine, you're not getting your money's worth out of the software.

Miller Freeman
1308 Orleans Drive
Sunnyvale, CA 94089
ISSN: 1076-7819
E-mail the editor, John Gross, at jgross@netcom.com.

❧ *NT Studio* is a new magazine dedicated to production tools for Windows NT platforms. Topics include industry news, tutorials, and hardware and software reviews for LightWave 3D and other packages. If future issues are anything like the premiere issue, it's worth reading.

NT Studio
201 E. Sandpointe Avenue, Suite 600
Santa Ana, CA 92707
http://www.ntstudio.com/

❧ *Post* is a post-production trade journal useful primarily for news on who's doing what. You should at least scan the promotional and help-wanted ads scattered throughout the magazine for production houses that may want to hire you.

Testa Communications
25 Willowdale Avenue
Port Washington, NY 11050

❧ *Video Toaster User* is a sister publication of *LIGHTWAVEPRO*, covering LightWave 3D in addition to NewTek's Video Toaster. There is usually at least one good LightWave 3D tutorial, and the rest of the magazine is informative on technical issues.

Miller Freeman
411 Borel Avenue, Suite 100
San Mateo CA 94402
ISSN: 1075-8704

Treasure Islands in the Net

In addition to the Web sites maintained by the magazines and studios listed above, there are a few general-purpose sites with useful information for CGI character animators and TDs.

CG-CHAR Home Page

The CG-CHAR home page is a collection of resources by and for subscribers of the CG-CHAR listserv. Galleries of art, works in progress, book reviews, shareware, and job postings are there now, and plans for the future include complete listserv archives and interactive chats.

To quote the founder and moderator of the listserv, Rick May,

> The CG (computer generated) Character Animation List was created for artists and TD's to share information and ideas on creating computer assisted character animation. We are hoping to discuss not only software and (a little) hardware, but techniques and ideas. Although we are applying our artistry through the computer—we welcome postings from people with cel or stopmo experience. A lot of people creating CG character work nowadays have cel or stopmo backgrounds anyway—techniques learned from these disciplines are always helpful. Traditional animators could also benefit from our list—perhaps learning how to use the computer in their animation work.

For more information, visit the Web site at http://www.cinenet.net/users/rickmay/CGCHAR/frameset.htm or e-mail Rick at rickmay@cinenet.net.

GWEB

"An Electronic Trade Journal for Computer Animators." This is a good all-around source for news, job listings, and résumés for the animation industry. Lots of links, too. Find it at http://www.gweb.org/.

3dsite

This site has a lot of links: production houses, publications, organizations, employment opportunities, ongoing research—you can spend some serious surfing time with this as your home port. Check it out at http://www.3dsite.com/.

NewTek

The home page of LightWave 3D itself, with many links to related Web pages: http://www.newtek.com/.

CGA—Computer Game Artists

A fledgling organization of and for game artists. Get in on the ground floor and help build it! Find it at http://www.vectorg.com:80/cga/.

The Digital Movie News™

An electronic journal of computer-assisted filmmaking. Lots of useful articles and links on everything from story development to locating financing: http://www.el-dorado.ca.us/~dmnews/.

Sample Script

The following script is included to assist you in completing the exercises in Chapter 19, in case you don't want to write your own script. The premise of the story is also the title, "Easy Come, Easy Go."

This script is copyright © 1996 Douglas A. Kelly. Your permission to use the script is subject to the following conditions:

- Permission is granted to purchasers of this book to use this script for educational purposes only.

- Purchasers of this book are specifically granted permission to use this script for completing the exercises in Chapter 19 in the production of a not-for-resale animated motion picture.

- If you use this script as is or in any revised or derivative form, you are required to display the phrase "Written by Doug Kelly" in the credits.

- If the finished work will be used for any commercial purpose or public display, including any advertisement or solicitation regarding animation services or employment, copyright law requires that you get my permission in advance.

- If you use this script to create a demo reel, you can secure my permission by sending me a letter of request and a copy of the demo reel.

Whether you use it or not, I hope you enjoy the story.

"EASY COME, EASY GO"

Written by

Doug Kelly

Doug Kelly   REVISED DRAFT
P.O. Box 16878   May 25, 1996
Rocky River, OH 44107

                                         kcc@apk.net

1

"EASY COME, EASY GO"

FADE IN:

EXT CLOSE SHOT PUDDLE DESERTED CITY STREET LATE AFTERNOON

Heavy rain is falling on a city sidewalk. Puddle reflects
blinking neon in ripples. NEON BUZZES. Rainfall tapers
off, stops.

Truck back, pan up to MEDIUM TRACKING SHOT of FRED.
Storefronts are brick with large plate glass windows. FRED
looks down on his luck. Almost emaciated, holes and tears
in clothing, dirty, unshaven, overlong hair peeking out
under a stoved-in hat, flapping shoe sole, glasses askew.
FRED walks along sidewalk, head down, dragging feet.

THREE-QUARTER MEDIUM SHOT FRED as he glances in darkened
shop window, then pauses. He sees his REFLECTION, stops and
faces window.

CLOSE SHOT REFLECTION over FRED's shoulder. Reflection
morphs to well-fed, well-dressed, happy-looking version of
FRED.

MEDIUM SHOT REVERSE ANGLE THROUGH WINDOW FRED as he perks
up, smiling, tips hat to reflection.

CLOSE SHOT REFLECTION over FRED's shoulder, as reflection
morphs back to Fred's current image.

MEDIUM SHOT REVERSE ANGLE THROUGH WINDOW FRED as he sighs,
slouches again. Fred turns and begins to walk out of frame.

MEDIUM TRACKING SHOT FRED as he shuffles along sidewalk.
Trash blows past. BILL blows into frame, plasters itself
across FRED's glasses. FRED staggers.

CLOSE SHOT FRED as he peels bill off glasses, tries to clear
glasses.

THREE-QUARTER CLOSE SHOT FRED as he looks at bill. FRED
blinks, momentarily baffled.

2

CLOSE SHOT over FRED's shoulder ZOOM to EXTREME CLOSE SHOT on BILL in FRED's hands. We can read bill as $1000.

THREE-QUARTER MEDIUM SHOT FRED as he looks at bill. Wild take, as he stretches bill flat between both hands.

THREE-QUARTER CLOSE SHOT FRED recovers, looks up and into the middle distance, as if at a wonderful vision.

CLOSE SHOT FRED'S FACE. FRED's eyes reflect images of dollar signs, then a rich dinner, then bubbling champagne, then the well-dressed image from the storefront.

THREE-QUARTER MEDIUM SHOT FRED clutching bill as he looks around, reading storefront signs. FRED sees shop he wants, anticipates and zips out of frame.

REAR MEDIUM SHOT FRED as he brakes to a screeching halt and performs a 90-degree zip into Restaurant doorway. DOOR SWINGING. ARGUMENT, ON RISING NOTE. Door opens forcefully as FRED reappears, arcing out of doorway in midair and landing on his rump in the middle of the sidewalk, still clutching bill. FRED protests. BOUNCER'S HAND appears from doorway, pointing to sign in window.

CLOSE SHOT SIGN with pointing hand. Sign reads, "PROPER ATTIRE REQUIRED" in elegant script.

MEDIUM SHOT FRED as BOUNCER'S HAND withdraws, SLAMMING DOOR. FRED gets to feet, dusts himself off, looking disgruntled, then transitions to determination. FRED looks around at storefront signs again. He sees the shop he wants across the street. FRED marches determinedly out of frame, stepping off the curb.

MEDIUM SHOT TAILOR SHOP as FRED marches up to door and enters.

HELD SHOT ON TAILOR SHOP. We hear MEASURING TAPE, SCISSORS, SEWING MACHINE, CASH REGISTER.

MATCH DISSOLVE TO:

MEDIUM SHOT BARBER SHOP with spinning barber pole. By the
light, it is visibly later in the evening, nearly sunset. We
hear SCISSORS, HAIR TONIC, LATHER BRUSH, RAZOR STROP,
SHAVING, CASH REGISTER. Door opens. FRED exits with a
jaunty strut, clean-shaven and with slicked-down, neatly-
parted hair. (Possibly insert humorous cameo from weiner-
dog) FRED turns to find restaurant again, and jauntily walks
out of frame, back across street.

MEDIUM SHOT RESTAURANT as FRED jauntily walks up and enters.

INT MEDIUM SHOT TABLE RESTAURANT EVENING

WAITRESS'S HANDS hold chair as FRED sits down. WAITRESS'S
HANDS present MENU. FRED peruses menu, making a great show
of it. FRED smiles broadly, holds menu open toward WAITRESS
(OS) and points to several items, nodding rapidly.
WAITRESS'S HANDS retrieve menu. WAITRESS'S HANDS serve
heaping plates of food, pour champagne.

MONTAGE

fred making pig of self, waistline expanding

drinking more

becoming boisterous

gesturing and calling to other tables (OS)

dishes stacking

champagne magnums accumulating

increasingly tight close shots on Fred, mouth opening wider
in eating and talking, actions more broad and out of control

loosening collar, clothing becoming disarrayed

CASH REGISTER RINGING repeatedly

MEDIUM SHOT TABLE FRED as WAITRESS' HANDS gesture Fred to
settle down. FRED transitions from gluttonous to irate,
then fascinated with WAITRESS(OS), then leering. FRED makes
grab for WAITRESS(OS). WAITRESS' HANDS withdraw, fending
off FRED, who nearly falls out of chair. FRED, grumbling,
resumes guzzling champagne. BOUNCER'S HAND reaches into
frame, tap FRED on shoulder. FRED looks up, bleary and
obviously in his cups. His reaction time is severely
impaired.

4

EXT MEDIUM SHOT RESTAURANT DESERTED CITY STREET NIGHT

CRASHING and THUDS. DOOR OPENS forcefully as FRED reappears, arcing out of doorway in midair. Camera tracks FRED, does zip pan as he COLLIDES headfirst with LAMPPOST. DOOR SLAMS forcefully. FRED defies gravity for a moment, then falls, SPLAT, facefirst onto sidewalk.

CLOSE SHOT MOVING HOLD FRED, left flat on face across sidewalk. Hat is now crumpled, clothing partially soiled from contact with sidewalk and lamppost. (Possibly insert another humorous cameo from weiner-dog) FRED slowly sits up, holds head and weaves a bit. FRED climbs shakily to his feet. He GAGS, but can't hold it in and the camera pans to follow his rush for the alley entrance next to RESTAURANT. FRED drops to knees with head and upper torso out of sight in alley, and GAGS repeatedly.

MEDIUM SHOT ALLEY FRED as he drags himself across the alley on hands and knees to a patch of wall between garbage cans and props himself there.

CLOSE SHOT FRED TRASH CANS His color is slightly better, although still pale. His clothing is now thoroughly soiled and torn. His eyelids flicker a few times, then fall shut as FRED begins to snore.

DISSOLVE TO:

MEDIUM SHOT ALLEY FRED as morning light filters into the alley, showing all the damage. FRED's snoring changes, he wakes, blinks repeatedly, winces at the light, shakes his head and immediately clutches it in pain. He is badly hung over.

FULL SHOT ALLEY RESTAURANT SHOP as FRED staggers onto sidewalk in front of store.

CLOSE SHOT FRED as he transitions from bewilderment to total recall, and then to crushing remorse. His shoulders sag.

THREE-QUARTER MEDIUM SHOT FRED as FRED glances in darkened shop window. He sees his reflection again, and turns to face window.

CLOSE SHOT MOVING HOLD REFLECTION over FRED's shoulder. Reflection morphs to well-fed, well-dressed version of FRED. REFLECTION's expression is stern and disapproving, an

5

unflinching glare.

THREE-QUARTER MEDIUM SHOT FRED as REFLECTION morphs back to real reflection. FRED SIGHS, slouches further.

MEDIUM TRACKING SHOT FRED as he turns, SIGHS again, and shuffles down the sidewalk, very much as we first saw him, holes and tears in clothing, dirty, unshaven, hat stoved in and glasses askew. TRACKING slows to let FRED pass gradually out of frame.

FADE OUT

Sample Storyboard

The following storyboard is included to assist you in completing the exercises in Chapter 19, in case you don't want to draw your own storyboards. These story sketches follow a revised version of the script in Appendix D, so you may find small differences where shots were cut, added, or changed. This enables you to see how the story changed during script revisions.

Gaps or additional letters in the shot numbering show where shots were deleted or added in the storyboard sessions; shots 3, 36, 37, 49, 63, and 72 were cut, and shots 18A, 19A, 28A and B, 34A, 49A through M, and 71A were inserted. The storyboard reproduced here is very close to the final version used to produce the film.

I used standard screenwriting abbreviations in the script and storyboard. For complete details on style and abbreviation usage, I recommend Irwin Blacker's *Elements of Screenwriting*, listed in the Bibliography. In these storyboard captions, the abbreviations EXT, INT, and OS mean, respectively, Exterior, Interior, and Offscreen.

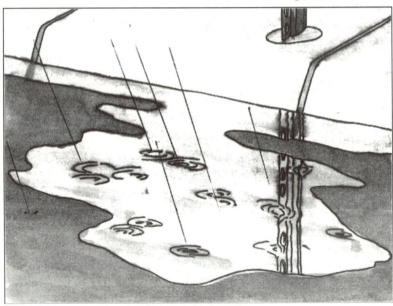

Shot 1: FADE IN: EXT CLOSE SHOT PUDDLE DESERTED CITY STREET NIGHT. Heavy rain is falling on a city sidewalk. Puddle reflects blinking neon in ripples. NEON BUZZES. Rainfall tapers off, stops.

Shot 2: Truck back, pan up to MEDIUM TRACKING SHOT of FRED. Storefronts are brick with large plate glass windows. FRED looks down on his luck. Almost emaciated, holes and tears in clothing, dirty, unshaven, overlong hair peeking out under a stoved-in hat, flapping shoe sole, glasses askew.

Shot 4: THREE-QUARTER MEDIUM SHOT FRED as he glances in darkened shop window, then pauses. He sees his REFLECTION, stops, and faces window.

Shot 5: CLOSE SHOT REFLECTION over FRED's shoulder. Reflection morphs to well-fed, well-dressed, happy-looking version of FRED.

Shot 6: THREE-QUARTER MEDIUM SHOT THROUGH WINDOW FRED as he perks up, smiling, tips hat.

Shot 7: CLOSE SHOT REFLECTION over FRED's shoulder, as reflection morphs back to Fred's current image.

Shot 8: THREE-QUARTER MEDIUM SHOT THROUGH WINDOW FRED as face falls, he sighs, slouches again.

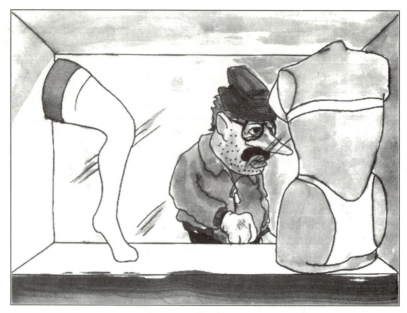

Shot 9: Fred turns and walks out of frame.

Shot 10: MEDIUM TRACKING SHOT FRED as he shuffles along sidewalk. Trash blows past.

Shot 11: BILL blows into frame, plasters itself across FRED's glasses. FRED staggers.

Shot 12: CLOSE SHOT FRED as he peels bill off glasses, tries to clear glasses.

Shot 13: THREE-QUARTER CLOSE SHOT FRED as he looks at bill. FRED blinks, momentarily baffled.

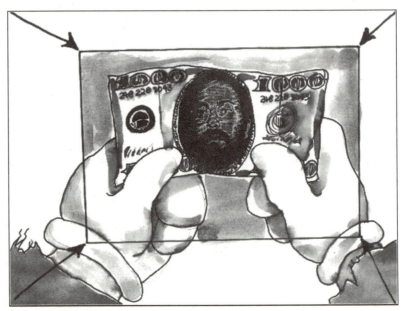

Shot 14: CLOSE SHOT over FRED's shoulder STAGGER ZOOM to EX-TREME CLOSE SHOT on BILL in FRED's hands. We can read bill as $1000.

Shot 15: THREE-QUARTER MEDIUM SHOT FRED as he looks at bill. Wild take, as he stretches bill flat between both hands.

Shot 16: FRED recovers, looks up and into the middle distance, as if at a wonderful vision.

Shot 17: CLOSE SHOT FRED'S FACE. FRED's eyes reflect images of dollar signs, then a rich dinner, then bubbling champagne, then the well-dressed image from the storefront.

Shot 18: THREE-QUARTER MEDIUM SHOT FRED clutching bill as he looks around, reading storefront signs.

Shot 18A: FRED sees shop he wants, anticipates, and zips out of frame.

Shot 19: REAR MEDIUM SHOT FRED as he brakes to a screeching halt and performs a 90-degree zip into restaurant doorway.

Shot 19A: DOOR SWINGING. ARGUMENT, ON RISING NOTE.

Shot 20: Door opens forcefully as FRED reappears, arcing out of doorway in midair and landing on his rump in the middle of the sidewalk, still clutching bill.

Shot 21: FRED protests.

Shot 22: BOUNCER'S HAND appears from doorway, pointing to sign in window.

Shot 23: CLOSE SHOT SIGN with pointing hand. Sign reads, "PROPER ATTIRE REQUIRED" in elegant script.

Shot 24: MEDIUM SHOT FRED as BOUNCER'S HAND withdraws, SLAMMING DOOR.

Shot 25: FRED gets to feet, dusts himself off, looking disgruntled, then transitions to determination.

Shot 26: FRED looks around at storefront signs again. He sees the shop he wants, across the street.

Shot 27: FRED marches determinedly out of frame, stepping off curb.

Shot 28: MEDIUM SHOT TAILOR SHOP as FRED marches up to door and enters.

Shot 28A: HELD SHOT TAILOR SHOP. We hear MEASURING TAPE, SCISSORS, SEWING MACHINE, CASH REGISTER.

Shot 28B: MATCH DISSOLVE TO MEDIUM SHOT BARBER SHOP, visibly later by lighting, now near dusk. SOUNDS continuous, bridge from TAILOR sounds to BARBER sounds.

Shot 34A: HELD SHOT BARBER SHOP with spinning barber pole. We hear SCISSORS, HAIR TONIC, LATHER BRUSH, RAZOR STROP, SHAVING, CASH REGISTER.

Shot 35: BARBER SHOP Door opens. FRED exits with a jaunty strut, clean-shaven and with slicked-down, neatly-parted hair.

Shot 38: FRED turns and scans storefronts, finds restaurant again.

Shot 39: FRED jauntily walks out of frame, back across street.

Shot 40: MEDIUM SHOT RESTAURANT as FRED jauntily walks up and enters.

Shot 41: INT MEDIUM SHOT TABLE RESTAURANT EVENING as WAITRESS'S HANDS hold chair as FRED crosses in front of table, makes slight bow to WAITRESS, sits down as WAITRESS places chair.

Shot 42: CLOSE SHOT TABLE FRED, as WAITRESS'S HANDS present MENU.

Shot 43: CLOSE SHOT MENU FRED as he peruses menu, making a great show of it.

Shot 44: CLOSE SHOT TABLE FRED *as he smiles broadly, holds menu open toward* WAITRESS (OS, RIGHT) *and points to several items, nodding rapidly.*

Shot 45: WAITRESS'S HANDS *retrieve menu.*

Shot 48: MEDIUM SHOT FRED TABLE as WAITRESS'S HANDS serve heaping plates of food, pour champagne.

Shot 49A-49M: MONTAGE: Fred making pig of self, waistline expanding, drinking more, becoming boisterous, gesturing and calling to other tables (OS), dishes stacking, champagne magnums accumulating, increasingly tight close shots on Fred, mouth opening wider in eating and talking, actions more broad and out of control, loosening collar, clothing becoming disarrayed, CASH REGISTER RINGING repeatedly. Evening light dims to night during montage.

Shot 50: MEDIUM SHOT TABLE FRED as WAITRESS'S HANDS (OS, RIGHT) gesture Fred to settle down.

Shot 51: FRED transitions from gluttonous to irate, then fascinated with WAITRESS (OS), then leering.

Shot 52: FRED makes grab for WAITRESS (OS). WAITRESS'S HANDS withdraw, fending off FRED, who nearly falls out of chair.

Shot 53: FRED, grumbling, resumes guzzling champagne.

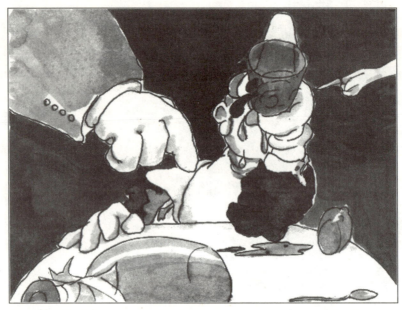

Shot 54: BOUNCER'S HAND reaches into frame from OS RIGHT, taps FRED on shoulder.

Shot 55: FRED looks up, bleary and obviously in his cups. His reaction time is severely impaired.

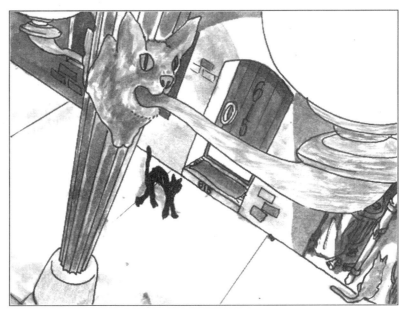

Shot 56: EXT MEDIUM SHOT RESTAURANT DESERTED CITY STREET NIGHT as we hear CRASHING and THUDS.

Shot 57: DOOR OPENS forcefully as FRED reappears, arcing out of doorway in midair.

Shot 58: Camera tracks FRED, does zip pan as he COLLIDES headfirst with LAMPPOST.

Shot 59: DOOR SLAMS forcefully.

Shot 60: FRED defies gravity for a moment, then rear end sags accordion-style down to sidewalk, followed by body, head, and hat.

Shot 61: FRED is left flat across sidewalk. Hat is now crumpled, clothing partially soiled from contact with sidewalk and lamppost. MOVING HOLD.

Shot 62: FRED slowly sits up, holds head, and weaves a bit.

Shot 64: FRED climbs shakily to his feet.

Shot 65: FRED GAGS, but can't hold it in and the camera pans to follow his rush for the alley entrance next to RESTAURANT.

Shot 66: FRED drops to knees with head and upper torso out of sight in alley, and GAGS repeatedly.

Shot 67: MEDIUM SHOT ALLEY FRED as he drags himself across the alley on hands and knees to a patch of wall between garbage cans and props himself there.

Shot 68: CLOSE SHOT FRED TRASH CANS. FRED's color is slightly better, although still pale. His clothing is now thoroughly soiled and torn. His eyelids flicker a few times, then fall shut as FRED begins to snore.

Shot 69: MATCH DISSOLVE to MEDIUM SHOT ALLEY FRED as morning light filters into the alley, showing all the damage.

Shot 70: FRED wakes, blinks repeatedly, winces at the light, shakes his head, and immediately clutches it in pain. He is badly hung over.

Shot 71A: THREE-QUARTER MEDIUM SHOT FRED ALLEY ENTRANCE as he staggers onto sidewalk in front of store.

Shot 73: CLOSE SHOT FRED as he transitions from incomprehension to total recall, and then to crushing remorse. His shoulders sag.

Shot 74: THREE-QUARTER MEDIUM SHOT FRED as FRED glances in darkened shop window. He sees his reflection again, and turns to face window.

Shot 75: CLOSE SHOT REFLECTION over FRED's shoulder.

Shot 76: REFLECTION morphs to well-fed, well-dressed version of FRED. REFLECTION's expression is stern and disapproving, an unflinching glare. MOVING HOLD.

Shot 77: THREE-QUARTER MEDIUM SHOT FRED as REFLECTION morphs back to real reflection. FRED SIGHS, slouches further.

Shot 78: MEDIUM SHOT SHOPFRONT FRED as he turns, SIGHS again.

Shot 79: FRED shuffles down the sidewalk and out of frame, very much as we first saw him, holes and tears in clothing, dirty, unshaven, hat stoved in, and glasses askew. FADE OUT.

Exposure Sheets

If you want to make as few mistakes as possible, plan your lip sync and synchronized action with an exposure sheet. The exposure sheet, or x-sheet, tracks most of the information the animator needs. The sheet is laid out with one line per frame and one column per type of information. Keeping track of these sheets is an important job; don't neglect it!

Different production houses use different forms. I've created an exposure sheet that I like to use for character animation with LightWave 3D. You can find it in the Appendix F directory on the Companion CD-ROM. It's in Microsoft Word (X_SHEET.DOC) and Adobe Acrobat (X_SHEET.PDF) formats. If you would like to customize it, or create your own exposure sheet, see Appendix G for a detailed how-to.

The last page of this appendix is a blank copy of the sample exposure sheet. You can photocopy this form, or laser print multiple copies from the CD-ROM files, and pencil in all your notes and changes. When you need to make revisions, you can easily erase the pencil marks while leaving the laser or photocopy form intact.

Label the sheets with enough information to keep them in order. At a minimum, you need the project name, the animator's name, and the scene number. The sheet number is required for shots over 3 seconds, and should be written "1 of 4," "2 of 4," and so on, so that you know how many sheets are attached.

The blank exposure sheet is long enough to hold 90 frames, or three seconds of NTSC video, on each page. Each column has different information:

- ❦ Column 1 is for a waveform image of the audio track. Refer to the "Planning for Lip Sync" section in Chapter 19, for details on inserting these waveform images. It is extremely helpful to work with exposure sheets that have the waveform printed on them.

- ❦ Column 2 is titled PH for phoneme. Here, you write in the phonetic spelling of the sound being pronounced, and mark duration and transitions as well. This is called *track analysis*, and you can learn more about it in Chapter 19 and Appendix H. If you are using replacement objects or color/bump/clip map sets, you can write in the actual filename instead of the phonetic spelling.

- ❦ Column 3, DIALOG, is for the dialog and sound effects from the script. These words are written with their usual spellings, and should begin on the frame when the word or sound begins.

- ❦ Column 4, ACTION, is for a written description of the action, marked at the correct frame. A door slamming, for instance, requires the complete closure of the door to be noted at the frame where the sound of the slam begins. If you are using LightWave 3D's Metamorph or MTSE functions for an action, you might specify object filenames and Metamorph percentages whenever the action is to match the soundtrack.

- ❦ Column 5, SMPTE, is for synchronizing the animation to film or video footage with SMPTE timecoding.

- ❦ Column 6, FRAME, is the frame count of the scene or shot. Only the last digit is preprinted on the form. Write in your own leading digits; usually only the tens line needs to be filled in.

- ❦ Column 7, BACKGROUND, provides a place for you to note any images or sequences to be used as backdrops. This is especially useful for compositing with other animations, digitized video, or "matched" stills.

❧ Column 8, CAMERA, is the place to put your notes about special camera, post-processing plug-in, or compositing effects. List changes in lens size and other parameters for camera zooms, tracking, and pans here.

The sample filled-in exposure sheets document a quote from the "Finest Hour" speech by Sir Winston Churchill. A three-second clip from the speech is digitized in the file THISHOUR.WAV, which can be found on the Companion CD-ROM. A longer version is in FINESTHR.WAV. Both are used in lip sync exercises in this book.

The full quote is: "So bear ourselves that if the British Empire, and its commonwealth, last for a thousand years, men will still say, 'This...was their finest hour.'" The shorter quote is: "This...was their finest hour."

PRODUCTION _____ ANIMATOR _____ SCENE _____ SHEET _____

WAVEFORM	PH.	DIALOG	ACTION	SMPTE	FRAME	BACKGROUND	CAMERA
					1		
					2		
					3		
					4		
					5		
					6		
					7		
					8		
					9		
					0		
					1		
					2		
					3		
					4		
					5		
					6		
					7		
					8		
					9		
					0		
					1		
					2		
					3		
					4		
					5		
					6		
					7		
					8		
					9		
					0		
					1		
					2		
					3		
					4		
					5		
					6		
					7		
					8		
					9		
					0		
					1		
					2		
					3		
					4		
					5		
					6		
					7		
					8		
					9		
					0		
					1		
					2		
					3		
					4		
					5		
					6		
					7		
					8		
					9		
					0		
					1		
					2		
					3		
					4		
					5		
					6		
					7		
					8		
					9		
					0		
					1		
					2		
					3		
					4		
					5		
					6		
					7		
					8		
					9		
					0		

Making Your Own Exposure Sheets

This appendix shows how to make exposure sheets like those shown in Appendix F and Chapter 19, and how to customize sheets for your particular needs and preferences.

Before you get started, take a look at the example exposure sheets in Appendix F. How much of that information will you want to have in your own sheets? What information do you need to track that doesn't appear here? How many frames do you need to fit on a single sheet? How small can you read and write? What size paper can your printer handle? These are all questions you should have definite answers to before you start building your own exposure sheet.

These instructions are specific to Microsoft Word 6.0, but the principles can be adapted to any word processor or spreadsheet manager that allows you to embed linked graphics.

1. Open a New document.

2. Choose File | Page Setup. The Page Setup dialog appears (see Figure G-1).

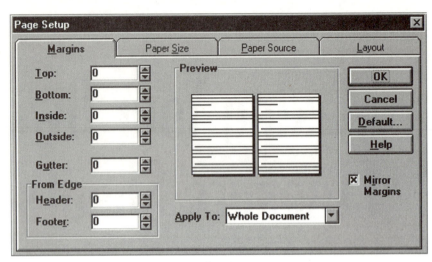

Figure G-1: Page Setup dialog with all margins set to zero.

You will want to use as much of each page as possible; you don't need much margin since your notes are supposed to fit in the exposure sheet itself.

3. Set all the margins to zero and click OK. A warning dialog gives you the option to use the Fix function. This automatically sets the page margins to the maximum printing area for your printer. Click the Fix button.

    Since there are many kinds of printers, there is no one set of dimensions guaranteed to work with all systems. This procedure finds the best dimensions for your particular system.

4. The margins will have changed to the minimum. Depending on your printer, the left margin may be less than 1/2 inch. Change the left margin to at least 0.5 if you want to hole-punch your exposure sheets for a loose-leaf binder. When you are finished, click the OK button.

    I tend to design all my working papers with a loose-leaf binder punch in mind. For most purposes, it's one of the better ways of keeping projects organized. The exception is original artwork, which no one in their right mind would punch holes through. I keep those items in binder-punched document envelopes.

5. Choose Edit | Select All. You want the next few steps to affect the entire document.

6. Choose Format | Columns. The Columns dialog appears (see G-2).

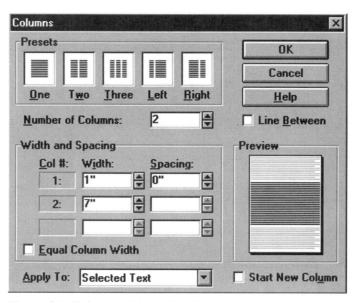

Figure G-2: Columns dialog with all settings made.

7. Choose 2 columns and turn off Equal Column Width. Set the first column to 1 inch wide with zero spacing. The second column defaults to the remainder of the print area. Make a note of the second column's width. Click OK.

   The first column is used for the waveform image file. The second column holds the table that organizes the rest of the exposure sheet's information.

8. Insert three carriage returns. After the second carriage return choose Insert | Frame.

   You'll be positioning a frame to hold the waveform image. It's not absolutely critical, but it makes the printed sheet look a little neater.

9. The cursor changes to the Frame crosshair. This tells you the program is ready for you to draw the frame. Click and hold in the upper left corner of the first column, and drag down and to the right, approximately the width of the first column. Release and the new frame is drawn in (see Figure G-3).

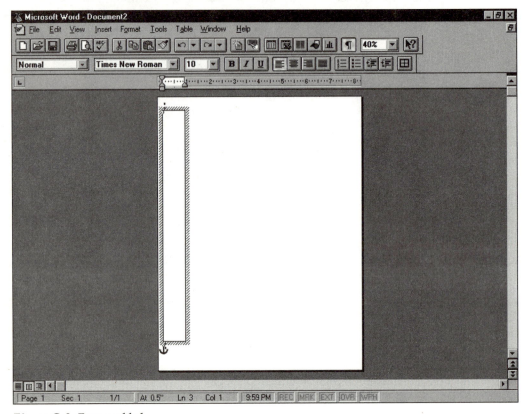

Figure G-3: Frame added.

10. Choose Format | Frame. The Frame dialog appears.

11. In the Frame dialog, set Horizontal | Left | Margin | Distance from Text=0, and set Vertical | 0" | Paragraph | Distance from Text=0. Set Size | Width | Exactly | 0.95", and set Size | Height | Exactly | 9.0". Click OK (see Figure G-4).

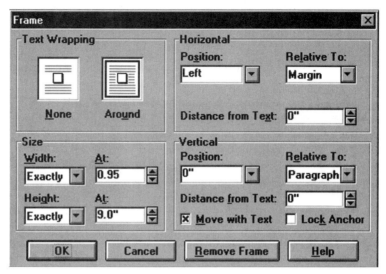

Figure G-4: Frame format settings.

Some of these settings will be changed later, but set them to this value for now. The goal is to have the frame aligned with the table as closely as possible, as if the waveform were actually printed as part of the table.

12. Position the cursor below the frame. Choose Insert | Break, then choose Column Break. Click OK.

    This leaves the frame in the first column, and starts the next column, where you'll be putting the table.

13. At the last paragraph mark, choose Table | Insert Table.

    Did you figure out how many columns you'd need before you started these instructions? If not, stop and get a definite answer now or you'll be wasting your time.

14. Set the number of columns and rows you want, then click the Autoformat button. The Autoformat Table dialog appears.

15. From the Formats list, select Grid1. Click OK.

    This draws a simple grid of fine lines around each cell of the table. This is easy to read and doesn't take up much space. You can choose something fancier if you like, but remember that form should follow function.

16. Remember the width of the second column from back in step 7? Calculate the total width of the second column, divided by the number of columns in the table. Set the table column width to this figure. You should have something like Figure G-5.

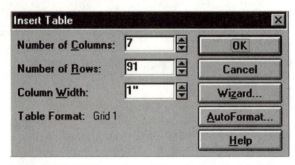

Figure G-5: Table settings. Where's the salad fork?

17. Click OK. Just a few more tweaks for the table, now. Choose Table | Select Table. Change the table font to Arial 7 point, or larger if you can fit it in. 7 point is the largest that would fit in a 91-row, 7-column table on standard paper for my system.

18. Choose Table | Cell Height & Width. Set the Row Height to Exactly 7 point, and leave Column Width to the value you set earlier, but set the space between columns to 0.1. Click OK.

19. Select the top row and click on the Center toolbar button. This centers the labels for the columns. Again, this is a personal preference; I think it's more legible and looks more professional.

20. Select the top cell of the first column. Type the column label. Repeat for the other columns. I prefer making the column labels all caps; at 7 point size, you need all the help you can get!

21. Select the column for the frame numbers, then click the Align Right toolbar button. This keeps the last digits of the frame numbers aligned. Select the top cell, containing the column label, and reset it to Center.

22. In the second row of the Frames column (assuming you have one), type the number **1**. Type **2** in the third row, and so on up to **0** in the 11th row. Select the 10 cells you just filled in and copy them. Select the next 10 empty cells and paste the copied values into them. Repeat until all the cells in the Frame column are filled in.

This gives you, preprinted, the last digit of each frame. You have only to pencil in the tens and hundreds digits. It is usually acceptable to pencil in the extra digits just at the frames ending in 0, as in the examples provided in Appendix F.

23. Drag each of the column markers in the ruler to set the width of the columns (see Figure G-6). Leave extra space for the columns you will have to write words in; leave less space if only numbers are needed.

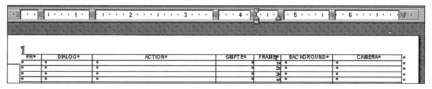

Figure G-6: Setting the table column margins.

24. Move the cursor to the top of the second column of the page, above the table. Type the sheet information labels and underscored blanks. Select the entire line and change the font to a readable style and size. I prefer Arial 10 point, as shown in the examples. Add a carriage return after the blanks to separate them from the table (see Figure G-7).

Figure G-7: Sheet information blanks.

The types of information you use to track your projects depends on the kind of work you do. If you are an independent or student, you may need little more than your name, the project, and the scene and shot. On the other hand, if you are one of several animators working on a long and complex animation project, you may need details like lead animator, technical director, and revision numbers.

Here are some examples of information that can be useful in heading an exposure sheet: producer, director, lead animator, animator, technical director, art director, layout artist, camera operator/rendering supervisor, assistants (various), project, client, agency, account or billing number, scene, shot, sheet number, date (start, due, and finish), and approvals/checkoffs/initials. And that's the short list!

25. Select the paragraphs above the frame in the first column. Change the font and size to match the changes you just made in the second column.

26. Add another carriage return above the frame. Select the paragraph immediately above the frame, and change the font and size to match the first row of the table. This should bring the top of the frame level with the top of the second row of the table.

27. Type the label **WAVEFORM** in the paragraph above the frame.
    This makes the frame look like an extension of the table, since it is now aligned with the other columns and headed in the same style. Now you're ready to add the waveform image.

28. Click on the inside of the frame to set the cursor. Choose Insert | Picture. The Insert Picture dialog appears (see Figure G-8).
    As noted in Appendix F and Chapter 19, it's a good idea to keep the waveform images in a temp file directory or similar location. Generally, the waveform images will be used only once, and there's no need to clutter your system with obsolete images. Since they are so similar, keeping them around can be a definite hazard to your track analysis.

29. Select the waveform image file to paste into the frame. Turn on the Link to File option. Turn off the Save Picture in Document option. Click OK.

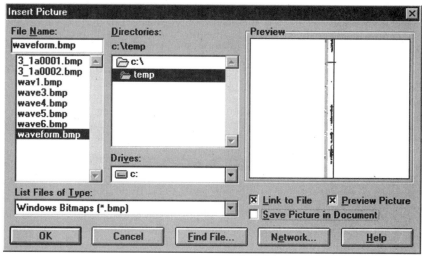

Figure G-8: Options for inserting the waveform picture.

30. Scroll to the bottom of the page. Select the frame. Drag the bottom of the frame until it is exactly level with the bottom of the table.

31. Choose Format | Frame | Lock Anchor (see Figure G-9).

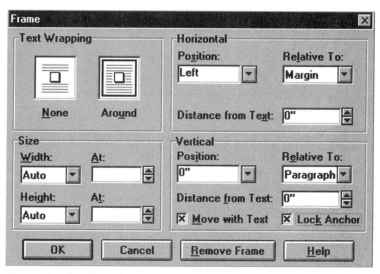

Figure G-9: Locking the frame anchor.

This should keep the frame the same size, even if the wave-form image changes size. This means you should not have to resize the frame or image each time you reload this document.

32. Choose Edit | Links. The Links dialog appears. Turn on the Locked option (see Figure G-10).

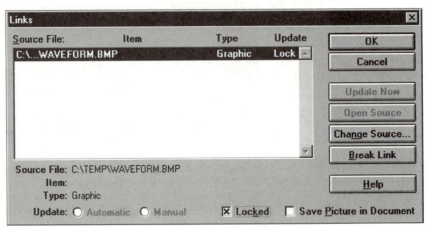

Figure G-10: Locking the picture link.

This tells Word to reload the image file every time something happens to either document. This is how the procedures in Appendix F can produce a stack of exposure sheets, complete with preprinted waveforms, so quickly. It's an example of an appropriate use of computers: automating repetitive work to free up human creative resources.

33. Save the document.

That's it. You are now the proud owner of a brand-new exposure sheet. Go find a track to analyze!

Track Analysis Using Magpie

CD-ROM

Magpie is a track analysis program written by Miguel Grinberg. The MAGPIE directory of this book's Companion CD-ROM contains a working version of the program. Magpie is copyrighted shareware and you may evaluate it for a period of no more than 30 days. After that time you must either register and pay for it or remove it from your system.

Failure to comply with this condition is a violation of international copyright law—not to mention being very rude to Mr. Grinberg, who has graciously made this software available to animators worldwide. If you use it, please pay for it.

For details on registering and free updates, please refer to the information files in the MAGPIE directory on the Companion CD-ROM.

To run Magpie, you need a PC-compatible computer running Windows NT or Windows 95, 16MB of RAM, about 5MB of free hard disk space, a true color graphics display, and an MCI device capable of playing 8- or 16-bit WAV audio files.

Review of Track Analysis Basics

Track analysis is not really difficult, just painstaking. There is a relatively small number of *phonemes*, or unique sounds, used by all spoken human languages. Track analysis is the art of transcribing exactly when each phoneme occurs in a voice track.

I highly recommend keeping a good dictionary handy while analyzing vocal tracks; it can save you a lot of time while you are developing your track-reading skills. Any good dictionary has a pronunciation guide that lists all the phonemes for the dictionary's language and explains the letters and diacritical marks used in phonetic spelling. I recommend that you use the following cheat until you can rely on your own skills.

Make up a copy of the script for the vocal track, double- or even triple-spaced so you can write legibly under or over each word. Look up each word in the dictionary. Copy the phonetic spelling of each word under the normal spelling in the script. Now you know exactly what phonemes you need and in what order.

This appendix shows you the basics of track analysis using Magpie. We'll be using a digitized sample from a speech by Sir Winston Churchill, THISHOUR.WAV, which you can find on the Companion CD-ROM. The phrase is, "This . . . was their finest hour." You can complete the following exercise more easily if you transcribe this phrase in phonetic spelling before you begin.

1. Follow the instructions for installing Magpie, which you can find in the MAGPIE directory of the Companion CD-ROM. When installation is complete, start Magpie.

    The Magpie window contains four panes: Waveform, Mouth, Preview, and Exposure Sheet.

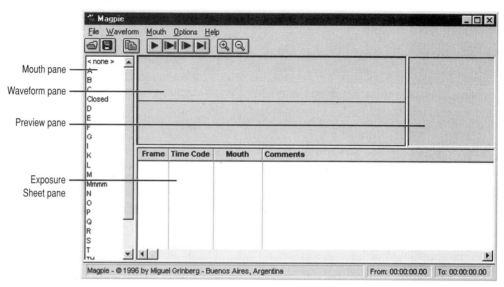

Figure H-1: The Magpie window.

The Waveform pane displays the sound file you will be analyzing. Magpie opens up with no sound file loaded.

2. Click the Open File button at the upper left of the window, or select File | Open. Choose the THISHOUR.WAV audio file from the Chapter 19 directory on the Companion CD-ROM and click Open.

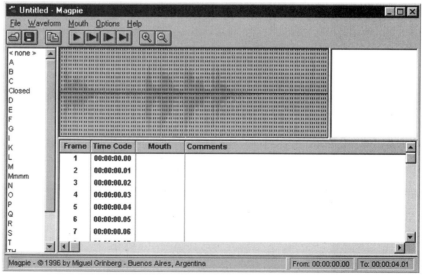

Figure H-2: THISHOUR.WAV file displayed in Magpie Waveform pane.

Opening up a new .WAV file automatically loads a clean Magpie session for you to work on.

3. Click the Play button to hear the .WAV file.

Each pair of vertical lines in the Waveform pane brackets a single frame.

4. Select the second frame from the left by clicking on it once. The frame turns red. Double-click on the frame to hear it played.

You can tell from your phonetic transcript (and from listening carefully) that the sound at this frame is a soft "th" sound, the first phoneme of the word "This."

5. The Magpie interface refers to phoneme images as Mouths. The Mouth pane runs along the left edge of the window, listing letters or words associated with images of mouth shapes. Double-click on the letters "TH."

Magpie copies the Mouth label TH to the second frame of the Exposure Sheet pane. The TH image appears in the Preview pane.

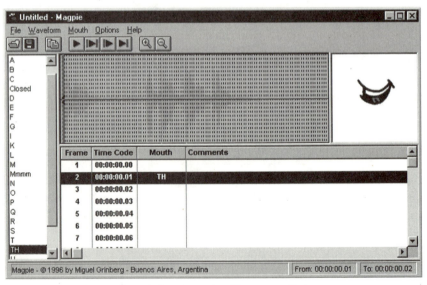

Figure H-3: TH Mouth copied to frame 2 of Exposure Sheet pane.

6. Repeat steps 4 and 5 for all the other frames, listening carefully and matching the sounds to your phonetic transcript.

At any time during this process you can use the different Play buttons to play the entire sound, only the selected frames, or everything up to or following the selected frames. As the sound plays back, the images matching the Mouths you selected also play back in the Preview window.

What you will be doing is looking—and listening—for characteristic shapes in the waveform that correspond to phonemes. Human speech is made up mostly of clicks, buzzes, and hisses. For example, a sharp spike—a click—can represent a plosive sound such as P or B. The word "baby" would therefore have two spikes, and you would mark the frames next to those spikes with the letter B. Buzzing phonemes like M or N show up as relatively even zigzags with very similar individual waveforms, sustained over a number of frames. Hissing Ses or Cs look a lot like static, just a little louder.

Rather than go into a rambling theoretical discussion of all the different phonemes and how they are produced, I'm going to encourage you to experiment and develop your own rules. This all goes back to the principles discussed in Chapters 7 and 8; you can take someone else's word for it, or you can observe and draw your own conclusions. Observing speech is a wonderful way to lose your preconceptions about how people communicate.

If you are working with a large audio file you may need to use the Zoom In and Zoom Out tools to see frames more clearly.

Find the plosives and clicks in the audio file. Look for peaks or other sharp changes within the word. Select and play them back until you can identify their start at a particular frame.

You can select more than one frame in the Waveform pane by dragging the mouse. All the selected frames should turn red. Double-clicking on a phoneme in the Mouth pane assigns that Mouth to all the selected frames.

Find the buzzes and hisses. They appear as relatively even areas, drawn out over several frames. Select all the affected frames and assign the appropriate Mouth shape.

The remaining phonemes are probably mostly vowels. They tend to fill in everywhere but the clicks, buzzes, and hisses. They are also the most visible mouth shapes to animate, as they are held longer and generally require more facial distortion.

7. When you are satisfied with your results, save the file. You should end up with something like Figure H-4.

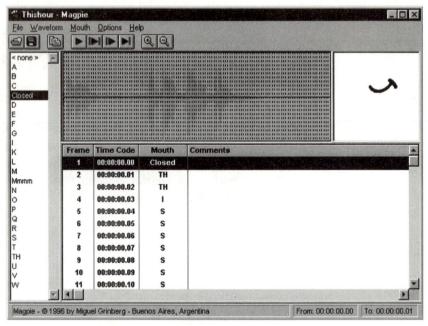

Figure H-4: THISHOUR.WAV, completely analyzed.

Magpie saves the session, including Mouth settings and the path to the original audio file, in a Magpie format with the extension .MPS.

Making Exposure Sheets With Magpie

Until Miguel Grinberg adds printing exposure sheets to Magpie's bag of tricks, here's a procedure you can follow that works nearly as well. With a little patience, you can paste the Exposure Sheet pane information straight into a custom exposure sheet document, as described in Appendix F.

1. When your track analysis is complete, click the Copy to Clipboard button. This copies the contents of the Exposure Sheet pane to the system clipboard, which is available to most other Windows applications.

2. Open a text editor, and paste the clipboard contents into a new (blank) document.

```
1····00:00:00.00······Closed··¶
····2····00:00:00.01········TH····¶
····3····00:00:00.02········TH····¶
····4····00:00:00.03········I·····¶
····5····00:00:00.04········S·····¶
····6····00:00:00.05········S·····¶
····7····00:00:00.06········S·····¶
····8····00:00:00.07········S·····¶
····9····00:00:00.08········S·····¶
···10····00:00:00.09········S·····¶
···11····00:00:00.10········S·····¶
···12····00:00:00.11········S·····¶
···13····00:00:00.12········S·····¶
···14····00:00:00.13········S·····¶
···15····00:00:00.14········S·····¶
···16····00:00:00.15········S·····¶
···17····00:00:00.16········S·····¶
···18····00:00:00.17········S·····¶
```

Figure H-5: Magpie export file sample.

The file structure contains a few redundant spaces, and nothing else separating the columns. This isn't compatible with the Word table layout I used to create my exposure sheets, so let's change it.

3. Using whatever global-find-and-replace tools your text processor supports, edit the file as follows:

   a. Replace two zeros following four spaces with two zeros following a tab.

   b. Replace a line break followed by four spaces with just a line break.

   c. Replace a line break followed by three spaces with just a line break.

   d. Replace two spaces with nothing.

   e. Replace a period followed by two numbers with the found characters followed by a tab.

This should result in a file of three columns, containing frame numbers, SMPTE timecode, and Mouth names, respectively, all separated by tabs. This is compatible with a copy-and-paste to a Word table.

4. Now you can follow the instructions in Appendix G to create a custom exposure sheet compatible with this format. You will need to set up the frame number column to the left of the SMPTE timecode column, and the Mouth, or Phoneme, column to the right of the SMPTE code column.

5. When the exposure sheet is ready, select the first 90 lines of the modified Magpie export file and copy them.

6. Select 90 rows of the appropriate three columns in the exposure sheet table, and paste. The Magpie data should copy smoothly into the exposure sheet.

7. Repeat the select, copy, and paste process for the rest of the export file until all the exposure sheets for the audio track are filled in.

FRAME.	SMPTE	PH	DIALOG	ACTION
1	00:00:00.00	Closed		
2	00:00:00.01	TH		
3	00:00:00.02	TH		
4	00:00:00.03	I		
5	00:00:00.04	S		
6	00:00:00.05	S		
7	00:00:00.06	S		
8	00:00:00.07	S		
9	00:00:00.08	S		
10	00:00:00.09	S		
11	00:00:00.10	S		
12	00:00:00.11	S		
13	00:00:00.12	S		
14	00:00:00.13	S		
15	00:00:00.14	S		
16	00:00:00.15	S		
17	00:00:00.16	S		
18	00:00:00.17	S		
19	00:00:00.18	S		
20	00:00:00.19	S		
21	00:00:00.20	S		
22	00:00:00.21	S		
23	00:00:00.22	S		
24	00:00:00.23	S		
25	00:00:00.24	S		
26	00:00:00.25	S		
27	00:00:00.26	S		
28	00:00:00.27	S		
29	00:00:00.28	S		
30	00:00:00.29	S		
31	00:00:01.00	S		

Figure H-6: The filled-in exposure sheet.

Ta daa! You have just learned a method of analyzing audio tracks that is faster, cheaper, and less work than most other methods. I'd say it's worth the software registration, wouldn't you?

Customizing Magpie

As you can see, Magpie's combination of visual and audible feedback is a great help to track analysis. You can also customize Magpie to better suit your own track analysis style and needs.

The version of Magpie on the Companion CD-ROM includes three default sets of Mouths, each having 11 image files. Each image file can be used for more than one Mouth. The MAGPIE.INI file controls image and Mouth assignments. You can edit this file directly with a word processor or interactively from within Magpie.

Here is the full text of a default MAGPIE.INI file:

```
[Settings]
FramesPerSecond=30

[Mouths]
Default=
Cartoon=
Billy=

[Default]
A=MOUTHS\DEFAULT\Ai.bmp
I=MOUTHS\DEFAULT\Ai.bmp
K=MOUTHS\DEFAULT\cdgk.bmp
N=MOUTHS\DEFAULT\cdgk.bmp
E=MOUTHS\DEFAULT\E.bmp
F=MOUTHS\DEFAULT\Fv.bmp
V=MOUTHS\DEFAULT\Fv.bmp
L=MOUTHS\DEFAULT\Lth.bmp
TH=MOUTHS\DEFAULT\Lth.bmp
D=MOUTHS\DEFAULT\d.bmp
M=MOUTHS\DEFAULT\MBP.bmp
B=MOUTHS\DEFAULT\MBP.bmp
P=MOUTHS\DEFAULT\MBP.bmp
O=MOUTHS\DEFAULT\O.bmp
U=MOUTHS\DEFAULT\U.bmp
Q=MOUTHS\DEFAULT\Wq.bmp
```

```
W=MOUTHS\DEFAULT\Wq.bmp
R=MOUTHS\DEFAULT\cdgk.bmp
Closed=MOUTHS\DEFAULT\closed.bmp
C=MOUTHS\DEFAULT\cdgk.bmp
G=MOUTHS\DEFAULT\cdgk.bmp
S=MOUTHS\default\Cdgk.bmp
T=MOUTHS\default\Cdgk.bmp

[Cartoon]
A=MOUTHS\CARTOON\Ai.bmp
I=MOUTHS\CARTOON\Ai.bmp
K=MOUTHS\CARTOON\cdgk.bmp
N=MOUTHS\CARTOON\cdgk.bmp
E=MOUTHS\CARTOON\E.bmp
F=MOUTHS\CARTOON\Fv.bmp
V=MOUTHS\CARTOON\Fv.bmp
L=MOUTHS\CARTOON\Lth.bmp
TH=MOUTHS\CARTOON\Lth.bmp
D=MOUTHS\CARTOON\lth.bmp
M=MOUTHS\CARTOON\MBP.bmp
B=MOUTHS\CARTOON\MBP.bmp
P=MOUTHS\CARTOON\MBP.bmp
O=MOUTHS\CARTOON\O.bmp
U=MOUTHS\CARTOON\U.bmp
Q=MOUTHS\CARTOON\Wq.bmp
W=MOUTHS\CARTOON\Wq.bmp
R=MOUTHS\CARTOON\cdgk.bmp
Closed=MOUTHS\CARTOON\closed.bmp
C=MOUTHS\CARTOON\cdgk.bmp
G=MOUTHS\CARTOON\cdgk.bmp
S=MOUTHS\CARTOON\cdgk.bmp
T=MOUTHS\CARTOON\cdgk.bmp

[Billy]
A=MOUTHS\BILLY\Ai.bmp
I=MOUTHS\BILLY\Ai.bmp
B=MOUTHS\BILLY\Mbp.bmp
M=MOUTHS\BILLY\Mbp.bmp
P=MOUTHS\BILLY\Mbp.bmp
C=MOUTHS\BILLY\Cdgk.bmp
Closed=MOUTHS\BILLY\Closed.bmp
D=MOUTHS\BILLY\Cdgk.bmp
E=MOUTHS\BILLY\E.bmp
```

```
F=MOUTHS\BILLY\Fv.bmp
G=MOUTHS\BILLY\Cdgk.bmp
K=MOUTHS\BILLY\Cdgk.bmp
L=MOUTHS\BILLY\Lth.bmp
N=MOUTHS\BILLY\Cdgk.bmp
O=MOUTHS\BILLY\O.bmp
Q=MOUTHS\BILLY\Wq.bmp
R=MOUTHS\BILLY\Cdgk.bmp
TH=MOUTHS\BILLY\Lth.bmp
U=MOUTHS\BILLY\U.bmp
V=MOUTHS\BILLY\Fv.bmp
W=MOUTHS\BILLY\Wq.bmp
S=MOUTHS\billy\cdgk.bmp
T=MOUTHS\billy\cdgk.bmp
```

The Mouth images supplied are good samples, but if you want to animate more accurate lip sync you'll want to customize your own Mouth sets. For example, the provided sets have no transition pose other than Closed. Ideally, you should also have Mouths shaped for the in betweens or transitions between each of the key Mouths. These in betweens can make the difference between a jerky, distracting lip sync and one that appears fluid and natural.

You can also make some of the key mouths more specific. The F and V Mouths, for instance, should have a slightly different placement of the upper front teeth against the lower lip. In the default sets, the two phonemes share one Mouth.

Creating Your Own Mouth Images

If you are animating lip sync with mapped images or image sequences, creating Magpie Mouth images is very simple.

1. Create a new directory inside the Magpie directory, named for the new Mouth set you are creating.

2. Copy all the map images to a new file in the new directory, with appropriate filenames.

3. Resize all the images to 128 by 128 pixels, and change the format (if necessary) to BMP.

4. Add a new section to the MAGPIE.INI file, using Notepad or another text editor. Use the default Mouth sets as a template.

You may have some difficulty selecting Mouth names that accurately describe the phoneme represented. Unfortunately, accurate diacritical marks are not available in the standard screen fonts. To make up for this deficiency, use more letters or even complete words to describe the phonemes. For example, either "e_macron" or "eee" clearly represent the long e phoneme.

The most important consideration is that you be able to quickly identify and choose among the available Mouths.

5. If you are animating lip sync using Replacement or Displacement techniques, you have one more step for each Mouth. You will have to set up a LightWave 3D scene with Camera and lights that clearly delineate the head object's mouth shape, then render 128 x 128 BMP files usable by Magpie.

The method I use to create these images is to pose and light the basic mouth model, then create an ObjList text file that will step through every mouth model in my library. Then I render the entire animation out to 128-pixel-square BMP files in the appropriate Magpie Mouth directory. After LightWave 3D finishes rendering, all I have to do is rename the image files by referring to the ObjList text file.

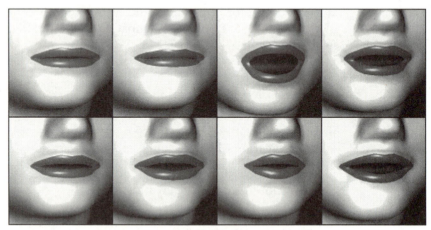

Figure H-7: Magpie-compatible Mouth images rendered from LightWave 3D.

To contact Miguel Grinberg—preferably to tell him how much you like Magpie, but also for technical support—you can send him e-mail at: mgrinberg@impsat1.com.ar.

The Latest Version of Magpie

There is now a newer version of Magpie lip sync software than the one on the Companion CE-ROM. Here is a brief list of the new features on it:

- **Print option**   You can print the exposure sheet on any installed printer.

- **Export option**   The old copy to clipboard option has been replaced with a powerful export option. You can define your own export formats or just use the default formats provided. The output can be directed to the clipboard, a file, or a printer. With no effort you can export text files matching the format of your favorite animation software!

- **Export to Hash Animation option**   Users of Hash Inc. animation software can save the exposure sheet directly into a muscle action file.

- **Mouth icons**   The Mouth List pane has new mouth icons to speed up the mouth selection process.

- **New waveform navigation controls**   You can move forward or backward in the waveform frame by frame or page by page.

- **Keyboard shortcuts**   Almost every command has a keyboard shortcut.

- **Scrubbing**   You can hear the frames of the sound clip as you drag the mouse over the waveform with the right button pressed. Great for fine tuning and checking.

- **New play options**   There are more play controls: loop play, play while select (same as scrubbing but during a frame range selection), and a stop button.

- **More frame rates**   You can use any frame rate (even non-standard rates!). Great for limited animation, multimedia productions, and so on.

- **Improved creation of mouth sets**   There's a new window for creating and modifying mouth sets. You can copy a mouth set with a new name and then modify it. No more creating mouth sets from scratch.

❧ **Keyframes** If you plan to use Magpie to lip sync dialogue for 3D characters, now can mark the keyframes in the exposure sheet. (You don't need this for cartoon animation; you must draw all the frames!). The Export and Hash Export options use the keyframe information.

This new version (and future versions) is available only for registered users. Don't worry, it's really cheap software!

If you've never heard about Magpie, and want to take a look at it, you can download Magpie version 0.9 from the CG-CHAR web site at: http://www.cinenet.net/users/rickmay.

If you want more information about this new version, e-mail Miguel Grinberg at mgrinberg@impsat1.com.ar and he'll send you a more detailed feature list via e-mail.

Glossary

16mm   A smaller film size for educational and film festival use.

35mm   The standard film size for motion pictures in wide release.

Academy field ratio   A standardized ratio for the film frame. Created in 1930, it began at 1:1.33 (height v. width), currently stands at 1:1.85.

Academy leader   A length of film appended at the beginning of a reel to assist the projectionist in framing and focusing.

acceleration   Increase in velocity.

action   Any visible change in a scene; movement, rotation, size, or deformation of an object.

action axis   See *line of action.*

algorithm   A procedure or set of rules for solving a problem. An algorithm is implemented by a programmer to create software.

aliasing   The stairstep pattern seen along the edge of a curve or diagonal border when presented in a raster display, as in a computer monitor or print. See also *antialiasing*.

alpha   In software, the first draft of a computer program, before the faults have been corrected.

alpha channel   A grayscale or black-and-white rendering of a scene, used as a matte in compositing.

altitude   Rotation on the X, or left-to-right horizontal axis. In LightWave 3D, the Pitch rotation.

animation   Any technique which makes inanimate objects move on screen.

animation cycle   See *cycle, motion*.

animation hierarchy   The sequence of levels, from root to outer extremities, followed to efficiently animate a complex character (see Chapter 6).

animator   The person who sets the frame by frame timing and posing of the objects in a scene.

antialiasing   A technique for blending color values near an aliased border to visually smooth it out for raster display. In LightWave 3D, this requires rendering multiple passes and blending aliased areas.

anticipation   A brief action in the opposite direction, preceding and foreshadowing the main action.

aperture (lens aperture)   In cinematography, the size of the lens opening divided by the focal length, expressed as an f-stop (e.g., f/8, f/11).

arc   See *slalom*.

armature   An internal skeleton designed to support and hold the pose of the outer material of a stop-motion puppet.

aspect ratio   The ratio of width to the height of a film frame. In CGI, it also refers to the ratio of the resolution.

AVI Audio Video Interleaved is a playback compression format designed for the Microsoft Windows operating systems.

azimuth Rotation on the Z-axis. In LightWave 3D, the Heading rotation.

back light See *rim light*.

back projection In cinematography, projecting footage onto a screen placed behind the action as a means of compositing in the camera.

background An image or sequence rendered behind all the objects in a scene.

backplane An object sized and positioned to act as a background.

ball and socket joint A rotational joint with three degrees of freedom (e.g., human hip).

ballistics The branch of mathematics describing behavior of falling bodies.

banding Borders between areas of similar color or brightness, visible because the image does not contain enough colors to shade the border more smoothly.

bank Rotation on the front-to-back horizontal axis.

bar sheet Diagrams similar to sheet music, used to set the broad timing for long sequences of animation.

beta (software) The next generation of software after alpha, ideally with fewer faults, but not yet ready for public release.

beta tester An optimist who believes they can do production work with faulty software. One who tests beta software.

Betacam A family of VTR formats developed by Sony.

BG In cinematography, abbreviation for background.

bit The smallest unit of information processed by a digital computer, a 1 or 0. Bits are grouped into bytes.

blocking   In stage or cinema direction, setting marks or positions for actors.

bluescreen   See *chroma key*.

bouncing ball   Basic animation exercise demonstrating timing, squash, and stretch.

breakdown drawings   See *inbetweens*.

bug   An error in computer software that produces an unintended result
(a.k.a. fault).

byte   A group or word of bits, a unit of digital data. Computer files are usually measured in thousands (kb) or millions (mb) of bytes.

CAD   Computer Aided Design is the use of computers and graphics software to design products, partially automating traditional drafting and engineering tasks.

camera   A machine designed to expose photosensitive film to a focused image for a controlled period of time to create an image on the film. In cinematography, a machine to perform this operation repeatedly for successive frames to create a motion picture. In LightWave 3D, the point from which the scene is rendered, emulating a physical camera.

camera animation   Animation performed exclusively with the camera, as pans, dollys, zooms, or other changes, while photographing a scene or image with no other action.

camera back   The part of the camera that holds the film. Motion picture and film recorder camera backs can hold many feet of film.

camera body   The main part of the camera between the back and the lens, containing the shutter and film transport. Film recorder and stop-motion camera bodies have very accurate pin registration for the film sprocket holes to ensure that each image is recorded in precisely the same position.

camera shake   See *pan, zip*.

cameraless animation   Animation that is drawn or etched directly on film stock.

caricature Exaggeration of the peculiarities or unique attributes of a person or thing. In character animation, the exaggeration of the essentials of a motion to create unrealistic but truthful action.

cel Acetate sheets used in cel animation.

cel animation Animation drawn or painted on transparent acetate sheets and layered with foreground and background cels or images.

center of gravity Abbreviated CG, the center of an object's balance.

CG See *center of gravity*.

CGI Computer Generated Imagery is any graphic image created with the assistance of a computer.

character In CGI, an object that displays volition and personality in a scene.

character animation In CGI, the process of timing and posing a character object to create the illusion of life.

character model In CGI, an object or objects to be animated as a character.

charts In traditional animation, graphic notes or diagrams to show the timing for inbetweens or camera motion. In LightWave 3D, motion graphs.

cheating Repositioning objects between shots to improve a composition without tipping off the audience that the scene has been changed.

chroma key Keying a composite layer by color, typically blue or green.

clay animation Stop-motion cinematography of clay or other plastic material that is manually deformed by the animators for each pose. Clay can be used alone or supported by an armature.

clean plate A live-action shot with no actors in it, to be used in compositing CGI effects.

climax In drama, the most important crisis in the story.

close-up   Literally, a shot of the subject face alone. Generally, considered to be any close shot.

code   Part of a program as written by a programmer.

collision detection   An algorithm used in some CGI software to detect when one object intersects another.

color depth   The number of bits used to store color information for each pixel in an image. 1-bit is black and white; 8-bit can be color or grayscale having 256 different values; 24-bit has 8-bit values for red, green, and blue, approximating the color depth of a television screen.

color key   See *chroma key*.

commercial   A brief advertisement, generally intended for television. Typically 15, 30, or 60 seconds in length (a.k.a. a spot or ad).

compression   Removing redundant information from a data file to make it smaller, often used for storing or playing back images and animations. Different algorithms and software have different definitions of "redundant."

computer   A machine capable of running a program to produce the intended result. A machine that can't run a program correctly is sometimes referred to as a boat anchor.

computer animation   Animation timed and posed by a human and inbetweened and rendered by a computer. If a non-animator is ignorant enough to say something like, "The computer does all the work," the nearest animator is entitled to whup them upside the head with a blunt instrument.

computer graphics   See *CGI*.

conflict   In drama, the collision between character and circumstance that drives the story.

coordinates   In geometry and CGI, a set of numbers that describes a location from the origin of the local system. In LightWave 3D, XYZ coordinates are used to describe the location of an object in world coordinates (from the Layout origin), and the location of each point in an object's local coordinates (from the object's Pivot).

coverage   Additional camera angles and setups rendered to give the editor more leeway in assembling the final cut. Almost never used in traditional animation, and rarely used in CGI animation.

crane   Vertical movement of the camera (a.k.a. boom).

crawl   Very slow camera move intended to build tension (a.k.a. creep).

creeping titles   Also known as scrolling titles. Titles that move across the screen, typically from bottom to top, making it easier for the audience to read credits that are displayed briefly.

crisis   In drama, a decision point where a character's actions determine the direction of the story.

crossing the line   Shifting the camera to the opposite side of the line of action, which can confuse the audience if not handled carefully.

CRT   Acronym for cathode ray tube, a common type of computer or video display.

CU   In cinematography, a close-up.

cut   The act of moving from one shot to another through the editing process.

cutting height   In cinematography, the height where the bottom of the frame intersects the actor(s).

cutting on the action   Changing from one camera position to the next during the character's action. This relieves the *visual jar*, since the audience focuses its attention on the action, not the shot composition.

cycle   See *motion cycle*.

default scene   A LightWave 3D default scene contains a single character with all its associated textures, Bones, hierarchies, motion plug-ins, and lights set up and ready to animate.

delta   A change in color or luminance values for each pixel from one frame of an animation to the next. Large deltas make animations more difficult to compress for direct computer playback.

depth of field   The area in which objects are in focus (see Chapter 9 exercises).

dialog   Any soundtrack, script, or storyboard incorporating an actor's vocal performance.

digitizer   A device, often a computer peripheral, for converting analog signals to digital data. In CGI, typical source materials are 3D models, film or video footage, or still images.

direct to video   A growing market segment of videotape sales and rentals, of films that have never been theatrically released. A potential opportunity for independent animators.

director   The person who oversees the big picture of the production, and who generally has final creative control over the look, story, timing, and editing of an animated film.

displacement   A class of animation techniques based on posing or deformation of a single object. Contrast with *replacement*.

display buffer   A section of RAM that contains the current image.

dissolve   A special effect shot transition where the first shot gradually fades out and is replaced by the second shot fading in. See also *wipe*.

dither   Scattering pixels of one value over the border into an area of a different value, to visually blend the two areas together. See also *banding*.

dolly   Camera move as if on a dolly, truck, or other horizontally mobile platform (a.k.a. track, truck).

dope sheet   See *exposure sheet*.

double-take   See *take*.

drawn-on-film   See *cameraless animation*.

dubbing   The process of correcting mistakes in dialog or soundtrack by rerecording. In animation, the process of adding sound to the silent animation.

dynamic balance   Constantly hanging, but balanced equilibrium between mass, inertia, and energy in a character. If the combination of mass, inertia, and energy in the lower body is equal to the mass, inertia, and energy in the upper body, the body as a whole is in dynamic balance.

dynamics   The motions that connect each key pose. Different parts move at different rates, accelerating and decelerating in a complex balancing act.

ECU   In cinematography, extreme close-up.

edge   In LightWave 3D, a line connecting two points, the boundary between one polygon and the next.

editor, film editor   The person who assembles shots in sequence and synchronizes the soundtrack(s) according to the director's instructions.

effects animation   Animation created to mimic phenomena such as fire, smoke, clouds, rain, or anything else that moves but is not a character or prop.

effects track   A soundtrack containing sound effects rather than music or dialog.

elevation   A side or front view of a set design.

ELS   In cinematography, extreme long shot.

encoder   Also known as scan converter.

ergonomics   Design of objects to fit the user's shape and actions, to prevent injury and increase comfort and efficiency.

establishing shot   Shows the audience the general environment in which the action will take place.

exposition   In drama, necessary background information communicated to the audience, usually by dialog, sometimes by a title sequence or insert shot, that would be difficult or impossible to convey by a character's actions.

exposure sheet   A form filled out by the animator with frame-by-frame information for character action, lip sync, backgrounds, and camera.

extreme take   A gross distortion of a character to show surprise.

eye movements   Animation of the eyes and eyelids used to define the character and foreshadow actions.

eyelights   In cinematography, lights set up specifically to bring out a highlight spot in an actor's eyes.

fade   A dissolve to or from a solid color, usually black or white.

fade in   The process where an image gradually appears from a blackened screen by lightening up to scene.

fade out   The opposite of fade in.

fair use   The doctrine of copyright prevalent in the United States that says a duplicate of a copyrighted work may be made for personal, educational use.

fault   An error in a computer program that produced unwanted or unintentional results. Less scrupulous developers may document the behavior of a fault and call it a feature.

FG   In cinematography, foreground.

fill light   A light used to soften shadows and make hidden details visible without washing out the key light.

film grain   Tiny imperfections in an image produced by the crystals in film emulsion.

film recorder   A system that uses a camera to record digital images from a high-resolution CRT or laser. For motion picture film, the camera must have a pin-register film transport.

flicker fusion   The visual phenomenon that blends a rapid series of still images into the illusion of continuous motion. The frame rate at which flicker fusion occurs varies widely, from as low as 15 fps to over 100 fps. See also *Showscan*.

focal length   The length of a camera lens assembly, measured from the rear nodal point to the focal plane. After all, it's not the size of the lens, it's how you use it.

focal plane   Also known as film plane. The plane behind the camera lens where the image is in sharpest focus.

focus   The sharpness and clarity of an image.

focus pull   Animating the depth of field to match the area of sharp focus to an object's movement.

foley   Sound effects recording by professional noisemakers.

follow through   Animation to mimic inertia during deceleration. A character coming to a rapid stop must overshoot the target slightly to show follow-through.

foot slippage   Unless the grounded foot is the root of the animation hierarchy, changes to a character's pose can cause the foot to slip forward or back inconsistently with the character's overall motion. A forward slip is called skating, a backward slip is called moonwalking.

footage   In cinematography, exposed film from a camera, measured in feet.

fps   Acronym for frames per second, the rate at which images are projected to create the illusion of motion in film, video, or other media. See also *frame rate.*

frame   In cinematography, the boundaries of the projected image.

frame rate   The speed at which separate images are viewed in a motion picture or other device for creating the illusion of motion. See also *sound speed, silent speed, flicker fusion, fps.*

frame-accurate   A VTR with a tape transport that can accurately record a single frame or field at a time. Used until recently to record animation to tape, now largely replaced by digital recorders.

fricative   A class of phonemes including f and v.

front projection   Projecting an image into a scene from the front, used to composite in the camera. Contrast with *rear projection.*

full animation   Animating a complete character on ones or twos, the highest quality of cel animation. See also *limited animation*.

gag   A visual joke or humorous situation.

going ballistic   An uncontrolled emotional outburst. In animation, when a character leaves the ground in a ballistic trajectory or parabola.

good take   A live action shot or soundtrack recording good enough to use.

graphics   See *CGI*.

hardware   Computer equipment that you can see and touch, in contrast to software, which is intangible.

heading   See *azimuth*.

heel strike position   A character's pose in a walk cycle where the leading heel first contacts the ground. One of three key poses for a standard walk cycle. See also *squash position, passing position, motion cycle*.

held cel, hold cel   In cel animation, an image duplicated for a number of frames.

Hi-8   A consumer video format developed by Sony and popular for camcorders, providing higher image quality than 8mm or VHS.

hidden line removal   An algorithm that removes lines not visible to the camera from a wireframe rendering, producing a cleaner image.

hinge   The simplest rotational joint, having only one degree of freedom.

hit   A musical beat or sound effect used to synchronize the action.

hold   A pose or shot repeated over a number of frames.

hold, moving   A pose held by a character for a number of frames, animated to vary slightly to keep the character visually alive.

hookup   Match the beginning and ending poses in a motion cycle so the cycle can be looped. See also *loop, motion cycle*.

inbetweener In traditional 2D animation, the junior or assistant animator who draws the inbetweens.

inbetweens Frames between key poses that show the smallest changes.

index of refraction A number representing how much a material bends or refracts the light passing through it.

inertia The tendency of objects to keep doing what they've been doing.

ink and paint The transfer of original drawings to ink on acetate sheets, and filling the outlined areas with the correct colors.

inking The first step in *ink and paint*.

input communicating information to a computer.

input devices Peripherals designed to make it easier to communicate information to a computer. Common examples include the mouse, keyboard, pen and tablet, scanner, and digitizer.

insert shot A shot filmed or rendered separately from the master shot, usually a close-up for exposition or from a character's POV, and edited into the main shot.

inter-cut Shots edited together in a sequence.

inverse kinematics Usually abbreviated IK, this is a class of algorithms for determining the posing of a hierarchical chain by the positioning of the end links. Drag a finger, the arm follows along.

iris The colored portion of the eye surrounding the pupil.

iris out In cinematography, a transition in which a circular *matte* shrinks until the entire frame is obscured. Iris in is the reverse.

joystick An input device usually relegated to games, but occasionally useful in CGI.

key animator Also known as lead animator. The senior animator trusted with creating the key poses.

key drawings In cel animation, drawings of the key poses.

key light   The primary light in a scene, providing most of the illumination.

key pose   One of the extreme positions of a character that defines an action.

key sounds   Points in the soundtrack used to match the animation (e.g., footsteps).

keyframe animation   Setting key poses and interpolating between the keys to create animation. Contrast with *procedural animation*.

lateral   A sideways camera move.

leica reel   See *story reel*.

level   Status in an animated character's hierarchy, determining when in the animation process a part is posed. Generally, the root of the hierarchy is posed first and the extremities last.

limited animation   Animating on fours or more, or holding the majority of an image while animating a small part of it. A lot of television animation is limited.

line of action   Re posing characters; an imaginary line drawn through the character's center and any limbs protruding beyond the body's silhouette. Ideally, there should only be one line possible for a key pose, and the line should have a pronounced curve that directs the audience's eye to follow the action.

line of action   In cinematography, the main line (or slalom) of the action. The camera should stay on one side of the line of action during a sequence to avoid confusing the audience.

line test   See *pencil test*.

lip sync   Coordinating a character's facial animation to a sound track to create the illusion that the character is speaking.

live action   Footage shot in the real world.

local coordinates   In LightWave 3D, XYZ values calculated from the Pivot of an object, rather than the origin of the entire virtual world.

lockdown   In puppet animation, a fastener inserted into a puppet's foot to keep it in place on the set. In cinematography, securing the camera so it does not move during a shot. In LightWave 3D, setting several identical values with Linear in adjacent frames of a motion graph, to prevent any interpolated movement.

long shot   A shot in which the entire figure, as well as a good deal of the background, is visible.

loop   Repeat a motion cycle within a shot. See also *hookup, motion cycle*.

LS   In cinematography, long shot.

luma key   Similar to *chroma key*, but composites images based on luminance or brightness rather than color.

master shot   A shot that establishes the entire environment of a sequence, laying out a visual map for the audience. A camera setup wide enough to encompass an entire scene.

match   See *move matching, dissolve*.

match dissolve   A dissolve from one image to a similar image to show the passage of time or other gradual change or to smooth the transition.

matte   A mask used to block part of an image for compositing.

MCU   In cinematography, medium close-up.

mittens   The tendency to pose all of a character's fingers side-by-side in an undifferentiated lump. Closely related to *twins*.

mocap   Abbreviation of *motion capture*.

model sheet   In cel animation, a collection of drawings showing the character in a variety of poses. In CGI animation, screen shots or test renders of the character from several angles and in a variety of poses, with notes from the technical director.

modeling   In CGI, creating objects by manipulating points, edges, and faces.

modulus of elasticity   A number representing the ability of a material to return to its original shape after being deformed.

moonwalk   See *foot slippage*.

motion blur   Motion occurring while the camera shutter is open produces a blurred image; CGI can reproduce this effect by rendering and compositing images of a moving object's position between frames.

motion capture   See *mocap, Satan's Rotoscope*.

motion cycle   An action that you can repeat by connecting duplicates end-to-end (e.g., walking, running, hammering a nail, or any other repetitive action). See also *loop, hookup*.

motion study   Detailed, sustained analysis of the movement of a subject, necessary to realistic or caricature animation.

mouse   Input device, common but not well suited for character animation. See also *pen and tablet*.

mouth action   See *phoneme*.

move matching   Matching the CGI camera movements and settings to live action footage in order to render CGI elements that will merge seamlessly with the live action.

moving hold   A pose that a character must maintain for at least several frames, with slight changes to avoid losing the illusion of life.

MPEG   A lossy compression format popular for direct computer playback of animation and live action.

MS   In cinematography, medium shot.

natural path   See *slalom*.

noodle   Tweaking settings back and forth and repeatedly creating previews long past the point of diminishing returns.

NTSC   The standard for television signals used in the United States.

object animation   Traditional stop-motion animation of objects instead of puppets or clay.

omniscient observer   In cinematography, a camera directed as if it were an invisible, all-seeing actor in a scene.

on-axis cut   Abrupt change in camera setup on the long axis of the lens, either closer to or farther from the subject.

ones, twos, or fours   The number of frames exposed for a single composition. The fewer the frames, the smoother and more expensive the animation.

one-shot   One subject fills the frame (a.k.a. single).

optical printer   A machine that produced a film print by combining two or more prints, used for transitions and other compositing effects.

opticals   Effects produced by an optical printer.

origin   The center of the coordinate system, where X, Y, and Z all equal 0.

OTS   In cinematography, over the shoulder.

out of sync   Soundtrack running behind or ahead of the animation.

out take   A shot that is not included in the final print of the film.

overlapping action   Animating a part of the character to show flexibility, mass, and inertia, separate from the character's main body.

PAL   A standard for television signals used in the U.K. and Europe.

palette   The range of colors available to a display device. A 24-bit palette reproduces as many shades of color as an average person can sees.

pan   Abbreviation of panorama. Horizontal camera rotation around a fixed point; a Y-axis rotation.

pan, truck   A pan executed by moving the camera sideways rather than rotating it.

pan, zip   A caricatured camera motion representing a fast stop, as if the entire camera is vibrating rapidly.

parabola A mathematical curve describing the path of a projectile in a gravity field.

passing position One of the three main poses for a walk or run in which the trailing leg is rotated past the supporting leg. See also *walk cycle*.

pen and tablet A more artist-friendly substitute for the standard computer mouse, which simulates the behavior of a pen on paper (a.k.a. stylus).

pencil test A preliminary rendering of an animation used to test an action, often created without color, maps, or background objects. Originally sketched with pencil, shot on film, and viewed as a negative image. See also *Preview*.

pencil test reel See *story reel*.

peripherals Additional equipment for a computer (e.g., external hard drives, pen and tablet, film recorder, or digitizer).

persistence of vision See *flicker fusion*.

personality The collateral effect of animated actions, creating the illusion that a character has unique motivations, volition, and thoughts.

phoneme Also known as mouth action or phonic shape. The shape of the mouth when pronouncing a particular sound.

pin registration Securing the film precisely in an animation camera or film recorder with a set of pins to ensure that each frame is registered exactly like all the others.

Pitch In LightWave 3D, the left-to-right rotational axis. A character's head nods on the Pitch axis.

pixel Contraction of Picture Element. The smallest individual dot visible on a computer monitor. Rows and columns of pixels together make an image.

pixilation Stop-motion animation created by posing living actors frame-by-frame.

plan A top or overhead view of a set design.

point   One set of XYZ coordinates that defines the end or intersection of an edge (a.k.a. vertex).

point of view   See *POV*.

polygon   A surface defined by three or more edges and three or more points (a.k.a. face, surface).

pose   In LightWave 3D, the total of all Bone and object translations and transforms for a character in a particular keyframe.

pose-to-pose   Animating by setting all the key poses first, then going back over the animation and tweaking the inbetweens.

POV   Abbreviation of point of view. A camera directed to show the scene as it would appear to one of the characters.

premise   A very brief summary of the point of a story, generally a sentence or two at the most (e.g., "easy come, easy go").

Preview   A rapidly rendered part of an animation, created as a test.

procedural animation   Movement or other animation that is controlled by an algorithm (e.g., Dynamic Realities's Impact plug-in). Contrast with *keyframe animation*.

propeller head   A term applied to CGI artists who come from a more technical, especially computer science, background. Can be comradely or pejorative, depending on usage.

pull-back   See *zoom*.

puppet animation   Stop-motion animation techniques using jointed or flexible puppets.

puppet   A jointed or flexible figure designed either to be animated or manipulated in a real-time performance.

push-in   See *zoom*.

rack focus   Directing the audience's attention by animating the depth of field to change the area of sharp focus (see Chapter 9 exercises).

RAM   Random Access Memory, the type of memory used to hold program information for fast access. Equivalent to having information on your desk, rather than filed in a drawer. CGI requires a lot of RAM.

range of movement   The limits to which a character can be posed before they distort unacceptably. Part of the information that the TD should write on the character's model sheet.

raster   Data generated or displayed one row of points at a time, adding rows to create a matrix or image. In CGI, the data is usually an image or scanner dataset.

raytracing   A class of CGI rendering algorithms that calculates the value of each pixel by mathematically tracing the path of a ray from the pixel through all the reflections and refractions it would encounter in a scene.

real-time   "Live" or in a 1:1 temporal ratio, in contrast to animation or computer time.

rear projection   Projecting images or sequences on a screen behind the actors in a scene, to composite the image and live action in the camera.

repeat   See *loop*.

replacement   A class of animation techniques in which objects or parts of objects are sequentially replaced to create the illusion of changing shape or pose. Contrast with *displacement*.

resolution   The number of pixels in an image, usually expressed as the width by the height (e.g., 640x480).

rev. (revision)   In software, a new or improved edition of a program, presumably superior to, or at least not as flawed as, the preceding revision.

reveal   Moving the camera to gradually expose more of a scene.

reverse angle   Cutting from one camera angle to another nearly 180 degrees from the first. See Shots 5 through 9 in the example storyboards.

rim light   A light used to highlight the edges or rim of the subject.

room tone   The ambient or background sound and acoustic nature of a space where recording is done. Room tone is recorded for dubbing into blank spaces in the track, since completely blank spots in the soundtrack would be noticed by the audience.

Rotoscope   A technique originally patented by the Fleischer studio, in which live action footage was traced over to create cel animation. See also *Satan's Rotoscope*.

rough cut   The first complete edit of the film. It still needs to be fine-tuned.

RSI, RMI, CPS   Repetitive Stress Injury, Repetitive Motion Injury, Carpal Tunnel Syndrome. Occupational hazards of animation workers, can permanently disable the victim's hands. Prevention is the best cure.

run cycle   Action of a running character that has hookup frames suitable for looping.

Satan's Rotoscope   Term coined by Ken Cope, Jeff Hayes, and Steph Greenberg.

scene   In LightWave 3D, a file containing all the settings from Layout necessary to create a series of images. In cinematography, a collection of shots in the same set and in a close temporal series.

sclera   The visible white portion of the eyeball, surrounding the iris.

script   The written plan for a film, including dialog and some stage direction. The precursor to the *storyboard*.

sentence measurement   Transcribing the timing of each take in a vocal recording session, to be used in selecting takes for track analysis.

sequence   A number of shots, in order, that tell part of the story.

set   The place where a scene is shot.

setup   In cinematography, the positions of actors and camera; equivalent to LightWave 3D scene file frame 0.

short   Film with running time from 2 to 20 minutes. Classic cartoon shorts usually ran between 6 and 7 minutes.

shot   The basic unit of film. A continuously exposed unedited piece of film. In CGI, an uncut sequence of frames.

shot on twos   In traditional animation, exposing two frames of film for each change in the animation, so a 24 fps projection speed will only show 12 new images per second.

shot volume   The space contained in the pyramid formed by the lens (the apex) and the four corners of the frame. The apparent volume of the shot ends at the central object or character.

Showscan   A projection system combining 65 fps frame rate and a widescreen format to enhance perceived realism.

sibilant   A class of phonemes including the consonants s and z.

SIGGRAPH   The Association for Computing Machinery's Special Interest Group on Computer Graphics.

sightlines   An actor or character's line of vision, from the center of the eyeball through the pupil to the point being observed.

silent speed   16 fps, the minimum required to prevent strobing.

silhouette   The filled outline of a character in strong contrast to the rest of the scene, usually black and white. Useful for evaluating poses. In LightWave 3D, created by rendering an alpha channel image.

skate   See *foot slippage*.

skeleton   The arrangement and hierarchy of Bones in a LightWave 3D character that enables the animator to pose it. See also *armature*.

slalom   The path followed by any system, natural or machine, that can correct its movement toward a goal.

slip   Moving the soundtrack forward or back in relation to key sounds, deliberately modifying the sync so the action reads better.

snap   Rapid, energetic changes within an action, the opposite of ease.

sneak   A caricatured action of attempting to move quietly on tiptoe.

software   The set of instructions, or programs, used to control a computer.

sound effects   See *foley.*

sound speed   24 fps.

soundtrack   The dialog, music, and sound effects from a film.

special effects animation   Smoke, water, or other non-character visual effects, generally animated in LightWave 3D by a specially designed plug-in.

speed lines   In traditional animation, drybrush lines drawn to show the path of a quickly-moving object or character. Superseded in CGI by motion blur.

sprocket hole   An evenly space series of holes matching the sprocket that pulls film through a camera or projector.

squash-and-stretch   Exaggerated distortion of an animated object, intended to emphasize compression (squash) in deceleration or collision and elongation (stretch) in acceleration.

squash pose   In a take, the key pose in which a character or their face is most compressed in recoil.

squash position   In a walk cycle, the key pose in which the body is at its lowest, and the supporting leg is bent to absorb the impact of the heel strike.

stagger   A caricatured rapid oscillation of a character, especially after striking or being struck.

staging   Animating a character to foreshadow the main action, making it easier for the audience to read.

static balance   Balance achieved with no ongoing adjustments or changes in mass, inertia, or energy. See also *dynamic balance.*

still shot   Also known as lock down. A shot in which the camera doesn't move.

stop-motion   Action created by stopping the camera, making changes to the scene or camera settings, and starting the camera again. Originally used to create dissolves and other optical effects in addition to animation; now generally used to describe clay or puppet animation.

storyboard   A sequence of story sketches depicting the major actions and layout for each shot. Often pinned to a large board or wall for group review and critique. See Appendix F for an example.

story reel   An animation composed of story sketches synchronized to the soundtrack. Usually, each sketch is replaced with finished sequences as production proceeds.

straight ahead action   In 2D animation, drawing each pose as you come to it, working out timing and posing on the fly. Contrast with *pose-to-pose*.

stretch   Deforming all or part of a character to show acceleration. Contrast with *squash*.

stretch pose   In a take, the key pose immediately following the squash, in which the character's recovery from the squash is exaggerated beyond the original pose.

stride length   The distance a character travels with each step.

strobing   Changes between frames that are too extreme, catch the audience's eye, and destroy the illusion of smooth movement.

stroboscopic photography   Capturing a series of images on a single film frame by leaving the shutter open and firing a sequence of flashes or strobes, often used to capture a complex or rapid motion.

studio animation   Animation produced by specialists within a larger organization, so the product is more of a team effort than an individual creative achievement.

stylus   See *pen and tablet*.

successive breaking of joints   When a higher joint starts to rotate, there should be a slight lag before the lower joints start to rotate as part of the same action. This means the rotation of a child object should begin, peak, and end some time after the Parent performs the same actions.

sweatbox   Projection room in an animation studio used to review and critique animation. Term originated at Disney studios due to lack of air conditioning.

sync   Short for synchronization, the matching of sound to action on film or videotape.

synchronization   See *sync*.

synopsis   A brief summary of a script.

tablet   See *pen and tablet*.

take   A character's recoil of fear or surprise. See also *stretch pose*, *squash pose*.

telephoto lens   A camera lens assembly constructed so its focal length is significantly longer than its physical length.

television animation   Animation designed for the limitations of the television cutoff and safe-titling areas and (sometimes) for the higher frame rate.

television cutoff   The outside border of the television image that is visible on studio monitors but is not displayed by many home televisions.

television safe-titling   The area within the television image that is safe for titles and other written communication.

test   See *pencil test*.

three-shot   Three subjects fill the frame.

thumbnail   A smaller version of an image, used for convenience or, in CGI, to save memory.

tie-down   In traditional 3D animation, usually a threaded rod with a keyed head that locks into the bottom of a character's foot. The animator passes the rod through a hole in the stage and tightens it down with a wingnut, securing the puppet in place.

tilt   Vertical equivalent of pan. See *pan*.

time encoding   Adding time code to a videotape to enable accurate measurement and reference down to the frame and field, generally using the SMPTE standard HH:MM:SS:FF.

time sheet   See *exposure sheet*.

track analysis   The transcription of a vocal track to a series of phonemes in an exposure sheet (a.k.a. track breakdown).

track breakdown   See *track analysis*.

track reader   The specialist who performs track analysis.

transfer   In cinematography, a moving object carries the audience's attention across the frame (a.k.a. hand-off). In editing, duplicating images or sound from one media format to another.

transform   In CGI, a change in shape, size, or attributes. LightWave 3D's Metamorph and Size functions are transforms. Contrast with *translate*.

transition   In drama, a visible change from one dominant emotional state to another. In editing or cinematography, the effect or cut used between shots.

translate   In CGI, to change position. LightWave 3D's Move function translates items in Layout. In general computer usage, changing data to a different file format, as when LightWave 3D imports a 3DS or DXF file and saves it in LWO format.

transport   The mechanism in a VTR used to move the tape past the recording and playback heads. A very accurate and expensive transport can reliably position the tape to within one frame, enabling single-frame recording for animation.

transportation animation   Walking or other means of moving the character around within the shot.

treatment   A short form of a script, used by some studios when considering a production.

trucking, truck pan   See *dolly*.

tweak   To make fine adjustments or changes to settings. See also *noodle*.

twins   Posing a character to appear symmetric in the frame. To be avoided, as it makes the character look stiff and lifeless.

two-shot   Two subjects fill the frame (a.k.a. double).

twos   See *shot on twos.*

U-matic   An industrial videotape format, rarely used in consumer or entertainment venues.

union shop   A studio or production house that has signed an agreement with a union to hire only members of that union. Non-union workers can (sometimes) still get a job there, but may have to join the union to keep it.

universal joint   Rotational joint having two degrees of freedom.

user-friendly   A matter of opinion regarding the utility of computer software, as people have different cognitive and working styles. Hostile for some is friendly for others.

vector graphics   Images drawn on a screen by lines connecting points. Good for outlines and wireframes, not good for color images of solid objects.

vertex   In LightWave 3D, a point.

VGA-to-NTSC converter   An adapter which converts the VGA output of a computer to the NTSC standard video signal used by most video equipment. Inexpensive ones have inferior video signals; you should test them before buying or renting. See also *encoder.*

VHS   A consumer-grade videotape format using half-inch tape in a cassette, having a maximum resolution of approximately 400 lines.

visual jar   A sudden change in shot volume or camera orientation that momentarily disorients the audience.

voice track   The part of the sound track that contains dialog.

voice-over   An offscreen voice dubbed over footage, which does not need to be lip synched. A fast and cheap way to make changes after animation is completed.

VTR   A Video Tape Recorder of any format, usually VHS, S-VHS, or BetacamSP. Frame-accurate VTRs can be used to record animations as they are rendered, one frame at a time, under computer control.

walk cycle   A walk action that has hookup frames suitable for looping.

WAV   A file format for digitized sound, commonly used with the Microsoft Windows operating systems.

wide angle lens   A lens having a focal length shorter than the diagonal measure of the image at the focal plane.

wide-screen   A film format designed for a higher aspect ratio, producing panoramic images.

wild wall   A wall or other object in a set that can be deleted or moved when not in camera range to make room for lighting or camera movement.

wipe   A special effect shot transition where the first shot is gradually replaced by the second shot, with a relatively sharp dividing line. A wipe can go from any direction, but typically moves top-to-bottom or left-to-right. See also *dissolve*.

wipe the frame   Passing a foreground object in front of the camera at the moment of a cut, usually used to smooth a transition.

wire frame   An abbreviated representation of an object, showing just the edges defining the object's polygons. Computer can draw wireframes very fast, so they are widely used for previews and tests.

workstation   Marketing term for a more powerful personal computer system.

world coordinates   A coordinate system of measuring translation from a single origin for all items.

WS   In cinematography, wide shot.

x-sheet   See *exposure sheet*.

XYZ   Coordinate axes of three-dimensional space; in LightWave, the Y-axis is up-and-down, the Z-axis is front-to back, and the X-axis is side-to-side.

zip pan   See *pan, zip*.

zoom   Using a lens capable of various focal lengths to change a shot.

Bibliography

Arijon, Daniel. *Grammar of the Film Language.* Hollywood, CA: Silman-James Press, 1991. ISBN: 1-879505-07-X.

An exhaustive guide to the visual narrative techniques that form the "language" of filmmaking regarding the positioning and movement of players and cameras, as well as the sequence and pacing of images. Heavily illustrated with line drawings. In print for nearly 20 years in several languages. Highly recommended.

Blair, Preston. *Cartoon Animation.* Wilton, CT: Walter Foster, 1994. ISBN: 1-56010-084-2.

Best collection of caricature motion studies in a form easily adapted to 3D computer animation. Especially useful for character design regarding head and hands.

Blacker, Irwin R. *The Elements of Screenwriting.* New York, NY: Collier Books, 1986. ISBN: 0-02-000220-3.

One of the best, and certainly the most compact, source about writing for film or video. This book is the absolute minimum necessary for the amateur to understand the mechanics of writing usable scripts. Not a bad reminder for the experienced screenwriter, either!

Blinn, Jim, Mark Henne, John Lasseter, Ken Perlin, and Chris Wedge. "Animation Tricks." *ACM SIGGRAPH Course Notes* 1 (1994). P.O. Box 12114, New York, NY 10257. Annual.

   A collection of short lectures from some of the top working professionals. These tips and tricks are the hard-won lessons of experience. Required reading.

Bogner, Jonathan, prod., and Mike Bonifer, dir. *The Making of Toy Story*. Burbank, CA: Walt Disney Co., 1995. Videocassette.

   A little light on the animation side and proportionally heavier on the celebrity voice talent, but some good quotes and a little behind-the-scenes at Pixar. Originally shown on The Disney Channel around Toy Story's opening.

Bordwell, David, and Kristin Thompson. *Film Art: An Introduction.* 4th ed. New York: McGraw-Hill, 1993. ISBN: 0-070-06446-6.

   A more historical and theoretical, if shallower, approach to Arijon's subject, with stills and sequences from Hollywood and foreign films. Also covers sound and film criticism.

Chan, Alan. *The FX Kit for LightWave*. Lancaster, CA: Lightspeed, 1995.

   Writing and publication quality are spotty, but this 300+ page collection of tutorials (and its version 5.0 Addendum) are a useful supplement to the NewTek manuals.

Cook, David A. *A History of Narrative Film*. 3d ed. New York: W. W. Norton, 1996. ISBN: 0-393-96819-7 (pbk.).

   Good basic history of film, especially cinematic technique and influences.

Culhane, Shamus. *Animation: From Script to Screen*. New York: St. Martin's Press, 1990. ISBN: 0-312-05052-6.

   Ex-Disney animator with sixty years of industry experience describes the whole animation process, including production details, setting up a studio, storyboards, character animation, business issues, and more. One of the "traditional" craftsmen who has embraced the computer as a labor-saver for the animator.

Egri, Lajos. *The Art of Dramatic Writing*. New York, NY: Simon & Schuster, 1960. ISBN: 0-671-21332-6.

The best source on how to write an interesting, dramatic story. Lots of guidelines for developing convincing characters.

Faigin, Gary. *The Artist's Complete Guide to Facial Expression*. New York, NY: Watson-Guptill Publications, 1990. ISBN: 0-823-01628-5.

Useful for modeling and animating facial expressions, especially the more realistic. For the exaggerated or caricatured, refer to Blair.

Jones, Chuck. *Chuck Amuck: The Life and Times of an Animated Cartoonist*. 1st ed. New York, NY: Farrar Straus Giroux, 1989. ISBN: 0-240-50871-8.

Halas, John. *The Contemporary Animator*. Boston, MA: Focal Press, 1990. ISBN: 0-240-51280-4.

Excellent survey of the art up to 1990. Dated in areas pertaining to computer graphics, but a wealth of information on the various styles and techniques of animation. Worth tracking down for the glossary alone.

Hoffer, Thomas W. *Animation: A Reference Guide*. Westport, CN: Greenwood Press, 1981. ISBN: 0-313-21095-0.

Exhaustive reference and critical bibliography on the genre. Probably more information than you'd normally want, but if it's about animation and it existed prior to 1979 it's in here.

Katz, Steven D. *Film Directing: Shot by Shot*. Studio City, CA: Michael Wiese Productions, 1991. ISBN: 0-941188-10-8.

Excellent resource on the creation and use of storyboards for directing a film.

_____. *Film Directing—Cinematic Motion: A Workshop for Staging Scenes*. Studio City, CA: Michael Wiese Productions, 1992. ISBN: 0-941188-14-0.

Less important (for animation, anyway) resource on the actual composition techniques used in directing a film. Staging, choreography, blocking, and so on, plus meaty interviews with professionals like John Sayles and Ralph Singleton. A good complement to Arijon's book, with a different perspective.

Kelly, Douglas A. "Natural Camera Movement." *3D Artist*, 18 (1995): 33. P.O. Box 4787, Santa Fe, NM 87502. Irregular. ISSN: 1058-9503.
How to avoid the Steadicam Syndrome in CG animation.

Lasseter, John. "Principles of Traditional Animation Applied to 3D Computer Animation." *Computer Graphics*. 21:4 (1987), 35-44. Association for Computing Machinery, 1515 Broadway, 17th Floor, New York, NY 10036. ISSN: 1069-529X.
Lasseter translates the principles of animation taught at Disney (see Thomas and Johnston) to 3D computer animation, and also introduces the concept of layering or "hierarchical" animation . Solid gold; if you skip everything else in this list, get a copy of this paper.

Lasseter, John, and Steve Daly. *Toy Story: The Art and Making of the Animated Film*. New York, NY: Hyperion Press, 1995. ISBN: 0-7868-6180-0.
A wonderful collection of production art and interviews with the principal creators, both at Pixar and Disney. A must-have for 3D CGI enthusiasts and professionals.

Laybourne, Kit. *The Animation Book*. New York: Crown, 1979. ISBN: 0-517-52946-7.
Beginner's guide to most of the film-based techniques, from drawing on film to sand and clay stop-motion.

Lee, Stan, and John Buscema. *How to Draw Comics the Marvel Way*. New York, NY: Simon & Schuster, 1984. ISBN: 0-671-53077-1.
Useful as a study guide for constructing humanoid characters, strong poses, and dramatic scene composition. 2D drawing exercises translate well to 3D modeling.

Levitan, Eli. *Handbook of Animation Techniques*. New York, NY: Van Nostrand Reinhold, 1979. ISBN: 0-442-26115-2.
Focused on production for television advertising, this is a very nuts-and-bolts volume. While technically dated, it contains solid production advice which should be taken seriously by anyone trying to do business in animation. Direct and written in plain English, with a minimum of philosophizing.

Lewis, Verin G. "Storyboarding." *3D Artist*, 18 (1995): 32-33. P.O. Box 4787, Santa Fe, NM 87502. Irregular. ISSN: 1058-9503.

Concise argument for the necessity of storyboarding commercial 3D animation and a brief overview of storyboard production.

LightWavePro Compilation Book. Sunnyvale, CA: Avid Media Group, 1996.

A collection of 100 tutorials from LightWavePro magazine. Worth acquiring, even though there isn't much on version 5.0.

London, Barbara, and John Upton. *Photography*. 5th edition. New York, NY: Harper Collins, 1994. ISBN: 0-673-52223-7.

Useful for chapters on lighting, composition, color, lenses, and film vocabulary, all of which are readily adapted to 3D computer animation.

Malkiewicz, Kris. *Film Lighting: Talks with Hollywood's Cinematographers and Gaffers*. New York, NY: Prentice Hall Press, 1986. ISBN: 0-671-62271-4 (pbk.).

This is the working expertise of an impressive collection of lighting professionals. Not exactly an easy read, but lots of information. Derived almost entirely from live-action production, a lot of the hardware specifics won't apply to CG work, but the principles are the same.

Martino, Stephen Michael. *Storyboard Design for Computer Generated Animation*. Master's thesis. Columbus, OH: Ohio State University, 1989.

Well written and adequately illustrated, this is one thesis that won't put you to sleep. The author had previously worked as a designer and animator at Cranston/Csuri in Columbus and as a director at Metrolight Studios in Los Angeles. Storyboard examples include Dow "Scrubbing Bubbles," and KTLA, NBA, and HBO logos, among others. Solid practical advice on dealing with clients, too.

Morris, Desmond. *Bodytalk: The Meaning of Human Gestures*. New York, NY: Crown Publishers, 1994. ISBN: 0-517-88355-4.

A readable popular version of scholarly research on informal gestural communication. Excellent resource for animators, either for practice or to build up a library of reusable motions.

Morrison, Mike. *Becoming a Computer Animator*. Indianapolis, IN:
Sams, 1994. ISBN:
0-672-30463-5.

A brief history of computer animation and assessment of technology
as of 1994. Basic tutorials using Caligari's trueSpace. Includes information for finding employment and an overview of animation schools.
There is one chapter each on television, feature films, visualization,
forensic, and game animation. Includes a CD-ROM of animation clips
and (now dated) software demos.

Muybridge, Eadweard. *The Human Figure in Motion*. New York, NY:
Dover Press. ISBN: 0-486-20204-6.

_____. *Animals in Motion*. New York, NY: Dover Press. ISBN: 0-
486-20203-8.

Muybridge took carefully measured sequences of photos of animal
and human movement in the late 1800s. These sequences are a great
help for anyone trying to make something move realistically, or to
derive the essentials of an action for caricature.

Peck, Stephen Rogers. *Atlas of Facial Expression: An Account of Facial
Expression for Artists, Actors, and Writers*. New York, NY: Oxford University Press, 1987. ISBN: 0-195-04049-X.

Excellent technical reference on the facial structure and the uses of
muscles in emotional and vocal communication.

Thomas, Frank, and Ollie Johnston. *Disney Animation: The Illusion of
Life*. New York, NY: Abbeville Press, 1981. Reprinted Hyperion Press,
1995. ISBN: 0-7868-6070-7.

Referred to as "the Animation Bible" due to its size and the value
of its contents. The Disney "rules of animation" and many other
useful rules-of-thumb are included. Recently reprinted, with some
loss of color and image quality since the '81 edition, but still well
worth the price.

Thompson, Frank T. *Tim Burton's Nightmare Before Christmas: the Film,
the Art, the Vision: With the Complete Lyrics From the Film*. 1st ed. New
York, NY: Hyperion, 1993. ISBN: 1-562-82774-X.

A really good behind-the-scenes book, about one of the most technically challenging puppet animation films ever. This is an excellent
idea-generator for replacement modeling and armature construction
that applies to CG as well as traditional methods.

Vince, John. *3D Computer Animation*. New York, NY: Addison-Wesley, 1992. ISBN: 0-201-62756-6.

Introductory technical animation theory for programming. Recommended for TDs.

Watt, Alan, and Mark Watt. *Advanced Animation and Rendering Techniques*. New York, NY: Addison-Wesley, 1992. ISBN: 0-201-54412-1.

An excellent technical text, covering important implementation theory and details. Recommended for TDs.

Weil, Jerry, Neil Eskuri, Andy Kopra, John McLaughlin, and Kathy White. "Tricks of the Trade: Computer Graphics Production." *ACM SIGGRAPH Course Notes* 5 (1995). P.O. Box 12114, New York, NY 10257. Annual.

A gold mine of production rules of thumb, collected from technical directors at different production houses. Recommended for TDs, animation supervisors, and anyone else who needs to produce CGI animation on time and within budget.

Whitaker, Harold, and John Halas. *Timing for Animation*. 1st ed. New York, NY: Focal Press, 1981. ISBN: 0-240-51310-X.

An absolute treasure trove of information on timing. Difficult to find, but well worth it.

Wilson, Steven S. *Puppets and People*. London: Tantivy Press, 1980. ISBN: 0-498-02312-5.

A history, filmography, and a smattering of basic nuts-and-bolts for the motion picture techniques of compositing live-action with stop-motion puppets. Examines the work of Willis O'Brien, Ray Harryhausen, Phil Tippett, and others. Lots of photos, and since the physical models tend to decay or be salvaged for parts, a collection of information hard to find elsewhere. Worth looking for, if only to use the extensive bibliography pointing to primary sources in the industry press.

Zaloom Mayfield Productions, prod. *The Making of Jurassic Park.* Universal City, CA: Amblin Entertainment, 1994. Videocassette.

A good collection of behind-the-scenes information and interviews, featuring Steven Spielberg, Stan Winston, Phil Tippett, Dennis Muren, Michael Lantieri, Mark Dippe, Steve Williams, and others. Includes a sequence on the techniques used for matching animation to live-action footage from a moving camera, plus the use of animal motion studies. Originally broadcast on NBC.

Index

Design Online!

Interactive Web Publishing With Microsoft Tools

$49.99, 818 pages, illustrated, part #: 462-6

Take advantage of Microsoft's broad range of development tools
to produce powerful web pages; program with VBScript; create
virtual 3D worlds; and incorporate the functionality of Office
applications with OLE. The CD-ROM features demos/lite versions
of third party software, sample code.

Looking Good Online

$39.99, 450 pages, illustrated, part #: 469-3

Create well-designed, organized web sites—incorporating text,
graphics, digital photos, backgrounds and forms. Features studies
of successful sites and design tips from pros. The companion CD-
ROM includes samples from online professionals; buttons,
backgrounds, templates and graphics.

Internet Business 500

$39.95, 450 pages, illustrated, part #: 287-9

This authoritative list of the most useful, most valuable online
resources for business is also the most current list, linked to a
regularly updated *Online Companion* on the Internet. The
companion CD-ROM features a hyperlinked version of the entire
text of the book.

The Comprehensive Guide to VBScript

$39.99, 864 pages, illustrated, part #: 470-7

The only encyclopedic reference to VBScript and HTML commands
and features. Complete with practical examples for plugging
directly into programs. The companion CD-ROM features a
hypertext version of the book, along with shareware, templates,
utilities and more.

 Books marked with this logo include *Online Udates*™, which include free
additional online resources, chapter updates and regularly updated links
to related resources from Ventana.

Web Publishing With Adobe PageMill 2

$34.99, 450 pages, illustrated, part #: 458-2

Here's the ultimate guide to designing professional web pages. Now, creating and designing pages on the Web is a simple, drag-and-drop function. Learn to pump up PageMill with tips, tricks and troubleshooting strategies in this step-by-step tutorial for designing professional pages. The CD-ROM features Netscape plug-ins, original textures, graphical and text-editing tools, sample backgrounds, icons, buttons, bars, GIF and JPEG images, Shockwave animations.

Web Publishing With Macromedia Backstage 2

$49.99, 500 pages, illustrated, part #: 598-3

Farewell to HTML! This overview of all four tiers of Backstage lets users jump in at their own level. With the focus on processes as well as techniques, readers learn everything they need to create center-stage pages. The CD-ROM includes plug-ins, applets, animations, audio files, Director xTras and demos.

Web Publishing With QuarkImmedia

$39.99, 450 pages, illustrated, part #: 525-8

Use multimedia to learn multimedia, building on the power of QuarkXPress. Step-by-step instructions introduce basic features and techniques, moving quickly to delivering dynamic documents for the Web and other electronic media. The CD-ROM features an interactive manual and sample movie gallery with displays showing settings and steps. Both are written in QuarkImmedia.

Web Publishing With Microsoft FrontPage 97

$34.99, 500 pages, illustrated, part #: 478-2

Web page publishing for everyone! Streamline web-site creation and automate maintenance, all without programming! Covers introductory-to-advanced techniques, with hands-on examples. For Internet and intranet developers. The CD-ROM includes all web-site examples from the book, FrontPage add-ons, shareware, clip art and more.

Make it Multimedia

Microsoft SoftImage|3D Professional Techniques 🌐

$69.99, 524 pages, illustrated, part #: 499-5

Create intuitive, visually rich 3D images with this award-winning technology. Follow the structured tutorial to master modeling, animation and rendering, and to increase your 3D productivity. The CD-ROM features tutorials, sample scenes, textures, scripts, shaders, images and animations.

LightWave 3D 5 Character Animation f/x 🌐

$49.99, 760 pages, illustrated, part #: 532-0

Master the fine—and lucrative—art of 3D character animation. Traditional animators and computer graphic artists alike will discover everything they need to know: from lighting, motion, caricature, composition, rendering ... right down to work-flow strategies. The CD-ROM features everything you need to complete the exercises in the book including working scripts, example rendered animation, models and much more.

3D Studio MAX f/x 🌐

$49.99, 552 pages, illustrated, part #: 427-8

Create Hollywood-style special effects! Plunge into 3D animation with step-by-step instructions for lighting, camera movements, optical effects, texture maps, storyboarding, cinematography, editing and much more. The companion CD-ROM features free plug-ins, all the tutorials from the book, 300+ original texture maps and animations.

Looking Good in 3D 🌐

$39.99, 400 pages, illustrated, part #: 434-4

A guide to thinking, planning and designing in 3D. Become the da Vinci of the 3D world! Learn the artistic elements involved in 3D design—light, motion, perspective, animation and more—to create effective interactive projects. The CD-ROM includes samples from the book, templates, fonts and graphics.

TO ORDER ANY VENTANA TITLE, COMPLETE THIS ORDER FORM AND MAIL OR FAX IT TO US, WITH PAYMENT, FOR QUICK SHIPMENT.

TITLE	PART #	QTY	PRICE	TOTAL

SHIPPING

For all standard orders, please ADD $4.50/first book, $1.35/each additional.
For "two-day air," ADD $8.25/first book, $2.25/each additional.
For orders to Canada, ADD $6.50/book.
For orders sent C.O.D., ADD $4.50 to your shipping rate.
North Carolina residents must ADD 6% sales tax.
International orders require additional shipping charges.

SUBTOTAL = $ _____
SHIPPING = $ _____
TAX   = $ _____
TOTAL   = $ _____

**Or, save 15%—order online.
http://www.vmedia.com**

Mail to: Ventana • PO Box 13964 • Research Triangle Park, NC 27709-3964 ☎ 800/743-5369 • Fax 919/544-9472

Name _____
E-mail _____ Daytime phone _____
Company _____
Address (No PO Box) _____
City_____ State_____ Zip_____
Payment enclosed ___VISA ___MC ___ Acc't # _____ Exp. date_____
Signature _____ Exact name on card _____

Check your local bookstore or software retailer for
these and other bestselling titles, or call toll free: **800/743-5369**